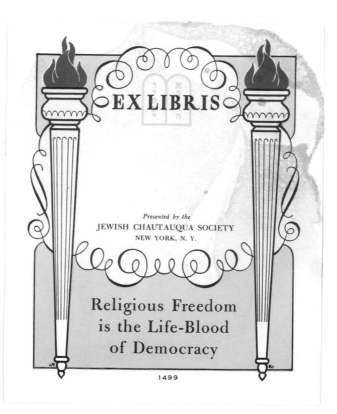

THE GENESIS OF FAITH

THE GENESIS
OF
FAITH

THE DEPTH THEOLOGY OF
ABRAHAM JOSHUA HESCHEL

JOHN C. MERKLE

MACMILLAN PUBLISHING COMPANY
A Division of Macmillan, Inc.
NEW YORK
Collier Macmillan Publishers
LONDON

Macmillan Publishing Company
866 Third Avenue, New York, N. Y. 10022

Collier Macmillan Canada, Inc.

Sections of this book are drawn from the following articles by John C. Merkle:

"Religious Experience through Conscience in the Religious Philosophy of Abraham Joshua
Heschel," *Louvain Studies* 6 (Fall 1977).

"The Sublime, the Human, and the Divine in the Depth Theology of Abraham Joshua Heschel,"
The Journal of Religion 58 (October 1977).

"Tradition, Faith, and Identity in Abraham Joshua Heschel's Religious Philosophy,"
Conservative Judaism 36 (Winter 1982–1983).

"The Meaning and Status of Torah in the Theology of Abraham Joshua Heschel," *Religious
Studies Bulletin* 4 (January 1984).

Permission has been granted for the use of extended quotations from the volumes cited:

America, volume 128, copyright 1973.
Central Conference of American Rabbis Journal, volume 18, copyright 1971.
Union Seminary Quarterly Review, volume 21, copyright 1966.
Who Is Man, by Abraham J. Heschel, reprinted with the permission of the publisher, Stanford
University Press. Copyright © 1965 Abraham J. Heschel.

Library of Congress Catalog Card Number: 84–14356

Printed in the United States of America

printing number
1 2 3 4 5 6 7 8 9 10

Library of Congress Cataloging in Publication Data

Merkle, John C.
  The genesis of faith.

  Bibliography: p.
  Includes index.
  1. Heschel, Abraham Joshua, 1907–1972.   I. Title.
BM755.H37M47 1984   296.3'092'4   84–14356
ISBN 0-02-920990-0

This book is dedicated with love and gratitude to my mother, Susanna Dougherty Merkle, and to my father, Hugh, of blessed memory, who inspired the genesis of my own faith in God. They made it easy for me, and a sheer delight, to observe what Heschel called the heart of the Ten Commandments: "Revere thy father and thy mother."

Contents

PART TWO
THE SOURCES OF FAITH

PART THREE
THE ANTECEDENTS OF FAITH

Foreword

The writings of the late Abraham Joshua Heschel contain a wealth of religious inspiration and theological insight not only for his fellow Jews but also, and perhaps even especially, for contemporary Christians. In spite of the relatively wide diffusion of some of his shorter and more popular works, the riches that Heschel has to offer to Christian faith and theology have remained largely unexplored hitherto.

Heschel offers us important insights on the reconciliation of tradition and personal authenticity in faith, on that mediation of the human encounter with God which Christians call sacramentality, and on the relationship between reason and revelation in the day-to-day living of a life of faith. Most of all, as a philosopher, an outstanding Jewish scholar, and a man of deep personal faith and compassion, Heschel shows how the modern person, surrounded by world catastrophes, secularism, cynicism, psychological and intellectual fatigue, and social-political discouragement, can find the way to faith.

Dr. John Merkle's penetrating and delightful study of Heschel focuses specifically on the question of the genesis of faith. There is probably no English-speaking Christian who understands Heschel better than Professor Merkle, the organizer and guiding genius of the epoch-making Heschel Symposium of spring 1983, to be published under the title *Abraham Joshua Heschel: Exploring His Life and Thought*.

This is a rewarding book which should have a wide appeal among clergy, religious educators, and all who reflect seriously on religious questions. Pleasantly written in a very readable style, the book combines an immense amount of scholarly research with directness and simplicity of presentation and with a certain discreet spontaneous piety that conveys the spirit of Heschel himself. It can be strongly recommended to all who are concerned to discover, deepen, or foster religious faith in our times.

MONIKA K. HELLWIG
Professor of Theology
Georgetown University
Washington D.C.

Preface

Abraham Joshua Heschel, one of the greatest Jewish philosophers and theologians of our time, does not fit easily into one of the categories used to classify religious thinkers for reference in academic circles. His poetic and evocative style of writing has led many readers to be edified by the spiritual grandeur of his books and essays, while overlooking the fact that Heschel was a skilled thinker whose original presentation of Judaic faith is meant to be read as a coherent and rigorous study of Judaism.

Trained from early childhood in traditional modes of rabbinic study and hasidic piety, Heschel later mastered the techniques of phenomenological analysis to assist him in his understanding and exposition of Judaism. And while presenting his philosophy of Judaism, he dealt with the challenges of Greek philosophers and medieval rationalist theologians, as well as with the onslaughts of modern secularism and naturalism against faith in the God of the Bible.

It is the merit of John C. Merkle to have written the best and most detailed systematic work on Heschel's thought. I am convinced it will become the definitive magisterial work on this important thinker for the foreseeable future. Dr. Merkle brilliantly, yet painstakingly, presents the "depth theology" beneath the dogmas and traditional formulations of the Judeo-Christian traditions which so often have served as substitutes for the root experiences of biblical faith. He has not only mastered the subtleties and frequently unexpressed or merely hinted assumptions in Heschel's writings, but presents them clearly in their mutual interrelationships. Thus Heschel, who did not write theology *more geometrico,* emerges in this study as the consistent thinker he really was.

Heschel's thought is of equal importance to Jews and Christians as an authentic philosophy of religion based on biblical and post-biblical categories of thought. John Merkle's book is a significant contribution to the very substance of that which ought to unite Christians and Jews, the renascence of that religious thought which is the common heritage of all those who have been disenchanted with the ideologies and pseudo-religions of our secularized culture. It is one of the most exciting and hopeful developments for all those who wish to make religion relevant and responsive to our age.

This book will enable specialists as well as laymen and women to gain a sympathetic yet not uncritical understanding of the thought of a great and authentic Jewish theologian. It is also a remarkable contribution by a young

Catholic theologian to the recovery of the common heritage of faith seeking understanding, when both Jews and Christians in this post-modern world are looking for a way that will enable honest seekers to set out once again on the mind's journey to God.

FRITZ A. ROTHSCHILD
Professor of Jewish Philosophy
The Jewish Theological Seminary
* of America*
New York, New York

Acknowledgments

"Genuine reverence for the sanctity of study is bound to invoke in the pupils the awareness that study is not an ordeal but an act of edification; that the school is a sanctuary, not a factory; that study is a form of worship." What Rabbi Heschel here claims, I have learned well from my mentor at the Catholic University of Louvain, Professor Benjamin Willaert. I am deeply grateful for his wise and faithful guidance of my research on Heschel, and for his enlightened teaching that inspired me to seek his counsel.

My years in Louvain were a blessing for a lifetime. I am indebted, in particular, to Professor Maurits Sabbe for his gracious hospitality as President of Paus Adriaan VI College, where I had the privilege and pleasure to reside.

Likewise I am indebted to Rev. Robert Bilheimer, Executive Director of the Institute for Ecumenical and Cultural Research, Collegeville, Minnesota, and to the Institute's board of directors for the research fellowship they granted me. Their support enabled me to pursue a good deal of my research under most favorable conditions.

My heartfelt gratitude goes to Sylvia Heschel, esteemed widow of Rabbi Heschel, and to Susannah Heschel, for their gracious hospitality and for cherished memories they shared with me.

I thank my professors at Louvain, my friends and colleagues at the College of Saint Benedict and elsewhere, and my family, all of whom have encouraged and inspired me in the course of my research and writing.

I am especially indebted to Maxine Andraschko for typing this manuscript. Her expert assistance made pleasant what might have been a tedious final stage of work.

Finally, a special word of thanks to Monika Hellwig and Fritz Rothschild for writing the foreword and the preface to this book.

JOHN C. MERKLE
St. Joseph, Minnesota
April 27, 1984

Introduction

"For an adequate concept of religion, we . . . should turn to those whose mind is bent upon the spiritual, whose life *is* religion."[1] It is for this very reason that I have turned to the man who offered this advice, Abraham Joshua Heschel. Rabbi Heschel's life was so profoundly religious that the great Reinhold Niebuhr called him "the most authentic prophet of religious life in our culture."[2]

Not only was Heschel's life genuinely religious, he was a religious author whose books "read like *seforim*—holy books."[3] For more than a decade now I have had the privilege and the joy of carefully studying these works. I offer this book as the fruit of my study, with the hope that it will leave readers hungry for Heschel's holy books.

An adequate concept of religion involves an adequate understanding of religious faith. This, in turn, demands an adequate understanding of the sources and antecedents of faith. Heschel himself was especially concerned with this and I have made it the focus of my study. And since Heschel was a spokesman for the Jewish faith, this book deals particularly with the sources and antecedents of Jewish faith. While much of what is discussed herein applies to other religions, especially Christianity, all of it applies to Judaism.

In one of his first essays written in English, Heschel made a claim that set the tone for nearly all of his subsequent writings. It is a claim that so many of his later works elaborated and explained. The claim to which I refer is this: "Faith is not a stagnant pool. It is rather a fountain that rises with the influx of personal experience. Personal faith flows out of an experience and a pledge. For faith is not a thing that comes into being out of nothing. It originates in an event.[4]"

A personal experience that gives rise to faith is what Heschel calls in later writings an antecedent of faith. More than two decades after making the above claim, Heschel told a congress of Catholic theologians: "The hour calls for a renewal of the antecedents of faith . . . because it is useless to offer conclusions of faith to those who do not possess the prerequisites of faith."[5] The antecedents or prerequisites of faith of which Heschel speaks are "certain insights, attitudes, and emotions, . . . acts that happen within the depth of the person, moments that necessitate groping for faith."[6] These subjective happenings are elicited by objective realities which, because of what they evoke, may be called sources of faith. To understand the meaning of the antecedents of faith it is essential to understand the meaning of the sources to which they are responses. Part Two of this book (chapters 3, 4, and 5) deals with what appear in Heschel's writings to be the primary sources of faith. Part Three (chapters 6, 7, and 8) deals with Heschel's principal antecedents of faith.

Part One of this book (chapters 1 and 2) is an introduction to Heschel's life and works and to his depth theology. Heschel calls his work "depth theology" in order to distinguish it from what is often meant by "theology." Theology deals with the content of belief, with what we have seen Heschel refer to as the "conclusions of faith." Depth theology deals with the act of faith as well as with the experiences that precede and nurture faith, the "antecedents of faith." Heschel's depth theology is found in works of profound theological depth, and these works are the fruit of a faith sown in the depth of a seasoned religious life. Chapter 1 focuses on that life and those works. Chapter 2 examines the nature and purpose of the depth theology that is so congruent with Heschel's life and works.

The sources of faith dealt with in Part Two are: the sublime mystery of creation (chapter 3); the divine glory present in the world (chapter 4); the wellsprings of the Jewish tradition—revelation, the Bible, and rabbinic midrashim—and the principal foci of that tradition, God, Torah, and Israel (chapter 5).

The antecedents of faith dealt with in Part Three are: wonder and awe (chapter 6), which are the responses to sublimity and mystery; indebtedness and praise (chapter 7), the responses to divine glory; remembrance and mitsvah (chapter 8), the responses to the wellsprings and the foci of the Jewish tradition.

In and throughout this study I examine why and in what sense the realities and experiences mentioned above are sources and antecedents of faith. While Heschel has explored these sources and antecedents of faith, his treatment of these is not strictly systematic or analytical. In fact, his insights about them are often scattered aphoristically amidst his various works. Therefore, one of the principal tasks of this study is to systematize and analyze Heschel's insights concerning the sources and antecedents of faith and to thereby advance the work of depth theology.

Another of the major tasks of this book is to raise questions that Heschel himself did not raise and to offer answers that are implied in his writings or, where no such implications can be found, are in the spirit of his thinking or, at least, in the spirit of his search for truth. One of the main questions raised herein is that of the difference between antecedents of faith and aspects of faith. Heschel uses the phrase "antecedents of faith" both for those experiences and acts which obviously are not in themselves aspects of faith and for those that at first sight are aspects of faith. Even an experience or act that Heschel speaks of in one context as the quintessence or climax of religious existence is referred to by him in another context as an antecedent of faith. How can an experience or act that is a constitutive element of faith, even a quintessential aspect of faith, be an antecedent of faith? This book aims to answer that question and to explain why certain experiences and acts that are commonly viewed as aspects of faith are also considered antecedents of faith by Heschel. It also intends to show why other experiences and acts that are not in themselves aspects of faith may function as antecedents of faith in Heschel's view.

Heschel claims that "all philosophy is an *apologia pro vita sua.*"[7] His own religious philosophy or depth theology is no exception. In exploring the sources and antecedents of Jewish faith, Heschel offers a rationale for allowing such faith to emerge. His task is to disclose the meaningfulness and truth of Jewish faith. As such, it is an *apologia pro vita judaica.* This book therefore includes the endeavor to present and analyze systematically the cogency of Heschel's apologetics.

In dealing specifically with Heschel's understanding of the genesis of religious or Jewish faith, this study addresses most of the major themes found in his works since they have a bearing on the sources, the antecedents, and the phenomenon of faith. In short, this book is focused on a particular problem while at the same time it is a comprehensive study of Heschel's religious world view.

Soon after Rabbi Heschel's death in 1972, Fritz Rothschild eulogized him as "the outstanding Jewish thinker of his generation."[8] More recently, Jacob Neusner hailed him as "the most productive and by far the best theological mind in modern and contemporary Judaism."[9] Yet, despite such acclaim, Heschel's contribution to theology is still virtually unexplored. This book is an attempt to remedy this situation.

PART
ONE

Heschel's Life, Works, and Depth Theology

1

Life and Works

There are no proofs for the existence of the God of Abraham. There are only witnesses.[1]

Abraham Heschel not only spoke and wrote about witnesses for God, he himself was such a witness. Those who had the privilege to know him or simply to hear him speak or lead them in prayer consistently testify to Rabbi Heschel's profound witness to the presence of God.

"Here was a man for whom God was real," said Robert McAfee Brown of Heschel. "It is not very often these days that one finds a person who communicates this reality, even among theologians."[2] Heschel communicated this reality of God to such an extent that after his death on December 23, 1972, one of his disciples, Byron Sherwin, was moved to say: "Now you dwell in paradise. But while you were alive, paradise dwelt within you. . . . God found a home in your deeds. Now you are gone. The *Shekinah* once more is cast into exile."[3] Another disciple, recognizing the depth of Heschel's holiness, said of him: "Perhaps he was a *'lamed Vov,'* one of the 36 righteous people of every generation who dwell on the earth anonymously saving it from destruction by their presence."[4] Another said: "It was the love of God that was personified in him. The harp of this *zaddik's* heart played day and night the echo of God's message."[5]

While Heschel claimed there are no proofs, but only witnesses, for the existence of God, he nonetheless launched persuasive arguments on behalf of God. As his life was a profound testimony to God, his writings are an eloquent *apologia* for monotheistic faith, especially Judaism. Heschel the witness was also Heschel the scholar and theologian.

Fearing that Heschel would be remembered only as a holy man and a public spokesman for peace and social justice, Jacob Neusner said: "The story of his life is not what matters. Theologians and scholars should have no biographies: their work is all that matters."[6] Neusner's apprehension is understandable. Many who saw Heschel blaze with righteous anger or who felt a healing peace in his presence may be unaware of his rigorous scholarship and creative contribution to the world of theological research. Nevertheless, Heschel's work cannot be separated from his life. Heschel was not only a scholar and theologian; he was first and foremost a religious person, an exemplary Jew, and he should be remembered as such. Neusner knows this, for he himself has also said of Heschel: "To remember him is to learn what we are not, but might become."[7]

Perhaps what Neusner is really telling us when he says "the story of his life is not what matters" is that the whole of Heschel's life matters greatly— his scholarship included. Neusner is justifiably concerned that Heschel's luminous intelligence and scholarly contribution may be obscured by his public, more easily accessible, personality. Yet it would be wrong to view that contribution as something apart from Heschel's personality.

This book deals primarily with Heschel's work as a theologian. But since that work was born and nurtured in a life of prayer and religious action, this first chapter is presented as an introduction to his life, one too rich to describe adequately, yet for that reason too significant to bypass.

Life and Works in Europe

Slightly more than half of Heschel's near sixty-six years of life were lived in Europe. Almost two-thirds of his European years were spent in Poland, one-third in Germany, and less than a year in England.

HASIDIC BACKGROUND

Abraham Joshua Heschel was born in Warsaw on January 11, 1907, to Rabbi "Moishele" Mordecai, the Peltzovizner *rebbe,* and Reisel Perlow Heschel. He was the descendant of a long line of scholars and religious leaders, a rabbinic family that can be traced back to the late fifteenth century. For the last seven generations all of Heschel's male ancestors have been Hasidic rabbis.[8] Most famous among his paternal ancestors are: Rabbi Dov Ber of Mezeritz (d. 1772), known as "the Great *Maggid,*" the foremost disciple and successor of the Baal Shem Tov (d. 1760), the founder of Hasidism; Rabbi Abraham Joshua Heschel (d. 1825), the "Apter *Rav,*" who was generally accepted as the leader of his generation;[9] and Rabbi Israel of Rizhyn (d. 1850), the princely *rebbe* who has been called

"Hasidism's favorite child and the last undisputed leader."[10] On his mother's side, Heschel's ancestors include Rabbi Pinhas of Koretz (d. 1791), accepted by the Baal Shem "more as a companion than as a disciple,"[11] and Rabbi Levi Yitzhak of Berditchev (d. 1809), "the Compassionate One" of whom it is said that "no European Diaspora Master since the Baal Shem has left so profound a mark on the Jewish imagination."[12] It has been said that Heschel was related "to almost every important Hasidic 'dynasty' in Europe.[13]

With ancestry like that, it is not surprising that Heschel grew up in an atmosphere of genuine Hasidic piety and learning, nurtured by a great wealth of Hasidic traditions and tales. In the introduction to his last book, *A Passion for Truth,* Heschel writes: "The earliest fascination I can recall is associated with the Baal Shem, whose parables disclosed some of the first insights I gained as a child. He remained a model too sublime to follow yet too overwhelming to ignore."[14]

Also influential in Heschel's early religious formation was another great and legendary Hasidic master, Menahem Mendl of Kotzk (d. 1859). Says Heschel: "It was in my ninth year that the presence of Reb Menahem Mendl of Kotzk, known as the Kotzker, entered my life. Since then he has remained a steady companion and a haunting challenge. Although he often stunted me, he also urged me to confront perplexities that I might have preferred to evade."[15]

In many ways, the Kotzker was the antithesis of the Baal Shem, and their dual influence upon the young Heschel perhaps accounts for much of the polarity and paradox in Heschel's later writings. The Baal Shem found God everywhere and rejoiced in God's presence. The Kotzker was dreadfully aware of God's absence and stormed the heavens, accosting God for permitting evil to exist in the world. The Baal Shem taught people to find a trace of heaven on earth. The Kotzker told people they were living in the chamber of hell. The Baal Shem inspired joy and ecstasy, the Kotzker fear and trembling. The Baal Shem emphasized love, the Kotzker truth. Reflecting upon the influence of both the Baal Shem and the Kotzker on his life, Heschel writes:

> Years later I realized that, in being guided by both the Baal Shem Tov and the Kotzker, I had allowed two forces to carry on a struggle within me. One was occasionally mightier than the other. But who was to prevail, which was to be my guide? Both spoke convincingly, and each proved right on one level yet questionable on another.
>
> In a very strange way, I found my soul at home with the Baal Shem but driven by the Kotzker. Was it good to live with one's heart torn between the joy of Mezbizh [the home of the Baal Shem] and the anxiety of Kotzk? To live in both awe and consternation, in fervor and horror, with my conscience on mercy and my eyes on Auschwitz, wavering between

exaltation and dismay? Was this a life a man would choose to live? I had no choice: my heart was in Mezbizh, my mind in Kotzk.

I was taught about inexhaustible mines of meaning by the Baal Shem; from the Kotzker I learned to detect immense mountains of absurdity standing in the way. The one taught me song, the other—silence. The one reminded me that there could be a Heaven on earth, the other shocked me into discovering Hell in the alleged Heavenly places in our world.[16]

The dilemma that Heschel faced concerning the "two forces" he had allowed to carry on a struggle within him stayed with him throughout his life. Never did he answer the question "Who was to prevail, which was to be my guide?" by opting for one or the other, either the Baal Shem or the Kotzker. "I must admit," says Heschel, "that during my entire life I struggled between being a hasid of the way of the Baal Shem or the way of the Kotzker Rebbe."[17] Perhaps this accounts for Heschel's uniqueness and wisdom: he combined within himself the spirit of two such divergent masters. Though single-minded, he was never one-sided. Throughout his life and in all his works, Heschel kept alive the principle of polarity. Perhaps this is what accounts for the depth and breadth of insight found in his writings. It was precisely because Heschel allowed neither the Baal Shem nor the Kotzker to prevail one over the other as his guide that Heschel's depiction of human existence and of Jewish faith is so penetrating and complete. In an interview about fourteen months before his death, Heschel expressed his belief that the principle of polarity is essential to Judaism and he revealed that he consciously decided that it was his task "to find some kind of calculus by which to establish a polarity of the Kotzker and the Baal Shem—or of Judaism altogether."[18]

While Heschel's religious imagination and sensitivity were nurtured by tales of Hasidic masters, most of his youthful years were devoted to classical Jewish learning: the study of biblical and rabbinic literature. And by the age of ten he was not only at home in the world of the Bible and the Talmud, he had also been exposed to the world of Jewish mysticism, the *Kabbalah*.[19] According to Professor Fritz Rothschild, Heschel achieved in his youth not only "*knowledge* of the Jewish religious heritage" but also "*understanding* for the realness of the spirit and for the holy dimension of all existence." This, says Rothschild, "was not primarily the result of book learning but the cumulative effect of life lived among people who 'were sure that everything hinted at something transcendent'; that the presence of God was a daily experience and the sanctification of life a daily task."[20]

As a teenager in Poland, Heschel sought a modern education and entered the secular Yiddish "Realgymnasium" in Vilna. There he developed his literary talents and became a co-founder of the "Yung Vilne" movement of writers and poets. After his graduation in July 1927, Heschel was eager to further his education at the university level. In the fall of that year he left Poland to enroll at the University of Berlin.

UNIVERSITY YEARS

Concerning Heschel's university years, Franklin Sherman writes: "While appreciatively absorbing the riches of the modern intellectual tradition, he remembered with equal appreciation the world of fervent faith and piety from which he had come; and he resolved to try to hold the two worlds together. He would neither forsake his faith in order to adjust to the modern world, nor retreat from the world in order to preserve his faith. Rather, he would allow each element to criticize as well as fructify the other."[21] Concerned as he was to allow such an encounter of diverse worlds to occur within him, it is understandable that Heschel enrolled not only at the University of Berlin but also concurrently at Berlin's Hochschule für die Wissenschaft des Judentums. His dual enrollment signifies what was to become his lifelong task: to combine the fruits of modern Western scholarship with a faithful and profound understanding of his Jewish heritage.

While Heschel acquired a broad liberal education in Berlin, his major fields of academic concern were philosophy and Semitics, preparing him well for the synthesis he would attempt. But such a synthesis was not one that the university would easily recognize as possible. It was up to Heschel to work it out for himself, for his experience and understanding of God and religion were greatly different from what was expounded at the university. Heschel explains:

> I came with great hunger to the University of Berlin to study philosophy. I looked for a system of thought, for the depth of the spirit, for the meaning of existence. Erudite and profound scholars gave courses in logic, epistemology, esthetics, ethics, and metaphysics. . . . Yet in spite of the intellectual power and honesty which I was privileged to witness, I became increasingly aware of the gulf that separated my views from those held at the university. . . . To them, religion was a feeling. To me, religion included the insights of the Torah which is a vision of man from the point of view of God. They spoke of God from the point of view of man. To them God was an idea, a postulate of reason. They granted Him the status of being a logical possibility. But to assume that He had existence would have been a crime against epistemology.[22]

Commenting on this experience of Heschel's, Fritz Rothschild writes:

> The result of this confrontation was Heschel's attempt to examine the classical documents of Judaism anew in order to discover their relevance for

contemporary man. In this enterprise he made use of the conceptual tools of academic philosophy, especially the techniques of phenomenology. But he was careful to refrain from forcing upon biblical thought categories derived from Greek metaphysics and neo-Kantian philosophy, which in his opinion distorted the meaning of the biblical message. In his doctoral dissertation he developed a novel conceptual framework that became the nucleus of his later philosophy of Judaism.[23]

Heschel's dissertation, *Die Prophetie*, is an analysis of prophetic consciousness from the standpoint of comparative religion and from literary, phenomenological, and theological perspectives. The University of Berlin awarded him the doctoral degree in philosophy in February 1933, and his dissertation was published in 1936. This study, recognized by biblical scholars as an outstanding contribution, forms the basis of the latter half of Heschel's monumental book, *The Prophets*, published in English in 1962.

In the introduction to *The Prophets*, Heschel explains what it was that influenced him to examine the thought of the prophets for his doctoral dissertation:

What drove me to study the prophets?
In the academic environment in which I spent my student years philosophy had become an isolated, self-subsisting, self-indulgent entity, a *Ding an sich*, encouraging suspicion instead of love of wisdom. The answers offered were unrelated to the problems, indifferent to the travail of a person who became aware of man's suspended sensitivity in the face of stupendous challenge, indifferent to a situation in which good and evil became irrelevant, in which man became increasingly callous to catastrophe and ready to suspend the principle of truth. I was slowly led to the realization that some of the terms, motivations, and concerns which dominate our thinking may prove destructive of the roots of human responsibility and treasonable to the ultimate ground of human solidarity. The challenge we are all exposed to, and the dreadful shame that shatters our capacity for inner peace, defy the ways and patterns of our thinking. One is forced to admit that some of the causes and motives of our thinking have led our existence astray, that speculative prosperity is no answer to spiritual bankruptcy. It was the realization that the right coins were not available in the common currency that drove me to study the thought of the prophets.
Every mind operates with presuppositions or premises as well as within a particular way of thinking. In the face of the tragic failure of the modern mind, incapable of preventing its own destruction, it became clear to me that the most important philosophical problem of the twentieth century was to find a new set of presuppositions or premises, a different way of thinking.[24]

To explicate that "different way of thinking" that Heschel found in the prophets was to become the "major effort" of his lifework. In an address to a group of Jewish educators, Heschel explained why this effort became his primary enterprise:

> We are essentially trained in a non-Jewish world. This is where we obtain our general training. We are inclined to think in non-Jewish terms. I am not discouraging exposure to the non-Jewish world. . . . A non-Jewish philosophy is fine. But we would also like to have in our thinking a Jewish view of things. . . . May I say to you personally, that this has been my major challenge, ever since I have begun working on my dissertation, that is: How to think in a Jewish way of thinking? This was the major concern and the major thesis of my dissertation *Die Prophetie.* Since that day I consider this to be my major effort.[25]

Thus, the religious philosophy that Heschel developed is a biblical or Jewish philosophy based on the prophetic experience of divine concern. The title of Heschel's major work of religious philosophy, *God in Search of Man,* expresses what he considers to be the most fundamental insight of prophetic and rabbinic Judaism, that the initiative in the divine–human relationship is on God's part, and it is this insight upon which he builds his philosophy of Judaism.[26] The divine initiative reflects God's loving concern for human beings. By basing his philosophy on the experience of God's concern, and on the insight that this concern involves God's being affected and moved by the plight and the deeds of human beings, "Heschel has propounded a truly revolutionary doctrine, challenging the whole venerable tradition of Jewish and Christian metaphysical theology."[27] God, as the Supreme Subject in search of human beings, as One who is compassionate toward them, affected by them, is not the Unmoved Mover of classical metaphysical theology, but is, in Fritz Rothschild's apt expression, the Most Moved Mover of biblical consciousness. It is this consciousness of God that lies at the foundation of Heschel's religious thought; it is the explication of this consciousness that was the "major effort" of his lifework.

LAST YEARS IN EUROPE

Heschel's first book was published in 1933, the year of his doctoral defense. Entitled *Der Shem Hameforash: Mentsh* (Man: God's Ineffable Name), it is a collection of sixty-six of Heschel's poems written in Yiddish.[28] Throughout his life, Heschel was a scholar and a poet; his scholarly works are cast in a poetic prose that signifies the inseparability of theology and spirituality. That the publication of his religious poems coincided with the defense of his scholarly research was indicative of an ingenious style that would endure for a lifetime.

In 1934 Heschel assumed his first teaching position as an instructor in Talmud at the Hochschule in Berlin where he had studied.[29] In 1935 the publication of his *Maimonides: Eine Biographie* "established his reputation as a fine scholar, a gifted and imaginative writer, and a master of German prose."[30] In 1937, the year in which his *Don Jizchak Abravanel* was published, Heschel was chosen by Martin Buber to be his successor at the Central Organization for Jewish Adult Education and the Jüdische Lehrhaus, founded by Franz Rosenzweig, in Frankfurt am Main. There Heschel taught and directed educational activities until October 1938, when he was deported by the Nazi Regime.

Heschel was one of thousands of Polish Jews being sent back to their native country. But when the train carrying them reached the border, Poland refused to let them come home. Heschel and others were placed in a detention camp along the border. It was not long, however, before Heschel's relatives had him freed and he returned to Warsaw where he taught for the next eight months at a rabbinical seminary, the Institute for Jewish Studies.

In April 1939 Heschel received an invitation to join the faculty of the Hebrew Union College in Cincinnati, Ohio. That summer, just six weeks before the Nazi invasion of Poland, Heschel left for England en route to his new post in the United States. Although he lived in London for only a short time, while there Heschel founded the Institute for Jewish Learning.

Life and Works in America

Heschel was thirty-three years of age when he came to the United States in 1940. There he lived for almost another thirty-three years before his death in 1972. The first five of Heschel's American years were lived in Cincinnati; the remaining twenty-seven years in New York.

"A BRAND PLUCKED FROM THE FIRE"

Heschel never forgot the horror of his last months in Germany and Poland. Twenty-five years later, upon assuming the Harry Emerson Fosdick Visiting Professorship at the Union Theological Seminary in New York, he spoke these words:

> I speak as a member of a congregation whose founder was Abraham, and the name of my rabbi is Moses.
> I speak as a person who was able to leave Warsaw, the city in which I was born, just six weeks before the disaster began. My destination was New

York, it would have been Auschwitz or Treblinka. I am a brand plucked from the fire, in which my people was burned to death. I am a brand plucked from the fire of an altar of Satan on which millions of human lives were exterminated to evil's greater glory, and on which so much else was consumed: the divine image of so many human beings, many people's faith in the God of justice and compassion, and much of the secret and power of attachment to the Bible bred and cherished in the hearts of men for nearly two thousand years.[31]

Suffering can either embitter or ennoble the person who suffers; it depends on what one does with the suffering. Heschel's own suffering was ennobling, for through it he realized a deep empathy and care for others who were afflicted. "Abraham Heschel felt within himself the world's pain, which most of us can conceive only in the mind."[32] Heschel's prophetic outcries against all forms of racism, against the American war policy in Southeast Asia, his pleas for aid to the Jews being persecuted in Russia, and for the State of Israel when threatened with annihilation—these were born out of an identification with, and a compassion for, the poor and persecuted throughout the world.

A NEW BEGINNING IN CINCINNATI

In the spring of 1940 Heschel reached Cincinnati where he was appointed Associate Professor of Jewish Philosophy and Rabbinics at the Hebrew Union College, a position he held for five years. While there Heschel continued the study of medieval Jewish philosophers that he had begun in Berlin and wrote his first book in English, *The Quest for Certainty in Saadia's Philosophy*. Published in 1944, this work is a penetrating study of the major questions explored by the father of medieval Jewish philosophy; questions with which Heschel continued to grapple throughout the course of his life and to which he offered his own unique replies; questions such as the meaning of truth, the source of religious knowledge, revelation and reason, doubt and faith. What Heschel said of Saadia Gaon may be said of Heschel himself as he pursued the task of what he later called depth theology: "He penetrated below the deep mines of Bible and Talmud, where he had unearthed a wealth of wisdom and learning in order to ascertain what lay in the substratum."[33]

Heschel remained forever grateful to those at the Hebrew Union College who had secured his exodus from Poland. Yet while there he became increasingly aware of the fact that his philosophy of Judaism was not in full accord with the teachings of the college. This center of Reform Judaism was not the place for this scion of Hasidic Judaism who "followed Jewish law punctiliously."[34] In 1945 Heschel resigned his position at the Hebrew Union College.

PROFESSORSHIP AND MARRIAGE

In 1945, the year in which he became a citizen of the United States, Heschel joined the faculty of the Jewish Theological Seminary of America in New York, where he taught until the time of his death in 1972.

When asked once what type of Jew he was, Orthodox, Conservative, or Reform, Heschel replied that he "was not a noun in search of an adjective."[35] Yet by teaching for the last twenty-seven years of his life at the Jewish Theological Seminary, the world's center of Conservative Judaism, Heschel aligned himself with the Conservative movement. "He supported the Conservative movement," claims Sylvia Heschel, his widow; "he thought it necessary for Judaism."[36] This is most likely because of the movement's appreciation for both the authority and the dynamism of Jewish law.[37]

During his years at the Jewish Theological Seminary, Heschel was Professor of Jewish Ethics and Mysticism. And he not only held this chair, he embodied its meaning, and in so doing gave yet another testimony to the polarity of Judaism. According to Robert McAfee Brown, "The real importance of Heschel is symbolized . . . by his title at the Jewish Seminary." He explains:

> Now the words "ethics" and "mysticism" are tough ones to define or dissect (let alone the word "Jewish"), and I will not attempt that task here. But we find today that most of the people who are engaged in the religious enterprise tend to get preoccupied, if not swallowed up, in one of those two areas to the virtual exclusion of the other. An ethicist we can understand even if we don't like his ethics, a mystic we know something about even if we can't follow him in his approach to reality; but an *ethical* mystic or a *mystical* ethicist? That is a strange breed. What would such a person look like? My friend, let me tell you something. I have an answer. I have been writing about him in every paragraph.[38]

In 1946, the year after he joined the seminary faculty, Heschel married Sylvia Straus, a gifted concert pianist from Cleveland, Ohio, whom he had met while teaching in Cincinnati. Perhaps it was his marriage to a musician that moved Heschel, whose own speaking and writing had such a melodious quality, to make the following autobiographical observation:

> Listening to great music is a shattering experience, throwing the soul into an encounter with an aspect of reality to which the mind can never relate itself adequately. . . . The shattering experience of music has been a challenge to my thinking on ultimate issues. I spend my life working with thoughts. And one problem that gives me no rest is: do these thoughts ever rise to the heights reached by authentic music? . . . Music leads to the threshold of repentance, of unbearable realization of our own vanity and frailty and of

the terrible relevance of God. I would define myself as a person who has been smitten by music, as a person who has never recovered from the blows of music.[39]

Together with their one daughter, Susannah, the Heschels made their home on Riverside Drive, several blocks from the seminary.

During his tenure at the Seminary, Heschel also served as a visiting professor at several universities. In the spring semester of 1960 he lectured at the University of Minnesota and in the following year at Iowa State University. In 1963 he delivered the Raymond Fred West Memorial Lectures at Stanford University in California. In the 1965–1966 academic year he became the first Jewish theologian to assume a visiting professorship at Union Theological Seminary in New York, located just across the street from Jewish Theological Seminary, at Broadway and 122nd Street. There he drew more students to his classes than any other visiting professor in the school's history. But it was not only the students who came to Heschel; he reached out to them as well. According to J. A. Sanders, a professor at Union, "Heschel made himself available to students and colleagues in ways that put the rest of the faculty to shame. Like the God of whom he spoke so warmly, Heschel was always there."[40]

THE INFLUENCE AND RANGE OF HESCHEL'S BOOKS

While his tenured post and the visiting professorships that Heschel assumed were highlights in his academic career, the chief milestones in his career were, as Franklin Sherman points out, the publication of his books.[41] This view is confirmed by Moshe Starkman, a Yiddish writer and historian: "It soon became evident that American Jewry had long awaited such a figure as Abraham Joshua Heschel. . . . Every new book by Heschel intrigued Jews searching for roads back toward Judaism. More than anyone else in our time, he helped the seeking Jews gain vision to see the *maor sheb'yahadut,* the bright and brilliant within Judaism, the humanism and universalism within *Yiddishkeit.*"[42]

The influence of Heschel's books, however, extends far beyond his Jewish audience. Referring to Heschel as "an apostle to the Gentiles," J.A. Sanders writes: "His influence on Christianity, especially since the publication in 1951 of *The Sabbath* and *Man Is Not Alone,* has been remarkable. . . . Heschel's greatest influence upon Christian thinking in the post-war period was *God in Search of Man.* For the first time, many Christian thinkers learned that God already was, and had been for a long time, what traditional Christian dogma taught was revealed only in Christ. . . . In Christian idiom, Heschel had an incarnational faith without the Incarnation."[43] Explaining why Heschel's books and essays became "the devotional reading of myriads of non-Jews," the renowned scholar W. D. Davies writes:

> Through his faith in the God beyond all mystery he ministered to our ultimate human need and, therefore, to us all. In his books and speeches, in which the cadences and rhythms and patterns of ancient synagogal prayers and sermons reverberate, his very prose is instinct with a poetry that strangely recalls us to primordial certainties. In all these he called into being the emotions which he described, and summoned, not only Jews, but non-Jews also, to the depth of awe, wonder and mystery that life should evoke in all men.[44]

The concern and interest that fills Heschel's books is as wide as the appeal and impact those books enjoy. Since Heschel's books are known primarily for the depth of wisdom they convey, the breadth of issues they contain is astounding. Heschel's books and essays deal with biblical and rabbinic theology, medieval philosophy, Jewish mysticism, Hasidism and its great masters, Eastern European Jewry, the meaning of Israel, the Sabbath, prayer and symbolism, time and space, the philosophy of being, the meaning of being human, the philosophy of religion and of Judaism in particular, applied religious ethics, social justice and racial equality, war and peace—to name but a few of his concerns. Not only did Heschel deal intelligently with these various issues, he made major contributions to the understanding of many of them.[45] Moreover, the variety of Heschel's works does not indicate a lack of integration to his scholarly endeavors. Rather, it bespeaks his realization that an interpretation of the classical sources of Judaism is a necessary prerequisite for the development of a creative religious or Jewish philosophy for our time. Jacob Neusner, a critical scholar who is seldom complimentary toward contemporary theologians, confirms this view in a statement of unrestrained praise of Heschel's contributions: "What is remarkable is that he knew everything he had to know to do what he wanted to do. . . . In point of fact, there is not a single record of Jewish religious experience, not a single moment in the unfolding of the Jewish spirit, which Heschel did not take into his own being and reshape through the crucible of his own mind and soul."[46] It was because of such breadth of learning and depth of understanding that Reuven Kimelman claimed that to encounter Heschel "was to witness a three thousand year tradition rolled up into one soul."[47]

HESCHEL'S MAJOR WORKS

It is a telling fact that the first of Heschel's books to appear after World War II and the Holocaust that accompanied it was entitled *The Earth Is the*

Lord's: The Inner World of the Jew in East Europe. Published in 1950, this book is an eloquent tribute to the people from and with whom Heschel learned to develop his own inner life as a Jew. "It is a primary document," writes Franklin Sherman about this book, "which itself represents the spirit and the style of life that it depicts."[48] In the book's preface, Heschel claims that "the East European period . . . was the golden period in Jewish history, in the history of the Jewish soul."[49] And with this book, says Jacob Neusner, "Heschel writes its obituary."[50]

While Heschel wrote the obituary for one age of Jewish history, his books represent for a new age what Will Herberg calls "a renascence of Jewish religious thinking."[51] And the brilliance of Heschel's religious thinking is expressed nowhere more beautifully than in *The Sabbath: Its Meaning for Modern Man,* published in 1951. The title and the subtitle reflect what Sherman calls "a typical Heschel enterprise,"[52] linking an ancient and venerable Jewish heritage, the Sabbath, with the situation of contemporary people.

It is not only in *The Sabbath,* but in each of his books, that Heschel demonstrates the relevance of the Jewish heritage for the modern world. The next two books are primary examples of this and their titles aptly summarize the essence of Heschel's philosophy of Judaism. Whereas in the wake of World War II and the Holocaust many people spoke of humanity's dreadful aloneness in a world that had been abandoned by God, Heschel, son of the now extinct Warsaw Jewish community, brought from the depths of his anguished soul the affirmation expressed in *Man Is Not Alone,* and held fast to his faith in *God in Search of Man.* In these books, published as companion volumes in 1951 and 1955 respectively, Heschel explores the basis for faith in God and suggests ways of developing rapport with God's presence. Upon the release of the first of these, Reinhold Niebuhr predicted that Heschel would become "a commanding and authoritative voice not only in the Jewish community but in the religious life of America."[53] Since prior to that publication Heschel was not well known outside the world of Jewish scholarship, Fritz Rothschild notes that Niebuhr's prediction "sounded more like a pious wish than a realistic expectation." But Rothschild goes on to acknowledge that "two decades later Heschel had emerged as the outstanding Jewish thinker of his generation, a major spiritual force in contemporary America and a recognized spokesman for Judaism among theologians and informed laymen."[54] Referring to *Man Is Not Alone* as a "masterly analysis of faith," Niebuhr wrote: "The volume is so impressive because it is the work of a poet and mystic who has mastered the philosophical and scientific disciplines and who with consummate skill reveals the dimension of reality apprehended by religious faith."[55] Reviewing *God in Search of Man,* Niebuhr continued his praise of Heschel: "This new volume . . . enhances the gratitude of all readers who sense the authentically religious quality of his mind, in which Biblical thought is blended with the mystic quality of the Hasidic tradition in which he was nurtured."[56] Fifteen years after its publication, Jacob Neusner called *God in Search of Man* "the single best introduction to the intellectual heritage of Judaism."[57]

While the two books last mentioned are commonly considered Heschel's *magna opera* as a creative philosopher and theologian, his two-volume Hebrew work, *Torah min ha-šhamayim be-ispaḳlaryah šhel ha-dorot* (Torah from Heaven in the Light of the Generations), is generally regarded as his *magnum opus* as a historian of theology. In these volumes, which appeared in 1962 and 1965 respectively,[58] Heschel explores and expounds the major issues of revelation according to different strands of rabbinic theology. Claiming that "every page yields a new insight into some passage in Rabbinic literature," Seymour Siegel hails this work as "an achievement of great significance in the history of Jewish thought," as "an epoch-making event in the history of Rabbinic scholarship."[59] Jacob Neusner, himself a renowned rabbinic scholar, claims that "this work will remain absolutely essential for all future studies of rabbinic theology."[60]

The publication of *The Prophets* in 1962 was a great milestone both in Heschel's career and in the history of biblical scholarship. According to Bernhard Anderson, a famous biblical scholar, Heschel's monumental work on the prophets is "the most penetrating study of the subject that has appeared."[61] It is in this book more than any other, including the much slimmer *Die Prophetie* of 1936, that Heschel expounds what Fritz Rothschild called his "truly revolutionary doctrine" of divine pathos.

The West Memorial lectures which Heschel had delivered at Stanford were published in 1965 as a book entitled *Who Is Man?* An eloquent defense of the uniqueness of being human, this book persuasively counters all forms of anthropological reductionism and shows that genuine human living involves openness to transcendence and partnership with God. Maurice Friedman recommends *Who Is Man?* as "the clearest and most cogent statement of Heschel's philosophy."[62]

In addition to the forenamed books, two collections of Heschel's addresses and essays have been published. *Man's Quest for God: Studies in Prayer and Symbolism* (1954) contains what Will Herberg calls "one of the most penetrating discussions of prayer and one of the most devastating critiques of the secularism consuming Jewish religious life in America to appear in many years."[63] Says another critic: "This book may well turn out to be the most important book dealing with the theology of praying that has been published in our time."[64]

The Insecurity of Freedom: Essays on Human Existence (1966) is a collection of twenty essays dealing with issues such as race relations, medical care, the plight of the elderly, ecumenism, and religious education.

More than any of his other books, this work shows the practical ramifications of Heschel's religious philosophy.

Aside from these two collections of essays, there is an anthology of Heschel's writings entitled *Between God and Man: An Interpretation of Judaism*. Published in 1959, it is a work composed of sections of Heschel's previous books and of manuscripts of his then-forthcoming works. It is superbly edited and introduced by Fritz Rothschild and it provides a good overview of Heschel's theology.

All of Heschel's books are answers to appeals, spoken or not, of those who are searching for the meaning of human existence and of religious faith. Two of his books, *Vietnam: Crisis of Conscience* (1967) and *Israel: An Echo of Eternity* (1968) are answers to explicit requests by others for Heschel's help. Robert McAfee Brown's explanation of how Heschel became involved in co-authoring the book on Vietnam reveals much about Heschel and how he acted upon his conviction that "at this hour Vietnam is our most urgent, our most disturbing religious problem, a challenge to the whole nation as well as a challenge to every one of us as an individual."[65] After explaining how he and Michael Novak conceived to write a book on Vietnam which would be addressed to the American religious communities in an attempt "to create a climate of opinion that would make it politically feasible to deescalate the then escalating war," Brown relates why and how Heschel was invited to be a co-author, as well as Heschel's brief but telling response:

> We needed a Jew as a co-author since we already represented between ourselves the Catholic and Protestant traditions. Did we dare approach Heschel, the great man with so many other pressing demands upon his time? We decided to dare, though without much hope. So I phoned Heschel the next morning, outlined our concern and our project, and asked with great temerity whether he would consider uniting with two younger and less well-known colleagues in the production of such a book. His reply was instantaneous: "My friend, I am at your disposal."[66]

Heschel also put himself at the disposal of the Anti-Defamation League when its leadership requested his help. After the Six Day War of 1967, when Israel was once again faced with the threat of annihilation, the League felt the urgent need to convey to Christians just what Israel means to the Jewish people. "The best person to do this was Abraham Joshua Heschel," claimed an ADL spokesperson. "When our office approached Dr. Heschel with a request that he write a paper on Israel for the Christian community, he readily agreed and put aside his work on Mendl of Kotzk. The Kotzker was dear to his heart, but Israel was paramount."[67] The result was far more than expected: a beautifully written book expressing the significance that Israel holds for Jews everywhere.

Heschel returned to his work on the Kotzker, which resulted in a two-volume book in Yiddish, *Kotzk: In gerangl far emesdikeit (Kotzk: The Struggle for Integrity)*, and *A Passion for Truth*, described as "probably the best book on Hasidism to appear in the English language."[68] Both works were completed just days before Heschel died and were published in 1973. These are Heschel's most disquieting books, wherein his own struggle for integrity and passion for truth are evident on every page. Jack Riemer describes *A Passion for Truth* as "a work of solid scholarship" and "an essay in comparative culture" and then adds "it is essentially spiritual autobiography, disguised as research."[69] The bold spiritual wrestling and the prophetic challenge found in Heschel's previous books are intensified here. Recalling that Heschel submitted the test to the publisher the very day before he died, Riemer writes: "It is in many ways a summary of how he lived and what he stood for."[70] Eugene Borowitz agrees: "With this work, Heschel wrote his own magnificent epitaph."[71] Concerning the significance of Heschel's last work being primarily in the field of Hasidism, Reuven Kimelman writes:

> Heschel's work reached its climax in his study of mysticism and Hasidism. Although he left Hasidic life to go to Berlin, Hasidism never really left him. For some strange reason, which only his disciples sense, he put off making his major contribution to the understanding of Hasidism. Previously, he had written on specific Hasidic masters, and had described their lives in *The Earth Is the Lord's*. And yet, it was not until the last week of his life that he finished a full-length portrait of Rabbi Mendl of Kotzk with whom he compared the Baal Shem Tov. It was with this book that he repaid his debt to the world of Hasidism and was laid to rest.[72]

"A JEWELER OF WORDS"

Although Heschel has been laid to rest, what he said of the Kotzker may now be said of him: "He has not fled from us by dying. Somehow his lightning persists."[73] This is so not only because of the sublime message he left behind but also because of the poetic grandeur by which he conveyed that message. "His poetic images not only shine; they burn. They sear our soul with the urgency with which God seeks man."[74]

Heschel believed that "music is the soul of language" and that "a sentence without a tone, without a musical quality is like a body without a soul."[75] He made sure that the language he employed and the literary corpus he produced was full of soul. "His works are like enchanted forests," writes Fritz Rothschild. "If only we take the effort to enter into them, we shall find them both enchanted and enchanting."[76] Thus do Heschel's works evoke the religious sensitivity of which he writes. Literary scholar Edward Kaplan explains this well:

> When we start to read a book by Abraham Heschel, we enter a universe of excitement and wonder, an electric atmosphere where words sing and thoughts dance. We enter the domain of written love, of a love that writes itself, loves as it expresses itself, loves as it weaves sentences to celebrate God. When we read Abraham Heschel, we enter a poetic universe which takes God seriously.
>
> If we allow ourselves to follow the movement of his thought, we ourselves begin to seek God, and even attempt to experience God's presence. It is the poetic aspect of Heschel's writings that conveys a feeling for the divine presence in human experience.[77]

Heschel's works are things of beauty precisely because he took great pains to make them so. Recalling the care with which Heschel wrote, Mrs. Heschel relates how sometimes when she would ask him at night how his work went that day he would reply: "I wrote a good sentence today."[78] It is understandable, then, that Balfour Brickner would call Heschel "a Jeweler of words."[79] Judith Herschlag Muffs, who was privileged to help Heschel prepare the text of *Israel: An Echo of Eternity,* confirms this view while providing us with a rare glimpse of how Heschel worked:

> I saw the meticulous care with which he chose every word. I saw him climbing the footstool in his study, going from volume to volume to find the right quotation, the right nuance. His study was warm, cluttered and overflowing. The thesaurus and dictionary were always at hand. . . . Often when I came, he would hand me several sheets of paper with what he had written "between visits." Sometimes each sheet would contain just one sentence. Later he would string the sentences together as a necklace.[80]

"Words must not fall off our lips like dead leaves in the autumn," said Heschel. "They must rise like birds out of the heart into the vast expanse of eternity."[81] Heschel's own words did as much, and, if we let them, they may carry us with them into the eternal dimension they celebrate.

SOCIAL ACTION AND LEADERSHIP

Heschel's writings are genuinely religious because his was an authentic religious life: a harmony of prayer, study, and action. Heschel's action consisted primarily in the unsung *mitsvot* of a pious Jew. But he also took a public stand on social issues, even to the point that, according to *Newsweek*'s Kenneth L. Woodward, "Heschel assumed a role of social leadership seldom attained by a man of prayer."[82] Thus it was not simply from reading Heschel's books that Reinhold Niebuhr was moved to call Heschel "the most authentic prophet of religious life in our culture."[83]

"Reflection about the prophets gives way to communion with the prophets," writes Heschel.[84] And it was communion with the prophets of Israel that compelled Heschel, the great expositor of prophetic religion, to take a prophetic stand on behalf of the poor, the neglected, and the oppressed people in our world. In a nationally televised interview, taped shortly before his death, Heschel acknowledged the fact that his exploration of the prophets changed his life: "Early in my life, my great love was for learning, studying. And the place where I preferred to live was my study. . . . I've learned from the prophets I have to be involved with the affairs of man, in the affairs of suffering man."[85] Realizing that Heschel has been acclaimed by many to be a prophet for our time, NBC's Carl Stern asked Heschel frankly, "Well, are you a prophet?" Heschel's response: "I wouldn't accept this praise, because it's not for me to say that I am a descendant of the prophets, . . . what is called *Bnai Nevi'im*. So let us hope and pray that I am worthy of being a descendant of the prophets."[86] To his disciples, Heschel was indeed one of the *Bnai Nevi'im*. Bernhard Anderson has said of him what Heschel himself suggested was the mark of a prophet, "that his life was a prophetic sympathy with the pathos of God."[87]

While acknowledging that affinity with the prophets thrust Heschel into a prophetic role, W. D. Davies suggests that it was also Heschel's experience in Europe, where he witnessed the silence of so many otherwise decent people in the face of Nazi crimes, that lent special urgency to his awareness of having to "speak out" and take a public stand on social and political issues. Says Davies: "Abraham Heschel felt that it was important, not only that one protest against evil, but that one be seen to protest, even at the risk of being misinterpreted and misunderstood."[88] Heschel suffered the risk and the subsequent criticism because in his view: "Indifference to evil is more insidious than evil itself. . . . A silent justification, it makes possible an evil erupting as an exception becoming the rule and being in turn accepted."[89] Byron Sherwin would agree with Professor Davies that it was the silence of many in the face of the Holocaust, as well as his communion with Israel's prophets, that prompted Heschel to wage a prophetic protest against evil and against indifference to evil. In Sherwin's words: "Memory of the lost Atlantis of European Jewry was always with him" and "was a motivating force behind his words and deeds."[90]

Heschel's prophetic protest started early in his life and was particularly evident in an anti-Nazi lecture that he delivered in Frankfurt am Main in March 1938.[91] Several years later, soon after arriving in the United States, Heschel tried to persuade leaders of American Jewry to intercede to help save European Jewry.[92] Yet it was only in the last decade of his life that Heschel emerged as a recognized ethical leader of national prominence.

This began in 1963 when Heschel delivered the keynote address at the National Conference on Religion and Race which led to widespread clergy participation in the great "march on Washington."[93]

Heschel was passionate and persistent in his support of civil rights and in his condemnation of racism which, as an "unmitigated evil," he considered as "worse than idolatry."[94] Acting on his belief that "one must be seen to protest" against evil, Heschel appeared with Martin Luther King on numerous occasions and he marched by his side from Selma to Montgomery.

Heschel also protested the American involvement in the Vietnam war. Not only was he one of the earliest opponents of that war, he was, claims Robert McAfee Brown, "*the* supreme Jewish voice and leader on Vietnam."[95] "To speak about God and remain silent on Vietnam is blasphemous," said Heschel.[96] And in the last years of his life Heschel seemed to speak as much about Vietnam as he did about God. John C. Bennett, past president of Union Theological Seminary, remembers how Heschel "never stopped pressing those questions" about how the American people could allow our country to perpetrate the atrocity of the Vietnam war. "Two days before his death, the last time I was to hear his voice," recalls Dr. Bennett, "he spoke about the intensified bombing of North Vietnam, of the agony of Vietnam and of the shame of America and of the conflict in her soul."[97] Along with Dr. Bennett, Heschel had been one of the founders and a national co-chairman of Clergy and Laity Concerned about Vietnam, an organization that helped to bring the horror of this war, and its moral and religious implications, to the attention of the American people. It was largely in connection with this organization that Heschel spent an enormous amount of time and energy in the service of peace.[98]

Heschel was also the first major Jewish figure to urge world Jewry to come to the aid of the Jews in the Soviet Union. "Early in the 1960's," writes Reuven Kimelman, "when Heschel was forging concern for Vietnam, he was simultaneously lighting the spark for one of the greatest protest movements of Jewish history—Soviet Jewry."[99] Speaking about the same issue, Maurice Friedman claims: "What is today a widespread movement of protest Heschel began as an almost singlehanded fight."[100] It was on September 4, 1963, at a convocation of the Rabbinical Assembly in New York, that Heschel sounded the battle cry against the "spiritual genocide" being inflicted on Jews in the Soviet Union. "The six million are no more," cried Heschel. "Now three million face spiritual extinction. . . . Let the twentieth century not enter the annals of Jewish history as the century of physical and spiritual destruction! If I forget thee, O Russian Jewry. . . ."[101] Recalling Heschel's address to the Assembly, Fritz Rothschild writes: "His passionate plea for massive public action received wide publicity in the press and led to the subsequent formation of the American Conference on

Soviet Jewry."[102] It is largely because of the persistent efforts of Heschel and those he inspired that Russian Jewry has not been forgotten and that the lot of many Russian Jews has been improved.

These are but a few of the humanitarian causes to which Heschel was actively dedicated and, along with the cause of religious ecumenism, are the ones in which he assumed the task of prophetic leadership. About Heschel's involvement, W. D. Davies writes: "His will be an enduring Jewish presence in the history of the protest movements of our day."[103]

ECUMENICAL IMPACT

Heschel was also very active on the ecumenical front. Most noteworthy is the prominent role he assumed in the negotiations between Jewish organizations and the hierarchy of the Catholic church before and during the Second Vatican Council. In Rome during the council, Heschel represented the American Jewish Committee in its effort to improve Jewish–Christian relations and to eliminate anti-Judaism from church teachings. The American Jewish Committee realized that the church's attitude toward Jews was related to basic questions of theology and therefore chose Heschel, on the basis of his theological acumen, to represent the committee at the council. In December 1961 Heschel met with Augustin Cardinal Bea, the head of the Secretariat for Christian Unity, who invited Heschel to submit suggestions to the Ecumenical Council to improve Catholic–Jewish relations. Concerning Heschel's response to Bea, Fritz Rothschild writes:

> Heschel's memorandum, prepared in cooperation with the American Jewish Committee, made three important recommendations. It urged the Council "to reject and condemn those who assert that the Jews as a people are responsible for the crucifixion. . . ." It suggested that the Council "acknowledge the integrity and permanent preciousness of the Jews and Judaism" so that the Jews be accepted *as Jews*. This meant that the Church would reconsider its missionary attitude and refrain from regarding Jews primarily as potential converts. And finally, it called for programs "to eliminate abuses and derogatory stereotypes" by promoting scholarly cooperation and the creation of church agencies to combat religious prejudice.[104]

Throughout the remaining four years of Vatican II, Heschel remained the most influential American Jewish delegate at the council. Although the final conciliar decree on the Jews did not fulfill Heschel's original expectations, "he nevertheless felt that it was a landmark in Jewish–Catholic relations and opened the path for a new era of better understanding and mutual respect.[105] This "landmark" was largely due to Heschel's presence and effort at the council.

While Heschel enjoyed significant influence in "official" interfaith relations, he also had far-reaching ecumenical influence by working in an "unofficial" capacity. Simply by living and teaching as he did, placing himself where he was in relation to non-Jews, particularly Christians, Heschel may have done more to inspire an enhanced appreciation of Judaism among non-Jews than any other Jew in post-biblical history. Although other Jews have represented the grandeur of Judaism, perhaps as much as Heschel did, he seems to have communicated the splendor of his tradition to non-Jews, particularly Christians, more than others have been able to do. Only in recent decades have Christians finally begun turning to Jews for their interpretation of Judaism rather than to Christian critics of Judaism, and in doing so they have found that "the entire range of the holy books of Judaism speaks, in particular, through Heschel."[106]

Speaking of Heschel's influence on Christians and on himself in particular, Robert McAfee Brown states:

> Heschel's contribution to Christians consisted in his being such a good Jew, and this did not separate him from us but enabled us to work together more closely on the things that concerned us all. He has always left me finally disquieted, however, for when I have been in his presence and have talked with him and have heard him pray, I have been moved to ask myself, "What have I got to tell this man about God?" and thus far I have never found an answer. At this stage of the Christian–Jewish dialogue I remain content to learn.[107]

To have inspired an outstanding Christian theologian to such an extent that he felt he had nothing to tell Heschel about God and was therefore "content to learn" from him was for Heschel to perform a major feat for Judaism vis-à-vis Christianity. And what he did for Brown, Heschel did for many other Christians as well. A Christian biblical scholar, W. D. Davies, says of Heschel: "To encounter him was to 'feel' the force and spirit of Judaism, the depth and grandeur of it. He led one, even thrust one, into the mysterious greatness of the Jewish tradition."[108] Still another outstanding Christian thinker, John C. Bennett, confirms this view of Heschel's ecumenical significance: "Abraham Heschel belonged to the whole American religious community. I know of no other person of whom this was so true. He was profoundly Jewish in his spiritual and cultural roots, in his closeness to Jewish suffering, in his religious commitment, in his love for the nation and land of Israel, and in the quality of his prophetic presence. And yet he was a religious inspiration to Christians and to many searching people beyond the familiar religious boundaries."[109]

As "a religious inspiration to Christians" Heschel has helped them gain a vision of the enduring grandeur and validity of Judaism and thereby reject the anti-Judaism that has often inflamed the horror of racist anti-Semitism. Dr. Bennett explains: "I truly believe that there has been a radical break in the minds and consciences of both Protestants and Catholics with their evil past of anti-Judaism, which so often helped to create the climate in which brutal racist anti-Semitism has flourished. I have great confidence that this turning has at last come, this turning away from so cruel and wicked a history, and Abraham Heschel has had an enormous influence in what one may call the consolidation of this change."[110]

If Heschel's influence on Christians and on their understanding of Judaism has been as great as these scholars claim, it is not simply because Christians have turned to Heschel for their understanding; it is also because he made the effort to speak to them. Although he made no attempt to convert non-Jews to Judaism, Heschel's task was "to transform the hearts and minds not only of Jews but also of Christians and of all men."[111] In this effort, Heschel not only helped Christians overcome their anti-Jewish prejudice and gain instead an appreciation for the greatness of Judaism, but he also nourished them in their own faith in the living God. All of this adds up to what Harold Kasimow calls "Heschel's as yet immeasurable impact on the Christian world."[112]

Heschel's ecumenical significance is also evident in the way he helped his fellow Jews deepen their appreciation for the validity and significance of religions other than their own, particularly Christianity. He also helped Jews realize the importance of interfaith encounter: how Jews could be spiritually enriched by the encounter just as they could help enrich the lives of people in other traditions. Professor Kasimow goes so far as to claim: "A thorough analysis of the Jewish attitude to the other religions from Biblical times to the present reveals that Heschel's position . . . promises to be the most meaningful position if dialogue between Judaism and other religions is really to take place."[113]

Heschel taught that "in this aeon diversity of religions is the will of God" and in this context asked: "Does not the task of preparing the kingdom of God require a diversity of talents, a variety of rituals, soul-searching as well as opposition?"[114] Since "the majesty of God transcends the dignity of religion," Heschel asked, "should we not regard a divergent religion as His Majesty's loyal opposition?"[115]

The essence of Heschel's approach to interfaith dialogue is perhaps best summarized in the following excerpts:

> *No religion is an island.* We are all involved with one another. Spiritual betrayal on the part of one of us affects the faith of all of us. Views adopted in one community have an impact on other communities. . . .

We fail to realize that while different exponents of faith in the world of religion continue to be wary of the ecumenical movement, there is another ecumenical movement, world-wide in extent and influence: nihilism. We must choose between interfaith and inter-nihilism. Cynicism is not parochial. Should religions insist upon the illusion of complete isolation? Should we refuse to be on speaking terms with one another and hope for each other's failure? Or should we pray for each other's health, and help one another in preserving one's respective legacy, in preserving a common legacy? . . .

Over and above mutual respect we must acknowledge indebtedness to one another. . . .

The purpose of religious communication among human beings of different commitments is mutual enrichment and enhancement of respect and appreciation rather than the hope that the person spoken to will prove to be wrong in what he regards as sacred.[116]

Reflecting on Heschel's openness toward and respect for religions other than his own, W. D. Davies writes:

Here is the paradox of Abraham Heschel: he was most Jewish and yet most universal. . . . Polish-Hasidic transplant in some sense he always remained. And yet this Polish Hasid in his inaugural address at Union Theological Seminary provided a basis for loyalty to other traditions than his own. In particular, rooted in his own faith, he recognized that despite its failures the Christian faith had had a role in the redemption of all men.

How was this possible? It was possible because Abraham Heschel never lost the certainty given him in Hasidism. As he had entered the strange and sophisticated world of western European culture and learning, in Germany and later in this country, he always carried with him the simplicity, wonder and richness of Hasidic faith. Above all, he never abandoned the depth of its certainty in the reality of the Living God in whose image all men were created and are being made. Throughout his life he continued to make dazzlingly clear and luminous and alive the concept of the One God, belief in whom we have all owed to Israel for close on three millennia. In the certainty that beyond all mystery is God, beyond the darkness of our human pilgrimage, however horrendous, the Light of the Lord, Abraham Heschel discovered a ground for being open to recognize the common element, nay the common need, behind all the religious differences of men. He always insisted on the universal need of men for the Living God; and so it was that he was most human as he was most Jewish: Israel and humanity for him were concentric.[117]

By word and example, this "most Jewish and yet most universal" man inspired loyalty to one's own tradition and reverence for different traditions. In so doing, Heschel made a monumental contribution to ecumenism and interfaith accord.

"LOYALTY OF ALL MY LOYALTIES"

The life and works of Abraham Joshua Heschel reveal him to have been a man of many commitments and diverse achievements. Yet his life and works had but one center that held together all that concerned him, all that consumed him. That center was God. In Heschel's own words: "My life is shaped by many loyalties—to my family, to my friends, to my people, to the U.S. constitution, etc. Each of my loyalties has its ultimate root in one ultimate relationship: loyalty to God, the loyalty of all my loyalties. That relationship is the covenant of Sinai. All we are we owe to Him. He has enriched us with gifts of insight, with the joy of moments full of blessing. He has also suffered with us in years of agony and distress."[118]

Heschel was fond of saying "God is of no importance unless He is of supreme importance."[119] In his own life and works, Abraham Joshua Heschel revealed the supreme importance of God as well as what it is like to live with faith in God. It is appropriate, then, that we explore Heschel's depth theology to learn what he thought it was that sparked the genesis of such faith.

2

Depth Theology

The purpose of depth theology is not to establish a doctrine but to lay bare some of the roots of our being, stirred by the Ultimate Question. Its theme is faith in status nascendi.[1]

Why attempt "to lay bare some of the roots of our being"? Why explore the genesis of faith? Because to do so is to fulfill a basic human obligation: to strive for truth, the truth of what it means to be human. This obligation includes the responsibility to seek to know whether one's faith is rooted in truth. The purpose of what Abraham Heschel calls "depth theology" is "to explore the depth of faith, the substratum out of which belief arises," in order to discover, as far as possible, "the truth of religion" as well as "man's capacity to sense the truth of religion."[2]

Heschel knows that the way to truth is not without trial. He is quite aware of the human tendency toward self-deception: "We are indignant when we are fooled by others but live comfortably with our unconscious desire for self-deceit, being effusive when we flatter our own selves, deriving pleasure from wishful thinking."[3] Depth theology entails the confrontation with this secret desire for self-deceit. In the opening chapter of *God in Search of Man,* Heschel's most comprehensive work of depth theology, he recalls a pertinent teaching of Rabbi Bunam of Przyscha: "Now this is the law: Thou shalt not deceive thy fellow-man (Leviticus 25:17). A hasid goes beyond the law; he will not even deceive his own self."[4] Heschel's depth theology is the work of a religious thinker who, as an observant Jew, is careful not to deceive others and, as a true hasid, is careful not to deceive himself.

The purpose of this chapter is to examine Heschel's conception of depth theology and its relation to the philosophy of religion and to theology per se. This examination is meant to illustrate the precise nature of Heschel's inquiry into the substratum of religion and faith. As such, it serves as an introduction to the remaining chapters of this book which explore what Heschel considers to be the sources and antecedents of religious faith.

The Study of Religion

Depth theology is the study of religion, particularly the sources and antecedents of religious existence and faith. It is a study that demands remembrance of religious tradition as well as personal religious insight. It focuses on those for whom religion is a way of life and seeks to penetrate their consciousness in order to perceive the reality that stirs them. Its method is that of "situational thinking," thinking within the context of those situations that give rise to the ultimate questions to which religion is an answer.

WHAT IS RELIGION?

What is the essence of religion? Where is religion found? How should it be studied? To what and to whom should we turn in order to study religion? In what spirit should we approach religion in order to understand its proper mode of being?

Do rituals and myths constitute the essence of religion? Is religion found in sacraments and scriptures? Does a careful study of religious deeds and doctrines expose the proper nature of religion? To what extent does the study of institutional structures disclose the truth of religion? Is it possible to discern the essence of religion by taking cross-cultural surveys of opinions and attitudes concerning religion? Is religion best studied in a spirit of impartial analysis or detached speculation?

Rituals and myths, sacraments and scriptures, deeds and doctrines, as well as the contexts or institutions in which these are found, are vital components of religion. As such, they must be studied in order to arrive at a proper understanding of religion. Yet what of the dimension that gives rise to religious actions and words and to the institutions that preserve them? Is it not imperative to explore the innerness or intimacy of religious living in order to attain insight into the meaning and truth of religion? Heschel believes it is.[5] For him, ritual without reverence is like language without tone. Deed without depth is a body without soul. Creed without faith is an answer to a forgotten question.

"Religion is an answer to man's ultimate questions," says Heschel.[6] But many religious persons forget the questions that gave rise to their practices.

The decline of religion is due to the demise of ultimate questions within the hearts and minds of those who "practice" religion; it is due to religion devoid of life. This is the opening paragraph of Heschel's *God in Search of Man:*

> It is customary to blame secular science and anti-religious philosophy for the eclipse of religion in modern society. It would be more honest to blame religion for its own defeats. Religion declined not because it was refuted, but because it became irrelevant, dull, oppressive, insipid. When faith is completely replaced by creed, worship by discipline, love by habit; when the crisis of today is ignored because of the splendor of the past; when faith becomes an heirloom rather than a living fountain; when religion speaks only in the name of authority rather than with the voice of compassion—its message becomes meaningless.[7]

In order to discover religious meaning and truth, to resurrect the life of religion and faith, we must recover the situations in which religious insight and commitment were born. We must "rediscover the questions to which religion is an answer."[8] This is the task of depth theology. The rationale for this task and a brief description of it is stated thus by Heschel:

> Religion has been reduced to institution, symbol, theology. It does not affect the pretheological situation, the presymbolic depth of existence. To redirect the trend, we must lay bare what is involved in religious existence; we must recover the situations which both precede and correspond to the theological formulations; we must recall the questions which religious doctrines are trying to answer, *the antecedents of religious commitment,* the presuppositions of faith. . . . The inquiry must proceed both by delving into the consciousness of man and by delving into the teachings and attitudes of the religious tradition.[9]

Notice, what Heschel is speaking about is a twofold inquiry rather than two disparate projects. "Delving into the consciousness of man" involves a study of the traditions people have consciously assumed. "Delving into the teachings and attitudes of the religious tradition" requires a penetration of the human consciousness in which those teachings and attitudes were formed.

SOURCES OF RELIGIOUS THINKING

Depth theology, being the twofold inquiry that it is, draws on two sources of religious thinking: memory of tradition and personal insight.[10] Concerning the importance of memory for Jewish religious thinking, Heschel writes:

The essence of Jewish religious thinking does not lie in entertaining a concept of God but in the ability to articulate a memory of moments of illumination by His presence. . . . Reminders of what has been disclosed to us are hanging over our souls like stars, remote and of mind-surpassing grandeur. They shine through dark and dangerous ages, and their reflection can be seen in the lives of those who guard the path of conscience and memory in the wilderness of careless living.

Since those perennial reminders have moved into our minds, wonder has never left us. Heedfully we stare through the telescope of ancient rites lest we lose the perpetual brightness beckoning to our souls.[11]

Essential as it is, memory alone is not a self-sufficient source of Jewish religious thinking. Personal insight, or the striving for insight, is as indispensable as memory: "A great event, miraculous as it may be, if it happened only once, will hardly be able to dominate forever the mind of man. The mere remembrance of such an event is hardly powerful enough to hold in its spell the soul of man with its constant restlessness and vitality. There was wrestling for insight out of which Jewish faith drew its strength."[12]

These last two quotations show that, for Heschel, memory and insight are intimately connected sources of religious thinking and faith. The memory of miraculous moments ignites the abiding wonder that sparks the quest for insight. Furthermore, the miraculous moments that are remembered were themselves moments of illumined insight. And these remembered moments gave rise to a tradition comprised not simply of dogmas and laws, teachings and facts, but to one that is itself "a heritage of insight. What is the ultimate nature of the sacred words which tradition preserves? These words are not made of paper but of life. The task is not to reproduce in sound what is preserved in graphic signs; the task is to resurrect its life, to feel its pulse, so that the life within the words should reproduce its kind within our lives. Indeed there is a heritage of insight as there is a tradition of words and rituals."[13]

There is "life within the words" of tradition because the words were born of "the living insights" of impassioned souls: "Beneath the calm surface of creed and law the souls were astir. Our task, then, is to go beneath the tranquility of creed and tradition in order to overhear the echoes of wrestling and to recapture the living insights."[14] The "heritage of insight" of which Heschel speaks is "a tradition transmitted from soul to soul, inherited like the power to love, and kept alive by constant communion with the Word."[15] Such a tradition flourishes only in the lives of those who personally share in the tradition's reservoir of insight by way of personal insight. In order "to recapture the living insights" we must have personal insight, since "in the realm of the spirit only he who is a pioneer is able to be an heir."[16] We must therefore venture into situations akin to those in which the living insights were born; we must ask those ultimate questions which preceded the answers of creed and law that we have inherited. "To overhear the echoes of wrestling" we ourselves must wrestle for insight. There is no understanding by standing aloof; only if we "go beneath the tranquility of creed and tradition" will we be able truly to understand.

Heschel himself explored the depth of the Jewish tradition and wrestled with the insights that brought it forth. The extent to which his own religious thinking is rooted in both memory and personal insight is best summarized by Jacob Neusner: "There is not a single record of Jewish religious experience, not a single moment in the unfolding of the Jewish spirit, which Heschel did not take into his own being and reshape through the crucible of his own mind and soul."[17]

HOW TO STUDY RELIGION

Although a genuine understanding of religion comes only to those who "go beneath" its surface and explore its depth, there are those who seek to know and evaluate religion without such involvement. "Having attained supreme critical detachment from their subject matter, some scholars apply to religion a paleontological method," says Heschel, "as if it were a fossil chiseled from the shale or a plant brought home by an expedition from exotic lands."[18] One way of maintaining "critical detachment" while attempting to study religion is "by submitting questionnaires to a typical group of people or by taking the views and mentality of an average person as a perspective of judgment."[19] While such projects may be worthwhile as sociological studies, they must not pretend to capture the essence or worth of religion, a right understanding of which can not be found by surveying "typical" groups or "average" persons, many of whom may be neutral or indifferent with regard to religion. On the contrary, it is by turning to religious persons, "to those whose mind is bent upon the spiritual, whose life *is* religion,"[20] that an accurate idea of religion may be formed. "It [religion] can only be studied in its natural habitat of faith and piety, in a soul where the divine is within reach of all thoughts. . . . By penetrating the consciousness of the pious man, we may conceive the reality behind it."[21] A survey of religious behavior and opinions does not necessitate religious sympathy and engagement on the part of the researcher. But a detached analysis is insufficient for those who would penetrate "the consciousness of the pious man," as it is for those who would penetrate the meaning of a sacred text. "Only those will apprehend religion who can probe its depth, who can combine intuition and love with the rigor of method."[22]

But is not a certain detachment or disinterestedness essential to a rigorous method, an unprejudiced analysis? And, if so, how does one "combine intuition and love with the rigor of method"? The sympathetic study of religion for which Heschel calls is not one that includes sympathy for a preconceived idea but rather for the phenomenon being studied. "The principle to be kept in mind is to know what we see rather than to see what we know."[23] To do this we may have to "unthink many thoughts."[24] The detachment or disinterestedness that is required for an objective or unbiased study is the detachment from preconceived notions and the disinterest in proving such notions. And this attitude is required precisely in order to be truly involved with the object of research and to attain insight into its meaning. "It is in being involved with a phenomenon," explains Heschel, "being intimately engaged to it, courting it, as it were, that after much perplexity and embarrassment we come upon *insight*—upon a way of seeing the phenomenon from within."[25] Detachment from preconceived ideas is a prerequisite for genuine involvement with a phenomenon. But after involvement with a phenomenon occurs, impartiality or neutrality vis-à-vis its existence and its relevance does not yield understanding of its meaning. In a sentence that summarizes Heschel's approach, he claims: "To comprehend what phenomena are, it is important to suspend judgment and think in detachment; to comprehend what phenomena mean, it is necessary to suspend indifference and be involved."[26]

"To suspend judgment and think in detachment"—the first step of Heschel's approach to study—reflects the method of phenomenology conceived by Edmund Husserl inasmuch as it entails the emancipation from preconceived notions and the suspension of personal beliefs about the phenomena being studied.[27] Even the question of the existence of the phenomena, whether they exist outside the mind or only therein, is suspended. Apparent in Heschel's distinction between "what phenomena are" and "what phenomena mean" is the philosophical distinction between essence and existence; apparent in the first step of his methodology is the concern of phenomenology with the former to the point of "bracketing" the question of the latter. What are analyzed and described are the objects or contents of consciousness, the essences of experience. For example, concerning his analysis of prophetic consciousness and experience, Heschel writes: "It is my claim that, regardless of whether or not their experience was of the real, it is possible to analyze the form and content of that experience."[28]

While Heschel maintains the soundness of the phenomenological method, he employs it only as a first step in his study of religion. Concerned as he is not only with the essence of phenomena, but also with their existence, meaning, and relevance, he sees the need to go beyond the method of phenomenology. He explains this in connection with his study of the prophets: "While I still maintain the soundness of the method described above, which in important aspects reflects the method of phenomenology, I have long since become wary of impartiality, which is itself a way of being partial. The prophet's existence is either irrelevant or relevant. If irrelevant, I cannot truly be involved in it; if relevant, then my impartiality is but a pretense. Reflection may succeed in isolating an object; reflection itself cannot be isolated. Reflection is part of a situation."[29]

Notice that the impartiality of which Heschel has become wary is not impartiality vis-à-vis preconceived notions about phenomena but rather impartiality concerning their existence and relevance. But what if one of the preconceived notions about a certain phenomenon was the prereflected idea that it exists? It seems that Heschel would maintain the position that the essence of the phenomenon can be known by suspending all preconceptions about it, even the idea of its existence, while the existence of the phenomenon can be known only by suspending indifference about its existence, taking it for real, and becoming involved with it. It also seems that Heschel would admit that there must be good reasons for taking a "leap of faith" concerning the existence of a phenomenon. He would probably suggest that among the reasons for accepting the existence of a phenomenon is the pressure it exerts upon consciousness or the resistance it offers to solipsistic pretensions. For when Heschel claims that the ineffable dimension of life is an objective reality, existing independent of the subjective perception of it, he says: "Just as material things offer resistance to our spontaneous impulses, and it is that feeling of resistance that makes us believe that these things are real, not illusory, so does the ineffable offer resistance to our categories."[30] And when he claims that "awareness of the divine . . . intrudes first as a sense of wonder gleaming through indifference," Heschel speaks of how we know that the "enforced concern" we experience "is not our own" but has an origin and a reality outside ourselves: "It is a pressure that weighs upon us as well as upon all men"; it is "an unbearable concern that deprives us of complacency and peace of mind, forcing us to care for ends which we do not wish to care for, for ends which have no appeal to our personal interest."[31] It is precisely this kind of reason, for example, that moves the student of the prophets from a phenomenological analysis of the essence of prophetic experience to a concerned involvement with prophetic existence:

> While the structure and the bare content of prophetic consciousness may be made accessible by an attitude of pure reflection, in which the concern for their truth and validity is suspended, the sheer force of what is disclosed in such reflection quietly corrodes the hardness of self-detachment. The magic of the process seems to be stronger than any asceticism of the intellect. Thus in the course of listening to their words one cannot long retain the security of a prudent, impartial observer. The prophets do not offer reflections about ideas in general. Their words are onslaughts, scuttling illusions of

false security, challenging evasions, calling faith to account, questioning prudence and impartiality. . . . Reflection about the prophets gives way to communion with the prophets.[32]

When "the sheer force of what is disclosed . . . corrodes the hardness of self-detachment" the method of phenomenology is transcended. "Communion with the prophets" represents the second step in Heschel's study of religion.

SITUATIONAL THINKING

"To suspend indifference and be involved"—the second step of Heschel's methodology—is to engage in what Heschel calls "situational thinking," as contrasted with "conceptual thinking."[33] The latter deals with concepts by way of detached analysis; the former deals with situations by way of concerned involvement. By "conceptual thinking" in this sense, Heschel does not simply mean thinking in concepts, which even situational thinking must include, but thinking about concepts rather than the situations that account for them, or thinking about phenomena in a purely speculative way. By "situational thinking" Heschel means thinking about situations, not only the concepts that arise from them, by way of situational involvement, not only conceptual interest.

Conceptual thinking is an adequate and important way of dealing with many intellectual questions. But the ultimate questions with which human beings are confronted are not merely intellectual. Ultimate questions are existential problems. Situational thinking is necessary when dealing with these problems:

> No genuine problem comes into being out of sheer inquisitiveness. A problem is the outcome of a situation. It comes to pass in moments of being in straits, of intellectual embarrassment, in experiencing tension, conflict, contradiction.
>
>   To understand the meaning of the problem and to appreciate its urgency, we must keep alive in our reflection the situation of stress and strain in which it comes to pass, genesis and birth pangs, motivation, the face of perplexity, the varieties of experiencing it, the necessity of confronting and being preoccupied with it.[34]

To "keep alive in our reflection the situation" in which the problem "comes to pass" is to be engaged in situational thinking. However, it is easier to keep alive the conceptualization of the problem and the conclusions based thereon than it is to keep alive the situation in which the problem emerged. And it is easier to spawn a conceptual problem than it is to grapple with a situational problem. But the conceptualization of a problem is not the problem itself and is often a distortion thereof. It is one thing to entertain or comprehend a certain concept; it is another thing to experience an actual situation and to perceive a real problem. Thus, says Heschel:

> Too often speculation becomes analysis-by-long-distance of sounds trans-mitted over a poor connection. We formulate and debate the issues while oblivious to, and alienated from, the experiences or the insights which account for our raising the issues.
>   The predicament of much of contemporary philosophy is partly due to the fact that ongoing conceptualizations have so far outdistanced the situations which engender philosophizing that their conclusions seem to be unrelated to the original problems.[35]

Situational thinking focuses on "the human situation"[36] and its "original problems" more than on concepts or speculations about human nature. And the only way to understand the human situation is to explore concrete human situations. Depth theology—as an instance of situational thinking—focuses on "the religious situation"[37] and its "ultimate questions" more than on concepts or speculations about the nature of religion and its doctrines. And the only way to understand the religious situation is to explore concrete religious situations. The task is best summarized in Heschel's own words: "Our primary concern is not to analyze concepts but to explore situations. The religious situation precedes the religious conception, and it would be a false abstraction, for example, to deal with the idea of God regardless of the situation in which such an idea occurs. Our first goal, then, is not to evolve the philosophy of a doctrine, interpretations of a dogma, but the philosophy of concrete events, acts, insights, of that which is a part of the pious man."[38]

Each of Heschel's books is a result of situational thinking, of the exploration of concrete religious situations. Whether he was studying the prophet Isaiah or Rabbi Akiba, the philosopher Maimonides or the Kotzker Rebbe, Heschel always attempted to place himself in the situation of the religious person whose life and thought he was examining and to experience anew the "concrete events, acts, insights, of that which is a part of the pious man." What Heschel explains about the study of the prophets is an example of the situational thinking he employed in the study of other religious persons as well:

> Pure reflection may be sufficient for the clarification of what the prophet's consciousness asserts—but not for what his existence involves. For such understanding it is not enough to have the prophets in mind; we must think as if we were inside their minds. For them to be alive and present to us we must think, not *about,* but *in* the prophets, with their concern and their heart. Their existence involves us. Unless their concern strikes us, pains us, exalts us, we do not really sense it. Such involvement requires accord,

receptivity, hearing, sheer surrender to their impact. Its intellectual rewards include moments in which the mind peels off, as it were, its not-knowing. Thought is like touch, comprehending by being comprehended.[39]

To think "*in* the prophets," to sense the meaning of their existence as "their concern strikes us, pains us, exalts us," presupposes an experience akin to the prophets: sensitivity to evil, longing for redemption, feeling the approach of God. Moreover, "to evolve . . . the philosophy of concrete events, acts, insights of that which is a part of the pious man"—which is, as we have seen, the "first goal" of depth theology's situational thinking—presupposes an experience and a life of piety: "To understand love it is not enough to read tales about it. . . . One must be inspired to understand inspiration. Just as we cannot test thinking without thinking, we cannot sense holiness without being holy."[40] To understand religion, then, one must be religious.

Depth theology, as religious thinking in search of understanding, therefore requires religious preparation. Since the ultimate questions to which religion is an answer are not simply a matter of intellectual curiosity but of existential concern, religious understanding presupposes the cultivation of concern for such questions. "We think the way we live," writes Heschel, and since "it is only a concern that initiates religious thinking,"[41] if we are to achieve religious understanding we must live with religious concern. Heschel makes this clear in the following reflection:

> The urgent problem is not only the truth of religion, but man's capacity to sense the truth of religion, the authenticity of religious concern. Religious truth does not shine in a vacuum. It is certainly not comprehensible when the antecedents of religious insight and commitment are wasted away; when the mind is dazzled by ideologies which either obscure or misrepresent man's ultimate questions; when life is lived in a way which tends to abuse and to squander the gold mines, the challenging resources of human existence. The primary issue of theology is *pre-theological;* it is the total situation of man and his attitudes toward life and the world.[42]

It is only by placing oneself in situations wherein "the antecedents of religious insight and commitment" are nurtured, and where "the challenging resources of human existence" are realized, that one will be able to engage adequately in depth theology and achieve religious understanding. A study of religion that would seek to probe its depth and to understand its truth requires engagement in those situations that give rise to the ultimate questions to which religion is an answer.

> A legitimate question represents more than what it says. It represents a radical situation which accounts for its coming into being, a *raison d'être* for the presence of the question in the mind. . . .

We must, therefore, not deal with the ultimate question apart from the situation in which it exists, apart from the insights in which it is evoked and in which it is involved. Apart from its human and personal setting it withers to a mere speculative issue. Yet it is as a religious concern that we are dealing with it here.

The ultimate question, moreover, is a question that arises on the level of the ineffable. It is phrased not in *concepts* but in *acts,* and no abstract formulation is capable of conveying it. It is, therefore, necessary to understand the inner logic of the situation, the spiritual climate in which it exists, in order to comprehend what the ultimate question implies. It is a situation in which we are challenged, aroused, stirred by the sublime, the marvel, the mystery and the Presence. . . .

The ultimate insight is the outcome of *moments* when we are stirred beyond words, of instants of wonder, awe, praise. . . . It is at the climax of such moments that we attain the certainty that life has meaning, that time is more than evanescence, that beyond all being there is someone who cares.[43]

"The sublime, the marvel, the mystery and the Presence," along with the religious tradition that nurtures the responses to them, are what Heschel regards as the sources of religious faith. How they are such will be explored in Part Two of this book. "Wonder, awe, praise," these are the responses to the sublime, the mystery and the Presence and are, therefore, some of the antecedents of faith. How they are such will be explored in Part Three.

Philosophy of Religion

As an instance of situational thinking, a matter of thinking within the context of the religious situation, depth theology corresponds to the first of Heschel's three definitions of philosophy of religion. Heschel suggests that in the phrase "philosophy of religion," the word "religion" may be used not only as an object but also as a subject.[44] Thus, philosophy of religion is not simply philosophy about religion; it is also religion's own philosophy, that is, religious philosophy; furthermore, it includes religion's critique of philosophy. Accordingly, Heschel defines philosophy of religion as: 1) *"radical self-understanding of religion in terms of its own spirit";* 2) *"critical reassessment of religion from the point of view of philosophy";* and 3) *"critical reassessment of philosophy from the perspective of religion."*[45] In order to discover the meaning and truth of religion and to judge the authenticity of religious faith, thereby avoiding religious self-deception, Heschel seeks to understand religion from inside, while remaining open to criticism from outside. His own philosophy of religion is primarily one of religious self-understanding, yet it includes philosophical critique of religion as well as religious critique of philosophy.

RELIGIOUS SELF-UNDERSTANDING

As *"radical self-understanding of religion in terms of its own spirit,"* philosophy of religion is "religion's reflection upon its basic insights and basic attitudes."[46] In this sense, philosophy of religion "is an effort at self-clarification and self-examination."[47] Concerning the former, Heschel writes: "By *self-clarification* we mean the effort to remind ourselves of what we stand for, to analyze the experiences, insights, attitudes, and principles of religion; to uncover its guiding features, its ultimate claims; to determine the meaning of its teachings; to distinguish between principles and opinions."[48] Self-clarification in this sense refers not so much to the clarification of the self's religious perceptions as to the clarification of what the religious tradition itself perceives and teaches. "To remind ourselves of what we stand for" is to discover what our tradition holds dear. To do this we must carefully study, in the manner previously explained, the lives and the writings of the guardians of our tradition. But while the emphasis is on the clarification of religion by turning "to those . . . whose life *is* religion," to the sages and saints of our tradition, we should also analyze our own religious experiences, insights, and attitudes to see if they accord with the "guiding features" of religion as otherwise perceived or if they teach us things about religion that are otherwise imperceivable.

Concerning philosophy of religion's effort at self-examination, Heschel writes: "By *self-examination* we mean the effort to scrutinize the authenticity of our position. Is our religious attitude one of conviction or a mere assertion? Is the existence of God a probability to us or a certainty? Is God a mere word to us, a name, a possibility, a hypothesis, or is He a living presence? Is the claim of the prophets a figure of speech to us or a compelling belief?"[49] Whereas, in this context, self-clarification means the effort to understand what we mean by what we confess, self-examination means the effort to know whether or not we believe what we confess. The self-examination for which Heschel pleads demands that we question our own faith and, for example, ask ourselves what God means to us: "Is He an alibi for ignorance? The white flag of surrender to the unknown? Is He a pretext for comfort and unwarranted cheer? A device to cheat despondency, fear or despair?"[50]

As noted above, the goal of depth theology is to discover, as far as possible, "the truth of religion" as well as "man's capacity to sense the truth of religion." Since philosophy of religion, at least Heschel's first definition of it, is a synonym for depth theology, its goal is the discovery of religious truth which, as depth theology, entails the confrontation with the human tendency toward self-deceit. Self-examination is a necessary practice for the purpose of attaining truth because it is so easy to deceive oneself.[51] This is particularly true in the sphere of religious existence:

Religious thinking, believing, feeling are among the most deceptive activities of the human spirit. We often assume it is God we believe in, but in reality it may be a symbol of personal interests that we dwell upon. We may assume that we feel drawn to God, but in reality it may be a power within the world that is the object of our adoration. We may assume it is God we care for, but it may be our own ego we are concerned with. To examine our religious existence is, therefore, a task to be performed constantly.[52]

The self-examination of religious existence, so crucial to the overcoming of self-deception, is for the purpose of attaining truth through intellectual honesty. According to Heschel, philosophy of religion is meant to serve this end.[53]

PHILOSOPHY'S CHALLENGE TO RELIGION

Philosophy of religion, as espoused by Heschel and described above, is first and foremost a matter of religious self-understanding; it is philosophy from the point of view of religion. Yet philosophy of religion is also a *"critical reassessment of religion from the point of view of philosophy."* As such, philosophy of religion challenges religion to demonstrate its validity, to justify its claims. "If a religion claims to be true," says Heschel, "it is under obligation to offer a criterion for its validity either in terms of ideas or in terms of events."[54]

Although philosophy should not be identified with rationalism, philosophy does include the art of reasoning. To speak of philosophy's challenge to religion, then, is to speak of reason's challenge to religion. While Heschel maintains that "religion is not within but beyond the limits of mere reason," he also claims that the "rejection of reason is cowardice and betrays a lack of faith."[55] Although religion surpasses reason, it must not suppress reason. While transcending reason, religion must not contradict reason. Polarity, not rivalry, should mark the relationship between religion and reason. This is particularly true with regard to monotheism. Belief in one God implies the conviction that reason and the revelation to which religion is a response are both derived from the same source. "Yet what is one in creation is not always one in our historic situation," admits Heschel. "It is an act of redemption when it is granted to us to discover the higher unity of reason and revelation."[56] It is our obligation to attempt to discover this unity of reason and revelation if for no other purpose than to make sure that what we believe to be revelation does not conflict with the truth as perceived by reason. "What is contained in the divine message can neither misrepresent reality nor contradict any truths taught by science, since both reason and revelation originated in the wisdom of God who created all reality and knows all truth."[57] Although "reason is not the measure of all things,"[58] religion should heed its critique. "Truth has nothing to fear from reason" and a religion that is true would "never compel reason to accept that which is absurd."[59]

Since religion is liable to become distorted and corrupt, it is imperative that religious believers heed the criticism of reason leveled against religion. Heschel explains: "Superstition, pride, self-righteousness, bias, and vulgarity, may defile the finest tradition. Faith in its zeal tends to become bigotry. The criticism of reason, the challenge, and the doubts of the unbeliever may, therefore, be more helpful to the integrity of faith than the simple reliance on one's own faith."[60]

The philosopher of religion must therefore constantly challenge the authenticity of religion from the point of view of reason and philosophy. It must be kept in mind, however, that the term "philosophy" must always be qualified, since there are many different philosophies, any one of which is but a given perspective on reality. It would be naive to assume that the validity of any one philosophical system is established beyond dispute. While a particular philosophy may offer a credible perspective on reality, it remains only one possible perspective. Thus, Heschel modifies his second definition of philosophy of religion accordingly: it is a "critical reassessment of religion from the perspective of a particular philosophical situation."[61] But granted the limitations of any one philosophical system, philosophy, as classically conceived, is the human attempt to achieve a synoptic view of things. Therefore, concludes Heschel, "it is the task of philosophy of religion to place religious understanding in relation to the entire range of human knowledge."[62]

RELIGION'S CHALLENGE TO PHILOSOPHY

While religion may benefit from the challenge of philosophy, philosophy may benefit from its encounter with religion. "The role of religion is to be *a challenge to philosophy*," says Heschel, "not merely an object of examination."[63] Thus, Heschel advances yet another description of philosophy of relition as a *"critical reassessment of philosophy from the perspective of religion."*[64]

It is a mark of reason to know its own limits. But just as religion can become distorted, reason's value can be inflated. While reason must criticize religious fundamentalism and check religious fanaticism, religion must counter the overestimation of reason. Although reason performs an invaluable service in relation to faith, it can neither penetrate the depth of faith's insight nor soar to the summit of its wisdom. While reason lends form to faith's knowledge, helps faith communicate itself, and even curbs its excesses, reason is not the measure of faith's worth. In Heschel's words:

"Evaluating faith in terms of reason is like trying to understand love as a syllogism and beauty as an algebraic equation."[65]

"All power corrupts, including the power of reason," says Heschel. "When such corruption or arrogance sets in, it must be checked."[66] Reason becomes arrogant vis-à-vis religion when it presumes to evaluate its worth and control its life. Such arrogance may be checked by religion as it challenges reason with the force of its own unequalled insights: "Reason in testing religion is testing itself; examining its own premises, scope, and power; proving whether it has advanced enough to comprehend the insights of the prophets. Indeed, there are insights of the spirit to which our reason comes late, often too late, after having rejected them."[67] While seeing to it that religion receives the critique of reason, philosophy of religion must make sure that reason is met with the challenge of religion.

In order to succeed at facilitating a fruitful encounter between religion and philosophy, "philosophy of religion must keep in mind both the uniqueness and the limitations of both philosophy and religion."[68] But, as Heschel points out, religion is often reduced to philosophy[69] and philosophy is frequently mistaken as religion.[70] However, since thinking is not an adequate substitute for communion, philosophy is not a genuine substitute for religion.[71] The themes of philosophy are not born so much in philosophy itself but in the events and insights that precede and enlighten philosophy, including the events and insights of religion. Within the context in which it arises, philosophy is vitally important; detached from its roots it is virtually impotent. Philosophy is sterile when it begins and ends with its own concepts. It is presumptuous when it casts judgment upon religion but does not open itself to the judgment of religion.

> Philosophy is more creative in symbiosis with life than in preoccupation with themes born of its own reflection. Philosophy of religion remains, accordingly, a method of clarification, examination, and validation, rather than a source of ultimate insights. It must, furthermore, elucidate the essential difference between philosophy and religion. Its task is not only to examine the claim of religion in the face of philosophy, but also to refute the claim of philosophy when it presumes to become a substitute for religion, to prove the inadequacy of philosophy as a religion.[72]

Philosophy of religion, as a "critical reassessment of philosophy from the perspective of religion," does not, however, simply indicate the limits of philosophy. It also helps philosophy reach its outer limits. Philosophy of religion leads the philosophical mind onto new heights. "The task of philosophy of religion is to lead the mind to the summit of thinking; to create in us the understanding of why the problems of religion cannot be apprehended in terms of science; to let us realize that religion has its own scope, perspective and goal; to expose us to the majesty and mystery, in the presence of which the mind is not deaf to that which transcends the mind."[73]

By recognizing and pursuing the three functions of philosophy of religion as explained above, Heschel envisions and engages in a project that protects and promotes the integrity and the scope of both philosophy and religion. Obversely, Heschel's project prevents the subjugation of either philosophy or religion to its counterpart. Philosophy of religion, thus conceived, is a system of "checks and balances," checking the misuse of either philosophy or religion and balancing the two in proper relation to each other.

PHILOSOPHY OF JUDAISM

Just as the term "philosophy" must always be qualified, so too must the term "religion." Even if there are universally common religious characteristics, there is no such thing as a generalized religion, but rather a host of specific religions. While Heschel's philosophy of religion may have universal relevance and appeal, it is first and foremost a philosophy of one particular religion: Judaism.

Moreover, just as the term "religion" in the phrase "philosophy of religion" may be used as either an object or a subject, so with the term "Judaism" in the phrase "philosophy of Judaism." Accordingly, philosophy of Judaism may be described along the lines by which Heschel describes philosophy of religion, as: 1) *radical self-understanding of Judaism in terms of its own spirit;* 2) *critical reassessment of Judaism from the point of view of philosophy;* and 3) *critical reassessment of philosophy from the perspective of Judaism.*[74]

Heschel's own philosophy of Judaism is primarily, though not exclusively, one of Jewish self-understanding.[75] As such, it seeks to clarify and examine the meaning of the events and ideas essential to Judaism. It presents a Jewish view of God, humanity, and the world that has its roots in what Heschel calls "the biblical view of reality."[76] It is a view of reality that has been neglected in the history of Western philosophy but which, if assimilated, would enhance our philosophical thinking: "It would be an achievement of the first magnitude to reconstruct the peculiar nature of Biblical thinking and to spell out its divergence from all other types of thinking. It would open new perspectives for the understanding of moral, social and religious issues and enrich the whole of our thinking."[77]

What Heschel claims "would be an achievement of the first magnitude" is precisely what he himself accomplished, according to biblical scholar Bernhard Anderson: "He has opened up an authentic understanding of the Bible, one that not only could revolutionize biblical theology but, if taken seriously, could overcome the "eclipse of the Bible" which he regarded as the sign of the hollowness of modern life and the sterility of western civilization."[78] Moreover, as Judaism is based on more than the Bible, Heschel's philosophy of Judaism opens up more than "an authentic understanding of the Bible." In Jacob Neusner's judgment, "the entire range of the holy books of Judaism speaks, in particular, through Heschel."[79] It is precisely because Heschel creatively synthesizes and interprets the entire range of Judaism's holy books that Fritz Rothschild speaks of "Heschel's original philosophy of Judaism."[80]

In the course of this book we shall examine what Heschel holds to be "the biblical view of reality" and "a Jewish view of things" as we explore the meaning of the sublime mystery of creation, the glory of God in the world, and the main features of the Jewish tradition. We shall likewise explore some of the attitudes and actions which the Jewish tradition fosters as responses to these realities: wonder and awe, indebtedness and praise, remembrance and *mitsvah*. Each of these attitudes or actions is, for Heschel, an antecedent of faith. So by exploring Heschel's philosophy of Judaism we shall be probing what he believes accounts for the genesis of faith. In fact, Heschel claims that it is precisely this problem of faith that is the principal concern of Jewish philosophy: "The central thought of Judaism is *the living God*. It is the perspective from which all other issues are seen. And the supreme problem in any philosophy of Judaism is: what are the grounds for man's believing in the realness of the living God? Is man at all capable of discovering such grounds? . . . Is there a way of developing sensitivity to God and attachment to his presence?"[81] What Heschel describes as the supreme problem in any philosophy of Judaism is, as we have already seen and shall continue to examine presently, also the primary concern of Heschel's depth theology.

To explore "the grounds for man's believing in the realness of the living God" is to explore 1) the facts and events, the attitudes and actions that provoke the emergence of faith and 2) the rationale for allowing such faith to emerge. Thus, Heschel's philosophy of Judaism or depth theology is not simply a matter of analyzing and describing the phenomenon of faith or the phenomena that spark faith; it is also a matter of testing the sources, antecedents, and phenomenon of faith. Moreover, it involves philosophically defending the faith perceived to be true. Indeed, Heschel is speaking autobiographically when he claims: "All philosophy is an *apologia pro vita sua*."[82] Concerning Heschel's philosophical apologetics, Fritz Rothschild writes:

> Heschel does not stop at the level of phenomenological description and analysis. He claims that the basic truths and insights revealed in the depiction of Jewish faith are not merely the idiosyncracies of a particular religious outlook. He believes that if sympathetically presented, they will be

found relevant to the problems of sensitive men beyond the circle of previously committed traditionalists. The endeavor to present this universal aspect of Jewish thought constitutes the main part of his philosophy of religion.[83]

"The endeavor to present the universal aspect of Jewish thought" is an effort to disclose the meaningfulness and truth of Judaism. As such, it is an *apologia pro vita judaica.*

Another important dimension of Heschel's apologetics is his evocation of the religious situation by means of sublime poetic prose. About this Edward Kaplan writes:

Heschel often functions as a poet who takes a philosophical approach to religious problems. . . .

An important part of Heschel's mission as writer is to place the reader in a *situation* in which he may sense the presence of God: poetry aids us to open our ear to God. Heschel's assumption is that poetic imagination, an experience that transpires within the mind of an attentive reader, can then be extended to enrich his experience of the outside world. . . .

To my mind, as a person outside the intellectual community of traditional Judaism, the greatest value of Heschel's writings is that they present in a most concrete way the fundamental and crucial issues of religious belief and practice. . . . Heschel's poetry is a direct and intimate communication of the inner life of religion. He has mastered the gift of combining a profound philosophical and traditional Jewish culture with the passion of poetry and beautiful prose. The poetic character of Heschel's language can be characterized thus: it is metaphysics condensed into passion, love compressed into acts and words, a poetry of faith. . . .

Heschel's books, his life and his poetry, remind us to preserve our aspiration toward God. His poetry is meant to bring us closer to the emotions which have accompanied his own search, and the dormant passion in the holy words of religious literature. Our sensitivity to the *tone* (the inward life and vibration) of such words, combined with a lucid rational appreciation of the religious concepts they express, should bring us into full fellowship with the creative language of religion. In Heschel's writings, poetry endows philosophy with a living pulsebeat, and makes the reader more receptive to the inner, personal dimension of his own quest for God.[84]

To read Heschel carefully, sympathetically, is to gain sensitivity for what it is like to live in faith, to feel drawn toward the life of faith. Through his "poetry of faith" Heschel inspires believers to enrich their life of faith and he sparks the desire in less committed readers to take a "leap" into the world of faith—not a blind leap into the dark but one made clear by the light that Heschel sheds on the life of faith.

Since Heschel's philosophy of Judaism is a combination of pheno-menology and apologetics, this book not only explores what he considers to be the sources, antecedents, and phenomenon of faith but also examines the credibility of faith in light of its sources and antecedents.

Depth Theology

Heschel refers to his work as "philosophy of religion," "philosophy of Judaism," and "depth theology." The latter functions as a synonym for the first two insofar as they are endeavors at religious self-understanding and Jewish self-understanding. However, "depth theology" has a special connotation; it is the effort at religious or Jewish self-understanding by way of an exploration of "the depth of faith, the substratum out of which belief arises."[85]

Heschel calls this task "depth theology" in order to distinguish it from what is often meant by "theology." Theology deals with the *content* of belief; depth theology deals with the *act* of faith as well as with the experiences that precede and nurture faith.[86] Accordingly, Heschel distinguishes between faith and belief as well as between faith and creed, the content of belief. Both of these distinctions are specifications of a more fundamental distinction that Heschel makes between insight and expression. In order to situate and understand Heschel's distinction between depth theology and theology, we shall first examine these prior distinctions.

INSIGHT AND EXPRESSION

"We have an awareness that is deeper than our concepts," writes Heschel; "we possess insights that are not accessible to the power of expression."[87] This is particularly true of the "ultimate insights" of religion which have their roots "on the level of wonder and radical amazement, in the depth of awe, in our sensitivity to the mystery, in our awareness of the ineffable."[88] Religion's ultimate insights are rooted thus because the ultimate questions to which religion is an answer arise in moments of wonder and awe, on the level of the ineffable: "The realm of the ineffable rather than speculation is the climate in which the ultimate question comes into being, and it is in its natural abode, where the mystery is within reach of all thoughts, that the question must be studied. In its native state the ultimate question is different in form from the logical contour to which it is trimmed when brought to the abstract level of speculation."[89]

Implicit in this last quotation from Heschel is the already-cited distinction between situational thinking and conceptual thinking which relates to the distinction between insight and expression. Conceptual thinking deals with concepts, the content of which we can comprehend and express clearly. Situational thinking deals with situations, the content of which "we apprehend but cannot comprehend,"[90] with experiences that include insights that are beyond the reach of expression. Heschel says: "In our religious situation we do not comprehend the transcendent; we are present at it, we witness it. Whatever we know is inadequate; whatever we say is an understatement. . . . The entire range of religious thought and expression is a sublimation of a presymbolic knowledge which the awareness of the ineffable provides. That awareness can only partly be sublimated into rational symbols."[91]

The fact that the awareness of the ineffable can "be sublimated into rational symbols," even if "only partly," means that 1) the ineffable is not a synonym for the inexpressible but for that which cannot be adequately expressed; and 2) the ineffable insights of religion which cannot be fully expressed are nonetheless not inimical to expression. "It is difficult [but not impossible] to transpose the insights phrased in the presymbolic language of inner events into the symbolic language of concepts."[92] In fact, according to Heschel, the attempt at such a transposition is necessary: "The sense for the power of words and the sense for the impotence of human expression are equally characteristic of the religious consciousness."[93]

Religious language has the power to communicate religious insight, but only partially. Thus, depth theology attempts "to keep alive the metasymbolic relevance of religious terms."[94] Theologians must therefore participate in the ineffable events of which, paradoxically, they speak. Recognizing the ambivalent nature of the task, Heschel says: "The issue at stake will be apprehended only by those who are able to find categories that mix with the unalloyed and to forge the imponderable into unique expression."[95] This paradoxical endeavor shows that for Heschel there is a certain incongruity but not a radical discontinuity between insight and expression.[96]

The process of forging "the imponderable into unique expression" is, to say the least, a delicate task, as Heschel vividly suggests when describing the type of preparation that is needed:

> If, nevertheless, we attempt to ponder about the ultimate question in its logical form, we should at least treat it like a plant which is uprooted from its soil, removed from its native winds, sunrays and terrestrial environment and can survive only if kept in conditions that somewhat resemble its original climate. This is why even when our thinking about it takes place on the discursive level, our memory must remain moored to our perceptions of the ineffable, and our mind abide in a state of awe without which we never acquire a common language with the spirit of the question, without which the original nature of the problem will not disclose itself to us.[97]

While Heschel is aware of the fact that "religious insights have to be carried over a long distance to reach expression, and [that] they may easily shrivel or even perish on the way from the heart to the lips," he also believes that "to say how our thoughts detect the patina of the holy on the surface of the common is worth spending a lifetime."[98] He therefore offers, perhaps reluctantly, the following "standards of expression" concerning religious insight, standards which, given the sublimity of his writing, he himself must have followed:

> We must beware lest we violate the holy, lest our dogmas overthink the mystery, lest our psalms sing it away. The right of interpretation is given only to one who covers his face, "afraid to look at God," to one who, when the vision is forced upon him, says: "I am undone . . . for mine eyes have seen the King." We can only drink the flow of thoughts out of the rock of their words. Only words that would not be trite in the presence of a dying man, only ideas that would not pale in the face of the rising sun or in the midst of a violent earthquake: "God is One" or: "Holy, Holy, Holy is the Lord of Hosts . . ." may be used as metaphors in speaking of God.
>
> The ineffable will only enter a word in the way in which the hour to come will enter the path of time: when there shall be no other hours in the way. It will speak when of all words only one will be worthwhile. For the mystery is not always evasive. It confides itself at rare moments to those who are chosen.[99]

A word that has been entered by the ineffable is an expression worthy of the insight it reflects. Religious language has value insofar as it points beyond itself. Heschel's depth theology is an attempt to penetrate the beyond, the realm of the ineffable, to be stirred by ultimate questions, inspired with ultimate insights. It seeks to regain contact with preconceptual religious experience, to participate in the situations in which religious faith germinates prior to its transposition into belief and creed.

FAITH AND BELIEF

"Faith is not the same as belief, not the same as the attitude of regarding something as true."[100] Belief is a mental assent to a proposition or to an alleged fact, the truth of which is acknowledged on the basis of authority or evidence. Faith, on the other hand, is far more than an attitude of the mind. "Faith is an act of the whole person, of mind, will and heart. Faith is *sensitivity, understanding, engagement* and *attachment.*"[101] As such, "faith is not the assent to an idea, but the consent to God."[102]

When we say that we "believe in" someone or something we may mean that we have faith in that person or that reality, that we trust in, rely upon, and strive to be faithful to the object of our belief. But such *belief in* a reality is quite different from the *belief that* a reality exists or that a proposition is true.[103] Belief that something exists or is true is an act of the intellect; faith, or belief in a reality, "is an act of the whole person, of mind, will and heart."

"Faith is a relation to God; belief a relation to an idea or a dogma."[104] Belief, therefore, refers to what is known or comprehended; faith refers to a reality that transcends human comprehension. An idea, even an idea about God, is comprehensible; but reality itself, especially the reality of God, is something "we apprehend but cannot comprehend."[105]

Furthermore, belief is a self-conscious act, while faith is an act that transcends the awareness of the self. "In saying: 'I believe,' there is the awareness that it is the *self* that accepts something as true. . . . Yet, in the diffidence and awe in which faith is born there is no place for self-awareness."[106] This does not mean that faith is a less personal act than belief. On the contrary, perhaps our acts are most personal when self-awareness is not a part of them, when we are "lost" in contemplation, and response to, the other in whom we have faith.[107]

Judaism, like other religions, calls for belief, belief in God and in certain basic teachings. But it is faith, not belief, that is "the central demand of Judaism."

> The first demand of Judaism is to have faith in God, in Torah and in the people Israel. It is by faith and love of God that find expression in deeds that we live as Jews. Faith is attachment, and to be a Jew is to be attached to God, Torah, and Israel. . . .
>   Not the confession of belief, but the active acceptance of the kingship of God and its order is the central demand of Judaism. . . . Thus our relation to God cannot be expressed in a belief but rather in the accepting of an order that determines all of life.[108]

Faith presupposes belief, but belief is no substitute for faith, and faith is not reducible to belief. If belief is separated from faith it is but a formal and spiritually meaningless assent. And if faith does not formulate its belief it is an unintelligible act. As an ineffable insight that seeks expression, faith seeks to declare its belief in the form of creed.

FAITH AND CREED

"The soul rarely knows how to raise its deeper secrets to discursive levels of the mind. We must not, therefore, equate the act of faith with its expression."[109] A creed of dogmas is an expression of faith, not to be confused with faith itself. Faith, as we have seen, is an act of the whole person, involving insight, trust, and fidelity. Creed is an act of the mind, an affirmation of the truth perceived in faith. On the relationship between faith and creed, Heschel writes:

Faith becomes a dogma or a doctrine when crystallized in an opinion. In other words, what is expressed and taught as a creed is but the adaptation of the uncommon spirit to the common mind. Our creed is, like music, a translation of the unutterable into a form of expression. The original is known to God alone.

Faith is an act of spiritual audacity, while in employing terms we necessarily come to terms with our desire for intellectual security, for steadiness, tranquility.[110]

Given this relationship between faith and creed, Heschel calls creed "the diminutive of faith"[111] without undermining its significance. In fact, he maintains that creed or dogmas have an "indispensable function" in the life of faith. "There are . . . many strata of faith for which we have no dogmas,"[112] and dogmas can even "stand in the way of authentic faith"[113] if they are presumed to capture its fullness; yet dogmas can, if properly employed as allusions rather than descriptions, preserve, communicate, and even illumine the insights of faith. Heschel explains:

Are dogmas unnecessary? We cannot be in rapport with the reality of the divine except for rare, fugitive moments. How can those moments be saved for the long hours of functional living, when the thoughts that feed like bees on the inscrutable desert us and we lose both the sight and the drive? Dogmas are like amber in which bees, once alive, are embalmed, and they are capable of being electrified when our minds become exposed to the power of the ineffable. For problems remain with which we must always grapple: How are we to communicate those rare moments of insight to all hours of our life? How are we to commit intuition to concepts, the ineffable to words, communion to rational understanding? How are we to convey our insights to others and unite with them in a fellowship of faith? It is the creed that attempts to answer these questions.

The adequacy of dogmas depends on whether they claim to formulate or to allude; in the first case they flaunt and fail, in the second they indicate and illumine. To be adequate they must retain a telelscopic relation to the theme to which they refer, must point to the mysteries of God rather than picture them. All they can do is indicate a way, not mark an end, of thinking. Unless they serve as humble signposts on the way dogmas are obstacles. . . .

Unless we realize that dogmas are tentative rather than final, that they are accommodations rather than definitions, intimations rather than descriptions; unless we learn how to share the moment and the insight to which they are trying to testify, we stand guilty of literalmindedness, of pretending to know what cannot be put into words; we are guilty of intellectual idolatry. The indispensable function of the dogmas is to make it possible for us to rise above them.[114]

While Heschel recognizes the value of dogmas, he also recognizes "the danger of dogmas lies in their tendency to serve as *vicarious faith*."[115] But dogmas, no matter how true, are no substitute for the struggle, the intimacy, and the insights of faith. Heschel is wary of the human tendency to idolize dogmas, to serve them rather than the God to whom they are meant to testify. When the value of creed is inflated, people of different creeds often replace faith with suspicion, prejudice, and inquisition.[116] When the primacy of faith is acknowledged, people of different creeds tend to unite in the search for truth.[117]

One of the primary goals of religious existence, according to Heschel, is to keep alive the polarity of faith and creed and to maintain a proper balance between them.[118] Without creed, faith will be vague and private. Yet "the overgrowth of creed may smash and seal the doom of faith," says Heschel. "A minimum of creed and a maximum of faith is the ideal synthesis."[119]

DEPTH THEOLOGY AND THEOLOGY

The distinction between depth theology and theology is based on the distinctions we have just examined.[120] Depth theology deals with religious insights, with the antecedents and the act of faith; theology deals with religious expressions, with the beliefs and dogmas born of faith. Depth theology attempts to evoke the religious situation that gives rise to insight and faith; theology tries to systematize and articulate religious beliefs and dogmas that are compatible with insight and faith.

Depth theology and theology are as disparate and as interdependent as insight and expression, faith and creed. While dogmas "telescope" the mysteries of faith, "theology is the crystallization of the insights of depth theology."[121] Each needs the other for its own prosperity. Depth theology is the wellspring of theology; theology, the harvest of depth theology. Theology needs depth theology to supply it with the insights from which to yield its concepts; depth theology needs theology to provide it with the concepts in which to preserve its insights.

Theology, in dealing with religious expressions, beliefs, and dogmas, must retain contact with the living insights of faith from which they were spawned, if it is not to become so abstract as to lose its viability. Depth theology, in dealing with the insights of faith, must retain close contact with established beliefs and dogmas, if it is not to become so subjective as to lose its credibility. Theology apart from depth theology may result in a fossilization of concepts rather than a crystallization of insights. Depth theology apart from theology may result in an atrophy of insights rather than a burgeoning into concepts. Theology apart from depth theology is conceptual thinking without the inspiration of situational thinking. Depth theology apart from theology is situational thinking that fails to find appropriate conceptualization.

The intrinsic relation between theology and depth theology is indicated by Heschel when he says: "The primary issue of theology is *pretheological*."[122] In other words, depth theology, which explores the pretheological religious situation, is the issue of theology. The task at hand is to go beneath theological formulations and to reflect upon those "acts which precede articulation and defy definition," says Heschel.[123] "The time has come to break through the bottom of theology into depth theology."[124]

EXPLORING THE SOURCES AND ANTECEDENTS OF FAITH

"The hour calls for *the renewal of the antecedents of faith* . . . because it is useless to offer conclusions of faith to those who do not possess the prerequisites of faith."[125] The antecedents or prerequisites of faith of which Heschel speaks are "certain insights, attitudes, and emotions, . . . acts that happen within the depth of the person, moments that necessitate groping for faith."[126] These subjective happenings are elicited by objective realities which, because of what they evoke, may be called sources of faith. To understand the meaning of the antecedents of faith it is essential to understand the meaning of the sources to which they are responses. Part Two of this book deals with what appear in Heschel's writings to be the primary sources of Jewish faith: the sublime mystery, the divine glory, and the Jewish tradition. Part Three deals with Heschel's principal antecedents of faith: wonder and awe, indebtedness and praise, remembrance and *mitsvah*. One of the primary tasks in the remaining chapters is to examine why and in what sense these realities and experiences are sources and antecedents of faith. Another major task of this book is to explain the difference between antecedents of faith and elements of faith, something that Heschel did not attempt to do. It is obvious that wonder and awe before the sublime mystery of nature are not in themselves elements of monotheistic faith, since such faith is a response to God rather than to the majesty of God's creation. It is also understandable how the remembrance of a religious tradition, perhaps by way of study, may take place prior to the actualization of faith. Yet it seems that indebtedness to God, the act of praising God, and the performance of *mitsvot* would be better described as elements of faith. Especially perplexing, for example, is the fact that Heschel claims that praising God is both an antecedent of faith[127] and the quintessence or climax of religious life.[128] It is therefore one of my intentions to engage in an exegesis of Heschel's use of the word "faith" in relation to what he calls antecedents of faith in order to discover in what sense he considers acts such as praising God to be antecedents of faith.

Moreover, while it is obvious, as mentioned, that wonder and awe in the face of nature, as well as the remembrance of tradition, are not in themselves elements of faith, it nevertheless must be shown why these experiences give rise to faith. So, on the one hand, I attempt, with Heschel, to show why certain experiences which are obviously not in themselves aspects of faith are nevertheless antecedents of faith. And, on the other hand, I attempt to explain something that Heschel himself did not explain: why certain experiences that are commonly considered elements of faith are regarded by Heschel as antecedents of faith.

PART
TWO

*The Sources
of Faith*

3

The Sublime Mystery

Faith will come to him who passionately yearns for ultimate meaning, who is alert to the sublime dignity of being.[1] Faith is the response to the mystery, shot through with meaning.[2]

The seed of faith grows in the soil of a soul sensitive to the sublime mystery of existence.

The perception of the sublime involves an awareness of mystery, and the feel for mystery a taste for the sublime. Still, Heschel makes a distinction between the sublime and mystery. We will therefore examine the meaning of each, concentrating on their significance for the genesis of faith.

The Sublime

"How does one find the way to an awareness of God through beholding the world here and now?"[3] This is Heschel's opening question in his chapter entitled "The Sublime" in *God in Search of Man*. The answer which he expounds in that chapter and elsewhere may be summarized as follows: By recognizing aspects of reality that are often, if not usually, ignored; by beholding the sublime and mysterious dimensions of this world, one may find a way to an awareness of God who is beyond, yet present in, this world. An elaboration of this summarized answer must begin by analyzing what Heschel means by the sublime and by the recognition of the sublime.

THE SILENT ALLUSION

"The grand premise of religion is that *man is able to surpass himself,"*[4] and it is in perceiving and appreciating the sublime dimension of reality that

self-transcendence begins to occur. So Heschel begins his depth theology or philosophy of religion where religion itself begins—with the sense of the sublime or with what he also calls the awareness of grandeur.[5] In fact, the very first lines of Heschel's original work of religious philosophy, *Man Is Not Alone,* read as follows: "There are three aspects of nature which command man's attention: power, loveliness, grandeur. Power he exploits, loveliness he enjoys, grandeur fills him with awe."[6] While the experience of nature's power, loveliness, and grandeur may coincide, Heschel nevertheless avoids reducing grandeur, the sublime, to the vast and mighty or to the aesthetic; he also refrains from viewing the sublime in opposition to the beautiful.[7] The sublime is a unique dimension of nature or reality that may be sensed in the small and the great alike, in things of beauty, in human deeds, and in historic events.[8] And when we do sense the sublime we are on our way to an awareness of the divine, for the sublime is "the silent allusion of things to a meaning greater than themselves."[9] It is the tacit referral of things to an ultimate meaning from which they derive their own raison d'etre, their own purpose and destiny. "What we encounter in our perception of the sublime, in our radical amazement, is a spiritual suggestiveness of reality, an *allusiveness* to transcendent meaning. The world in its grandeur is full of a spiritual radiance."[10]

Since the allusion to transcendent meaning is "silent," since the grandeur is a "spiritual radiance," it often remains unperceived. The attention of any person or any civilization may focus or even fixate on a particular aspect of nature, which in turn may yield a given human talent or life-style. Sadly enough, our age is preoccupied with nature's power to such an extent that—while some appreciation of beauty remains—the sublimity of nature is hardly recognized. Consequently, nature's resourcefulness or usefulness is deemed its foremost characteristic; and industry or exploitation is considered our chief reply to nature's wealth. But it is unworthy of us to disregard the sublime, the sense of which is "the root of man's creative activities in art, thought and noble living"[11] and as such is a necessary requirement of being human. The fixation on the power aspect of nature and the consequent lack of appreciation for the sublime leads to an attenuation of being human. Heschel explains:

> *The obsession with power* has completely transformed the life of man and dangerously stunted his concern for beauty and grandeur. We have achieved plenty, but lost quality; we have easy access to pleasure, we forget the meaning of joy. But what is more serious is the fact that man's worship of power has resurrected the demon of power.
>
> Not only do we distort our sight of the world by paying attention only to its aspect of power; we are reducing the status of man from *a person* to that of *a thing.* We have locked ourselves out of the world by regarding it only as material for the gratification of our desires. There is a strange cunning in the

fact that when man looks only at that which is useful, he eventually becomes useless to himself. In reducing the world to an instrument, man himself becomes an instrument. Man is the tool, and the machine is the consumer. The instrumentalization of the world leads to the *disintegration of man.*

The world is too sublime to be a tool, and man is too great to live by expediency alone. The mode of living which is becoming universal is rapidly depriving man of his sense of significance. . . . An extreme crisis calls for radical efforts, for a radical reorientation.[12]

This radical reorientation toward the sublime dimension of life, which is a prerequisite of genuine human living, requires the cultivation of what Heschel calls "a sense for the inexpedient."[13] The way of expediency, or of exploitation and manipulation, which is the result of fixating our attention on the power aspect of nature, prevents us from recognizing and appreciating the grandeur of nature. In order to sense the sublime we must "cultivate a stillness in the soul,"[14] which discloses "the fallacy of absolute expediency."[15] The grandeur of nature unveils itself to a contemplative spirit, rather than to a calculating mind; to a person who seeks to commune with nature, not simply to control it. "Stand still and behold!" says Heschel. "Behold not only in order to explain, to fit what we see into our notions; behold in order to stand face to face with the beauty and grandeur of the universe."[16] Such beholding is a way of wonder and appreciation, which is Heschel's alternative to the prevalent way of expediency and manip-ulation.[17]

The exercise of power may, of course, under certain circumstances be a legitimate goal. And the enjoyment of beauty may indeed be a noble pursuit. But wonder before the sublime will yield the greater meaning for life. Through the exercise of power we may indeed find a certain proximate meaning in life. And through the enjoyment of beauty we may discover even deeper meaning. But it is only when we apprehend the sublime that we are on our way toward the ultimate meaning for which we long and in relation to which our lives will be fulfilled. If we are to prevent the demise of being human, and instead truly to "come of age," we must respond to the grandeur of reality that surrounds and pervades us. "If the ultimate goal is power," says Heschel, "then modern man has come of age. However, if the ultimate goal is meaning of existence, then man has already descended into a new infancy."[18]

The fact that Heschel calls the sublime a "silent allusion" is significant because, as we have seen, it means that the sublime can be easily ignored. The fact that it is silent does not, however, make it any less real, except to those who equate the real with the blatant. Moreover, this poetic description of the sublime as a "silent allusion" has the further significance of suggesting that the sublime is not a physical quality but a spiritual radiance. It is precisely, though unfortunately, for this reason that it is so often ignored. But how, we may ask, can an aspect of nature be a nonphysical reality?

Although Heschel maintains that the sublime is an aspect of nature and even speaks of "the sublime in the sensuous,"[19] for him the sublime is not a physical quality of nature, it is not in itself something sensuous. Rather it is an aspect of nature in the sense that it is the significativeness of nature; the sublimity of nature is nature's "standing for" or "pointing to" that which is greater than itself. The sublime is in the physical inasmuch as the physical is imbued with or alludes to transcendent significance. But this allusion is not a sense datum, not something seen by the naked eye. If the sublime were, as Burke and Kant described it, that which is vast and powerful, then the sublime would be a physical quality of nature which could be physically perceived. But for Heschel, the sublime, as an allusion to transcendent meaning, is the "spiritual suggestiveness" of nature. Thus, the sense of the sublime is not a bodily sense but a nonsensuous perception. For this reason, for example, while two people may gaze at the same phenomenon of nature it is possible that only one of them will perceive the allusiveness of nature while the other will see only the physical structures and qualities of nature.[20]

The spiritual dimension of nature of which Heschel writes is attested to by another great philosopher, Alfred North Whitehead: "When you understand all about the sun and all about the atmosphere and all about the rotation of the earth, you may still miss the radiance of the sunset and the glory of the morning sky."[21] If it is possible to "miss the radiance," then it must be something more than physical luminosity. It is, rather the "celestial light" of which Wordsworth writes:

> There was a time when meadow, grove and stream,
> The earth, and every common sight,
> To me did seem
> Apparell'd in celestial light.[22]

As such, the sublime is "not the quantitative aspect of nature [like power] but something qualitative."[23] It is "the immense preciousness of being . . . which is not an object of analysis but a cause of wonder."[24] It is the wondrous splendor of reality that coerces us into asking: "Wherefore? For whose sake?"[25]

By referring to the sense of the sublime as a nonsensuous perception, I wish to stress the fact that, for Heschel, to sense the sublime is to perceive the sublime, not merely to conceive of it.[26] Heschel himself speaks of the "perception of the sublime" which is "a perception at the end of perception."[27] To say that we perceive the sublime, rather than simply conceive it, is to say that we really have contact with the sublime; we do not merely infer its reality. The sublime is apprehended in and through and with the sensuous; it is not inferred from sense data. The sense of the sublime is thus an experience of the sublime, not merely a notion of it. Of course, the processes of inferring and conceptualizing may and should be based on experience or may even be considered elements of experience, though secondary ones, but perceiving is a primary mode of experiencing.

Moreover, because the sublime is perceived, the evidence for its realness is much greater, at least for those who in fact perceive it, than if it were merely inferred or conceived. The allusiveness of nature is "seen" to be as real as the physical structures and qualities of nature; "it is a fact within all facts."[28] But how can we know whether the allusiveness we perceive is really a fact within other facts or simply a fact within our minds that we project into other facts? Granted that we perceive the sublime rather than simply conceive of it, how do we know whether it is an objective reality, as Heschel suggests, or something illusory?

According to Heschel, "the perception . . . is too consistent, staggering and universal to be illusory."[29] The staggering quality of the perception has to do in part with the resistance offered by what is perceived: "Just as material things offer resistance to our spontaneous impulses, and it is that feeling of resistance that makes us believe that these things are real, not illusory, so does the ineffable offer resistance to our categories."[30] Speaking of "the grandeur of the ineffable," and "the knowledge of its reality," Heschel admits "we cannot prove it."[31] But he also asks a question which suggests that, because of the staggering quality of ineffable grandeur, it is more reasonable to accept its reality than to dismiss it as an illusion: "Why in the world should man desire or postulate a marvel that he can neither master nor grasp, that fills him with terror and humility?"[32] The staggering quality of the perception, which indicates the realness of the sublimity perceived, has also to do with the type of response it provokes—an attitude of "unmitigated wonder" wherein we are shocked into realizing that "the world is too incredible, too meaningful for us" to have conceived it on our own: "In our unmitigated wonder, we are like spirits who have never been conscious of outside reality, and to whom the knowledge of the existence of the universe has been brought for the first time. Who could believe it? Who could conceive it?"[33]

Within such wonder, wherein we transcend self-interest and become lost in the wilderness of a world full of marvel, it seems ludicrous even to suspect that the marvel is there by the magic touch of the human mind. Within our wonder all solipsistic pretensions are torn asunder. Humbled in the presence of the sublime, we simply ask: "Who are we to scan the esoteric stars, to witness the settings of the sun, to have the service of the spring for our survival? How shall we ever reciprocate for breathing and thinking, for sight and hearing, for love and achievement?"[34]

Concerning the universal quality of the perception, the fact that countless human beings testify to the grandeur of reality is good evidence for the reality of grandeur: "To assert that the most sensitive minds of all ages were victims of an illusion; that religion, poetry, art, philosophy were the outcome of a self-deception is too sophisticated to be reasonable."[35] The fact that the perception is universal means not that every human being perceives the sublime but that it is perceived by "sensitive minds" throughout the world and that "it is potentially given to all men."[36] However, due to a preoccupation with power, "the awareness of grandeur and the sublime is all but gone from the modern mind."[37] Given this predicament, it is understandable that the perception of sublimity is now often considered an illusion. But since "contemporary experience is stunted experience, . . . largely devoid of the higher qualities of experience,"[38] Heschel suggests that the real illusion is the perception of nature devoid of the sublime. The perception of the sublime is not the product of a subjective impression, but rather its lack is the result of subjective deprivation: "an undeveloped sense for the depth of things."[39]

But why believe that those who champion the reality of the sublime are right, that there really is a "depth of things" beyond what the "modern mind" perceives? The "proof" of the perception is its produce. The disavowal of the sublime by means of an obsession with power spells human demise. The affirmation of the sublime by means of a cultivation of wonder yields the enrichment of human life. "Within our wonder," writes Heschel, "we become alive to our living in the great fellowship of all beings, we cease to regard things as opportunities to exploit."[40] Within our wonder—our response to the sublime—we seek, instead, to reciprocate, and *the dignity of human existence is in the power of reciprocity.*"[41] Is it not reasonable to believe that a perception that provokes dehumanization is the real illusion and that a perception that fosters human dignity the real truth?

THE SUBLIME, THE HUMAN, AND THE DIVINE

In his chapter entitled "The Sublime," Heschel points out that in the oldest known treatise on the subject Longinus regarded the ability to respond to the sublime as the sign of the inward greatness of the human soul.[42] Heschel indeed supports this view, as elsewhere he says: "Our tendency to make everything explicit, to explain the world as though everything were level and smooth, flat and bare, deprives the world of its aspect of grandeur which is *indispensable to the ennoblement of man.*"[43] Any philosophical anthropology that does not take into account the fact that to be human involves being-toward-grandeur—and as we shall see, reaching-beyond-grandeur—is, for Heschel, inadequate. But when industry and exploitation become primary human concerns it is not surprising that "man" is defined merely as a "toolmaking animal" or, worse still, in terms of a machine. Heschel was distressed by such reductionist interpretations of human existence. His anguish gave rise to *Who Is Man?*, a book in which he rejects any doctrine of human existence that, by attempting to comprehend human beings in comparison with animals, fails to give priority to the category of the human. "We can attain adequate understanding of man," says Heschel, "only if we think of man in human terms, *more humano*, and abstain from employing categories developed in the investigation of lower forms of life."[44] Thus, any doctrine that describes human beings as qualified animals, whether toolmaking or rational, civilized or political, precludes a genuine understanding of human existence. As Heschel explains: "Man in search of self-understanding is not motivated by a desire to classify himself zoologically or to find his place within the animal kingdom. His search, his being puzzled at himself is above all an act of disassociation and disengagement from sheer being, animal or otherwise. . . . Man is a peculiar being trying to understand his uniqueness. What he seeks to understand is not his animality but his humanity."[45]

Priority must therefore be given to the category of the human. "The attribute 'human' in the term 'human being' is not an accidental quality, added to the essence of his being. It is the essence. Human being demands being human."[46] Humans may at times act like toolmaking animals, or rational animals, or even like machines, but defining human existence in such terms by no means does justice to the essential meaning of being human. Instead, such descriptions "contribute to the gradual liquidation of man's self-understanding," says Heschel. "And the liquidation of the self-understanding of man may lead to the self-extinction of man."[47]

Thus, in *Who Is Man?* Heschel addresses himself to the question, "What is human about human being?"[48] He is concerned with proper self-understanding and with the preservation and promotion of authentic human living. Openness to the sublime dimension of reality is a requisite attitude for such authentic living; it is, as we have seen, "the root of man's creative activities in art, thought and noble living." So Heschel passionately calls attention to the sublime, thereby awakening us to our fundamental human vocation—that of caring for transcendent meaning: "The secret of being human is care for meaning. Man is not his own meaning, and if the essence of being human is concern for transcendent meaning, then man's secret lies in openness to transcendence. Existence is interspersed with suggestions of transcendence, and openness to transcendence is a constitutive element of being human."[49] This openness to transcendence, this care for transcendent meaning, begins with the recognition of the sublime which is the allusion to the transcendence with which "existence is interspersed." As Heschel says elsewhere, when we are "faced with the mind-surpassing grandeur of the universe, we cannot but admit that there is meaning which is greater than man."[50]

This recognition of and care for transcendent meaning is also a premise of religious living and faith. This is because the transcendent meaning to which grandeur alludes and for which we must care if we are to actualize our true humanity is really a transcendent being that cares for us; God is our ultimate transcendent meaning. But the question arises: "How do we go from the allusiveness of the world—to a being to whom the world alludes?"[51] It is because we are aware not only of the world's allusiveness but also of a transcendent presence that pervades the world. In our awareness of the world's allusiveness, its sublimity, we are aware of the reality to which the world alludes—an ultimate meaning revealed as a personal presence: "we sense His presence behind the splendor."[52] We do not infer God from the splendor, the sublime, but rather we are aware of God in and through the sublime, "behind the splendor." God is a presence distinct from the sublime, yet without an awareness of the sublime we would not be aware of God.

Only a personal God who cares for us could qualify as our ultimate transcendent meaning because "the cry for meaning is a cry for ultimate relationship, for ultimate belonging."[53] In view of this, "ultimate meaning as an idea is no answer to our anxiety" since "humanity is more than an intellectual structure; it is a personal reality."[54] Only a personal reality may serve as the ultimate transcendent meaning for another personal reality. Therefore, the ultimate question is not, "What is the meaning of human being?"—which is "a willful reduction of the meaning of being a person to a thing or an idea"—but rather, *"Who is man's meaning?"*[55] In other words, who is the personal God of humanity? It obviously cannot be nature, since, unlike humanity, nature is not "a personal reality." Neither can it be humanity itself, nor any human being or group of human beings. This is because no human being nor humanity itself is the source of the meaning with which human existence is graced. Being human involves responding to meaning not made by human beings. It is by responding to this transcendent meaning that humanity rises to higher levels of existence; it is by failing to respond that humanity sinks below the level of the human. Spellbound by the splendor of existence, by the marvel of our own existence; humbled by the fact that we often fail to realize the meaning within the marvel, we human beings must confess that we are not sovereign in the realm of being, that we have not authored the realm of meaning. Only a reality beyond the world of nature and humanity can be the ultimate source of all being and meaning. And only an ultimate presence—a transcendent, personal reality—can be ultimately meaningful to the personal reality of humanity. Therefore, says Heschel, "the pursuit of meaning is meaningless unless there is a meaning in pursuit of man."[56]

Yet how do we know that there is a meaning in pursuit of us and, thus, that our search for meaning is not meaningless? Is it perhaps because we find ourselves involved in the quest for meaning rather than simply craving it? This is what Heschel suggests: "Just as reasoning about and exploring the reality of the world are inconceivable without being in the world, reflecting about meaning is inconceivable without being involved in meaning. We are concerned because we are involved. Meaning, therefore, is more than a logical presupposition of our reflection; it is meaning that drives us to think about meaning."[57] Finding ourselves involved in the context of meaning, we come to realize that meaning is a reality we discover rather than something we simply crave or invent. Moreover, we realize that the discovery of meaning is the result of the revelation of "meaning that drives us to think about meaning." And realizing this, we become aware of the fact that "man's anxiety about meaning is not a question, an impulse, but an answer, a response to a challenge."[58] The challenge must issue from a source that transcends humanity because all human beings, individually and collectively, stand under the challenge. Thus, the challenge we face issues from "a transcendence called the living God."[59] Meaning is found in responding to the challenge which is, essentially, a challenge "to care for ends which we do not wish to care for," to have "concern for the unregarded."[60]

We become aware of the personal reality of God because the transcendence that we encounter "is not a passive thing; it is a challenging transcendence."[61] This challenging transcendence betokens "transcendent concern" because "there would be no call [challenge] to man without a concern for man"[62] and because, as noted, the challenge is to have "concern for the unregarded." This challenging and concerned transcendence is what Heschel means by God. As such, God is the ultimate transcendent meaning in whose presence we find meaning by responding to the divine challenge to share in divine concern.

Thus, in Heschel's view, the human quest for meaning, which is, consciously or not, a quest for God, is really a response to "God in search of man." The human pursuit of meaning is meaningful because ultimate meaning, the divine being, is in pursuit of human beings.

"What is human about human being?" The quest for meaning; openness to transcendent meaning; responsiveness to the challenge and concern of divine being. "To exist as a human is to assist the divine," says Heschel.[63] "The destiny of human being is to articulate what is concealed. The divine seeks to be disclosed in the human."[64]

This sublime vision of Heschel's is rooted in his sense of the sublime dimension of reality, in that dimension which introduces us to the transcendent meaning that is eventually recognized as divine. This sublime dimension is perceived not only by human beings, but especially in human beings. This is because, as we have seen, "the essence of being human is concern for transcendent meaning" and because we human beings are able to enact wondrous deeds of concern which are more meaningful than those of any other creature known to us.

The sense of the sublime is not only the root of creative human activities; many of the things human beings create are also sublime: words that "are a repository of the spirit,"[65] that call forth "ideas unheard of, meanings not fully realized before";[66] songs that carry our souls "to heights which utterable meanings can never reach," to "the world of unutterable meanings";[67] music that is "an attempt to convey that which is within our reach but beyond our grasp"[68] and that "endows us with moments in which the sense of the ineffable becomes alive";[69] noble deeds, *mitsvot,* that "lead us to wells of emergent meaning, to experiences which are full of hidden brilliance of the holy"[70] and evoke in us "the awareness of living in the neighborhood of God."[71]

In caring for transcendent meaning and by enacting meaningful deeds, human beings are a sublime reflection of the divine. For the human concern for meaning is experienced as a concern with which we are endowed rather than one which we ourselves initiate on our own accord; and the meaningful acts of concern we perform are experienced as deeds empowered by a transcendent spirit that we acknowledge as divine. Thus, in Heschel's words: "The human is the disclosure of the divine, and all men are one in God's care for man. Many things on earth are precious, some are holy, humanity is holy of holies. To meet a human being is an opportunity to sense of image of God, *the presence* of God."[72]

The presence of God is experienced primarily in human beings not only because human concern is divinely empowered but also because the awareness of God's challenge is awakened through the appeal of other persons. "God is a challenge, speaking to us in the language of human situations."[73] God's voice is experienced as the absolute claim upon our conscience, as the objective challenge to overcome inequity, injustice, suffering, and oppression. Throughout his writings Heschel stresses the fact that God's challenge is perceived primarily in the pleading of other human beings, in the anguished cry of the oppressed, and in the prophetic outcry made on their behalf. In responding to their appeal we are, knowingly or not, responding to God's command "to do justice, to love mercy, and to walk humbly with thy God" (Micah 6:8): "Human life is holy, holier even than the scrolls of the Torah. . . . Reverence for God is shown in reverence for man. The fear you must feel of offending or hurting a human being must be as ultimate as your fear of God. An act of violence is an act of desecration. To be arrogant toward man is to be blasphemous toward God."[74] God's challenge is a call to responsibility, and the supreme responsibility of being human is to protect, promote, and enhance human being. However, "there is no sense of responsibility without revernce for *the sublime in human existence.*"[75]

While many things on earth are sublime and thereby allude to God, human beings are the sublime image of God. The awareness of the sublime, in both the natural and the human, is, then, not only a necessary requirement of being human but a prerequisite of religious faith.

BEYOND THE GRANDEUR

Recognizing the urgent need of an education for the sublime, Heschel turns to the biblical view of reality as a guide, for as he says, "the theme of Biblical poetry is not the charm or beauty of nature; it is the grandeur, it is *the sublime* aspect of nature which Biblical poetry is trying to celebrate."[76] The most significant fact of the biblical understanding of the sublime is, as already indicated, that the sublime is not the ultimate but rather alludes to the ultimate. "To the Biblical man, the sublime is but a form in which the presence of God strikes forth. . . . The grandeur of nature is only the beginning. *Beyond the grandeur is God.*"[77] Thus, biblical religion never regards nature, for all its majesty, as an object of adoration but calls upon nature to adore the living God. God alone can save us and alone is worthy of adoration. "Nature is herself in need of salvation,"[78] so communion with nature cannot be a saving encounter: "To Judaism, the adoration of nature is as absurd as the alienation from nature is unnecessary. . . . One of the great achievements of the prophets was the repudiation of nature as an object of adoration. . . . Yet the *desanctification of nature* did not in any way bring about an alienation of nature. It brought man together with all things in a fellowship of praise."[79]

The world in its grandeur is a thoroughfare to God rather than "a wall between us and God" as long as we remember that nature is sublime because it is created by God and as such alludes to its Creator. "Sublime, magnificent is the world. Yet if it were not for His word, there would be no world, no sublimity and no magnificence."[80] Therefore, according to Heschel, the sublime is not properly described as a quality of things but as an act or creation of God, and it is this of which the biblical person is primarily aware.

> It is not the sublime as such of which the Biblical man is aware. To him, the sublime is but a way in which things react to the presence of God. It is never an ultimate aspect of reality, a quality meaningful in itself. It stands for something greater. . . .

> The sublime is not simply there. It is not a thing, a quality, but rather a happening, an act of God, a marvel. . . . What seems to be a stone is a drama; what seems to be natural is wondrous. There are no sublime facts; there are only divine *acts*.[81]

All things are sublime because they are divine acts of creation and because their continuous being is a way of obeying the Creator, though a way which is often beyond choice or decision. According to Heschel, being presupposes the creation of being, and the creation and duration of being presuppose the concern for being. God is that transcendent concern for being.[82] Thus, nature is not a closed, self-sufficient reality, but is open to and dependent on the God who surpasses nature. As such, nature alludes to the divine; and this is precisely what is meant by the sublime aspect of nature.

This, however, does not mean that worldly things are symbols of the divine; they are not symbols of God, they are responses to God. "The existence of things throughout the universe is a supreme ritual."[83] The fact that the world as sublime is an immense allusion to the divine does not make it a symbol of the divine. That the glory of God is sensed in the grandeur of the world does not, as some would have it, make the world in its grandeur the self-expression of God. According to biblical faith, Heschel reminds us, the world is God's creation, not God's self-expression:

> Now, the Bible does not regard the universe as a mechanism of the self-expression of God. For the world did not come into being in an act of self-expression but in an act of creation. The world is not of the essence of God, and its expression is not His. The world speaks to God, but that speech is not God speaking to Himself. It would be alien to the spirit of the Bible to say that it is the very life of God to be bodied forth. The world is neither His continuation nor His emanation but rather His creation and possession.[84]

While here Heschel maintains that the created universe is not God's self-expression, elsewhere he does say that "creation is the language of God,"[85] a statement that reflects his belief that God communicates with us through creation. Heschel's claim that the world is not God's self-expression must not, therefore, be read as a denial of God's communication through the world. Read in context, it must be understood to mean that for Heschel, as for the Bible itself, the universe cannot serve as a visible symbol for God, that the world itself is not God "bodied forth," it "is not of the essence of God." And while Heschel emphasizes the fact that the world speaks *to* God, he would not deny that it also speaks *of* God. On the contrary, this is just what he means when he suggests that the world as sublime is an allusion to God.

Heschel rejects the idea that the world is a symbol of God because a symbol is usually understood as something that not only points to but somehow partakes of the reality that is symbolized and thereby directly reflects or represents that reality.[86] "What the prophets sense in nature is not a direct refletion of God but an allusion to Him," says Heschel. "Nature is not a part of God but rather a fulfillment of His will."[87]

After presenting his case against regarding the world or any worldly object as a symbol of God, Heschel nevertheless proceeds to make the following observation: "And yet there is something in the world that the Bible does regard as a symbol of God. It is not a temple nor a tree, it is not a statue nor a star. The symbol of God is *man, every man.* God created man in His image *(Tselem)*, in His likeness *(Demuth).*"[88] The fact that Heschel regards humanity as a symbol of God does not mean that he views the human as the "self-expression" or the "bodying forth" of the divine, for basic to his Jewish philosophy is the belief that "God is never human, and man is never divine."[89] Therefore, when he speaks of humanity as God's symbol, he must not mean by "symbol" all that he meant when he condemned the view that the world is a symbol of God. Nevertheless, Heschel does mean to suggest that humanity not only alludes to God, as does nature, but that human beings represent and reflect God, something that he would not claim on behalf of nature itself, nor of any other known reality within the world. "God is indeed very much above man, but at the same time man is very much a reflection of God."[90] As stated at the end of the preceding section, while many things on earth are sublime and thereby allude to God, human beings are the sublime image of God.

Since neither nature as a sublime allusion to God nor humanity as a sublime symbol of God are of the essence of God, to sense the sublime is not the same as to sense the divine; but it is in and through our contact with the sublime that we begin to perceive the divine.[91] Heschel may be interpreted to mean that the infinite or ultimate reality which is the divine speaks through the finite or proximate which is sublime. Just as we do not simply infer the sublime from the physical, but perceive it in and through and with the physical, neither do we infer the infinite from the finite, the ultimate from the proximate, but perceive the infinite and ultimate in and through and with the finite and proximate. We do not reason to a necessary source from a contingent object; in order to view something as contingent we must have a simultaneous knowledge of the necessary source. A reality is sublime in Heschel's sense because it is a gift from God and is dependent on God. In order to view it as such we must have a simultaneous apprehension or experience of the living and gracious God. In Heschel's biblical perspective, sublimity is perceived as divine activity.

But here we come upon an apparent ambiguity. On the one hand Heschel has maintained that it is by becoming sensitive to the sublime dimension of this world that we can find a way in this world to the God beyond it. Now, on the other hand, he is suggesting that things are experienced as sublime inasmuch as they are dependent on God and as such perceived to be "divine acts." In the first instance, recognition of the sublime precedes the awareness of God. In the second, knowledge of God is prior to or at least given with the knowledge that something is sublime. If the latter is the case, then the awareness of the sublime could not be said to be an antecedent of faith, except in the sense that it is a constitutive feature of faith. Rather, faith in God would be antecedent—at least logically—to the perception of things as sublime. Is this apparent contradiction resolvable? I think it is, and my explanation is as follows.

The sense of the sublime as the perception of an allusion to a meaning greater than itself is an antecedent of faith in that it prepares us to perceive that transcendent meaning as divine; God is the transcendent meaning to which the sublime alludes. In order to perceive the divine we must perceive that which alludes to the divine. So something is considered sublime in Heschel's sense first because it alludes to transcendent meaning. But once the transcendent meaning is perceived to be divine then we realize that all things are sublime because they are created by and dependent on the living God. We cannot apprehend the divine unless we apprehend that which alludes to the divine, unless we perceive the sublime dimension of reality. Yet once we apprehend the divine it is for this reason that we view all reality as even more sublime than we had previously perceived it to be.

Perhaps an example not of the sublimity of nature but of the sublimity of human love will shed some light on what I mean. Sometimes when a person falls in love with another, this person is led in and through this experience of human love to a love for God, to faith in God. This is because this love is of such great moment, because it is profoundly meaningful; it bespeaks a meaning that the lover cannot fully grasp. In this sense, human love is sublime, it alludes to a transcendent meaning. It is an antecedent of faith if in time the person comes to believe that the transcendent meaning of this love is divine. This happens if the person realizes that human love is spiritually empowered love, that the love with which we are moved is a love by which we are moved, that the source, guide, and goal of this love is the divine. Divine love is not experienced apart from human love, but it is the way in which human love is experienced that reveals the presence of divine love within it. Human love is experienced as a grace; one with which we must cooperate, but nonetheless a true grace. In fact, our very ability to cooperate with that grace is itself experienced as sheer grace. Those who know the wonder and mystery of being in love should be able to understand what Heschel means when he says that "our life is felt to be an overflowing of something greater than ourselves, the excess of a spirit not our own."[92] In reflecting on the meaning of love, Heschel says that when people love one another they enter "a union which is more than an addition, more than one plus one. To love is to attach oneself to the spirit of unity, to rise to a new level, to enter a new dimension, a spiritual dimension."[93] Whether this "spirit of unity" or "spiritual dimension" is God's own presence or whether it is the bond that God creates between those who love—in either case, it is particularly when we are in love that we feel "the excess of spirit not our own" and thereby experience the presence of God. "In the harmony of husband and wife dwells the presence of God."[94]

The love that was first experienced as sublime because it alluded to transcendent meaning is now experienced as sublime because it is known to be a gift from God, a divine creation which is dependent on God's loving support. The sublimity of love was first recognized in love's allusiveness; it is now recognized also in its createdness. In one sense, then, experiencing the sublimity of human love is an antecedent of discovering and loving God. In another sense, the discovery and love of God enables the person to experience human love as truly sublime. There are, then, different though not unrelated meanings of the sublimity of human love: love as allusive and love as God's creation or gift. So it is, I suggest, with the sublimity of nature. The sense of the sublime in nature precedes the apprehension of God and is thus an antecedent of faith. Yet the awareness of God or the experience of faith and the consequent realization that nature is the creation of God is an even greater reason for viewing nature as sublime. Someone who senses the sublime is more apt to apprehend the divine; thus the sense of the sublime is an antecedent of faith. Yet someone who apprehends the divine is apt to then view nature as sublime because it is of divine creation, because the things of nature are "divine acts"; the awareness of the divine is in this sense an antecedent of the perception of the sublime. There are, then, different though not unrelated meanings of the sublimity of nature: nature as allusive and nature as God's creation or gift.

Thus, by becoming sensitive to the sublime dimension of reality we find a way in this world that leads to the awareness of God who is beyond this world. But once we discover God who is beyond this world and realize that the world is utterly dependent on God, then we view the world as even more sublime than we had ever thought it to be.

But whether we experience the sublime as allusive or as created, in either case we are, in experiencing the sublime, led beyond the sublime. This, however, is contrary to Burke's classic description of the experience of the sublime. According to Burke, the astonishment of a human being before the sublime is such that "the mind is so entirely filled with its object that it cannot entertain any other."[95] But Heschel suggests that when faced with the sublime we cannot circumvent the questions: "Who is the great author? Why is there a world at all?"[96] From Heschel's point of view, our astonishment before the sublime is such that our mind soars beyond the object of our perception and we are compelled to ask: "Who lit the wonder before our eyes and the wonder of our eyes?"[97] Moreover, Heschel reminds us that "the Biblical man in sensing the sublime is carried away by his eagerness to exalt and to praise the Maker of the world. . . . 'Make his praise glorious: Say unto God: How sublime are Thy works!'"[98]

Furthermore, while Burke describes the reaction to the sublime as "terrifying astonishment" or "stupefaction of mind and senses," Heschel describes it as "wonder and amazement."[99] This is because for Heschel the sublime is not, as for Burke, the immense as such but rather "the immense preciousness of being," the recognition of which makes us "as certain of the value of the world as we are of its existence."[100] It is also because the biblical person views even the most exalted objects as dependent on the living God. Therefore, "in the face of threatening sights, the Biblical man could say; 'Though I walk through the valley of the shadow of death, I will fear no evil for Thou are with me!'"[101] Such is a confession of faith in God. The experience of the sublime is not an end in itself but a means to or a part of the experience of faith.

The Mystery

The perception of the sublime involves an awareness of mystery, for "what smites us with unquenchable amazement is not that which we grasp and are able to convey but that which lies within our reach but beyond our grasp."[102] Standing face to face with the grandeur of the world we are overcome with the realization that "the world is something *we apprehend but cannot comprehend,*" that "the world is itself hiddenness; its essence is a mystery."[103]

Moreover, the transcendent meaning to which the sublime alludes is "a meaning wrapped in mystery."[104] In other words, "transcendent meaning is a meaning that surpasses our comprehension."[105]

Monotheistic faith presupposes the realization that "the world is a mystery, a question, not an answer"[106] so that we find reason to look beyond the world for an answer to the world. It also presupposes the awareness of mysterious, incomprehensible meaning since faith is "*an act of spiritual ecstasy,* or rising above our own wisdom."[107]

THE MYSTERY OF BEING

There are people for whom life's exceptional events may contain an element of mystery but for whom life is for the most part explainable. Many human beings, and most of us at one time or another, act and talk as if being is something that can be taken for granted and that whatever is can be known and explained. Heschel counters this rationalist view, saying "To ex-plain means to make plain. Yet the roots of existence are never plain, never flat; existence is anchored in *depth*."[108] As such, existence is a mystery: "What *is*, is more than what you see; what *is*, is 'far off and deep, exceedingly deep.' *Being is mysterious*."[109] The sublime dwells not only in the extraordinary and the remote but in the commonplace and the intimate as well; and what is sublime is mysterious. "Everywhere we encounter the mystery: in the rock and in the bee, in the cloud and in the sea."[110]

But does not science pierce the aura of enigma that Heschel assumes surrounds all things? Does it not at least diminish the mystery of many things once thought unfathomable? On the contrary, "science extends rather than limits the scope of the ineffable," according to Heschel, who explains this view as follows:

> Science does not try to fathom the mystery. It merely describes and explains the way in which things behave in terms of causal necessity. It does not try to give us an explanation of logical necessity—why things *must* be at all, and why the laws of nature *must* be the way they are. . . . The knowledge of how the world functions gives us neither an acquaintance with its essence nor an insight into its meaning. . . .
>
> The theory of evolution and adaptation of the species does not disenchant the organism of its wonder. Men like Kepler and Newton who have stood face to face with the reality of the infinite would have been unable to coin a phrase about the heavens declaring the glory not of God, but of Kepler and Newton; or the verse: "Glory to man in the highest! for man is the master of things."
>
> Scientific research is an entry into the endless, not a blind alley; solving one problem, a greater one enters our sight. One answer breeds a multitude of new questions; explanations are merely indications of greater puzzles. Everything hints at something that transcends it; the detail indicates the whole, the whole, its idea, the idea, its mysterious root. What appears to be a center is but a point on the periphery of another center. The totality of a thing is actual infinity.[111]

As "an entry into the endless," scientific research dispels not the mystery of being but enhances our appreciation of it. Scientific discovery lends support to Heschel's contention that "the mystery is an ontological category," for "the deeper we search the nearer we arrive at knowing that we do not know."[112]

But is this all there is, mystery and nothing else? Is being ultimately inscrutable, the search for knowledge futile? Indeed not, for while everything abides in mystery, the mystery is not everything. "The world is both open and concealed, a matter of fact and a mystery. We know and we do not know—this is our condition."[113] This is also the starting point of

Heschel's religious thinking—the relation between what we know and what we do not know. So while "it is the mystery that evokes our religious concern," it is not the mystery in and of itself but *"the mystery within the order."*[114] Heschel's depth theology begins neither solely with the unknown nor with the known but with the tension between both: "Our point of departure is not the sight of the shrouded and inscrutable; from the endless mist of the unknown we would, indeed, be unable to derive an understanding of the known. It is the tension of the known and the unknown, of the common and the holy, of the nimble and ineffable, that fills the moments of our insights."[115] The unknown and the known are two aspects of the same reality; incomprehension and understanding are opposite sides of the same experience.

Mystery engulfs everything, but our quest for knowledge is not drowned by mystery. On the contrary, the encounter with mystery is a prerequisite for intellectual endeavor and for the acquisition of knowledge. "All creative thinking comes out of *an encounter with the unknown.* We do not embark upon an investigation of what is definitely known. . . . Thus the mind must stand beyond its shell of knowledge in order to sense that which drives us toward knowledge. . . . It is a fact of profound significance that we sense more than we can say. . . . It is in the awareness that the mystery we face is incomparably deeper than what we know that all creative thinking begins."[116] So the keener our sense of mystery is, the more acute our knowledge. And the more we attain true knowledge, the more we see mystery everywhere, even within our knowledge. Real knowledge, which is better called wisdom, is not a triumph over mystery but a rapport with the mystery and the meaning for which it stands.

To have "an encounter with the unknown" is, paradoxically, to somehow know the unknown; it involves an awareness without comprehension. Such an awareness, if it includes an insight into the meaningfulness of the mystery, might be called a "knowing ignorance." Heschel himself speaks of "two kinds of ignorance."[117] One is insipid, caused by negligence, oversight; the other is lucid, the result of diligence, insight. The one leads to vanity and complacency; the other to humility and understanding. A statement by Abraham Flexner, quoted by Heschel, captures the meaning of the knowing kind of ignorance: "We have become increasingly and painfully aware of our abysmal ignorance. No scientist, fifty years ago, could have realized that he was as ignorant as all first-rate scientists now know themselves to be."[118] To be *aware* of our ignorance before the splendor of being, to *realize* that we are ignorant of its essence, is to be en route toward wisdom.

To know the mystery is not just to sense its existence; yet it is not a matter of comprehending its essence. To know the mystery is to have an insight into its meaningfulness without being able to penetrate its meaning. In acknowledging the mystery we realize that we are meant "not to measure meaning in terms of our own mind" and we begin "to sense a meaning infinitely greater than ourselves."[119] To sense the sublime is, as we have seen, to perceive "the immense preciousness of being" and "an allusiveness to transcendent meaning." And that which is precious and alludes to transcendent meaning is itself meaningful. Since the perception of the sublime carries with it the awareness that we human beings have not endowed being with its preciousness and meaning, to sense the sublime is to sense that which lies beyond the scope of the mind—the ineffable. "The ineffable, then, is a synonym for hidden meaning rather than for absence of meaning."[120] The sense of the ineffable, therefore, is the sense of mysterious meaning or meaningful mystery. "In moments of sensing the ineffable we are as certain of the value of the world as we are of its existence."[121] Again, to know the mystery involves more than sensing its existence but less than comprehending its essence; it involves "being certain of the value" of a reality whose meaning is beyond human comprehension. This is why to know the mystery may be said to be a "knowing ignorance" of reality, about which Heschel appears to be speaking when he says:

> With the gentle sense for the divine in all existence, for the sacred relevance of all being, the pious man can afford to forego the joy of knowing. . . .
>   The spirit can afford to acknowledge the superiority of the divine; it has the fortitude to realize the greatness of the transcendent, to love its superiority. . . . This is the secret of the spirit, not disclosed to reason: the adaptation of the mind to what is sacred, intellectual humility in the presence of the supreme. The mind surrenders to the mystery of spirit, not in resignation but in love.[122]

The kind of knowing that "the pious man can afford to forego" is superseded by a deeper, more intimate kind of knowing, one that, while "not disclosed to reason," transcends human comprehension and is realized in what the spirit apprehends in love.

What the spirit apprehends in love is not just being itself but the mystery of being and "the sacred relevance of all being." Surprised by the unexpectedness of being, awed by its sacred relevance, we human beings must confess that we are not sovereign in the realm of being, that we have not authored the realm of meaning.[123] Perceived as a mystery, "being points to the question of how being is possible."[124] Perceived as a mystery filled with sacred relevance, being points to the question of whence being derives its meaning and worth. Sensitivity to such questions is fertile soil for the flowering of monotheistic faith.

THE MYSTERY OF HUMAN BEING

"Everything holds the great secret. For it is the inescapable situation of all being to be involved in the infinite mystery. We may continue to disregard the mystery, but we can neither deny nor escape it."[125] We certainly cannot escape the mystery by withdrawing into the confines of the self. As human beings we not only have a sense of mystery, we ourselves are a great mystery unto ourselves. "What we are, we cannot say; what we become, we cannot grasp."[126] That the mystery is not something apart from us, but a dimension of our own existence, is explained by Heschel as follows:

> The awareness of wonder is often overtaken by the mind's tendency to dichotomize, which makes us look at the ineffable as if it were a thing or an aspect of things apart from our own selves; as if only the stars were surrounded with a halo of enigma and not our own existence. The truth is that the self, our "lord," is an unknown thing, inconceivable in itself. In penetrating the self, we discover the paradox of not knowing what we presume to know so well.
>
> Man sees the things that surround him long before he becomes aware of his own self. Many of us are conscious of the hiddenness of things, but few of us sense the mystery of our own presence. The self cannot be described in the terms of the mind, for all our symbols are too poor to render it. The self is more than we dream of; it stands, as it were, with its back to the mind. Indeed, to the mind even the mind itself is more enigmatic than a star.[127]

In short, "the most intimate is the most mysterious."[128] The awareness of this fact prompts the realization that the self is not the lord—even unto itself—that it might have otherwise presumed itself to be. "In penetrating and exposing the self, I realize that the self did not originate in itself" and, therefore, "that existence is not a property but a trust," that "I am what is not mine."[129] Humbled by this realization, I am moved to ask: How did the self that I am originate? Who "owns" the existence with which I have been entrusted? To whom does the self that is not mine belong?

Did I originate from my parents? Were they the ultimate source of my self? "In generating life, we are the tools not the masters," says Heschel. "We are witnesses rather than authors of birth and death."[130]

Does the self belong to any human being, to any society of human beings, or to humanity as such? If there is any principle of which we human beings are intuitively certain it is that no person belongs to any other person, to any society, or even to the human race itself. If my self—or any human self I know—did not originate in itself, it is reasonable to believe that humanity did not originate in itself, since "mankind is not conceived as a species, as an abstract concept, stripped from its concrete reality, but as an abundance of specific individuals."[131] It is therefore just as legitimate to inquire to whom humanity belongs as it is to ask to whom the self belongs. Although we humans are accountable to each other, humanity and every human being or group of human beings—despite human freedom—belongs to or is accountable to the creative reality that transcends the human and that entrusts humanity with existence and that challenges human beings to be trustworthy in and with existence. The transcendent source of human existence is present to humanity—to individual human beings—as the challenge "to live in a way which is compatible with the grandeur and mystery of living"[132] and as the empowering spirit that animates life and enables human beings to live up to that challenge.

But what is this challenging and empowering source of human existence? Is it nature, or any other power in the world? Of this are we not certain—that although we live within the sphere of nature we somehow transcend nature?

> Man is given the choice of being lost in the world or of being a partner in mastering and redeeming the world.
>
> Man is from the beginning not submerged in nature nor totally derived from it. He is capable of rising above nature, of conquering and controlling it. . . .
>
> According to the Bible, the conquest of nature is a means to an end; man's mystery is a privilege that must be neither misunderstood nor abused.[133]

How could nature be the ultimate origin of a species that transcends the order of nature? And since "nature is deaf to our cries and indifferent to our values,"[134] how could it be said that ultimately we belong to nature? Moreover, since "there is no answer in the world for man's ultimate wonder at the world," must we not realize that "there is nothing in the world to deserve the name God"?[135]

Humanity is a personal reality. Since it does not originate in itself, humanity must originate in a personal reality that transcends the human. Since the world is not a personal reality, humanity must have its origin in a reality that transcends the world. We know the world is not the ultimate reality, that it is not divine, precisely because it is not a personal reality and because it cannot account for its own existence. Might it not be dependent on the same transcendent reality on which humanity depends? After all, although humanity has its origin in a source beyond the world, humanity also originates within the world. Is it not reasonable to assume that, since humanity originates within the world, the world has the same source as humanity? This, indeed, is what Heschel assumes. "Man and the world have a mystery in common: the mystery of being dependent upon meaning."[136]

The meaning to which Heschel refers is "a meaning beyond all conventional meanings"[137] or "the meaning of all meanings"[138] which throughout his writings Heschel calls "transcendent meaning" or "ultimate meaning." This insight—provoked by the awareness of the mystery of being and, in particular, the mystery of human being—accounts for the dawning of monotheistic faith, expressed by Heschel in these words: "The universe is not a waif and life is not a derelict. Man is neither the lord of the universe nor even the master of his own destiny. Our life is not our own property but a possession of God. And it is this divine ownership that makes life a sacred thing."[139]

BEYOND THE MYSTERY

From the above it is clear that, despite his profound reverence for the mystery of being and, in particular, for the mystery of human being, Heschel does not deify the mystery but sees it in all its sublimity as alluding to God. This is the distinctly biblical approach to mystery which Heschel contrasts with two other approaches, the fatalist and the positivist.[140]

To the fatalist, mystery is the ultimate. The world, humanity, and the gods are all subject to "an irrational, absolutely inscrutable and blind power that is devoid of either justice or purpose."[141] History is meaningless; "dark uncertainty" envelops the future. Humanity is without recourse; resignation is the only attitude to assume. Such a view, Heschel points out, is found in nearly all pagan religions and in many modern philosophies, as well as in popular thinking.

To the positivist, mystery does not exist. What is a puzzle today will be solved tomorrow. It is meaningless to appeal to anything transcendent in order to describe the nature of reality. The evident or explainable is alone meaningful.

The biblical person neither denies nor succumbs to the mystery of reality. According to the biblical view, mystery indeed exists, but it is not the ultimate. Beyond the mystery is the meaning, justice, and mercy of God: "To the biblical man was given the understanding that beyond all mystery is meaning. God is neither plain meaning nor just mystery. God is meaning that transcends mystery, meaning that mystery alludes to, meaning that speaks through mystery."[142] Moreover, *"God is a mystery, but the mystery is not God.* He is a *revealer of mysteries."*[143] As a revealer of mysteries, God is a knower of mysteries: "What is unknown and concealed from us is known and open to God."[144] Therefore, although Heschel often uses the terms "mystery" and "the unknown" interchangeably, there is a sense in which the two are not synonyms: "This, then, is the specific meaning of mystery in our sense. It is not a *synonym for the unknown* but rather a name for a *meaning which stands in relation to God.*[145] What is meaningful to God is also meaningful, though mysterious, to us. For Heschel, then, there is not only meaning beyond the mystery; the mystery itself is meaningful.

The conviction that "beyond all mystery is meaning" is the basis of monotheistic faith. "Faith is a mode of being alive to the meaning beyond the mystery."[146] In contrast to fatalism, such faith is, in turn, the foundation of human freedom, hope, and responsibility within history. With the realization that "God is meaning that transcends mystery" dawns the awareness that, rather than submitting to mystery, we should celebrate the presence of God in mystery and champion the cause of God in history.

The central and most recurring question in *God in Search of Man* is: "What are the grounds for man's believing in the realness of the living God?"[147] The initial stage of Heschel's answer is: "Certainty for the realness of God comes about as a response of the whole person to the mystery and transcendence of living."[148] In moments of such responsiveness we attain an intuitive awareness of the reality of God, for it is in responding to the mystery and transcendence of living that we transcend ourselves and encounter a presence whose glory is nothing less than divine. "It is through openness to the mystery that we are present to the presence of God, open to the ineffable Name."[149] Responsiveness to mystery is, then, a prerequisite of the responsiveness of faith.

4

The Divine Glory

The glory is the presence of God.[1] Faith in God presupposes an awareness of the presence of God.[2]

The sublime mystery of this world is not the ultimate reality of existence. Rather it alludes to the ultimate; it signals the divine. The sublime mystery of worldly reality provokes the genesis of Jewish faith inasmuch as it echoes the glory of God.

There are two crucial distinctions that Heschel makes concerning the glory: 1) although "the whole *earth* is full of His glory" (Isaiah 6:3), the glory is not an earthly or worldly phenomenon; and 2) although it is *God's* glory, the glory is not the same as the essence or existence of God. Rather, the glory is "a living presence or *the effulgence of a living presence.*"[3] Each of these distinctions shall be examined in turn.

The Glory Is Not of This World

Since the glory is not an earthly or worldly reality, biblical religion never regards nature, for all its majesty, as an object of worship. "To Judaism, the adoration of nature is as absurd as the alienation from nature is unnecessary."[4] So with full appreciation of the grandeur and mystery of nature, biblical persons are moved to extol the glory of God.

This distinction between the sublime mystery of nature and the glorious presence of God is crucial because upon it rests the distinction between pantheism and monotheism. There is no doubt where Heschel himself stands. As noted in the previous chapter: "Beyond the grandeur is God"[5] and while "God is a mystery, the mystery is not God."[6] But how do we know that God's glory is really beyond the grandeur and mystery of nature?

DISTINGUISHING THE DIVINE GLORY FROM THE SUBLIME MYSTERY

Is the distinction between God's glory and the sublime mystery of nature a matter of experience or is it a belief derived from experience? Is God experienced in and through and with the sublime mystery or is God inferred from it?

If religious experience were simply a matter of experiencing "something more" than what our bodily senses perceive, then there would be no experiential basis for making a distinction between the sublime mystery of the world and the divine glory surpassing the world.[7] The reason we speak of a divine glory is because religious experience is not simply an experience of the sublime mystery of nature but also an experience of a *spiritual presence* in and through nature. In Heschel's words, the religious situation "is a situation in which we are challenged, aroused, stirred by the sublime, the marvel, the mystery *and the Presence*."[8]

But even if we experience not only sublime mystery but also presence-in-mystery, how do we know that this presence transcends the world? Again, our knowledge is a matter of experience, or is at least a knowledge based on the prophetic experience that is the foundation of our religious tradition. The experience is not simply "a feeling of objective presence, a perception of what has been called 'something there,' but rather a feeling of subjective presence, a perception of what may be called *Someone here*."[9] While an "objective presence" would perhaps be indistinguishable from the grandeur and mystery of the world, a "subjective presence," the presence of a Someone, a transcendent Subject, is experienced not only in and through and with nature but also *in contrast to* nature, even in contrast to the spiritual dimension of nature.[10]

Human experience involves more than the apprehension of merely human and natural realities, even more than the apprehension of the spiritual constitution or sublime mystery of these realities. To experience a personal, trans-human presence in the world is to experience a presence not of this world; for the world of nature is not experienced as personal. Sun and moon, rivers and trees, are not known to be personal beings, but, in the biblical tradition, are perceived as the created gifts of a personal Being. The presence of the Creator is experienced in and through and with the things of nature as well as in contrast to them.

It is extremely important to realize that God's presence is experienced *both* in and through and with the sublime mystery of nature *and also* in contrast to nature. For if we keep this in mind we will avoid the danger of thinking that a presence that is in and through and with nature is somehow *a part of* nature, just as we will avoid the danger of thinking that a presence which is in contrast to nature is somehow experienced *apart from* nature. God's presence, though experienced directly, is nonetheless a mediated presence. But the presence that is mediated is not a part of the medium through which it is experienced, nor is the medium a component of the presence.

To maintain that the presence of God is experienced as "Someone here" means that we do not simply arrive at the belief in a Creator because the world is experienced as something given. According to Heschel, "the datum of the experience is not something given, but Someone Who gives."[11] And Someone who gives—that is, Someone who creates the world—is Someone who transcends the world. To perceive the world as given, as created, and therefore finite and contingent, involves the simultaneous perception or awareness, whether preconceptual or explicit, of Someone who gives, of a Creator whose very being is infinite and necessary, transcending the world of finite and contingent reality.

According to Heschel, we do not simply have an *idea* of Someone who gives derived from the awareness that life is given. Rather, we have an *awareness* or *"vision"* of this Someone. The vision of a supreme reality "upon which we stake our effort and ultimate hope" is "the vision of the One."[12] And "the One" of whom Heschel speaks is not "the All," "the Universe," but the God who transcends the universe.[13] We therefore have a sense not only for transcendent presence but also for the presence of the Transcendent One. "To the speculative mind the oneness of God is an *idea* inferred from the idea of the ultimate perfection of God; to the *sense* of the ineffable the oneness of God is self-evident."[14]

What Heschel is asserting here is that there is in human consciousness a sense for the Ineffable One, for the transcendent presence of One God. However, it is questionable whether the oneness of God is self-evident to the sense of the ineffable as such, as Heschel claims. On the same page from which the last quotation is taken, Heschel writes: "Plurality is incompatible with the sense of the ineffable. You cannot ask in regard to the divine: Which one? There is only one synonym for God: One." Now while I agree that there is indeed a sense for the presence of One God, I do not believe that the sense of the ineffable itself renders the insight that there is One God. For I would distinguish between the sense of the ineffable and the sense of the Ineffable One whose presence is experienced in the realm of the ineffable. After all, there are many mysteries in life, many ineffable realities. Is it not so that some people have a sense for the mysteries of life without necessarily having a sense of the one Ultimate Mystery, or of the mysterious Ultimate One? Even Heschel himself elsewhere points out that "the sense of the ineffable does not give us an awareness of God" but "only leads to a plane . . . where His presence may be defied but not denied."[15] In fact, I would insist that the distinction between the sense of the ineffable and the sense of the Ineffable One is implied throughout Heschel's writings inasmuch as he repeatedly distinguishes between the sublime mystery of life and the glory of God disclosed therein. So rather than saying that the oneness of God is self-evident to the sense of the ineffable, Heschel should perhaps say that God's oneness is self-evident to the sense of the supreme, to the sense of the ultimate. To the sense of the ineffable there are many ineffable realities; to the sense of the supreme there is only one ineffable God. Thus, plurality is not incompatible with the sense of the ineffable apart from the sense of the supreme. Yet with a sense of the supreme "you cannot ask in regard to the divine: Which one?"

But one may ask, what is the difference between the *idea of ultimate perfection* (from which is inferred the oneness of God) and the *sense of the supreme* (to which the oneness of God is self-evident)? The former is the result of speculative thinking which concludes that there must be a God in order to account for the world, and that, given the degrees of perfection in the world, this God must be ultimately perfect. The latter, rather than being the result of speculation, is an awareness of the one supreme reality, the intuition or metaphysical insight that there is one supreme unifying presence. The former leads to the idea of God's oneness as a necessary postulate of God's perfection. The latter apprehends the oneness of God in an experience of this one supreme reality. Yet are not the way of experience and the way of inference more closely related than is often assumed? In fact, experience is usually shot through with inference; and speculative thinking is probably founded more upon the experience of that which is thought to be merely inferred than is usually realized. Thus, the idea of ultimate perfection may well be bound up with an experience or sense of the supreme, even if many who have this idea do not think that they really experience the supreme reality of God (perhaps due to the fact that their notion of experience is too limited). In any case, there is, for Heschel, an experience not only of the ineffable realm but also of the Ineffable One. Therefore, contrary to what Maurice Friedman claims, Heschel does not make what appears to be "an unprepared transition from the sense of the ineffable to an acceptance of the unique authority of the Bible."[16] The transition that Heschel makes is not from the sense of the ineffable to the belief in the God proclaimed by the Bible, but from a sense of the presence of the Ineffable One to an acceptance of the biblical proclamation of this very same God.

To be sure, there is a sense in which the experience of the ineffable predisposes us to experience the revelatory presence of God. It fosters a change of inner attitude that awakens the realization that reality is neither grounded in our own minds nor is it simply the result of an immanent principle which human minds may tend to grasp. Realizing that reality is beyond our comprehension, we begin to realize that life and time are not our own property. The awareness of the ineffable, the realization that reality exceeds what we can comprehend, thus prepares us to hear the "voice" of the Ineffable One who is even further beyond our comprehension. Yet the transition that we make is not from the sense of the ineffable to the acceptance of biblical proclamation of God, but from the awareness of the Ineffable One, who speaks through the ineffable realm, to the acceptance of the biblical proclamation. The God whom the Bible acclaims is believed to be the same God whose presence we experience. Thus, the "transition" is not nearly as "unprepared" as Friedman assumes. Heschel claims that "a great event, miraculous as it may be, if it happened only once, will hardly be able to dominate forever the mind of man."[17] I take this to mean that the revelation of God as proclaimed in the Bible happens time and time again, even though each particular event of revelation may be unique, and even though the revelatory events recorded in the Bible are archetypical. That this is Heschel's position is clear when he says that "the idea of revelation [in its archetypal form] remains an absurdity as long as we are unable to comprehend the impact with which the realness of God is pursuing man, every man."[18] According to Heschel, then, there is a correlation between the revelation of God proclaimed by the Bible and the revelatory events that religious persons experience throughout history. The transition is from our experience of God to our acceptance of what the Bible acclaims to be the paradigmatic experience of God. Professor Rothschild is entirely correct when he interprets Heschel's view thus: "The event of *revelation* as described in the Hebrew Bible exhibits in archetypal form what normal religious consciousness has discovered on a lower level."[19]

But the question that arises at this point is whether or not we would ever interpret our religious experiences monotheistically if we did not already belong to a tradition that focuses on paradigmatic religious events that have been interpreted monotheistically. Would those experiences that we claim are experiences of the Ineffable One, and not just experiences of the ineffable realm, be described as such if we did not belong to a monotheistic tradition? Perhaps we would not interpret our religious experience monotheistically if we were not a part of a community that has such a tradition. Yet in accord with this tradition we are able to say: "Yes, that is what I experience or have experienced, though I might not have described it thus apart from this tradition." The correlation is not between the experience of the ineffable and the acceptance of the biblical message. It would be this if we could not grant the fact that our own experience really is of one supreme reality, one personal God. The correlation is between the biblical testimony and the experience of the Ineffable One, even if the Bible has prompted us to read our experience in this way. After all, we could say: "No, I do not experience the Ineffable One, only an ineffable dimension of existence." If our religious experience were simply of the ineffable, then upon hearing the biblical word we would not say: "That interprets my experience; that is in fact what I have experienced myself, though quite dimly in comparison."

The fact that the biblical tradition provides us with the means of interpreting our religious experiences in monotheistic terms does not mean that we have not really had monotheistic experiences. Experience usually precedes interpretation, at least adequate interpretation. Often there are ingredients of an experience which we are not conscious of at the time of the experience but which come to light at a later time. We may, for example, experience love without recognizing it at the time. Later, sometimes too late, we may realize that we were being loved without appreciating it for what it was. Later we may respond to an initiative that almost went unnoticed. Likewise, God may have been the "object" of our experience, or an "ingredient" within the flow of our experience, without our having been able to recognize God's presence. Later we may come to recognize that God was there all along. Often we need guidance to be able to interpret our experiences, especially our deep experiences. The biblical tradition offers us guidance in interpreting our religious experiences. What we might have assumed was simply an experience of a holy dimension of life is, upon hearing and reflecting on the biblical message, recognized as an experience of the Holy One, the "Someone who gives." So even if we have inherited the means of interpreting our religious experience from the biblical tradition, the correlation is still between the revelation which is recorded in the Bible and the experience of the God to whom the Bible bears witness. The transition is from the preconceptual experience of God to the acceptance of the biblical message because, upon hearing it, it enables us to understand that experience, to interpret it correctly.

Heschel would surely admit that not everyone, and perhaps not even most people, have the conscious experience of "Someone here," of "Someone who gives." (In fact, many people may not even consciously experience the world as "something given.") Yet the experience of this Transcendent Other is the experience not only of prophets and saints but of many other religious persons as well. As Heschel says, "the certainty of being exposed to a presence not of this world is a fact of human existence."[20] Some people may sense this presence at distant intervals in their lives, while others may have an abiding sense of the presence of God. Whatever the case may be, when human beings recognize the ineffable dimension of existence and begin to sense the presence of God therein, they may also realize, through the guidance of the biblical tradition, that this presence transcends the sublime mystery through which it is disclosed.

Thus, the criterion by which we distinguish between the sublime mystery and the divine glory is the fact that along with, and in contrast to, experiencing an ineffable dimension of existence we also experience the transcendent presence of "Someone here." We experience both the allusiveness of nature and the personal presence to which it alludes. But the question that may be asked at this point is: What is the criterion (or what are the criteria) for claiming that we do in fact experience this divine presence? In other words, what are the distinguishing signs of the divine presence?

SIGNS OF GOD'S PRESENCE

From Heschel's perspective, what signals the presence of the divine is the experience of a *transcendent concern* for being as well as a *transcendent challenge* to live in a way that is compatible with the sublime mystery of being. In fact, the transcendent concern and the transcendent challenge are experienced simultaneously; they are even experienced as being of one and the same transcendent reality. This is because the transcendent concern for being carries with it a challenge to live in a way that is worthy of that concern, to share that concern; and the transcendent challenge is itself an expression of concern, for the challenge to embrace a life of concern must itself be born of concern. When, for example, a parent or teacher challenges a child to care for others, that challenge is an expression of concern on the part of the adult for the child as well as for those with whom the child associates. What Heschel realizes is that any and every challenge to care for others does not originate in the human soul alone but ultimately comes forth from the living God who creates and sustains all that is. But how do we become aware of God's concern? Heschel acknowledges the fact that "the extreme hiddenness of God is a fact of constant awareness," yet he also maintains that God's concern is "revealed to man and capable of being experienced by him."[21] But in what, we may ask, do we experience the concern of God?

Divine concern is not experienced apart from human concern, but it is the way in which human concern is experienced that reveals the presence of the divine within it. Human concern is, for many persons, experienced as "enforced concern," something with which we are endowed rather than something we ourselves initiate on our own accord. It is, in other words, an empowered concern before it is empowering. As such, human concern is but a reflection of divine concern. Heschel describes how the awareness of the divine is born in and through the experience of enforced concern in the following way:

> Awareness of the divine that intrudes first as a sense of wonder gleaming through indifference, as a compulsion to be aware of the ineffable, grows, imperceptibly, like a hair, to uneasiness, anxiety, until it bristles with an unbearable concern that deprives us of complacency and peace of mind, forcing us to care for ends which we do not wish to care for, for ends which have no appeal to our personal interest. With all our might, pride and self-reliance, we try to defy, to suppress and combat that concern for the unregarded, for that which is unconfined by either mind or will or our own life. We would rather be prisoners, if only our mind, will, passion and ambitions were the four walls of the prison. There would, indeed, be no greater comfort than to live in the security of foregone conclusions, if not for that gnawing concern which turns all conclusions to shambles.
>
> What is the nature of that enforced concern we resist so vehemently? It is not our own; it is a pressure that weighs upon us as well as upon all men. It does not impart any words; it only asks, it only calls. It plants a question, a behest, in front of us, which our heart echoes like a bell, overpowering as if it were the only sound in the endless stillness and we the only ones to answer it. Our mind, our voice is too coarse to utter a reply. It is a question that demands our whole being as an answer.[22]

But how do we know that this enforced concern is indeed enforced by the divine? Even though it is experienced as a concern with which we are empowered, rather than as one which we ourselves inaugurate, thus making it an "enforced" concern, why must we think that it is God rather than simply nature or society or humanity that is the source of this concern? Nature cannot be that which implants the concern within us because nature itself, being an impersonal reality, knows not the beneficent power of concern. Nor can humanity or society be the ultimate source of our concern, for society or humanity as a whole is faced with the challenge to be concerned for the realm of being and with ends that stand in need of fulfillment. Not only individuals but society or humanity itself is challenged to embrace a life of concern. The concern that we are obliged to incarnate is enforced not only on us as individuals but on the entire human race: "it is a pressure that weighs upon us as well as upon all men." While the concern by which we live is mediated to us and cultivated in us by our fellow human beings, all of us together are confronted with the requirement to be concerned for each other and for the entire realm of being.

The enforced concern is a *challenge* to be concerned. As a challenge that does not originate in the human soul but as one with which we human beings, individually and corporately, are confronted, as a concern that we are required to embrace, this enforced concern is a *transcendent* challenge, a challenge from beyond nature and humanity, a challenge that issues from the divine source of all concern. We become aware of the presence of the divine, of "Someone here" who is a Transcendent Other, because the transcendence which we experience "is not a passive thing; it is a challenging transcendence,"[23] a transcendence that challenges us to have "concern for the unregarded." And this challenging transcendence betokens transcendent concern, for "there would be no call [challenge] to man without a concern for man."[24] The transcendent presence with which we are confronted "is astir with a demand to live in a way that is worthy of that presence."[25] That presence, astir with a demand that bespeaks concern, is the presence of the living God. This is why Heschel says that "God reaches us as a claim,"[26] that "God is a challenge rather than a notion."[27] and that "the meaning of God is precisely the challenge of 'how to be.'"[28] God, as the transcendent challenge to be concerned, is the transcendent concern who challenges.

God's challenge to us is an expression of divine concern for the beings with whom we are challenged to be concerned. God's challenge is also an expression of concern for those of us who are challenged, for it is only in being challenged to care for others, and in being empowered with the ability to care, that we are able to realize the dignity of being human which is found in transcending our own needs and interests. In Heschel's words: "Human is he who is concerned with other selves."[29] Ultimately, it is God who challenges us to be concerned with other selves. And since it is by responding to this challenge that we realize the meaning of being human, this challenge to be concerned is itself an act of God's concern for us.

While the transcendent concern we experience always carries with it a challenge, it is not only as a challenge that the transcendent concern is experienced. God's concern for us is known not only in God's command "to do justice and love mercy" but also in God's rendering of justice and mercy. Divine concern is experienced in the inspiration and guidance God provides, in the love and compassion God bestows, and in the freedom and peace God imparts, not only in the demand and challenge God issues. "Man is being called upon, challenged, *and solaced*" by God.[30] "The unique quality of biblical religion" is "an awareness of a God who *helps,* demands, and calls upon man."[31] But when and how do we experience the help and solace of God? The beginning of an answer has already been indicated: the concern we have for others, which enables us to realize our humanness, is experienced as a concern with which we are endowed, a blessing and a grace of transcendent origin.

Those who know that their concern for others is spiritually empowered concern will understand what Heschel means when, in speaking about the "yearning to serve," he says "it is not the I that trembles alone, it is not a stir out of my soul but an eternal flutter that sweeps us all."[32] Since Heschel realizes that "the concern for others often demands the price of self-denial,"[33] he maintains that such concern requires "inner freedom" or "the state of being beyond all interests and selfishness" which he calls *"spiritual ecstasy.'"[34]* But how could such spiritual ecstasy be attained if not for the fact that we are "a part of an eternal spiritual movement that conjures power out of a weary conscience, that, striking the bottom out of conceit, tears selfishness to shreds?"[35] Thus, the spiritual ecstasy that is realized in transcending ourselves through concern for others is the result of the divine eternal concern that "sweeps us all." Human concern is empowered by divine concern; our concern for God and for others is thus a reflection of God's concern for us.

Heschel's most sublime passages are those in which he describes the way in which we may become aware of the empowering reality of God's concern. The following excerpt is one of those passages:

> Man's walled mind has no access to a ladder upon which he can, on his own strength, rise to knowledge of God. Yet his soul is endowed with translucent windows that open to the beyond. And if he rises to reach out to Him, it is a reflection of the divine light in him that gives him the power for such yearning. We are at times ablaze against and beyond our own power, and unless man's soul is dismissed as an insane asylum, the spectrum analysis of that ray is evidence for the truth of his insight.
>
> For God is not always silent, the man is not always blind. His glory fills the world; His spirit hovers above the waters. There are moments in which, to use a Talmudic phrase, heaven and earth kiss each other; in which there is a lifting of the veil at the horizon of the known, opening a vision of what is eternal in time. Some of us have at least once experienced the momentous realness of God. Some of us have at least once caught a glimpse of the beauty, peace, and power that flow through the souls of those who are devoted to Him. There may come a moment like a thunder in the soul, when man is not only aided, not only guided by God's mysterious hand, but also taught how to aid, how to guide other beings.[36]

The "divine light" that empowers us to yearn for God and which sets us "ablaze against and beyond our own power" is "evidence for the truth" of the insight that, as Heschel puts it elsewhere, "beyond all being there is someone who cares."[37] This experience of an empowering divine light, of "what is eternal in time," is the experience of "His glory" which not only "fills the world" but which is especially evident in "the souls of those who are devoted to Him," particularly those who are "not only guided" but who are "also taught . . . how to guide other beings." This is the experience of God's concern which is far more than the experience of a transcendent challenge that implies transcendent concern. Not only the transcendent challenge, but also the "beauty, peace and power that flow through the souls of those who are devoted to Him" bespeak "the momentous realness of God." Those who are devoted to God know that whatever beauty, peace, and power they experience ultimately comes from God.

Perhaps there are no proofs for the existence of God, but there are witnesses,[38] and those who are devoted to God are witnesses; it is they who give evidence to God's overpowering and empowering reality, God's creative concern and glorious presence. These witnesses are those who faithfully pursue the path of piety, and it is when reflecting on the experience of "the pious man" that Heschel offers one of his most profound descriptions of a life lived in the presence of God and of the signs of God's presence revealed in and through such a life:

> The pious man is possessed by his awareness of the presence and nearness of God. Everywhere and at all times he lives as in His sight, whether he remains always heedful of His proximity or not. He feels embraced by God's mercy as by a vast encircling space. Awareness of God is as close to him as the throbbing of his own heart, often deep and calm but at times overwhelming, intoxicating, setting the soul afire. The momentous reality of God stands there as peace, power and endless tranquility, as an inexhaustible source of help, as boundless compassion, as an open gate awaiting prayer. It sometimes happens that the life of a pious man becomes so involved in God that his heart overflows as though it were a cup in the hand of God. This presence of God is not like the proximity of a mountain or the vicinity of an ocean, the view of which one may relinquish by closing the eyes or removing from the place. Rather is this convergence with God unavoidable, inescapable; like air in space, it is always being breathed in, even though one is not always aware of continuous respiration.[39]

Passages such as this indicate the fact that, for Heschel, God's presence is as real as the presence of those who give witness to God. Indeed, the very fact that we are at times struck by the question of God, shaken by the concern for the ultimate, is evidence enough of the reality of God, for there comes a time when the question about God is perceived as a question from God. In Heschel's words: "The more deeply we meditate the more clearly we realize that the question we ask is a question we are being asked; that *man's question about God is God's question of man.*"[40]

It is by examining the situation that accounts for the ultimate question of God that we come to realize that this question is one which is addressed to us, rather than simply one which we ourselves raise on our own accord. The situation that accounts for the ultimate question is not an academic situation in which we merely speculate about the ultimate cause of things; it is, rather, an existential situation in which we are stirred by the ultimate meaning of things. It is a situation in which we are stunned by the mysterious grandeur of the world, struck by the miraculous wonder of our own existence, smitten by the disturbing presence of a transcendent challenge, solaced by the supreme glory of a transcendent concern.

"It is not 'the finitude of being which drives us to the question of God,' but the grandeur and mystery of all being."[41] The question of God bursts forth in our soul when we are overcome by the realization that "you and I have not invented the grandeur of the sky nor endowed man with the mystery of birth and death."[42] In such a situation we cannot avoid asking, "Who created these?" Nor can we deny the feeling that this question, rather than being born out of our own soul, has "shuddered itself into the soul."[43] What drives us to the question of God "is not . . . the acceptance of our own bankruptcy, but, on the contrary, the realization of our own great spiritual power, the power to heal what is broken in the world."[44] Since this spiritual power is experienced as something instilled within us, rather than something we conjure up by our own might, for this reason we are *driven* to the question of God. Awestruck by the fact that we are the witnesses, not the authors of life, that our power to heal is not our own, we also realize that we are aroused and stirred by the question of God.

Moreover, not only do "we ask because the world is too much for us" but also "because the world is replete with what is more than the world as we understand it."[45] We ask because we "learn to sense that all existence is embraced by a spiritual presence," because we are "introduced to a reality which is not only *other* than ourselves . . . but which is *higher* than the universe."[46] The situation that accounts for the question of God is one in which we are confronted by a presence so supreme, so empowering, that there is no other name for it but God.[47] It is the presence of God, as well as the grandeur and mystery of all being, that drives us to the question of the reality of God and to the belief in God. It is in this way that we can understand Heschel's claim that "God is a presupposition as well as a conclusion. . . . God is the climax if He is also the basis. You cannot find Him in the answer if you ignore Him in the question."[48] We accept the reality of God as the conclusion, the climax, or the answer to the question of God, only if God is the basis for the question, only if God is the one who confronts us with the question. "Unless God asks the question, all our inquiries are in vain."[49]

Our question about the *reality* of God is the result of our being pursued by the questioning *presence* of God. The presence is not one which we ourselves take the initiative to confront but one with which we are confronted, one by which we are aroused, stirred, unsettled, challenged, and solaced. We know that we are pursued by the question of God because it remains with us, hounding us, even when we ourselves may not wish to pursue it any longer. We know that the question about God is ultimately a question from God because it is an "invincible question" that "demands our whole being as an answer." "We cannot question the supreme invincible question that extends in front of us, opening itself to us like time, unremittingly, and pleading with us like a voice that had been melted into stillness."[50] Who among us would dare to raise such a question on his or her own, a question that tears our world asunder, depriving us of all complacency and self-satisfaction? And who among us has enough spiritual strength to answer such a question? Is not such an invincible question evidence for the reality of a transcendent challenge? Is not our being able to answer that question evidence of the reality of an empowering transcendent concern? And could such a transcendent challenge and concern be anything but divine?

Indeed, the question of God is evidence enough of the presence and reality of God, for implicit within that question is the realization that "man's question about God is God's question of man." Such a realization gives rise to the conviction that the presence of God is as real as—even more real than—the presence of our own selves. Heschel describes this profound and shocking realization in a most striking and brilliant way:

> When we think with all our mind, with all our heart, with all our soul; when we become aware of the fact that the self cannot stand on its own, we realize that the most subtle explanations are splendid enigmas, that God is more plausible than our own selves, that it is not God who is an enigma but we. When all our mind is aglow with the eternal question like a face in gazing on a mighty blaze, we are not moved to ask: Where is God? for such a question would imply that we who ask are present, while God is absent. In the realm of the ineffable, where our own presence is incredible, we do not ask: Where is God? We can only exclaim: Where is He not? Where are we? How is our presence possible?[51]

This is the epitome of Heschel's religious insight: "God is more plausible than our own selves"; the presence of God is more credible than our own presence. And since "God's presence in the world is, in essence, His concern for the world,"[52] this means that God's concern for us is more real than our concern for God, however real our concern might be. It also means that our concern for God is but an echo of God's concern for us. "At the beginning is God's concern. It is because of His concern for man that man may have a concern for Him."[53]

It must be admitted that were we not a part of a biblical tradition which heralded the concern and challenge of God we might not interpret our religious experiences in terms of God's concern and challenge. But the fact that we have learned to interpret our religious experiences in these terms does not mean that we are merely foisting these interpretations upon experiences which do not in fact include what we interpret to be there.

Upon hearing the biblical message of God's concern and challenge we may come to realize that we too experience that same concern and challenge, even if we might not have recognized it for what it is apart from the guidance of our tradition. The same argument advanced above concerning the correlation between the biblical proclamation of God and our experience of God applies here. In fact, the reason why we are able to speak at all of experiencing the presence of God and not simply the ineffable dimension is because along with and in contrast to experiencing a transcendent dimension of the world we also experience a transcendent concern and challenge from beyond the world. Since the transcendent concern and the transcendent challenge are experienced as being of one and the same transcendent reality, we may speak of experiencing the presence of the Transcendent One.

But could not the manifold experiences of transcendent concern and challenge be said to testify to a multiplicity of concerned and challenging deities rather than to one and the same God? The answer is *no* for the following reason: Since the manifold experiences of the transcendent concern and challenge are all experiences of a unifying concern, of a challenge to love and "to keep aflame our awareness of living in the great fellowship of all beings,"[54] for this reason the manifold experiences must be testifying to the presence of one creative source of unity, one unifying force or power, one God. Although experienced in a myriad of ways, the transcendent concern and challenge that drives us toward oneness must be supremely one. As Heschel says, "political and moral unity as a goal presupposes unity as a source; the brotherhood of men would be an empty dream without the fatherhood of God."[55]

> How do we identify the divine? Divine is a message that discloses unity where we see diversity, that discloses peace when we are involved in discord. God is He who holds our fitful lives together, who reveals to us that what is empirically diverse in color, in interest, in creeds—races, classes, nations—is one in His eyes.[56]
> Oneness is the norm, the standard and the goal. If in the afterglow of a religious insight we can see a way to gather up our scattered lives, to unite what lies in strife—we know it is a guidepost on His way.[57]
> There is no insight more disclosing: *God is One, and humanity is one.* . . . God is every man's pedigree. He is either the Father of all men or of no man. The image of God is either in every man or in no man. . . . God's covenant is with all men, and we must never be oblivious of *the equality of the divine dignity* of all men.[58]

It is the transcendent concern and challenge we experience "that discloses unity where we see diversity" and empowers us "to unite what lies in strife." As such, the transcendent concern and challenge is the sign of the presence of God, of the one God before whom "humanity is one" and because of whom we come to appreciate "the equality of the divine dignity of all men."

DIVINE CONCERN AND THEOLOGICAL ONTOLOGY

It is obvious from the way Heschel describes the meaning of divine concern that he is depicting a lived experience of that concern rather than simply delineating a mere concept of it. Yet it should also be obvious from the above that Heschel believes that the divine concern is not only a genuine human experience but also a credible philosophical idea. Indeed, it is precisely because the experience is so compelling that the idea is so commanding. Yet it seems that Heschel also regards the idea of divine concern to be philosophically tenable even apart from the profound experience of it which he portrays. This is not to say that he would consider the idea to be plausible apart from *all* experience, but that he considers it to be reasonable even apart from the momentous experience which he describes. Prescinding from that experience, there seems to be a twofold reason—connected with the doctrine of creation—why Heschel regards the idea of divine concern to be philosophically cogent: 1) The idea of creation is more persuasive than the idea that the world is self-sufficient and 2) the creation of the world implies a transcendent concern for the world. Based on the idea of creation, then, the idea of divine concern is more convincing than the idea of divine apathy.

While the idea of creation is reasonable even apart from the overwhelming experience of God's challenge and concern as depicted by Heschel, it is not an idea that is divorced from all experience. On the contrary, it is rooted in the experiential "surprise of being,"[59] in the radical amazement "*at the unexpectedness of being as such,* at the fact that there is being at all."[60]

It is not *being as such* that is Heschel's philosophical point of departure; it is rather the *unexpectedness* or *mystery* of being as such. The philosopher who begins with the acceptance of being as such rather than with the mysterious surprise of being is guilty of taking being for granted and as such mistakes the problem for a solution. But the philosopher who begins with the mystery of being is aware of the problem of why there is being at all instead of nothing and may come to realize that the "solution" is not to be found in the theory of the self-sufficiency of the world's being but in the doctrine of creation.

> Being points to the question of how being is possible. The act of bringing being into being, creation, stands higher in the ladder of problems than being.

The mind dares to go behind being in asking about the source of being. It is true that the concept of that source implies being, yet it is also true that a Being that calls a reality into being is endowed with the kind of being that transcends mysteriously all conceivable being. Thus, whereas ontology asks about *being as being,* theology asks about *being as creation,* about being as a divine act. From the perspective of *continuous creation,* there is no being as being; there is only *continuous coming-into-being.*[61]

When Heschel speaks of the creation of being he is of course speaking of the creation of the cosmos and all therein. The creation of the world of being is indeed a mystery, yet the doctrine of creation is a more reasonable answer to the question of why there is being at all, why there is a world, than is the theory of the self-sufficiency of the world. In Heschel's words: "Is not self-sufficiency of nature a greater puzzle, transcending all explanations, than the idea of nature's being dependent on what surpasses nature? The idea of dependence is an explanation, whereas self-sufficiency is an unprecedented, nonanalogous concept in terms of what we know about life within nature. Is not self-sufficiency itself insufficient to explain self-sufficiency?"[62]

Being in the world is not just a matter of being as such, explained in terms of self-sufficiency, but of being as creation, explained in terms of dependency. And the creation of being is the expression of the concern for being. Being as creation points beyond itself to the transcendent concern by which it came into being and by which it is sustained in being. This transcendent concern for being is divine; and it is this divine concern that is the fundamental category of Heschel's theological ontology,[63] which is summarized concisely and profoundly in the following excerpt: "Being is either open to, or dependent on, what is more than being, namely, the care for being, or it is a cul-de-sac, to be explained in terms of self-sufficiency. . . . Being would cease to be if its duration were a matter of indifference to the power of being. Duration of being presupposes concern for being. Being is transcended by a concern for being. . . . There is a care that hovers over being. Being is surpassed by concern for being. Being would cease to be were it not for God's care for being."[64]

But divine concern is not only the fundamental category of Heschel's ontology. It is also, as we have seen, the primary datum of religious experience as he interprets it. Indeed, it is the *experience* of divine concern which Heschel emphasizes more than the *idea* of divine concern as implied in the concept of creation. Yet this latter idea, when shown to be philosophically tenable, may lend support to the faith in God which emerges from the experience of divine concern; it may support the belief that the experience of divine concern is genuine and not illusory. But philosophical support is no substitute for the belief that is supported, nor for the experience that gives rise to the belief. It is, therefore, divine concern as an experience which is, more than the idea of it, a source of faith.

The Glory Is Not the Existence or Essence of God

Although the glory is of God, the glory is not the same as the existence or essence of God. Rather, as cited at the outset of this chapter, "the glory is the presence of God."

Since Heschel says the glory is not the same as the existence or essence of God, it may at first appear that, while making a distinction between the glory of God and the existence or essence of God, he does not make a distinction between the existence of God and the essence of God. Yet while Heschel would agree that there is no distinction in God between essence and existence (since it is of God's very essence to exist), he would nevertheless admit that there is a rational distinction in our minds between the essence of God and the existence of God, between our understanding of *what* God is and our realization *that* God is.[65]

But if God is indivisibly one, then what is meant by the distinction between the glorious presence of God and the essence or existence of God? Is this distinction also only rational, only in our minds? Is it just as true to say that it is of God's essence to be present to the world as it is to say that it is of God's essence to exist? Is it just as true to say that God cannot exist without being present to the world as it is to say that God cannot exist apart from God's essence?

Surely the distinction between the presence of God and the existence or essence of God cannot mean that God's presence is somehow apart from God's existence or essence, for God is present precisely as an existent reality with the essential attributes that constitute who God is. But does this mean, conversely, that God's essence or existence cannot be realized apart from God's being present to the world?

Given the rational distinction between the existence and essence of God, we shall examine first the distinction between the glory and the existence of God and then the distinction between the glory and the essence of God.

THE GLORY AND THE EXISTENCE OF GOD

Since the distinction between the glory and the existence of God cannot mean that God's glory or presence is somehow apart from God's existence, then it must mean that although God is present as an existent reality, God's existence, nevertheless, precedes God's presence to the world (or could have preceded it) and may endure beyond it. Although God's presence is not apart from God's existence, divine existence does not depend on God being present to the world. Thus, in the only sentence in which Heschel suggests what he means by the distinction between the glory and the existence of God, he says: "The Psalmist's prayer, 'May the glory of God be forever' (104:31) cannot be taken to mean, 'May the existence of God continue forever'; this would be blasphemous."[66]

If God can exist without being present to the world, then there must be a distinction between God's presence and God's existence. But since God is present as an existent being (and there is no other way to be present!), then it makes no sense to think of divine presence as somehow apart from divine existence. To encounter the presence of God is to encounter the reality of God. Yet God need not be encountered in order to exist. If God were to withdraw the divine presence from the world God would not cease to exist. But the world would cease to exist if God departed from it, for the world is sustained in being by the creative presence of God. In Heschel's words: "There is a present moment because God is present."[67] As long as there is a world there is divine presence in the world.

But if this is so, that God's presence is always in the world, and if it is also true that there are special manifestations of God's presence in the world, then it seems that we must distinguish between the *omnipresence* of God which sustains the world and the specifically *revealed presence* of God which is disclosed at certain chosen times and places. Given this distinction, we may be inclined at first to think that by "the glory of God" Heschel is referring to the specifically revealed presence of God rather than the omnipresence of God. But this does not seem to be the case. For even though Heschel says that "the glory . . . is revealed, particularly to the prophets," he also claims in accord with Isaiah's vision that "the whole earth is full of His glory," that, in other words, "the glory is not an exception but an aura that lies about all being, a spiritual setting of reality."[68] As "a spiritual setting of reality," the glory is the omnipresence of God; as that which "is revealed, particularly to the prophets," the glory is the special revelatory presence of God. Thus, says Heschel: "'The whole earth is full of His glory' (Isaiah 6:3). Yet, although the Shekinah, the Presence, is everywhere, the experience of the Shekinah is always somewhere."[69] Since the Shekinah is the glory of God, we may paraphrase Heschel in the following way: Although the glory of God is everywhere (omnipresent), the glory is always revealed somewhere.

But whether the glory is omnipresent or revealed, it is not apart from the existence of God; God's existence is omnipresent and revealed. Yet God exists regardless of divine omnipresence to the world or divine revealing presence in the world. And it is because of this that Heschel must make a distinction between the glory and the existence of God.

Regarding the distinction between the presence and the existence of God, we may also consider the distinction and relation between *experiencing* the presence of God and *affirming* the existence of God. For Heschel, the affirmation of the existence of God is a consequence of having been stirred by the presence of God. Heschel accepts the Kantian doctrine that existence cannot be reached through thought alone, that there is no warrant for postulating the existence of a reality on the basis of an idea of that reality within the mind. And he applies this doctrine to the question of God's existence: "The most basic objection to the belief in the existence of God is the argument that such a belief passes from the mind's data to something that surpasses the scope of the mind. What gives us the assurance that an idea which we may find ourselves obliged to think may hold true of a reality that lies beyond the reach of the mind? Such an objection is valid when applied to the speculative approach."[70]

While such an objection is valid when applied to the speculative approach, Heschel repeatedly points out that the affirmation of God's existence, at least from the biblical perspective, is not the result of the speculative approach. It is, rather, the result of the experience of God's presence. In Heschel's words: "The certainty of the realness of God does not come about as a corollary of logical premises, as a leap from the realm of logic to the realm of ontology, from an assumption to a fact. It is, on the contrary, a transition from an immediate apprehension to a thought, . . . from being overwhelmed by the presence of God to an awareness of His existence. . . . In asserting: God is, we merely bring down overpowering reality to the level of thought. Out thought is but an after-belief."[71]

If "our thought is but an after-belief," our belief is but an after-experience. And this is obviously Heschel's position, evident in the preceding quotation and in what he goes on to say: "Our belief in the reality of God is not a case of first possessing an idea and then postulating the ontal counterpart of it; or, to use a Kantian phrase, of first having the idea of a hundred dollars and then claiming to possess them on the basis of the idea. What obtains here is first the actual possession of the dollars and then the attempt to count the sum. There are possibilities of error in counting the notes, but the notes themselves are here."[72] In other words, what obtains here is first the actual experience of the reality of God which in turn gives rise to our belief in the reality of God and our attempt to affirm or articulate (to "count the sum" of) that belief. The experience of God's presence is the experience of a real presence, it is the experience of God's reality. And so the affirmation and idea of the reality of God is a consequence of experiencing that reality. That is why Heschel maintains that our belief in God comes through "overwhelming moments of the awareness of His *existence.*"[73]

The reality of God, the reality of divine presence to us, or the experience of and belief in divine reality, rather than being a logical conclusion of speculative thinking, is the "ontological presupposition" of our ideas and statements about the reality or existence of God.[74] Thus, says Heschel, "the existence of God is not real because it is conceivable; it is conceivable because it is real."[75] Elsewhere Heschel says: "In the depth of human thinking we all presuppose some ultimate reality which on the level of discursive thinking is crystallized into the concept of a power, a principle or a structure. This, then, is the order in our thinking and existence: The ultimate or God comes first and our reasoning about Him second. . . . Just as there is no thinking about the world without the premise of the reality of the world, there can be no thinking about God without the premise of the realness of God."[76] This realness of God is a premise for our thinking about God precisely because we experience a presence so overpowering that its reality cannot be denied and so empowering that its divinity must be confessed.

THE GLORY AND THE ESSENCE OF GOD

Heschel also distinguishes between the glory of God and the essence of God: "The glory is the presence, not the essence of God; an act rather than a quality; a process not a substance."[77] This does not mean that the presence of God is somehow detached from God's essence; for as already stated, when present, God is so precisely as an existent reality with the essential attributes that constitute who God is. What Heschel must mean, then, or what we must interpret him to mean, is that it is not of God's essence to be present to this world, even though when God is present God's essential being is present.

The fact that God's essential being is present to us does not mean that we can comprehend the essence of God. Heschel claims that "no tongue may describe His *essence,* but every soul may both share His *presence* and feel the anguish of His dreadful absence."[78] But the fact that no tongue may describe God's essence does not mean, according to Heschel, that we cannot attain some *understanding* of divine essence, though at times he does seem to suggest this. In one instance, Heschel says: "The Bible tells nothing about God in Himself; all its sayings refer to His relations to man. His own life and essence are neither told nor disclosed. . . . The only events in the life of God the Bible knows of are acts done for the sake of man: acts of creation, acts of redemption (from Ur, from Egypt, from Babylon), or acts of revelation."[79]

Here Heschel seems to imply that what is meant by the "essence" of God is something about "God in Himself." But "God in Himself," that is, God apart from creation, is not the whole of what is meant by the essence of

God. Even if we cannot know anything about "God in Himself," unrelated
to creation, can we not know something about the divine nature inasmuch
as God is related to creation? God in relation to creation is a divine being
with essential attributes which—because of God's acts of creation,
redemption, and revelation—can be discerned and understood, no matter
how inadequately. Certain events are perceived as divine acts because in
and through these events the divine reality and nature of God are revealed.

That Heschel does in fact believe that we can attain some knowledge or
understanding of the nature or essence of God is clear from the following
passage: "Long before we attain any knowledge about His *essence,* we
possess an intuition of a divine *presence.* . . . We proceed from an intuition
of His presence to an understanding of His essence."[80] In this instance
Heschel does not reserve the word "essence" for "God in Himself," for God
in detachment from creation. Heschel reiterates the conviction that we can
attain some understanding of the divine essence when he claims: "Existence
is an indefinable concept, it cannot be imagined *per se,* unqualified, in utter
nakedness; it is always some particular, specific existent, or a mode of
existence, a being dressed in attributes, that we grasp."[81] Heschel makes this
last assertion at the beginning of a chapter entitled "The Divine Concern,"
wherein he goes on to say that "the essence of life is intense care and
concern"[82] and where he claims that the meaning of God's existence is
"transitive concern."[83] The existence of God that we apprehend is the
existence of "a being dressed in attributes." These attributes—such as
justice, mercy, compassion, and love—are the essential characteristics of
God's nature and can be summed up in the term "transitive concern."

The fact that "no tongue can describe His essence" and yet at the same
time we may attain some "understanding of His essence" means that we can
have an understanding of what we cannot describe. Yet Heschel does
attempt to articulate his understanding of the divine nature. This can be
accounted for by the fact that Heschel distinguishes between descriptive and
indicative words: "*Descriptive* words . . . stand in a fixed relation to
conventional and definite meanings, such as the concrete nouns, chair,
table, or the terms of science; and *indicative* words . . . stand in a fluid
relation to ineffable meanings and, instead of describing, merely intimate
something which we intuit but cannot fully comprehend. The content of
words such as God, time, beauty, eternity cannot be faithfully imagined or
reproduced in our minds. Still they convey a wealth of meaning to our sense
of the ineffable."[84] Relating this distinction to our present discussion, we
may say that the term "transitive concern," when applied to God, is an
indicative term, a term that gives us the intimation of what we "cannot fully
comprehend" but that does nevertheless "convey a wealth of meaning to our
sense of the ineffable." The term "transitive concern," when applied to God,
is a term that, like the word "God" itself, represents a meaning we cannot

fully comprehend but nonetheless is conveyed to our consciousness. It is a term of whose meaning we have some intuitive understanding without full comprehension.

Heschel is painfully aware of the inadequacy of all terms when applied to God, yet he is also cognizant of our genuine need to use words to indicate what we understand by the reality of God. "One must not forget that all our utterances about Him are woefully inadequate. But when taken to be allusions rather than descriptions, understatements rather than adequate accounts, they are aids in evoking our sense of His realness."[85] Thus, for Heschel, there are some words that are able to convey an understanding of God—no matter how inadequate the words and how deficient the understanding. He realizes that whatever we can say about God can only be said analogously, in the sense that our language about God combines elements of comparability and uniqueness.[86] Because our language about the divine contains an element of comparability with respect to the human it is anthropomorphic and thus inadequate with respect to the divine. Yet the very fact that we use anthropomorphic expressions does not mean that we necessarily conceive of God in human form. As Heschel reminds us: "There is a difference between anthropomorphic conceptions and anthropomorphic expressions. The use of the latter does not necessarily prove belief in the former."[87] The Bible, for example, is full of anthropomorphic expressions about God, but "the prophets had to use anthropomorphic language in order to convey His nonanthropomorphic Being."[88] For instance, the prophetic language about the "selfless pathos" of God "consists of human ingredients and a superhuman *Gestalt*":

> Absolute selflessness and mysteriously undeserved love are more akin to the divine than to the human. And if these are characteristics of human nature, then man is endowed with attributes of the divine.
>   God's unconditional concern for justice is not an anthropomorphism. Rather, man's concern for justice is a theomorphism. . . . The language the prophets employed to describe that supreme concern was an anthropomorphism to end all anthropomorphisms.[89]

Thus, while the prophetic language about God is anthropomorphic, the prophetic understanding of God is not. Even so, the prophetic understanding of God is not complete. So even if we share the prophetic understanding of God as inspired by the biblical tradition, our understanding is still very inadequate.

Since God radically transcends creation, our understanding of the nature of God is radically different from our understanding of created realities. Yet since there is also an "analogy between Creator and creature,"[90] our way of knowing God is analogous to our way of knowing creation. Even though our awareness of God is noncorporeal, it is still a perceptive awareness; it is an awareness born in the wake of a spiritual perception. When we perceive the presence of God we begin to attain a God-given understanding of the divine nature. We come to realize that God, being utterly transcendent, is a spiritual reality as well as the ultimate one. In fact, it is because the presence we perceive is the ultimate spiritual reality that we refer to this reality as God.[91] This reality is also alive. The "challenging transcendence" which confronts us is indeed a "living transcendence,"[92] "a transcendence called the living God."[93]

Moreover, this reality is personal. Heschel goes so far as to claim that "God is all-personal," that "God is absolutely personal—devoid of anything impersonal."[94] As such, God is also "all concern."[95] This means that God's concern "has the attribute of eternity."[96] Thus, Heschel claims that "justice is His nature," and that "being compassionate" is an expression of "His own nature."[97] Moreover, says Heschel, "His willingness to be intimately involved in the history of man," is "the essence of God's moral nature."[98] Clearly, Heschel is not simply speaking about God's acts—acts of creation, redemption, and revelation—but about the essential nature of the God who acts.

Since God is living and personal, since there is an "analogy between Creator and creature," does this mean that God is also a person? There are statements of Heschel's which, taken on their own, could lead us to believe that he would answer this question in the negative. For example, he says of God: "He is not *a being,* but *being in and beyond all beings.*"[99] As such, God is "the power of maintaining being" or "the transcendent care for being" as well as "the holy dimension" in which all beings abide.[100] Yet Heschel also maintains that God "is encountered not as universal, general, pure Being, but . . . as personal God to a personal man."[101] As such, God is "a personal Being," and "a Being Who wills and acts"; God is "the Supreme Being."[102] In this sense, God is "a Person," God is "the divine Person."[103]

But the question that arises, though one not raised in Heschel's writings, is: How can God be both "not a being" and yet "a Being" or "a Person?" Is not the awareness of God as "the holy dimension"—and thus as a reality which is "not a being"—incompatible with the awareness of God as the supreme being or divine person? Is not the awareness of "abiding in" God incongruent with the experience of "encountering" God?

In this connection, it is interesting to note that Franklin Sherman, who claims that, for Heschel, God is "a dimensional reality,"[104] also maintains that Heschel rejects the proposition that God is a person: "To move from the adjectival or descriptive phrase (God as 'personal') to the substantive or definitional one (God as 'a person') is a step he [Heschel] declines to take."[105] Sherman must have overlooked the references that I have cited. While Sherman proposes that the reason Heschel does not call God a person is because doing so would be limiting God to a human category, perhaps Sherman also supposes that the idea of a dimensional reality in which we dwell is antithetical to the idea of a person whom we meet, since the term "person" connotes a singular, individual, concrete being "over-against" other beings. Contrary to what Sherman suggests, to speak of God as a person is not, in my judgment, to reduce God to a human category anymore than to speak of God as personal would be a way of reducing God. In both cases it must be understood that the terms "person" and "personal" are being used analogously. God's personal concern and involvement transcend any personal activity that human beings can realize themselves, and divine personhood utterly transcends our human category of personhood. Edmond La B. Cherbonnier, another interpreter of Heschel's thought, takes a position contrary to that of Sherman: "The noun 'person' is logically prior to the adjective 'personal.' The former is primary, the latter derivative. Unless there is first a person, nothing can be personal. It is therefore playing with words to say that 'the personal' is included in something else [like being-itself]."[106] Thus, Cherbonnier maintains what I also hold, that in Heschel's view God is not only personal but a distinct person.

Another of Sherman's claims with which I contend is his view that, for Heschel, "God transcends the distinction between personal and impersonal."[107] (This even contradicts his own admission that, for Heschel, God is indeed personal, though not a person.) On the contrary, as we have seen, Heschel believes the "God is all-personal," that "God is absolutely personal—devoid of anything impersonal." To be sure, God transcends our notion of what it means to be personal, but God does not transcend the distinction between personal and impersonal—and Heschel never says that God transcends this distinction.

But the question remains: How can Heschel, short of contradiction, maintain in one context that God is "not a being" and claim in other instances that God is "a Being" or "a Person"? Is not the awareness of God as a dimensional reality in whom we dwell incompatible with the awareness of God as a divine person whom we encounter?

It indeed appears as if Heschel has contradicted himself, that he is speaking of God in terms that are incompatible. Yet in my judgment Heschel has only apparently contradicted himself. For when he says that God is "not a being" he means, I suggest, that God is not a being among other beings; that is, God is not a being like other beings, a being restricted by time and space. And when, on the other hand, Heschel speaks of God as "a Being" or "a Person" he does not mean to imply that God is simply "man writ large." In Heschel's words, "the likeness of God [in man] means the likeness of Him who is unlike man."[108] Heschel is quite aware of the fact that "to speak of God as if He were a person does not necessarily mean to personify Him, to stamp Him in the image of a [human] person."[109]

In order to support his contention that Heschel never calls God a person, Professor Sherman refers his readers to the page from which the last quotation is taken. In doing so, he probably is thinking especially of this quotation. Granted that Heschel says that "to speak of God *as if* He were a person" is not "to stamp Him in the image of a person." However, it is clear from the context that what Heschel means is that to speak of God as such is not to cast him in the image of a *human* person, for two sentences later Heschel places the terms "a person" and "human being" in apposition: "To most of us a person, a human being, seems to be the maximum of being, the ceiling of reality; we think that to personify is to glorify." Clearly, then, when Heschel says in this instance that "to speak of God as if He were a person does not necessarily mean to personify Him" he means that to speak of God thus is not to think of God in the image of a *human* person. Not to personify God is not to humanize God. But this does not mean that God is not a person, analogously speaking. In other words, there is a difference between *personifying* God and speaking analogously of God as a *person*.

Another page to which Sherman refers in order to support his claim that Heschel refrains from calling God a person includes the following statement which he must have had in mind: "To be a person is to have a concern for the nonself. It is in this limited sense that we speak of God as a personal Being: He has concern for nondivine being."[110] Rather than confirming Sherman's contention, this reference seems to counter it. True, Heschel says that we speak of God as a personal Being "in a limited sense." Nevertheless, by saying that "to be a person is to have concern for the nonself" and that God "has concern for nondivine being" is certainly to imply what Heschel explicitly says elsewhere: that God is a person. By saying that it is only in a "limited sense that we speak of God as a personal Being" Heschel does not mean that God, as Sherman contends, "transcends the distinction between personal and impersonal." Rather, he means that while God possesses the outstanding feature of personhood—that is, "concern for the nonself"— God does not possess all the features that make up human personhood. But this is not a limitation on God's personal being, since much of what is essential to human personhood would in fact be unnecessary and even limiting to God. Moreover, God possesses the attribute of transitive concern in a supreme way, unlike any human person. God, unlike human beings, is "all concern." God's concern, unlike ours, "has the attribute of eternity . . . as well as the attribute of universality."[111] And it is precisely because of this, because God's concern is so supreme, that God is the Supreme Being, the Divine Person.

In short, then, God is a *B*eing, not a *b*eing. When Heschel refers to God as a Being, he is well aware of the fact that "a Being who calls a reality into being transcends mysteriously all conceivable being."[112] God as a Being is the Transcendent Being, the Supreme Being. God as a Person is the

Transcendent Person, the Divine Person. So when Heschel claims that God is not a being, he does not deny that God is the Supreme Being. And when Heschel says that God is "being in and beyond all beings," he does not mean that God.is being-itself. In Heschel's view, God is the supreme, transcendent Being who is within all beings and transcends all beings. As the supreme, transcendent *Being,* the divine *Person,* God is analogous to human persons: singular, unique, and social. Yet as *supreme* or *divine,* as a thoroughly transcendent and spiritual Person, God does, unlike human beings, envelop and permeate all other beings while remaining distinct from them. God is individual, not all-inclusive; but God is not individual in the sense that a human being is; God is an individual reality in whom we abide. Thus, it is not impossible for God, as divine Being, to be both a dimensional reality and a singular, unique Person. God is a dimensional Person, a Person in whom we dwell. And though we "dwell within" God, we do nevertheless "encounter" God. On the one hand, encountering God is like "encountering" the sea while swimming beneath its surface, rather than like encountering another being while swimming within the sea. Yet because God, unlike the sea, is personal, encountering God is, on the other hand, more like encountering a fellow human being than like experiencing an impersonal sea. God is like a sea that is personal. God is a Being whose presence is a flood of concern and love; God is a Person whose presence embays us like a sea.

　　God is all-embracing, but not all-inclusive. Those who dwell within the Spirit of God are not a part of God but are surrounded by God's glory. If God were all-inclusive, if we were all parts of God's being, perhaps it would make sense to speak to our "dwelling within" God, but it would make little sense to speak of our "encountering" God. And if God were a person among persons it would perhaps make sense to speak of "encountering" God, but it would make no sense to speak of "dwelling within" God. But since God is a transcendent, divine Person, it makes sense to speak of encountering the God in whom we dwell. God is, once again, both a dimensional reality and a divine Person. But in saying this it is important to keep in mind that the terms "a dimensional reality" and "a person" are used analogously when applied to God. There is an analogy between the dimension of time and the dimension of God's glory, or between our relation to time and our relation to the glory: we dwell in time and we dwell in the glory of God. Likewise, there is an analogy between a human person and the divine Person, or between our relation to another human person and our relation to the divine Person: we encounter both a human person and the divine Person; both relationships are "characterized by a subject–subject structure."[113] We dwell within the glory of God, and also encounter God as a Person. We encounter the God in whom we dwell, in whom we live and move and have our being. The glory of the Holy One is our Holy Domain. As such, this divine glory is a source of our human faith.

5

The Jewish Tradition

Faith is the achievement of ages, an effort accumulated over centuries.[1]

Religious faith is awakened and cultivated not only by our personal experience of the sublime, the mystery, and the glory, but also by our participating in a tradition that bears witness to the sublime mystery of life and to the glory of God therein. In fact, it is by sharing in such a tradition that we develop a sense of the sublime mystery and the divine glory.

There is no such thing as a generalized religious faith. Religious faith is always rooted in a particular tradition. In this chapter we shall examine Heschel's understanding of the Jewish tradition as a source of Jewish faith.

The Dynamics of Tradition

The genesis of monotheistic religious faith is rooted in the personal experience of God's presence which is nurtured by the tradition that testifies to the revelation of God's presence. Were it not for the tradition in which we share, we would not experience God's presence as we do. For no experience is realized apart from a community that is formed by the tradition it inherits. Even solitary experiences are affected by the community and its tradition. Tradition fosters community, and the community informs the experiences of its individual members. The experiences of individual persons also in turn affect the life of the community which not only inherits but also fashions its tradition. Community is shaped by the tradition to which it lends further shape. Individuals are formed by the community they help form. The experience of individual persons is thus influenced by the community's tradition and that tradition is in turn affected by individual persons in the community.

Religious experience, like all human experience, comes about as a coalition—or as a collision—between traditional ways and personal initiatives. Religious faith is thus rooted in personal experience and a particular tradition.[2] More precisely, it is awakened in personal experience roused by, though not completely determined by, a particular tradition. In turn, the tradition is enhanced by the individual's faith.

FAITH AND THE GUIDANCE OF TRADITION

A balanced perspective on the interconnection of tradition and personal religious experience as forming the substratum of faith is found in Heschel's writings. Therein too is found insight that prompts reflection on the relation between tradition and the faith of a generation.

FAITH AND THE HERITAGE OF INSIGHT

Religious faith is enlivened by, among other things, the insight born in the wake of the experience of the sublime, the mystery, and the glory. And such personal insight is nurtured by "a heritage of insight,"[3] by a tradition that cultivates an appreciation for the sublime, the mystery, and the glory. For instance, the wonder with which we respond to the sublime is provoked not only by the presence of the sublime but also by the "legacy of wonder" which our "religious tradition holds in store for us."[4] The tradition teaches us how to recognize and respond with wonder to the presence of the sublime. If we did not really perceive for ourselves the reality of the sublime we would not know the experience of wonder. Yet were it not for the "legacy of wonder" we might never learn to perceive the sublime for ourselves. The correlation between the heritage of insight and the personally experienced insight enables the individual to attain a faith which is more than idiosyncratic or private. Rather, it is a faith that is both personal and communal.

INDIVIDUAL FAITH IN NEED OF GUIDANCE

Faith that arises in and from the individual's personal insight or experience is not self-sufficient. In Heschel's words, "it must be counter-signed by the dictate of unforgettable guidance."[5] The guidance of tradition that comes from the past is available to us not only in the sacred texts and liturgies that have been preserved through the ages but also in the lives of our contemporaries who remember, revive, recast, and renew that tradition.

The tradition that guides us in our quest for God, that alerts us to God's search for us, is a living tradition: a tradition from the past alive in the souls of men and women of our present age. To enjoy the guidance of our tradition we must turn to our forebears who have bequeathed this tradition to us and to our contemporaries who have imbibed this same tradition. Together with them we may learn to discern more adequately the guidance which our tradition conveys.

To experience the guidance of our tradition we must recall the past by heeding the interpretive word of the sages among us. It is they who embody the meaning and truth that the tradition imparts and that they perceive anew because they have learned from the tradition how to discern the will of God as it is manifest in the events of our present age. As the Talmud teaches us in recording the words of Rabbi Simon ben Lakish: "In the end, you only have the sages of your own generation."[6] But the sages of our own generation have been nourished in the way of wisdom by generations of sages. Authentic religious faith is not merely individual or private faith; it is shared faith: faith shared by a people who share a tradition that attests to the revelation of God's redemptive concern.

"Our own life is a movement in the symphony of ages," says Heschel. This is why "religious living is not only a private concern."[7] And this is why individual faith is insufficient for the individual: because the individual is not a strictly solitary, self-sufficient being. Just as every individual depends on others for physical and emotional well-being, so too does every individual depend on others for mental and spiritual growth. "The individual's insight alone [including the insight of faith] is unable to cope with all the problems of living. It is the guidance of tradition on which we must rely, and whose norms we must learn to interpret and apply."[8] In fact, the individual would be devoid of insight were it not for the guidance of tradition or the "heritage of insight" that provokes the individual's insight.

Personal insight springs from the reservoir of inherited insight, no matter how novel or even dissenting the personal insight might be. What Michael Polanyi demonstrates about the birth of new insight in science is equally true concerning the genesis of religious insight: "Discoveries are made by pursuing possibilities suggested by existing knowledge."[9] Just as scientific originality emerges from a scientific tradition while at the same time advancing or superseding it, religious innovation issues from a religious tradition while simultaneously enriching or surpassing it. Of course, insight, whether scientific, religious or otherwise, need not be, and usually is not, altogether novel or in anywise dissentient. An individual's insight may be either an original insight in the history of a tradition or, as is more common, a personal insight into the fund of knowledge that tradition has acquired and vouchsafes to those who seek it. Personal insight is often a matter of seeing what others have already seen, yet seeing it for oneself.

Heschel's words are apt: "Our mind has not kindled the flame, has not produced these principles. Still our thoughts glow with their light."[10] Whether our insight be novel or not, if we are to attain personal insight at all we must be nourished by a heritage of insight. Thus, again in Polanyi's words: "A society which wants to preserve the fund of personal knowledge must submit to tradition."[11]

Notice that the submission which Polanyi counsels is a submission that preserves or promotes personal knowledge; it is a submission for the sake of freedom and creativity. It is for this same reason that Heschel counsels solidarity with our forebears: "The endeavor to integrate the abiding teachings and aspirations of the past into our own thinking will enable us to be creative and expand, not to imitate or to repeat."[12] To become freely creative in anything we must first submit to an authority in that field who can teach us the discipline that yields creative expression. "By watching the master and emulating his efforts in the presence of his example the apprentice unconsciously picks up the rules of the art, including those which are not explicitly known to the master himself."[13] The apprentice may someday outdo the master, but only by first learning from the master. Each of us must be an apprentice in the art of religious faith if ever we are to express our faith creatively. The sages and saints of our tradition are the masters whose efforts we must emulate.

The individual person must rely on the guidance of tradition also because the individual is not simply a *hic et nunc* being. Heschel philosophizes as follows: "We cannot . . . analyze man as a being only here and now. Not only here, because his situation is intentional with the situation of other men scattered far and wide all over the world. Not only now, because his total existence is, in a sense, a summation of past generations, a distillation of experiences and thoughts of his ancestors. The authentic individual is neither an end nor a beginning but a link between ages, both memory and expectation."[14] Human beings cannot live significantly without solidarity with other human beings, nor without a history and a solidarity with those who have gone before them. "We are a people in whom the past endures, in whom the present is inconceivable without moments gone by."[15] We must recall the meaning of moments gone by in order to appreciate the full significance of the present moment. Just as the true significance of the life of an isolated individual is not fully realized, the true meaning of the present moment is not adequately understood if segregated from the past moments that have led to its occurrence. Tradition is the link between the past and the present, and participation in a tradition is what enables an individual and a community to understand the significance of the present.

Just as a plant withers when uprooted, so wilts the human soul when sundered from its heritage. Yet as a plant may be transplanted and continue to live, so may a human being draw sustenance from a tradition not one's own or find new life by adopting another tradition as one's own. The convert develops a new spiritual identity with all that it entails: new history, new commitments, and new destiny.

The question is not whether to live by a tradition or not, but by which tradition to live. The problem is not whether to have faith or not, but in what or whom to place our faith. We cannot live significantly without faith in someone or something that makes life worthwhile. And we cannot have faith without a tradition that evokes and sustains that faith.

TRADITION AND THE FAITH OF A GENERATION

Just as faith that arises simply from the personal experience of an individual is not self-sufficient, so too the faith of any one generation must not be considered sufficient if it is based entirely on the experience of that generation. The individual learns not only from personal experience but also from the experience of others. Likewise, a generation of people may learn not only from its own experience but also from the experience of previous generations. The experience of any one individual or any one generation may be spiritually impoverished experience; these individuals and generations need the wisdom of other people and other generations. But even where the experience of individuals or generations is not spiritually deprived, it is still wise for individuals and generations to heed the lessons taught by the history of human experience. The lessons of history are conveyed by tradition. Particular traditions convey particular lessons that may have universal significance.

As there are countless histories, there are innumerable traditions, including a host of religious traditions. The purpose of any religious tradition is to transmit the religious faith of a given people. It is the religious tradition that guides—or misguides—both the individual person and the single generation. If the tradition is founded upon truth and heralds a message of truth, that tradition is a valuable guide for individuals and generations in their quest for truth. If the tradition is of God, the tradition will be able to help individuals and generations find their way to God. Without guaranteeing the emergence of faith in the life of any given individual, or the preservation of faith for a generation of people, the religious tradition facilitates the perpetuity or rise of faith in the lives of those who inherit its guidance.

Incumbent upon each generation, as upon each person, is the obligation to decide whether or not to keep alive an inherited tradition. A religious tradition merits preservation if it contains a key to the meaning and truth of existence, a means by which to live nobly and righteously, to foster human dignity, and to build a just society. A religious tradition should be preserved if it provides a way of living in accord with God's challenge and concern, thereby advancing the divine and human task of redeeming the world.

Just as culture is not the accomplishment of any single generation, so it is with the life of faith. "Not the individual man, nor a single generation by its own power, can erect the bridge that leads to God. Faith is the achievement of ages, an effort accumulated over centuries."[16] In fact, the life of faith is a certain kind of culture, or it is the ultimate criterion by which to evaluate the grandeur of a culture. Heschel contends that we should gauge a culture not by its scientific and artistic achievements but by the extent to which reverence, compassion, justice, and holiness are found in the daily life of a people.[17] The Jewish tradition preserves religious culture to the extent that it cultivates the faith by which people incarnate the qualities that Heschel mentions. It is a tradition that inspires faith by which people strive to live in accordance with God's eternal care. "Instances of God's care in history come about in seeming disarray, in scattered fashion—we must seek to comprehend the unity of the seemingly disconnected chords."[18] The Jewish tradition conveys "the unity of the seemingly disconnected chords" of "God's care in history" and helps people share that divine care. This is the meaning of Jewish faith: to live in accord with God's redeeming care. It is such care, such faith, that the Jewish tradition evokes and guides.

Notice, the Jewish tradition "evokes and guides" faith; it does not simply bestow it. Faith is not simply transmitted from person to person, nor from one generation to the next. Each person and each generation must struggle anew with the ultimate questions of faith and must decide whether to affirm or discard the convenantal faith by which previous generations lived. Although there is a heritage of faith, the fact that faith involves struggle and decision means that faith cannot simply be inherited. Tradition cannot simply bequeath faith, but it can inspire the covenantal renewal of faith.

TRADITION AND PIONEERING FAITH

By conveying "the unity of the seemingly disconnected chords" of "God's care in history," the Jewish tradition evokes and nurtures the life of faith. Yet "authentic faith is more than the echo of a tradition."[19]

NO SURROGATE FOR TRADITION

The revelation of God's redemptive care in history is the primary message of the biblical or Jewish tradition, and the ways or observances of that tradition help us discern the traces of God's care in our own life histories. It is the discernment of God's care in our lives correlated with the recognition of God's care in history that kindles faith in God. If we did not perceive God's care in our own lives, it would be difficult to accept the biblical message of God's care in history. Yet were it not for the biblical message we would not detect as we do God's care in our lives.

Were we not a part of a community that has a monotheistic tradition, probably we would not interpret our religious experience in monotheistic terms. But the fact that the biblical tradition allows us to interpret our religious experience monotheistically does not mean that we do not really have monotheistic experience. The biblical tradition provokes our religious experience and at the same time equips us with the means of interpreting that experience monotheistically. The experience lends itself to the interpretation; the interpretation fits the experience. We need guidance not only to experience certain realities but also to grow in the understanding of what we are experiencing. The biblical tradition guides us in interpreting the religious experience it incites.

Since it is in and through tradition that we learn to discern God's care and are inspired to commit ourselves to God's redemptive cause, there is "no surrogate for tradition"[20] in attaining faith in God. It is God who calls forth faith in God, yet the call is mediated through the tradition which has been formed in response to the revelation of God's love and command. This revelation is what forged a community that formed a tradition that conveys the meaning of that revelation and facilitates the discernment of further revelation. God graces us with faith by blessing us with a tradition in and through which divine care is experienced. Thus is tradition an indispensable source of faith. In the life of faith, "only he who is an heir is qualified to be a pioneer."[21]

TRADITION IS NO SUBSTITUTE FOR FAITH

Heschel also claims the converse: "In the realm of spirit only he who is a pioneer is able to be an heir."[22] Only someone who boldly confronts the ultimate questions of life and contends with God is able to appreciate the meaning and the grandeur of the biblical tradition which that person is invited to share. Only such a person is worthy to be an heir to a tradition which has been formed and transmitted by those who grappled with the ultimate questions and wrestled with the living God.

The Jewish tradition, at its best, is a living, pioneering tradition. "We should be pioneers as were our fathers three thousand years ago."[23] Tradition, in this sense, has nothing to do with an obscurant traditionalism which is the unconditional acceptance of the past and the uncritical adherence to archaic ideas and practices. Despite his respect for tradition, Heschel claims: "To have faith does not mean . . . to dwell in the shadow of old ideas conceived by prophets and sages, to live off an inherited estate of doctrines and dogmas. . . . The wages of spiritual plagiarism is the loss of integrity. . . . Authentic faith is more than an echo of a tradition. It is a creative situation, an event."[24]

The fact that "authentic faith is more than an echo of a tradition" does not mean that it in no way echoes a tradition. Authentic faith echoes the tradition but also lends its own unique tone to the tradition. It involves the correlation of the witness of tradition and the unique encounter with God which the tradition may have fostered but which it previously did not include. Authentic faith may indeed reaffirm the old ideas, doctrines, and dogmas conceived by prophets and sages, but it does not merely "live off" these. Rather, authentic faith wrestles anew with the questions that gave rise to these ideas, doctrines, and dogmas; it seeks to experience anew the divine–human encounter akin to that which underlies the tradition's creed. Such faith bears witness to the ideas, doctrines, and dogmas of the tradition that illumine the present situation, and it likewise testifies to the impact of God's presence in the present situation and to whatever ideas, dogmatic or otherwise, may emerge as the result of that impact. Authentic faith bears witness to what God has revealed and to what God is revealing.

Religious believers may indeed accept and adhere to ancient ideas and practices without being obscurantists, without doing so simply because of the antiquity of the ideas and practices. Pioneers in the realm of faith may hold many ancient ideas and observe many ancient practices; what makes them pioneers is that they do so because they discern the significance of those ideas and practices and adhere to them with spirit, as well as the fact that they seek to experience the reality to which the ideas and practices allude. Believers may also be pioneers by contributing to the development of the tradition with innovations and reforms.

Pioneers in faith may still recall and celebrate past events, not because of their antiquity but because of their meaning, because of the impact these events had on the past and continue to exert on the present and the future. Therefore, it is not the entire past that is remembered and cherished but only the significant past. It is only the events from the past that lend meaning to the present and the future that are recalled and celebrated. The events with which the Jewish tradition is especially concerned are those considered revelatory, and concern with these events has to do with their abiding significance. Thus, living by way of tradition is not a way of entering into the past but a way of allowing the significant past to enter into and affect the present and the future.

From this perspective, the inherited tradition is not a refuge for those who are afraid to think and search for themselves but a point of departure for the pioneering venture that the life of faith entails. "Faith requires action, a leap. It is an enterprise, not inertia. It requires bold initiative rather than continuity. Faith is forever contingent on the courage of the believer."[25] Pioneering faith is provoked by a pioneering tradition of faith. Such a tradition is a challenge to mere traditionalism. It is the Jewish tradition to adapt, develop, and change itself in order to meet the unique demands that arise in new times and different places. True, there is a core to the tradition that remains permanent and intact throughout its history, but even this core may be expressed, elaborated, and incarnated in a variety of languages and cultures.

Such a tradition not only permits but calls forth innovators and reformers, prophets, and sages. At its best, the Jewish tradition nurtures the work of authentic innovation and renewal that is demanded by the fact that history is full of new challenges as God is full of surprises.

So while "there is no surrogate for tradition," when it comes to attaining faith, tradition must never be used as a substitute for bold and courageous faith. Tradition becomes that substitute when it ceases to be a renewing, protesting, pioneering tradition. Though at its best the Jewish tradition is an impetus for pioneering faith, Heschel claims that at times it shows signs of inertia and fails to realize its purpose.[26] When this happens, respect for tradition degenerates into a kind of traditionalism that stifles the life of faith. Genuine respect for the Jewish tradition accepts it for what it is meant to be: an impetus for pioneering faith.

The Wellsprings of Jewish Tradition

Even in a pioneering tradition not all things are subject to change. There is a core within the body of Jewish tradition that endures throughout history. Both continuity and change, conservation and adaption, are essential to Judaism. The core of the Jewish tradition is faith in one God, Creator and Redeemer of the world, who has revealed to human beings divine concern and challenge, grace and torah, especially in the events of the Exodus and Sinai and through the prophets of Israel. At the heart of the tradition, then, is the belief that God has entered an alliance with humankind and has sealed it through a special covenant with the people of Israel, a bond entailing mutual responsibility. God's commitment is to initiate and pursue the work of redemption for Israel and the world. Israel's commitment is to help God in the redemptive task by pursuing a life of Torah.

This faith that is the core of Judaism was initially evoked through revelatory events. Even today Jewish faith is sparked by recounting and celebrating these events, by demonstrating their significance for the present and future, and by relating them to the current experience of God's presence. These revelatory events are attested to in the Hebrew Bible, which in turn is interpreted throughout Jewish history by the sages of Israel, the most authoritative interpretations (*midrashim*) being in the Talmud. Therefore, in order to understand Heschel's view of the Jewish tradition, we must explore his understanding of the meaning of revelation, the Bible, and rabbinic commentary.

REVELATION

"Relevation is an ecstasy of God."[27] It is a divine event in which the glory of God becomes manifest. Revelation is thus an act of "God's turning to man."[28] Since there is often a distance between God and humanity, Heschel realizes that "revelation is an event that does not happen all the time but at a particular time, at a unique moment of time."[29] These assertions and their implications must be carefully examined.

RELEVATION AS ECSTASY

As "an ecstasy of God," revelation is a transitive act whereby God is "turning" to humanity. Does Heschel mean to imply by this assertion that God is not always in a transitive relation to human beings, not always turned toward them? If so, he is inconsistent. Heschel's more consistent approach is to suggest that God is always turned toward humanity, for transitive concern is, according to Heschel, an essential attribute of God's divinity.[30] What, then, could Heschel possibly mean by saying that revelation is "God's turning to man"? I suggest that what he means, or what we may interpret him to mean, is that although God is always turned toward humanity, there are certain events or moments in which God reaches human beings in special ways. Revelation happens when God makes this contact. Would it not be more precise to say that revelation, rather than being an act of turning, is a manifestation or communication of God's being forever turned toward humanity?

That Heschel would accept this interpretation is suggested by the fact that he claims that "revelation . . . is an act in God's search for man."[31] In other words, revelation is one of the acts of God's reaching toward humanity. The fact that Heschel believes that God's reaching out is continuous is indicated by his claim that "all human history as seen by the Bible is the history of *God in search of man*."[32] If all of human history is a history of the divine search for human beings, then revelation is a disclosure of that search. Heschel's claim that revelation is "God's turning to man" does not mean that divine concern is at times withheld but that it is sometimes concealed. Thus, revelation as "God's turning to man" is a matter of "God's turning from the conditions of concealment to an act of revealment."[33]

Unceasingly concerned for creation, God is forever ecstatic, forever "reaching out." Yet God's eternal ecstasy is revealed in fragments of time, episodes of history. Divine revelation is the historical manifestation of eternal ecstasy. And since ecstasy is enhanced in the disclosure thereof, revelation is a moment of heightened ecstasy. Thus may we understand that "revelation is an ecstasy of God."

REVELATION AS EVENT

It is important to take note of Heschel's claim that "revelation is an event." As such it is neither a process nor a part of a process; rather it is a happening. Heschel describes this distinction between a process and an event in the following way: "A process happens regularly, following a relatively permanent pattern; an event is extraordinary, irregular. A process may be continuous, steady, uniform; events happen suddenly, intermittently, occasionally. Processes are typical; events are unique. A process follows a law, events create a precedent."[34] Having made this distinction, Heschel goes on to point out that processes occur in the realm of nature, while events are what constitute history. God may be manifest in and through the processes of nature, but revelation according to the biblical tradition occurs primarily in and through historical events. And since "a process may be continuous" while "events happen suddenly, intermittently, occasionally," Heschel denies the possibility of a "continuous revelation."[35]

But why must historical events happen in this way? Are there no historical processes? Are there no historical events that are at the same time processes? Heschel would probably agree that there are historical patterns of events. In this sense he may recognize a series of events forming what may be called a historical process. Unlike a natural process, a historical process involves acts of freedom, decision, and responsibility. But even if Heschel were to acknowledge a kind of historical process—a pattern of events—would he also admit that there are single historical events that are processes? It is reasonable to assume he would grant not only the possibility but the existence of events that involve process-like characteristics. For example, the birth of a nation is in a sense a single historical event which may involve a long process of negotiation. So when Heschel contrasts events and processes we should understand him to be distinguishing between historical events, which may be events-in-process, and natural processes, which are not events since they do not include freedom, decision, and responsibility. It is not the fact that something occurs "suddenly, intermittently, occasionally" but rather that it is informed with freedom, decision, and responsibility that distinguishes it as an event as opposed to a natural process.

But if some historical events may at the same time be considered historical processes, then does this mean that revelation can also be considered a process? An affirmative answer seems reasonable. If God addresses human beings primarily in and through historical events, and if some events are events-in-process, then it is reasonable to speak of a process of revelation. This does not deny the eventful nature of revelation; it only affirms that the revelatory event, like other events, may be a process-event. As such, revelation is still a very different kind of process than any natural process. Revelation does not occur automatically. According to Heschel, in the biblical tradition, revelation is "not thought of as proceeding out of God like rays out of the sun"; rather it is "an act proceeding from His will and brought about by a decision to disclose what otherwise would remain concealed."[36] This, I contend, is what Heschel is really driving at when he claims that revelation is an event rather than a process. Again, it is will and decision that make it an event, not the fact that it happens suddenly, intermittently, and occasionally. Even a process-event may be informed by will and decision.

But even if revelation may be considered a process-event, does this mean that revelation may also be considered a *continuous* process? Not if by continuous is meant unending. To admit that a revelatory event may take the form of a historical event-in-process is not to concede that there is one uninterrupted process of revelation. There may be many revelatory process-events, but these do not constitute an uninterrupted revelation.[37]

But why can revelation not be continuous? Perhaps in principle it could be. But in fact it appears not to be the case. There seem to be revelatory process-events that occur from time to time rather than one long revelational process-event. Although God is always present, God's presence is not always manifest. Although God is always concerned with humanity, God's will is not always communicated to human beings. God's presence and will may be revealed through events-in-process, but that revelation does not seem to be unending. Why? Perhaps it is because human beings are not always open to the presence and will of God. There can be no revelation unless human beings are attentive to God. God may be forever calling out to human beings, but this does not mean that revelation is continuous. And not only do human beings fail to perceive God's call because of inattention; they also resist that call by way of arrogance. Heschel says: "The will of God is to be here, manifest and near; but when the doors of this world are slammed on Him, His truth betrayed, His will defied, He withdraws, leaving man to himself. God did not depart of His own volition; He was expelled. *God is in exile.*"[38] As true as this assessment may be, it does not seem to be the whole story. For there are many times when human beings are quite attentive, straining for a sign of God's presence, longing for a glimpse of the divine will, and yet receive no revelation from God. God may be ever present, but it seems that God is sometimes awfully silent. "My tears have been my food day and night, while they say unto me, where is your God?" (Psalms 42:3).

Heschel is aware of God's silence.[39] Thus, from his perspective, to speak of a continuous revelation is naive. But though there is no continuous revelation, there indeed may be a continuous faith. For faith is not simply the response to God at times of divine revelation but also a matter of being faithful to God during times of divine concealment. "Faith includes faithfulness, strength of waiting, the acceptance of His concealment, defiance of history."[40] The history that must be defied is the history that looks like "a stage for the dance of might and evil,"[41] a history in which God's presence is eclipsed. But faith *despite* the eclipse of God can only be attained *because* of a former divine revelation. Faith, as faithfulness, must rely on the remembrance of what has been disclosed. Through such faithful remembrance we give witness to the God who has been revealed. And in so doing we reveal God again. "Despair is not man's last word. Hiddenness is not God's last act."[42] Faith knows neither God's continuous revelation nor God's continuous silence. "God's silence does not go on forever,"[43] nor does the revelation of God. Faith is the art of responding to God in moments of revelation and of witnessing to God in moments of silence.

PROPHETIC REVELATION

To speak of the glory of God in this world, the subject of the preceding chapter, is to speak of both the omnipresence of God and the specifically revealed presence of God. As "a spiritual setting of reality,"[44] the glory is the omnipresence of God; in this sense, "the whole earth is full of His glory." As that which "is revealed, particularly to the prophets,"[45] the glory is the special revelatory presence of God. Thus, although the glory of God is everywhere, the glory is always revealed somewhere.

Notice that when speaking of the revelation of God's glory, as distinct from the omnipresence of glory, Heschel says that the glory is revealed *particularly* to the prophets, implying that it is revealed *not only* to the prophets, though to them especially. The revelation that the prophets experienced was the revelation of God's glorious presence, a presence which may, in principle, be revealed to all people. God's presence was experienced by the prophets primarily as divine concern and challenge, love and command. This, as we have seen in the preceding chapter, may be experienced by others as well. The revelatory events experienced by the prophets may have been unique and unprecedented, but these events were not totally different from revelatory experiences had by others.

"There is a grain of the prophet in the recesses of every human existence."[46] According to Heschel, what enabled the people of Israel to trust Moses and what enables us to accept the biblical message is that they and we share "a degree of the prophetic sense."[47] To share the prophetic sense is to share not only in the prophetic task but also, to some degree, the prophetic experience of the revelatory presence of God. In fact, it is the prophetic experience that gives impetus to the prophetic task. Nevertheless, Heschel believes that the experience of Israel's prophets was an extraordinary experience of God's revelation. As such, it stands as an archetypal experience of what others may have to a lesser extent. Even the call to be a prophet, which is but one form of revelation found in the Bible, is not totally discontinuous with the revelation experienced by others. Anyone sensitive to the divine approach may discover that he or she is being called to give prophetic witness to God.

Since Heschel regards the revelation described in the Bible as extraordinary, he tends to speak of it as unprecedented, "like no other event."[48] This could imply that he considers the biblical revelation as totally different from any other event. But the fact that it is unlike other events does not mean that other events are not analogous to biblical revelation. Unlikeness or difference is but one side of the coin of analogy; likeness or similarity is the other. So no matter how often Heschel may speak of biblical revelation as unlike any other event, it does not preclude his speaking of other revelatory events as analogous to biblical revelation. Heschel's writings are replete with the conviction that the revelation of God's concern and challenge is not limited to the biblical era and may even be experienced apart from an encounter with the biblical testimony. The prophetic experience may be quite unlike our own experience which is, nonetheless, somewhat like it. The experience of the prophets may be unattainable to us, but it is not alien to us. We, like they, live under the divine claim which has been mediated to us through their word. In Heschel's view, the prophetic experience is to our own experience as a flame is to a spark. By the very fact that we perceive but a spark of divine revelation we are able to understand that the prophets experienced revelation as a flame. But without at least knowing what a divine spark is like, we would never be able to imagine what it might be like to perceive a divine flame. The analogy and correlation between the prophetic experience of revelation and ours is expressed by Heschel as follows:

> Behind the radiant cloud of living, perplexing the unacquainted souls, some men have sensed the sound of *Let There Be,* in the fullness of being. In others not only a song but a voice, lifting the curtain of unknowableness, reached the mind. Those who know that the grace of guidance may be ultimately bestowed upon those who pray for it, that in spite of their unworthiness and lowliness they may be enlightened by a spark that comes unexpectedly but in far-reaching wisdom, undeserved, yet saving, will not feel alien to the minds that perceived not a spark but a flame.[49]

RESISTANCE TO REVELATION

The previous quotation is an attempt on Heschel's part to break down resistance to the idea of the possibility of revelation as attested to in the Bible. In Heschel's judgment, resistance to revelation in the modern era is due mainly to two diametrically opposed views of human existence and to a certain dogma about the nature of God: 1) the doctrine of human self-sufficiency; 2) the doctrine of human unworthiness; and 3) the dogma of God's absolute otherness and total silence.[50]

According to the first of these views, humanity is too great to be in need of divine guidance. Through the advancement of technology, humanity is gradually tending toward improvement, evolving toward its own true perfection. History is a perpetual progress, through trials and despite errors, toward human self-redemption; history in and of itself is a redemptive process. In Heschel's mind, such a view has been proven utterly specious in the wake of recent history.[51]

According to a second view which accounts for resistance to the idea of revelation, humanity is too insignificant in relation to the universe to warrant an address from the infinite spirit of God. Moreover, considering the atrocities that human beings have performed, it is difficult to believe that humanity is either capable or worthy of receiving a revelation from God. But according to Heschel, it is precisely because human beings are so "dangerously mighty" that revelation from the almighty God is so necessary and tenable.[52]

The third view is the obverse of the second; it is the assumption of God's absolute distance from humanity with the attendant dogma of God's total silence. Since the infinite God dwells in absolute distance from finite human beings, it is meaningless to speak of a divine–human encounter. Heschel is his usual imaginative self in responding to this view:

If the stream of energy that is stored up in the sun and the soil can be channeled into a blade of grass, why should it be *a priori* excluded that the spirit of God reached into the minds of men?

There is such a distance between the sun and a flower. Can a flower, worlds away from the source of energy, attain a perception of its origin? Can a drop of water ever soar to behold, even for a moment, the stream's distant source? In prophecy it is as if the sun communed with the flower, as if the source sent out a current to reach a drop. . . .

Are we, then, because of the indescribability of revelation, justified in rejecting *a priori* as untrue the assertion of the prophets that, at certain hours in Israel's history, the divine came in touch with a few chosen souls? That the creative source of our own selves addressed itself to man?

If there are moments in which genius speaks for all men, why should we deny that there are moments in which a voice speaks for God? That the source of goodness communicates its way to the human mind?

True, it seems incredible that we should hold in our gaze words containing a breath of God. What we forget is that at this moment we breathe what God is creating, that right in front of us we behold works that reflect His infinite wisdom, His infinite goodness.[53]

The belief that God dwells at an absolute distance from humanity involves the assumption that God is a total mystery. Such a view, says Heschel, "seems to be part of our pagan heritage."[54] From the biblical perspective God is not sheer mystery, unapproachable and unknown. Rather, "God is *meaning beyond the mystery.*"[55] Heschel even goes so far as to say: "He is not an enigma, but justice, mercy. . . . He is not the Unknown, but the Father, the God of Abraham."[56] By this Heschel does not mean that God is in no way enigmatic but that God is not sheer enigma. In Heschel's biblical perspective: "God is neither plain meaning nor just mystery. God is meaning that transcends mystery, meaning that mystery alludes to, meaning that speaks through mystery."[57] If the divine were pure mystery, we would be unable to attain any understanding of God. But since God is "meaning that speaks through mystery," some understanding is attainable.[58]

The belief that God is total mystery is accompanied by the dogma of God's total silence, a dogma not at home in biblical religion. From a biblical perspective, God may at times be silent, but that God is totally silent contradicts the very foundation of biblical faith. And this faith, though not founded on reason, is not contrary to reason. "Why should we *a priori* exclude the power of expression from the absolute being? If the world is the work of God, isn't it conceivable that there would be within His work signs of His expression?"[59] To exclude the power of expression from God would be to assume that the supreme power is virtually powerless in relation to creatures who know the power of expression. If God is unable to address the human spirit, then God is neither divine nor relevant to humanity, for human beings cannot enter into personal communion with that which does not commune with them.

But God is not totally silent. God is experienced as the living, challenging, demanding, and thus the expressive, transcendence that assaults the human conscience, as well as the empowering source of compassion enabling human beings to live according to the dictates of conscience. God's voice is experienced as the absolute claim upon conscience, as the objective challenge to overcome inequity, injustice, suffering, and oppression, and as the spiritual light empowering human beings to achieve these ends. This challenge or claim is known to issue from a source that transcends humanity because all men and women, both the prophets who articulate it and those whom they address, live under the challenging claim. The spiritual light is also known to radiate from a transcendent source because it is experienced as an empowering presence, as "an excess of spirit not our own."[60] The claim of the prophets is therefore not their own; it is a claim that confronts them as well as those whom they confront. As such it is a divine claim. And the spiritual light that emanates from the prophets is not their own; it is a light that enlightens them as well as those who heed their way. As such it, too, is divine. If God were totally silent, then human beings would be alone in the world without a transcendent presence to whom to relate. But, because of the challenging claim and empowering light that reaches the human spirit, Heschel can exclaim that "man is not alone"; that, on the contrary, there is a "God in search of man."

REVELATION AS MYSTERY

Despite the fact that Heschel speaks of our being able to understand the prophetic claim, he is nonetheless aware of the fact that revelation is a mystery to us. "Revelation is a mystery for which reason has no concepts. To ignore its mysterious nature is an oversight of fatal consequence. Out of the darkness came the voice to Moses; and out of the darkness comes the Word to us."[61] Not only the revelation to Moses (and to other prophets) but also the revelation to us is mysterious. Since it is "an event in the realm of the ineffable,"[62] Heschel claims that "it is only through our sense of the ineffable that we may intuit the mystery of revelation."[63] When we intuit this mystery we understand something of its meaning, for revelation is a meaningful mystery. Revelation is a mystery that imparts a meaning that cannot be fully comprehended but can be existentially understood, just as the mysterious meaning of love can be understood without being comprehended.

When Heschel speaks of understanding the God who is revealed, he realizes that God is understood as a mysterious reality. So too when he speaks of being able to understand revelation, he realizes that revelation is understood as a mysterious event. To understand the meaning of the revealing God is not to comprehend God's meaning but to be aware of the mysterious divine presence and what that presence means for our lives. Likewise, to understand the meaning of revelation is not to comprehend the revelatory event but to apprehend it as a meaningful mystery.

To reveal something is to make it known. But the fact that a mystery is made known does not render it comprehensible. The revelation of a mystery does not mean the unveiling of what was mysterious but the disclosing of what remains mysterious. The revelation of God does not mean that God becomes less a mystery but that the mysterious God becomes less distant and thereby more personally known. God's grace is more intimately felt, God's will more clearly known, but God's being remains a deep mystery. Likewise, the act of revelation is experienced, its meaning perceived, but its eventfulness remains an enigma. The revealing is as mysterious as the reality revealed.

In order to communicate the meaning of revelation, words are employed which in another context would be comprehensible but which in this context suggest the incomprehensible. The same words may be used in either a descriptive or indicative way. When used to communicate the meaning of revelation, words that are otherwise descriptive are used to indicate what cannot be described. Heschel offers the following example: "'And God said: Let there be light' is different in spirit from a statement such as 'And Smith said: Let us turn on the light.' The second statement conveys a definite meaning; the first statement evokes an inner response to an ineffable meaning. The statement, man speaks, describes a physiological and psychological act; the statement, God speaks, conveys a mystery. It calls upon our sense of wonder and amazement to respond to a mystery that surpasses our power of comprehension."[64]

In light of this example, it is clear why Heschel maintains that "literalmindedness" is "the surest way of misunderstanding revelation."[65] Literalmindedness is the failure to discern the unique connotations that otherwise-descriptive terms assume when used indicatively in the religious context. Words about God or revelation are intimations rather than definitions, allusions rather than descriptions. "When taken literally, they either turn flat, narrow and shallow or become ventriloquous myths."[66] But if words used to speak of revelation, such as "God spoke," must not be taken literally, neither should they be regarded as simply figurative or symbolic, if by this it is meant that God not really but only seemingly addresses human beings. God really does address humanity, even if the address is not perceptible to bodily senses. "It is not only by his ear that man can hear. It is not only the physical sound that can reach the spirit of man."[67] God's "speech" is an act that transcends human speech and is inaudible to the human ear; yet it is a reality that reaches the human spirit. This being so, "the speech of God is not less but more than literally real."[68] The expression "God spoke" is not a hyperbole; it is an understatement.

Since the words concerning divine revelation are not to be understood either literally or figuratively, they should only be understood responsively. This is summarized by Heschel in the following way:

> To take a word literally means to reproduce in our mind an idea which the word denotes and with which it is definitely associated in our memory. It is apparent that only descriptive words can be taken literally. To take a descriptive word figuratively is to assume that the author is speaking double talk; saying one thing, he means another. It is apparent that only metaphoric expressions must be taken figuratively. Indicative words must be taken responsively. In order to understand them we must part with

preconceived meanings; clichés are of no avail. They are not portraits but *clues,* serving us as guides, suggesting a line of thinking.

This indeed is our situation in regard to a statement such as "God spoke." It refers to an idea that is not at home in the mind, and the only way to understand its meaning is by *responding* to it. We must adapt our minds to a meaning unheard of before. The word is but a clue; the real burden of understanding is upon the mind and soul of the reader.[69]

We will understand the meaning of the biblical term "God spoke" when, responding to the biblical message, we are open to the impact of God's concern and challenge. "Revelation" is a term that represents a meaning which we cannot fully comprehend but which nonetheless is conveyed to our consciousness. It is a term of whose meaning we have some intuitive understanding without full comprehension.[70] The event of revelation is therefore a meaningful mystery, an event full of transcendent meaning. As a mystery, revelation is an event that cannot be proved rationally but can be understood existentially. And the existential understanding renders a greater assurance of the reality of revelation than could any rational proof.

In conclusion, Heschel's position on the mystery of revelation may be summarized as follows:

1. Since revelation is a mystery, *how* it happens cannot be explained; since it is a mystery that is experienced, *that* it happens may be stated.[71]

2. The *event* of revelation inspires a *message* of revelation; the message indicates rather than describes the event.[72]

3. The message may in turn evoke an experience of the event; the reality with which the prophets were confronted confronts the people who heed the prophets' words.[73]

4. There are no proofs for the truth of the message or for the reality of the event to which it alludes, there are only witnesses and a message which is its own witness.[74]

5. The goal is not to prove the reality of the event or the truth of its message but "to point to the difficulty of an outright rejection" of the prophetic witness; the aim is to show why it is not unreasonable—and indeed why it is credible—to accept the witness of the prophets.[75]

6. The "meaning for existence" which is found in the biblical message "gives firmness to all reasons" for accepting that message.[76]

Lest one think that this schema suggests a too-facile acceptance of the reality of revelation, it should be recalled that it is not only divine revelation that is accepted despite its being mysterious and incomprehensible. The same six-fold schema can be discerned, for example, in the acceptance of love:

1. That love happens—and that there is a mutual revelation in the experience of love—is a fact; how love happens cannot be explained.

2. The experience of love inspires a message of love; this message alludes to the reality of love.

3. The message—its words and deeds—may in turn evoke the experience of love.

4. There are no proofs for the truth of the message of love or of the reality of love itself; love identifies itself.

5. The goal is not to prove the reality of love or the truth of its message but to show why it is foolish not to accept love and its testimony.

6. Meaning for existence is found in love, and this validates all reasons for accepting and enacting love.

Like human love, divine revelation—which is, after all, the revelation of love—is a mysterious event filled with a meaning that can be understood by experiencing it.

REVELATION AND FAITH

Faith is rooted in the understanding that comes in the wake of revelation. To have faith in another person is a risk. Yet this risk may be a wise choice rather than a foolish chance if it is based on knowledge of the other person. And such knowledge is contingent upon the other's personal revelation. This is so whether the other person is human or divine.

Faith in God is a response to the revelation of God. In particular, Jewish faith is a response to God as revealed in the history of the Jewish people, especially in the historical events and personages that gave birth to the Bible.

THE BIBLE

"The presence of God is found in many ways, but above all God is found in the words of the Bible."[77] Responsiveness to the Bible is therefore an antecedent of faith in God. In particular, responsiveness to the Hebrew Bible is a prerequisite of Jewish faith.

Heschel does not claim that it is the sense for the presence of God in the Bible that rouses response to the Bible. Rather, it is by responding to the Bible that one may discern God's presence therein. This in turn may prompt faith in God. Moreover, the sense for the divine presence in the Bible may lead to the belief in the divine origin of the Bible.

RESPONSIVENESS TO THE BIBLE

It is not simply by reading but by heeding the words of the Bible that God's presence may be found within it. "We cannot sense His presence in the Bible except by being responsive to it. Only living with its words, only sympathy with its pathos, will open our ear to its voice."[78] But, we may ask, why respond to the Bible if God's presence therein is not sensed in the first place?

Even if we cannot sense God's presence in the Bible except by being responsive to it, we must sense something in it that arrests our attention and elicits our response which may in turn lead to an appreciation of God's presence in its words. Perhaps the claims made on behalf of the Bible by exemplars of holiness entice us to investigate the claims made by the Bible on behalf of God. Since the Bible "is the fountainhead of the finest strivings of man in the Western World" and "has given birth and shape to a myriad of precious things in the lives of individuals and peoples,"[79] it deserves the responsiveness of even those who are not convinced that God may be found within its pages. Perhaps our own spiritual hunger prompts us to live in accord with a message that has nourished the lives of millions of men and women. Maybe the suspicion that the Bible contains a message that can flood our lives with meaning stirs us to respond to its claims and thereby come to sense the reality of God in those claims. "The Bible is *the perpetual motion of the spirit,* an ocean of meaning, its waves beating against man's abrupt and steep shortcomings, its echo reaching into the blind alleys of his wrestling with despair."[80] We may sense God's presence in the Bible only by responding to the Bible, but we may first respond to the Bible because we sense, or at least suspect, that it contains a message, and perhaps even a presence, worth responding to.

But what, then, might Heschel mean when he claims that "to sense the presence of God in the Bible, one must learn *to be present* to God in the Bible"?[81] What would move someone "*to be present* to God in the Bible" if in the first place God's presence was not sensed therein?

Might we interpret Heschel to mean that by responding to the biblical message, even prior to sensing the divine presence in it, that we are in fact being present to God, even if unaware of God's presence? In human relationships, is it true that a person can be present to another only when the other is perceived as present? Or is there a sense in which someone might be present to another simply by longing for the other's presence? Prior to the statement of Heschel's we are presently considering, he writes: "To be able to encounter the spirit within the words, we must learn to crave for an affinity with the pathos of God."[82] If "to encounter the spirit" is synonymous with "to sense the presence," then "to crave for an affinity" is the same as "to be present." If this is true, then we may be present to God prior to sensing God's presence simply by craving for an affinity with God.

THE SENSE OF GOD'S PRESENCE IN THE BIBLE

Having answered the preceding questions, it is now appropriate to address the question of how we may come to really sense and accept the presence of God in the Bible.

To be responsive to the Bible means to heed the grandeur of its message and its appeal to conscience. Could such a personal appeal come from a source itself not personal? In responding to biblical words that speak to their heart, men and women come to sense the personal source of those words. Is that source merely human? Are the prophets of Israel, for example, the sole personal source of the words they speak? Those who live with the words of the Bible feel kinship with Jeremiah, Isaiah, and other prophets. But the words these prophets utter contain a glory and a challenge which the prophets themselves claim not to have authored and to which they themselves must submit.[83]

"The light with which a prophet is aglow casts into the shade his own powers of vision and self-awareness."[84] This is why prophetic words are prefaced or concluded with "Thus saith the Lord." It also accounts for the fact that those who are inspired and smitten by prophetic words believe them to convey a divine presence. Such words are too heart-rending and healing to be of human origin alone. The personal source of those words is too life-giving and demanding to be no more than human. "The light with which a prophet is aglow" not only "casts into the shade his own . . . self-awareness" but also the awareness of him by those whom he addresses. Whatever kinship may be felt with a prophet, those who respond to a prophet become more aware of the light with which a prophet is aglow than of the prophet himself. No matter how close may be the presence of a prophet, it is the transcendent presence to which the prophet bears witness that is felt more intimately. The personal presence or light conveyed through prophetic words is so overwhelming and empowering that it can be nothing other than divine. God is the presence encountered in biblical words, a presence known to transcend the prophets since they too must submit to its claim while at the same time being set aglow by its light.

To summarize: First we long for meaning. Then we respond to the Bible because of the meaning it is said and seen to convey. Then we find not only meaning but a presence that is the source of all meaning. We respond to this presence as we continue to respond to the Bible and its claims.

In the light of what has been said about how we come to sense and accept the presence of God in the Bible, it should be clear that such acceptance, while not the result of reasoning, is nonetheless compatible with reason. Is it not reasonable to accept as divinely inspired a message that presents itself as a claim that confronts the prophets as well as those whom they confront with it? And is it not reasonable to accept as divinely inspired that which impassions and empowers human beings to seek justice, love mercy, and live in holiness? And if it is reasonable to accept the presence of God in the Bible, is it not reasonable as well to believe in the origin of the Bible in God? To this question we now turn.

DIVINE AND HUMAN AUTHORSHIP

"More decisive than *the origin of the Bible in God* is the *presence of God in the Bible*. It is the sense for the presence that leads us to a belief in its origin."[85] When the spirit of God is encountered in the Bible it becomes possible to believe that "the spirit of His revealing power brought the Bible into being."[86] It is not a matter of proving the divine origin of the Bible but of recognizing that the ultimate source of a message filled with divine presence must also be divine. God is the name for the power that created the world and inspired the Word. And if God is the prime source of the Bible, it makes sense to claim that "the Bible is not primarily man's vision of God, but God's vision of man."[87]

Does the fact that the Bible is primarily God's vision mean that God is its sole author and that the human writers are no more than scribes? No, it only means that God is the primary source of inspiration for the human writers, that "the Bible reflects its divine as well as human authorship."[88] "God has a vision. The Bible is an interpretation of the vision."[89]

According to Heschel, there are in the Bible the words of men and women inspired by God as well as words that did not originate in the spirit of God. Concerning the former, God's Word is expressed in human words, according to how human beings, no matter how inspired by God, perceive the Word. Even "God's vision of man" is phrased according to what men and women are able to envision. "No man is able to hear the voice of God as it is. . . . God addressed every individual according to his particular power of comprehension."[90] Even the comprehension of the prophets expressed in the Bible does not reflect the divine vision as it is. "The words of Scripture are the only lasting record of what was conveyed to the prophets. At the same time they are neither identical with, nor the eternally adequate rendering of, the divine wisdom."[91] The Bible reflects its human authorship, even while proclaiming "God's vision of man," to the extent that the words of the prophets are an interpretation of the divine vision they perceived. It reflects its divine authorship inasmuch as the revelation of the divine vision is what inspires the prophetic interpretation.

Heschel claims not only that there are in the Bible words of men and women inspired by God but also words that were not divinely inspired. Obviously, not everything in the Bible is prophetic utterance.[92] Even the response of the prophets to God did not originate in the spirit of God in the same sense as did the claims that the prophets make on behalf of God and to which they respond. Yet, according to Heschel, the claims and the response to them are equally important. "What the prophet says to God when addressed by Him is not considered less holy than what God says to the prophet in addressing him."[93]

In short, there are in the Bible 1) divine claims cast in human terms according to human perceptions, 2) human words uttered in response to divine claims, and 3) words that express neither divine claims nor responses to God. All of this testifies to the fact "the Bible is more than the word of God; it is the word of God and man."[94]

THE BIBLE AND JEWISH FAITH

Although not every word of the Bible is inspired by God, response to the Bible is an antecedent of faith in God because the Bible contains the word of God. For Jewish faith in particular, attachment to the Bible is essential. Heschel writes: "What is unique about Jewish existence? The fact that ours is not a free association with the Bible. We are her offspring, her outcome. Her spirit is our destiny. What is our destiny? To be a community in whom the Bible lives on."[95] As Israel is the offspring of the Bible, the Bible lives on because of Israel. Israel must remain dedicated to the Bible in order for the Bible to remain a sublime challenge and source of illumination for the world.[96] "What would be missing in the world, what would be the condition and faith of man, had the Bible not been preserved?"[97] Since the Bible is "the frontier of the spirit" that "shows the way of God with man and the way of man with God,"[98] had the Bible not been preserved an invaluable pathway to God would be lost. Consequently, the condition and faith of humankind would be more spiritually impoverished than it already is. In fact, the current spiritual famine throughout the world is due largely to a "growing alienation from the Bible."[99]

"I believe there is a battle going on in the twentieth century which centers around the Hebrew Bible," says Heschel. "The prohibition and suppression of the Hebrew Bible in Soviet Russia is symbolic of that battle."[100] Heschel also believes:

Nazism in its very roots was a rebellion against the Bible, against the God of Abraham. Realizing that it was Christianity that implanted attachment to

the God of Abraham and involvement with the Hebrew Bible in the hearts
of Western man, Nazism resolved that it must both exterminate the Jews
and eliminate Christianity, and bring about instead a revival of Teutonic
paganism.

Nazism has suffered a defeat, but the process of eliminating the Bible
from the consciousness of the western world goes on. It is on the issue of
saving the radiance of the Hebrew Bible in the minds of man that Jews and
Christians are called upon to work together.[101]

"The radiance of the Hebrew Bible" must be saved because it offers a noble
alternative to the "contemporary nihilism" which has as one of its roots "the
age-old resistance to the Hebrew view of the world and of man."[102] This
Hebrew view has been resisted because it "has destroyed the illusion that
one can be an innocent bystander or spectator in this world" and it "has
destroyed the ancient tradition . . . in which gods accommodated themselves to our notions and standards, in which religion was above all a
guarantee."[103] The alternative that the Hebrew Bible offers is "a new vision
of man" as *a being in travail with God's dreams and designs,* with God's
dream of a world redeemed, . . . of a mankind which is truly His image,
reflecting His wisdom, justice, and compassion."[104]

"Scripture may have vanished from our hearts. Yet the miracle of re-
engagement is possible."[105] Judaism is committed to this re-engagement.
One of the essential tasks of Jewish faith is to preserve, and where need be
resurrect, the Bible and thereby to inspire the kind of faith that enhances the
human condition by reflecting divine wisdom, justice, and compassion.

RABBINIC MIDRASHIM

Although the essence of Jewish faith involves responsiveness to the
Bible, "Judaism is not only a Biblical religion."[106] "The concern for God
continued throughout the ages, and in order to understand Judaism we
must inquire about the way and the spirit of that concern in post-Biblical
Jewish history as well."[107] The way and the spirit of Jewish concern for God,
of Jewish faith in God, is epitomized in the literature of Israel's sages.

"As a report about revelation, the Bible itself is *a midrash.*"[108] Yet since
"the full meaning of the Biblical words was not disclosed once and for
all,"[109] this great midrash stands in need of subsequent midrashim. Thus,
revelation and the Bible are not the only wellsprings of the Jewish tradition
and the faith it conveys and inspires. In fact, says Heschel, "Judaism is
based upon a minimum of revelation and a maximum of interpretation,
upon the will of God and upon the understanding of Israel."[110] Likewise,
"the Bible is not an end but a beginning,"[111] the beginning of a heritage that

is only presaged in the Bible. "The Bible is the seed, God is the sun, but we are the soil. Every generation is expected to bring forth new understanding and new realization."[112] While this contribution is expected of every generation, it is especially the sages of each generation that convey and provoke the genuine understanding and realization of Israel. Moreover, to arrive at this, the people of Israel, including its latter-day sages, must pay special attention to the interpretations of the sages of those generations that created Israel's oral Torah and its Talmud. Heschel says: "We approach the laws of the Bible through the interpretation and the wisdom of the Rabbis. . . . The prophets' inspirations and the sages' interpretations are equally important. . . . The savants are heirs to the prophets; they determine and interpret the meaning of the word."[113]

It is important to stress the fact that the Bible is approached through the interpretations of the sages precisely in order "to bring forth new understanding and new realization" in our own day, not simply to reiterate the ancient interpretations. Just as "we must beware of the obscurantism of mechanical deference to the Bible,"[114] so must we beware of this attitude vis-à-vis the Talmud. The fact that the sages "determine and interpret the meaning of the word" does not mean that new meanings can no longer be determined, nor new interpretations advanced. On the contrary, this is precisely what is required in order for each generation "to bring forth new understanding and new realization."

In conclusion: Revelation inspired the Bible, which in turn provoked a wealth of sagacious midrashim. These are the great wellsprings of the Jewish tradition and of the faith it expresses and provokes.

The Principal Foci of the Jewish Tradition

The revelation to which the Bible and rabbinic midrashim attest is the revelation of God which includes the Torah that is directed primarily to Israel. Therefore, this study of what Heschel means by the Jewish tradition or by the core of that tradition must focus on three central issues: the meaning of God, Torah, and Israel. This is in keeping with what Heschel regards as the principal foci of the Jewish tradition. As he explains: "Judaism is a complex structure. It can neither be characterized exclusively as a theological doctrine, nor as a way of living according to the law, nor as a community. A religious Jew is a person committed to God, to his concern and teaching (Torah), who lives as part of a covenant community (Israel). Judaism revolves around three sacred entities: God, Torah, Israel. The Jew never stands alone before God; the Torah and Israel are always with him."[115]

GOD

The meaning of God is so central to Heschel's depth theology that it is discussed in and throughout this book. Yet a separate section on the meaning of God that focuses on Heschel's fundamental and revolutionary doctrine of divine pathos is nonetheless in order. That a revolutionary doctrine has its place in a chapter on tradition is due to the fact that, as Heschel would contend, it is rooted in the wellsprings of the tradition in question and is implicit in the piety of the faithful throughout the course of that tradition.

THE PATHOS OF DIVINE CONCERN

In discussing the meaning of God we have for the most part focused on the theme of divine concern as central to Heschel's religious philosophy. By examining the idea of divine pathos we are focusing on a topic that is central to the theme of divine concern. In Heschel's view, the idea of divine pathos is "*the* central idea in prophetic theology" and "is an explication of the idea of God in Search of Man" which is "the summary of Jewish theology."[116] The phrase "God in Search of Man" suggests God's concern for human beings. And, according to Heschel, concern for others—what he calls transitive concern—implies pathos, being moved or affected by others. God, whose transitive concern is infinite, is intimately affected by the objects of divine concern, particularly by human beings.[117]

The very fact that human beings are historical creatures means that God's involvement with them must be historical, entailing a dynamic relationship in which there is call and response on both sides. Since God is truly involved in the lives of human beings, God relates to them according to where they are and what they are feeling, thinking, willing, and doing. This means that the attitudes and actions of God vis-à-vis human beings are subject to change, as persons change in relation to God, each other, and the world. God's loving concern for human beings is eternal, but the expressions of that concern are historical, otherwise they would not signify God's involvement with historical beings. Thus it is that "whatever man does affects not only his own life, but also the life of God insofar as it is directed to man."[118] And this is so even to the point of suffering.

"God does not stand outside the range of human suffering and sorrow. He is personally involved in, even stirred by, the conduct and fate of man."[119] History is often the record of human misery, and since God is concerned for human beings and involved in their history, God must be involved in their suffering. "God's participation in human history . . . finds its deepest expression in the fact that God can actually suffer."[120] Pathos is concern unto suffering. And God's concern is full of pathos.

In Heschel's view, concern is the essence of life. But there are different kinds of concern that constitute life. Heschel makes a distinction between reflexive concern, which is directed toward self, and transitive concern, which is directed toward others.[121] As God's concern is transitive, so too is the pathos of that concern. The passion of reflexive concern is self-centered; the pathos of transitive concern is other-directed. As an expression of transitive concern, the pathos of God, though itself a form of passion, is unlike the selfish passions of the pagan gods.[122] God's pathos is realized in response to, and for the sake of, human beings.

Divine pathos, though an emotional response, is "understood not as an unreasoned emotion, but as an act formed with intention, depending on free will, the result of decision and determination."[123] Acts of passion can be devoid of reasoned purpose but they need not be; "emotion can be reasonable just as reason can be emotional."[124] The divine pathos is God's reason and will charged with passion, or it is God's passion informed by reason and will. Moreover, since "God is the source of justice," Heschel claims that "His pathos is ethical."[125] Thus, the inner law of divine pathos is the moral law. But this does not mean that divine pathos is a matter of "strict justice." God's pathos never disregards the standards of justice, but, as compassion and forgiveness, it transcends justice alone. "When the people seem to be doomed by their own deeds, the mercy and grace of God may save them from disaster. Divine pathos may explain why justice is not meted out in the world."[126] In the biblical tradition, injustice is condemned, strict justice is surpassed.

PATHOS AND ONTOLOGY

Heschel's idea of divine pathos is directly opposed to the classical and Jewish and Christian metaphysical theology inspired by Greek philosophy. Yet he believes this idea accords with the biblical understanding of God and renders a more accurate interpretation of the theology implicit in the piety of the Jewish tradition than does the classical doctrine of God's impassibility.

It is because of its being steeped in Greek philosophical presuppositions that classical metaphysical theology opposes the idea of divine pathos. These Greek presuppositions are both ontological and psychological. "The static idea of divinity is the outcome of two strands of thought: the ontological notion of stability and the psychological view of the emotions as disturbances of the soul."[127] Heschel examines each of these Greek strands of thought, shows their incompatibility with the biblical understanding of God and advances the doctrine of pathos as "a more plausible view of ultimate reality."[128]

Concerning ontology, Heschel points to the formidable influence of Parmenides on later philosophical theology. According to Parmenides, being is immovable; movement illusory. Although later Greek philosophy recognized the reality of change, as stressed by Heraclitus, it tended to restrict Heraclitus's theory to the world of sense perception. Classical metaphysical theology applied Parmenides' concept of unchangeable being to God, affirming the Greek assumption that change implies an imperfection that is incompatible with the divine being. Heschel responds to the ontology of Parmenides' Eleatic school and to the metaphysical theology based thereupon as follows:

> The Eleatic premise that true being is unchangeable and that change implies corruption is valid only in regard to being as reflected in the mind. Being in reality, being as we encounter it, implies movement. If we think of being as something beyond and detached from beings, we may well arrive at an Eleatic notion. An ontology, however, concerned with being as involved in all beings or as the source of all beings, will find it impossible to separate being from action or movement, and thus postulate a dynamic concept of divine Being. . . . Biblical ontology does not separate being from doing. . . . Here the basic category is action rather than immobility. Movement, creation of nature, acts within history rather absolute transcendence and detachment from the events of history, are the attributes of the Supreme Being.[129]

The fact that Heschel ascribes mobility or movement to God sets him apart from classical philosophical theology. Yet the fact that he claims that God is moved by nondivine reality sets him even further apart from such classical thought. Some of God's actions come in the form of reactions, responses to human actions. Not only is God self-moving, acting in relation to the world; God is also moved by other selves, reacting in relation to the world. This, precisely, is the meaning of divine pathos. "The divine pathos which the prophets tried to express in many ways was not a name for His essence but rather for the modes of His reaction to Israel's conduct which would change if Israel modified its ways."[130] Whether God is viewed as self-moving in relation to the world or as moved by beings in the world, in either case God is quite unlike the Unmoved Mover of classical theism. The God of Israel is "the Most Moved Mover."[131]

The fact that God is moved or in movement implies that there is "history in God,"[132] that God is somehow mutable. But does this mean that God in essence changes? Recall that Heschel says "the divine pathos . . . was not a name for His essence." He also claims "the divine pathos is not conceived of as an essential attribute of God . . . , but as an expression of God's will."[133] In other words, "a subject of pathos, God Himself is not pathos."[134] Yet a subject of pathos must be a possible subject (that is, a subject capable of being affected, able to feel and suffer, and thereby to experience change). Pathos may not be "an essential attribute of God," but Heschel would have to admit that passibility is. For pathos is only possible in a being that is in essence passible. But this does not mean that the divine essence is changeable. The fact that God's modes of reacting to the world are changeable does not mean that God changes in essence. To be in essence passible is not the same as to have a passible essence. To be in essence passible is to be by nature a being who may change modes of action and reaction; to have a passible essence is to have a changing nature—for example, now human, now divine, or now living, now inanimate. God's nature may be immutable while the modes of God's being-in-relation may change. Specifically, while God *is* the transcendent, transitive concern for being, the expressions of that concern are historical and subject to change.

One reason that classical theism refuses to acknowledge divine change is that God is viewed as perfect and change is thought to imply imperfection. Why change, so it is thought, unless one's present state of being is less than perfect? According to the philosophic definition of perfection as pure actuality, it must be admitted that a passible God is not perfect, for such a God has not yet actualized all the expressions of divine concern that await realization. Yet the Bible is not concerned with that kind of perfection. From a biblical perspective, pure actuality is no synonym for divinity; God suffers change not because of any imperfection but because different situations demand different divine replies. Nowhere does Heschel suggest that God changes for the better. Divine mutability need not imply that God is in the process of becoming more divine. If God is passible, it is because there is potential in God: the potential to be affected and to enact responses not yet actual. But this does not mean that God is thereby perfected. We may move God because God allows us to do so. We need not assume that by doing so we somehow enhance God's divinity. Mutability is no sign of imperfection, just as immutability is no sign of perfection. There is history in God not because of a divine imperfection but because God is perfectly responsive to the vicissitudes of history.

Pathos and Psychology

It is the acceptance not only of a Greek ontological presupposition but also of a Greek psychological presupposition that has caused classical theism to reject the idea of divine pathos. Classical theists such as Maimonides or Thomas Aquinas, unlike Aristotle from whom they derive philosophical inspiration, do not deny God's concern for creation. They simply deny that God is concerned to the point of being affected by creation. Yet to have concern for human beings while remaining unaffected by their actions, unmoved by their plight, would be to have a rather remote-like concern, if concern at all it be. Whatever can be said of such an attitude, it does not signify the existence of a genuine relationship. But according to Heschel's interpretation of the biblical testimony, the concern of God is "a feeling of intimate concern" because "God stands in a passionate relationship to man."[135]

Just as the Greek philosophy adopted by classical theism regards change as an imperfection, so does it consider passion or pathos, an affection implying change, as a sign of weakness. Self-sufficiency is a presupposed ideal of such a philosophy and "the dignity of man was seen in the activity of the mind, in acts of self-determination."[136] Since pathos is aroused by something outside the self, and since it is considered to be an emotional reaction rather than an intellectual act, it is viewed as an imperfection. This could only be so, of course, in a philosophical system wherein "reason is dissociated from the emotional life and sharply contrasted with it."[137] It was such dissociation of reason from emotion and "it was such preference [for reason] that enabled Greek philosophy to exclude all emotion from the nature of the Deity, while at the same time ascribing thought and contemplation to it."[138]

In genuine Hebraic thinking, on the contrary, self-sufficiency in the sense of the self being unaffected by realities outside the self is no ideal. Moreover, the dissociation of reason from emotion is alien to biblical thinking, as is the disparagement of emotion. In fact, says Heschel, "thought is part of emotion. We think because we are moved. . . . Emotion may be defined as the consciousness of being moved."[139] Moreover, emotion is indispensable to the life of action: "Great deeds are done by those who are filled with *ruah,* with pathos."[140] Given this positive appreciation of emotion or pathos in the Bible, "there was no reason to shun the idea of pathos in the understanding of God."[141]

Heschel's contrast between the apathetic God of classical theism and the biblical God of pathos is perhaps best summarized in the following excerpt:

> An apathetic and ascetic God would have struck biblical man with a sense, not of dignity and grandeur, but rather of poverty and emptiness. Only through arbitrary allegorizing was later religious philosophy able to find an apathetic God in the Bible.
>
> Impressive as is the thought that God is too sublime to be affected by events on this insignificant planet, it stems from a line of reasoning about a God derived from abstraction. A God of abstraction is a high and mighty First Cause, which, dwelling in the lonely splendor of eternity, will never be open to human prayer; and to be affected by anything which it has itself caused to come into being would be beneath the dignity of an abstract God. This is a dogmatic sort of dignity, insisting upon pride rather than love, upon decorum rather than mercy.

> In contrast with the *primum movens immobile*, the God of the prophets cares for His creatures, and His thoughts are about the world. He is involved in human history and is affected by human acts.[142]

It is clear that Heschel regards the idea of divine pathos as not only religiously important but philosophically credible, superior to the idea of divine impassibility and apathy. A God unaffected by human concerns, unmoved by human cries, would be religiously irrelevant to human beings and both ontologically and psychologically inferior to those same beings who themselves are able to respond to the concerns and cries of their fellows. What in this regard human beings may do humanly, the God of Israel does divinely, supremely. Such a God alone is God.

DIVINE PATHOS AND HUMAN FAITH

It is because of God's pathos for human beings that humans are moved to put their faith in God. If God ignored the outcry of human beings, it would be strange indeed for them to cry out to God in faith. A god who was unmoved by human plight and human deeds would not deserve the faith of beings who themselves are moved by other selves. Only a God who takes human beings seriously is worthy of their faith. And humans are taken seriously only if related to historically. Only a God who responds to human beings deserves their faith. And to respond to them is to be moved by their sufferings and joys, their dreams and deeds.

In short, only a God of pathos is worthy of the faith of human beings who themselves may express pathos for God. It is precisely because God is filled with pathos for human beings that they may respond with sympathy for God. According to Heschel, "the prophet may be characterized as a *homo sympathetikos*," as a person who has "sympathetic solidarity with God" as a result of being "moved by the pathos of God."[143] Prophetic faith is the sympathetic response to divine pathos. And since Jewish faith may be characterized as "faith with the prophets,"[144] the revelation of divine pathos is one of the sources of Jewish faith. This is why the God of pathos, rather than any impassible god, must be viewed as the primary focus of the Jewish tradition.[145]

TORAH

Since "torah" literally means revelation, and since it is often used as a synonym for the Bible, to that extent the meaning of Torah has already been discussed above. Yet there are a number of questions concerning Torah which remain to be studied.

Torah is often if not usually thought of exclusively in terms of law. Some people believe that the whole of Torah was revealed to Moses on Mount Sinai and that this Torah is an immutable code of laws. Heschel's views on these matters will be examined, as will his understanding of the place of the Torah in Jewish life and the status of Torah vis-à-vis God.

TORAH IS MORE THAN LAW

There are two senses in which Heschel thinks it is inappropriate to limit the word "torah" to law or to a system of laws.

In the first place, "the Torah is primarily *divine ways* rather than *divine laws.*"[146] By this Heschel means that the Torah contains not only divine laws by which human beings must live in relation to God but also that it represents the ways in which God lives in relation to human beings. For example, Judaism teaches that "justice is an obligation to God, *His way* not only His demand."[147] Heschel reminds us that "Moses prayed: 'Let me know thy ways' (Exodus 33:13)" and that "all that God asks of man was summarized: 'And now, Israel, what doth the Lord thy God require of thee . . . but to walk in all His ways' (Deuteronomy 10:12)."[148] In a biblical perspective, then, between God and human beings there is not only an analogy of being but also an analogy of doing.[149] Created in God's image, we may act in God's likeness. "It is within our power to mirror His unending love in deeds of kindness, like brooks that hold the sky."[150]

It is appropriate that Heschel says Torah is *primarily* divine ways rather than divine laws. For there is a sense in which these divine ways are also divine laws, not only for human beings but also for God. Recall, "justice is an *obligation* to God," not only to us. The Torah represents a covenant in which a responsibility lies on God as well as on us. Yet divine ways are for God more than divine laws since these reflect not only the responsibility God assumes but also the very being God is. That is why "the plea is not to obey what He wills but to *do* what He *is.*" Heschel explains: "It is not said: Ye shall be full of awe for I am holy, but: Ye shall be holy, for I the Lord your God am holy (Leviticus 19:2). . . . We live by the conviction that acts of goodness reflect the hidden light of His holiness."[151]

A second reason why Heschel views the Torah as more than law is that only a small portion of the Torah deals with legal matters. The Torah comprises both *halacha* (Jewish law) and *agada* (Jewish lore), whether it is understood in its narrowest sense as referring only to the Penteteuch, or as a synonym for the Bible, or in its broadest sense as meaning both Scripture and rabbinic teaching.

PAN-HALACHISM AND RELIGIOUS BEHAVIORISM

Judaism is "the way of Torah."[152] So if Torah is reduced to halacha, Judaism becomes merely the way of halacha, a religion of law. Such "pan-halachism," as Heschel calls it, is a misrepresentation of Judaism. "He who would restrict Judaism to *Halacha* will distort its image and deprive it of its grandeur."[153]

Love is the supreme principle of Jewish law: "All observance is training in the art of love."[154] And since genuine love involves the heart and soul of the lover, the law of love cannot be fulfilled by mere external compliance with the law. Moreover, says Heschel, "no religious act is properly fulfilled unless it is done with a willing heart and a craving soul."[155] Yet those who reduce Torah and Judaism to halacha tend also to reduce halacha to external conformity to the law. Pan-halachism leads to religious behaviorism.

Heschel is critical of pan-halachism because of his love for halacha. "The foremost sources of my own religious insight lie in reverence for halacha," confesses Heschel, "in my feeble effort to live by it. . . . The observation of the law is the richest source of religious experience."[156] Pan-halachism spells the demise of genuine halachic living because "halacha is ultimately dependent upon agada."[157] Agada is the inspiration behind halacha. The heart of the law may be love of God and neighbor, but it is not the law itself but rather agada that motivates such love.

Heschel is critical of the religious behaviorism which pan-halachism yields because he realizes the importance of *kavanah,* inner devotion, for genuine religious behavior. "The outward performance is but an aspect of the totality of a deed."[158] A genuine religious deed, a true *mitsvah,* is more like an artistic act than a mechanical accomplishment and therefore must be imbued with kavanah. "The music in the score is open only to him who has music in his soul. It is not enough to play the notes; one must *be* what he *plays.* It is not enough to do the mitsvah; one must *live* what he *does.*"[159]

THE POLARITY OF AGADA AND HALACHA

Agada and halacha are both essential components of the Torah and their interrelationship is the essence of Judaism. Agada tells of the sublime mystery of creation, of the glory of the Creator, and of how human beings are known to respond with wonder, awe, and praise. Agada bespeaks the marvel of the divine–human covenant, the joy of human relationships within the covenant. Narrating the love story between God and Israel, agada sets the soul aflame and rouses the thirst for God and for a life compatible with God's love. Agada inspires love for God's law; it teaches that the law was given as a sign of God's love; that enacting the law is not for its own sake but for the sake of honoring God and ennobling the human; that the law therefore is not meant as a burden with which to comply but a helpmate to cherish and embrace.

As revelation is the impetus toward redemption, agada, which attests to revelation, calls forth the halachic living that advances redemption. Apart from revelation, redemption would be an empty dream. Apart from agada, halachic living would be a motiveless routine.

As redemption is the goal of revelation, halacha, which is meant to advance redemption, is inspired by the agada that attests to revelation. Without redemption as its goal, revelation would be an inefficacious event. Without halacha as its offspring, agada would be an irrelevant story.

Halacha affirms the value of agada, as redemption confirms the validity of revelation. Human beings are not ennobled by visions alone. The world is not redeemed by dreams. Agada, the vision and the dream, needs halacha as the way.

From the revelation of divine love we learn that "man is not alone." From the revelation of divine law we learn that God chooses not to be alone in redeeming the world. From divine love we know of God's share in human life. And from divine law we know of our share in God's design for a world redeemed. Halacha is as indispensable to Torah as is agada, and their correlation is essential to Judaism. "Halacha is the string, agada is the bow. When the string is tight the bow will evoke the melody. But the string may jar in the fumbler's hand."[160]

THE LAW AS TRANSCENDENT

As we are not the authors of life, we are not the authors of the ultimate principle by which life is made holy. God gives us both life and the law by which life is redeemed. Heschel says: "We believe that the Jew is committed to a divine law; that the ultimate standards are beyond man rather than within man. We believe that there is a law, the essence of which is derived from prophetic events, and the interpretation of which is in the hands of the sages."[161]

Why does the Jew believe that the essence of the law of Torah is the will of God? Because this is the claim of the Bible? But why accept such a claim? Is it not because the love and compassion for which the Torah stands are and have been experienced by Jews and others as being not only ideals and values but also requirements? And must not the source of such requirements transcend the human since all human beings are obligated to enact them? Thus Heschel's claim: "The good is not an abstract idea but a commandment, and the ultimate meaning of its fulfillment is in its being *an answer* to God."[162]

But what of the many halachic laws that do not convey such high ethical standards or are not concerned with ethics as such? What of the dietary and ritual laws, for example, many of which are not experienced by otherwise faithful Jews as being as morally imperative as the primary ethical principles of halacha? Does Heschel believe that these other laws of halacha were revealed by God or are an expression of the will of God? Are these laws binding in Heschel's judgment, as are the primary ethical demands of halacha?

Were All Halachic Laws Revealed by God?

"The assumption that every iota of the law was revealed to Moses at Sinai," says Heschel, is "a theological exaggeration" and "an unwarranted extension of the rabbinic concept of revelation."[163] On the contrary, Heschel regards the authority of the sages to issue new ordinances as a basic element of Jewish belief sanctioned by Deuteronomy 17:11. And not only do the sages have the authority to issue new ordinances, "they have the power to set aside a precept of the Torah when conditions require it."[164] Heschel quotes from several classical sources to defend his position on the role of the sages concerning halacha, perhaps the most significant of which is from the *Jerushalmi Sanhedrin:* "Were the Torah given as a rigid immutable code of laws, Israel could not survive. . . . The law will be explained, now one way, now another, according to the perception of the majority of the *sages.*"[165]

But if Heschel does not believe that the whole of the Torah was revealed to Moses, does he believe instead, given his perspective on the authority of the sages, that all of halacha was nonetheless revealed by God regardless of to whom? Heschel does not address this question explicitly. But to support his contention that the entire Torah was not revealed to Moses he includes among his quotations a statement from the *Pesikta Rabbati* which does seem to favor the view that the sages were recipients of revealed legislation: "things not revealed to Moses were revealed to Rabbi Akiba and his colleagues."[166] Yet Heschel includes this quotation not to defend the position that all of halacha was revealed by God but rather to defend the view that not all of the law was revealed to Moses. In his statement quoted above, "We believe that there is a law, the *essence* of which is derived from prophetic events," does Heschel mean to suggest that it is only the essence of Torah or halacha that is derived from revelation? If so, what does he mean by the essence of the law? Does he mean the primary ethical values and demands such as found in the Decalogue as well as the law of love as found in Deuteronomy 6:5 and 10:12 and in Leviticus 19:18?

The closest Heschel comes to saying explicitly whether or not he believes that all of halacha is the result of revelation is in the following statement: "There are times in Jewish history when the main issue is not what parts of the law cannot be fulfilled but what parts of the law can be and ought to be fulfilled, fulfilled as law, as an expression and interpretation of the will of God."[167] It seems, from the course of his writing, that this is also an issue for Heschel: What parts of the law ought to be fulfilled as an expression of the will of God?

Whether or not Heschel regards all of the Torah and halacha as the revealed will of God, it is clear that he does not regard all of the laws as equally important. This will be evident in the response to the question: Does Heschel believe that all the halachic laws are as binding as the primary ethical demands of halacha?

ARE ALL HALACHIC LAWS EQUALLY BINDING?

Another idea that Heschel regards as theologically unwarranted and indeed inimical to the survival of Jewish law is the notion that "all of its rules are of equal importance; and if one brick is removed the whole edifice must collapse."[168] Heschel's response to this notion is as follows:

> Such intransigence, laudable as it may be as an expression of devoutness, is neither historically nor theologically justified. There were ages in Jewish history when some aspects of Jewish ritual observance were not adhered to by people who had otherwise lived according to the law. And where is the man who could claim that he has been able to fulfill literally the *mitzvah* of "Love thy neighbor as thyself"?
>
> Where is the worry about the spiritual inadequacy of that which admittedly should not be abandoned? Where is our anxiety about the barrenness of our praying, the conventionality of our obedience?
>
> The problem, then, that cries for a solution is not everything or nothing, total disregard or obedience to the law; the problem is authentic or forged, genuine or artificial observance. The problem is not *how much* but *how to* observe.[169]

One reason why some aspects of halacha have not been followed by otherwise faithful Jews is that not all laws are of perennial significance or equal merit. Heschel rejects the fundamentalist notion that makes "no distinction between the eternal and the temporal" and he points out that some of the laws of the Torah, such as found in Exodus 21, "do not represent ideals but compromises, realistic attempts to refine the moral condition of ancient man."[170] Heschel goes so far as to claim that "in the name of God's mercy, we . . . have the right to challenge the harsh statements of the prophets."[171] It would therefore follow that Heschel would affirm the right to challenge some of the laws of halacha, whether of prophetic or rabbinic origin. In fact, paraphrasing Rashi, Heschel claims: "Sometimes one should annul parts of the Torah to act for the Lord."[172]

But if we are to criticize biblical "passages which seem to be incompatible with our certainty of the compassion of God," Heschel reminds us that "the standards by which those passages are criticized are impressed upon us by the Bible, which is the main factor in ennobling our conscience and endowing us with the sensitivity that rebels against all cruelty."[173] It follows that if we are to criticize some halachic laws that we should keep in mind that the standards by which we do so are derived from the Torah itself. If some laws are deemed no longer binding it is precisely because they are no longer compatible with or pertinent to the forever binding essentials of halacha.

Does God Require More than the Torah's Essence?

Regardless of whether all halachic laws are derived from revelation or whether all of them are binding, Heschel does believe that just as God requires adherence to the essence of halacha, God may also will and expect observance of the other seemingly less important aspects of halacha. "Faith . . . cannot rest content with essences. Faith knows no boundaries between the will of God and all of life."[174] This is why "the days of the week, the food we eat, the holidays of the year, the deeds that we do—these are the frontiers of faith."[175]

Heschel is aware of the rationalist's reaction to this view and he responds as follows:

> From a rationalist's point of view it does not seem plausible to assume that the infinite, ultimate supreme Being is concerned with my putting on Tefillin every day. It is, indeed, strange to believe that God should care whether a particular individual will eat leavened or unleavened bread during a particular season of the year. However, it is that paradox, namely, that the infinite God is intimately concerned with finite man and his finite deeds; that nothing is trite or irrelevant in the eyes of God, which is the very essence of the prophetic faith.[176]

If we believe that God cares about human beings, why should we hesitate to believe that God is concerned with the way as well as the goal of human living? If we believe that God requires us "to do justice" and "to love kindness," why should we not believe that God requires us "to hallow the Sabbath?"[177] "Perhaps," says Heschel, "the question of what benediction to pronounce upon a certain type of food, the problem of matching the material with the spiritual, is more important than is generally imagined."[178]

Holiness does not signify an air that prevails in the solemn atmosphere of a sanctuary, a quality reserved for supreme acts, an adverb of the spiritual, the distinction of hermits and priests. . . . The strength of holiness lies underground, in the somatic. It is primarily in the way in which we gratify physical needs that the seed of holiness is planted. . . .

Judaism teaches us how even the gratification of animal needs can be an act of sanctification. The enjoyment of food may be a way of purification. Something of my soul may be drowned in a glass of water, when its content is gulped down as if nothing in the world mattered except my thirst. But we can come a bit closer to God, when remembering Him still more in excitement and passion.[179]

If indeed "we can come a bit closer to God when remembering Him" in the performance of mitsvot, including the mitsvot associated with eating and drinking, might it not be that God wills and asks for such remembrance?

Love is the essence and purpose of halacha and, as has been noted, "all observance is training in the art of love." Thus, claims Heschel: "To forget that love is the purpose of all *mitsvot* is to vitiate their meaning."[180] Affixing a mezuzah to the doorpost of a home, praying at prescribed hours, wearing tzitzit and tallit, abstaining from certain foods, koshering others, lighting Sabbath candles, each of these is meant as an act of love. True, people can love without performing such deeds, but these are reminders of the duty to love and are themselves ways of expressing love. "All mitsvot are means of evoking in us the awareness of living in the neighborhood of God."[181] And when such awareness is abiding, love of God and neighbor is less rare. Is it so difficult to believe, then, that God requires not only love but certain ways of expressing love, distinct reminders of our "living in the neighborhood of God"?

TORAH VIS-À-VIS GOD

Since sanctity is associated with the Torah as with God, there arises the question of the Torah's status vis-à-vis God. This is Heschel's position, for which he finds justification in classical rabbinic literature: "God is greater than the Torah. . . . As God transcends the world, he transcends the Torah. . . . The Torah is his, but he is not his Torah."[182] Yet as the world conveys the presence of God, "the Torah, which comes from God, carries the presence of God."[183] And as a vehicle of God's presence, "the Torah is not an end in itself."[184]

If one is tempted to identify the Torah with God, it is perhaps because the Torah is viewed as the wisdom of God. Yet although the Torah is God's wisdom, the Torah as we have it is not exactly wisdom as God has it. "The Torah in our hands is some of God's wisdom but not all of his wisdom."[185] The Torah is to be studied, observed, and cherished; God alone is to be adored. Yet since the Torah conveys the wisdom and the presence of God, love for the Torah is an antecedent of faith in God.

ISRAEL

Judaism, as "the way of Torah," is the enacted faith in God, lived in the context of the covenant community of Israel.

A PEOPLE BY VIRTUE OF GOD AND TORAH

According to Jewish belief, God has revealed the Torah to Israel and has chosen this people to reveal the Torah to all other peoples. In fact, in Heschel's view, Israel is a people only by virtue of its relationship to God and Torah. About this he is emphatic: "There is no Jewish people without God and Torah."[186]

It would be much more understandable, and indeed less radical, for Heschel to claim that there is no Judaism—rather than no Jewish people—without God and Torah, since Judaism is the faith of the Jewish people. Is this perhaps what Heschel means? Elsewhere he says: "Judaism is not a matter of blood or race but a spiritual dimension" that "comes to expression in events and teachings, in thoughts and deeds."[187] Would Heschel want to suggest that Israel's peoplehood is not a matter of blood and race? Since not all Jewish people accept and express the faith of Judaism, is there not a distinction between the Jewish people as an ethnic group and the Judaism that many members of that group profess?

Heschel knows well that there are Jews estranged from Judaism. And he would not deny that these Jews are members of the Jewish people. Yet from an evaluation of Heschel's writings, wherein he always uses the terms "the people of Israel" and "the Jewish people" in a religious sense, it is clear that Heschel really means what he says: "There is no Jewish people without God and Torah." But since there are "secular Jews" who are still somehow a part of the Jewish people, what can Heschel mean by this radical statement?

Does Heschel mean that without God and Torah, Israel would never have been formed as a people? He means at least that much: "God's vision of Israel came first and only then did we come into the world. . . . We have not chosen God; He has chosen us."[188] Does he also mean that were it not for allegiance to God and Torah, Israel would not have had the patience and the strength to endure for so long as a people? Again, he certainly means just that: "Experts in assimilation, the Jews could have disappeared even before the names of modern nations were known. Still we are patient and cherish the will to perpetuate our essence."[189] This essence as a people has to do with their religious vocation: "Let us not withhold from our children the knowledge that we shall only endure in the covenant with God. . . . Israel's strength lies in the knowledge that it is the people of the God of Abraham."[190] And does Heschel also mean that without adhering to God and Torah the people of Israel would lose its purpose, its destiny? "It is our destiny to live for what is more than ourselves. . . . Israel exists not in order to be, but in order to cherish the vision of God."[191] And since the Torah represents God's vision, Heschel can say: "The Torah is . . . the destiny of Israel."[192]

Perhaps the Jewish people would still, for awhile, be identified as Jews even if God and Torah were erased from the memory of history. But, says Heschel, "a Jew without Torah is obsolete" and "if there is no God, it is not worthwhile to be a Jew."[193] As long as Judaism exists there will be a Jewish people, and even "nonreligious" Jews may be considered a part thereof. But without Judaism there would be no Jewish people, no Israel with which even the estranged could identify. Without God and Torah there may still exist some Jewish persons but there would not be a Jewish people. "Our historic experience has taught us . . . that in order to be a people, the Jews must be more than a people."[194] "Israel was made to be a 'holy people,'"[195] a people devoted to God and Torah. Perhaps more than anywhere else, it is, appropriately, in a letter to Israel's Prime Minister David Ben-Gurion, dated December 18, 1958, that Heschel is most explicit about why he believes it futile to speak of a Jewish people apart from its religion: "Now that Israel [the State] is firmly established, the time has come to reexamine some ideas of our national movement. We should question the validity of the theory that religion is only a means to an end—a device for preserving the people. This theory is based on the premises originating in mental obtuseness. This people is an eternal people. Its very purpose is basically a religious one."[196]

REVELATION THROUGH ISRAEL

While there is no Israel without God and Torah, there is a sense in which there would be no God and Torah in this world without Israel. Heschel is fond of recalling a rabbinic midrash on a passage from Isaiah that suggests this view:

"Ye are my witnesses, says the Lord, and I am God" (Isaiah 43:12). A rabbi of the second century took the statement to mean, if you are my witnesses, I am God; if you cease to be my witnesses, I am not God. This is one of the boldest utterances in Jewish literature, a manifesto of meaning. If there are no witnesses, there is no God to be met. There is a mystery, an enigma, a darkness past finding out. For God to be present there must be witnesses. Without the people Israel, the Bible is mere literature. Through Israel, the Bible is a voice, a power and a challenge.[197]

In the spirit of this bold midrash, Heschel makes statements every bit as bold: "The fate of God is bound up with the fate of Israel" and "the fate of the Jewish people and the fate of the Hebrew Bible are intertwined."[198] It is one thing for Heschel to maintain that the response of Israel is as important as the revelation of God, that "the 'We will do and we will listen' is as important as the 'I am the Lord thy God.'"[199] It is quite another thing for him to claim that the fate of God and Torah hinge on the fate of Israel. Is this merely hyperbole? Surely Heschel knows that other peoples may bear witness to God and to the Torah.

When once asked, "What does a Jew expect from Christianity?" Heschel replied: "The first thing you can do for us is to be genuine to your Christian faith and to be a witness to the God of Abraham."[200] Yet only a few sentences later he told his interviewer: "A Christian should realize that a world that does not have Israel will not have the God of Israel."[201] If God must have witnesses in order to be present, and if Christians can witness to God, then why would a world without Israel be a world without God? Not only does Heschel recognize that Christians, as well as Jews, may bear witness to God, he also claims that Christians share with Jews the responsibility of preserving the Hebrew Bible: "It is on the issue of saving the radiance of the Hebrew Bible in the minds of man that Jews and Christians are called upon to work together."[202]

Heschel realizes that Christians can and do give witness to God and to the Hebrew Bible, but he seems to believe that without Israel Christian witness would atrophy. In fact, in another interview, wherein he applauded the fact that in the Catholic Church's Decree on Ecumenism, issued at the Second Vatican Council, there is no mention of a Christian mission to the Jews, he said: "This great, old, wise Church in Rome realizes that the existence of Jews as Jews is so holy and so precious that the Church would collapse if the Jewish people would cease to exist."[203] Whether or not this is part of the church's realization may be disputed. But the question here is, why does Heschel suggest that the church, as a people that bears witness to God and to the Bible, would collapse if Israel ceased to exist?

The answer seems to be that Heschel believes that the "dejudaization" of Christianity has weakened and distorted the power of its witness[204] and that in a world without Jews the dejudaization of Christianity would be complete. In other words, Christianity needs Israel as a reminder of its origin, purpose, and destiny: "Christian renewal should imply confrontation with Judaism out of which it emerged. Separated from its source, Christianity is easily exposed to principles alien to its spirit. The vital challenge for the Church is to decide whether Christianity came to overcome, to abolish, or to continue the Jewish way by bringing the God of Abraham and His will to the Gentiles."[205] "Separated from its source," Christianity would lose the vitality to carry out its purpose, that of "bringing the God of Abraham and His will [the Torah] to the Gentiles." Without Israel the Church would forfeit its destiny and collapse.

By claiming that a world without Israel would be a world without God and Torah, Heschel may also mean that such a world would be without an understanding of the true meaning of God and Torah. He seems to believe that, even with the Christian witness to God and the Bible, the world still needs the Jewish witness as a corrective to what may often be Christian misrepresentations. Since the Hebrew Bible is "indispensable to our existence" and since Christians have "made it an 'old' book of Law that very few people read" and since "the Jews have a good memory of what the Bible means,"[206] for these reasons Jews are indispensable to the survival of the true meaning of the Hebrew Bible *as Torah*. Moreover, since those who forget "the primacy of the Hebrew Bible" tend "to cherish one perspective of the meaning of God" to the exclusion of other vital perspectives, it is important that the Jewish people, attached to the primacy of the Torah, continue to exist and bear witness, correcting such one-sidedness.[207]

To say that a world without Israel would be a world without God and Torah is a negative way of claiming the positive fact that "revelation to Israel continues as revelation through Israel."[208] As God and Torah were revealed to Israel, Israel has been chosen to reveal God and Torah to the world.

A CHOSEN PEOPLE

If revelation continues through Israel it is because God has chosen Israel to be a vehicle of divine revelation. "God is in search of man," of every human being and of all people. In this divine search, God found or formed one people, Israel, chosen to bear witness to the divine search for all peoples.

There is perhaps no concept in Judaism that has been more misunderstood by its critics than the idea of Israel as a chosen people. Contrary to what many critics assume, the idea is not meant to imply that Israel is a superior people. Heschel writes: "The idea of a chosen people does not suggest the preference for a people based upon a discrimination among a number of peoples. We do not say that we are a superior people. The 'chosen people' means a people approached and chosen by God. The significance of this term is genuine in relation to God rather than in relation to other peoples. It signifies not a quality inherent in the people but a relationship between the people and God."[209]

Although its significance "is genuine in relation to God" and it signifies "a relationship between the people and God," the term "chosen people" is not meant to imply that Israel has an exclusive relationship to God. Heschel makes this clear when commenting on the meaning of "God of Israel," a phrase associated with the term "chosen people": "The saying 'God of Israel' has no possessive or exclusive connotation: God belonging to Israel alone. Its true meaning is that the God of all men has entered a Covenant with one people for the sake of all people."[210] Israel's relationship to God is special not because God favors Israel over other peoples but in the sense that God has charged Israel with the task of witnessing to God and Torah.

Israel has been chosen as a vehicle of divine revelation. But just as the term "chosen people" does not imply either Israel's superiority or its exclusive relationship with God, neither does it imply that Israel is the only vehicle of God's revelation. There are a number of ways in which Heschel indicates his belief that God is revealed not only through Israel, its individual members, and its community, but also through other persons and other peoples as well.

In the first place, Heschel believes that the divine is, or may be, revealed through each and every human being. "The human is the disclosure of the divine. . . . To meet a human being is an opportunity to sense the image of God, *the presence* of God."[211] Although Israel is chosen for a special type of witness, every human being, created in the image of God, is "chosen" or meant "to be *a witness for God.*"[212] Moreover, says Heschel, "God is to be found in many hearts all over the world; not limited to one nation or to one people, to one religion."[213] This means not only that God has somehow been revealed to the hearts of many people but that many people are known to reveal the God in their hearts.

Specifically concerning revelation through various religions, Heschel has this to say: "If we accept the principle that the majesty of God transcends the dignity of religion, should we not regard a divergent religion as His Majesty's loyal opposition? . . . The voice of God reaches the spirit of man in a variety of ways, in a multiplicity of languages. One truth comes to expression in many ways of understanding."[214] It is for this reason that Heschel believes that "in this aeon diversity of religions is the will of God."[215] If religious pluralism is God's will, does it follow that the peoples of various religions have been chosen by God for various tasks? Heschel seems open to such a view when, in the context of affirming religious diversity as a matter of God's will, he asks: "Is religious uniformity desirable or even possible? . . . Does not the task of preparing the kingdom of God require a diversity of talents, a variety of rituals, soul-searching as well as opposition?"[216]

Even if the peoples of other valid religions have been "chosen" for other divine tasks or for contributing to the one great redemptive task in other ways, the uniqueness of Israel's chosenness remains. Israel has been chosen to bear witness to God in a unique way, the way of Torah.

A HOLY PEOPLE

Israel is a chosen people, meant to be a holy people: "'Ye shall be unto me a kingdom of priests, a holy people' (Exodus 19:6), was the reason for Israel's election."[217] Israel is meant to be holy because the God whom Israel has been chosen to represent is holy (cf. Leviticus 19:2).

The word "holy," *kadosh,* denotes "set apart" or separate. In usage it signifies divinity or a divine-like quality derived from contact with divinity.[218] God is the Holy One, the Transcendent Other, separate from creation even though in touch with it. When used in reference to God, *kadosh* suggests not only God's ontological transcendence but also God's moral transcendence or ethical excellence. As a holy people, set apart from the pagan world, Israel is meant to call attention to God's ontological and moral transcendence by mirroring the ethical excellence of God.

As the Holy One is separate from creation while nonetheless in contact with it, Israel, as a holy people, is meant to be set apart from the world without withdrawing from it. By its way of Torah, Israel is meant to separate itself from the ungodly ways of the world. Yet the Torah is meant to be lived in the midst of the world, inspiring the peoples of the world to turn to God. Israel has been chosen to be a holy people in order to lead other peoples to holiness.[219]

Just as Israel's status as a chosen people does not mean that Israel is superior to other peoples or has an exclusive relationship to God or is the only vehicle of God's revelation, Israel's consecration as a holy people does not mean that Israel alone is holy. "Holiness is not the monopoly of any particular religion or tradition."[220]

There are at least two senses in which Heschel sees holiness existing in all peoples. In the first place, "human life is holy, holier even than the Scrolls of the Torah."[221] But even though "just to live is holy," simply "being alive is no answer to the problem of living."[222] Therefore, the holiness of being must be incarnated in the holiness of doing. In the second place, then, "whenever a deed is done in accord with the will of God, whenever a thought of man is directed toward Him, there is the holy."[223] Human *life* is holy by virtue of its being created in the image and likeness of God. Yet human *living* is holy by virtue of human beings thinking and acting in harmony with the holiness of God. Human beings are able either to reflect or distort the image of God in which they are made, either to affirm or deny the holiness with which their beings are blessed. This applies to Israel and to all the peoples of the earth.

Israel has been set apart as a holy people so that all peoples may be set apart in holiness through the service of God. Redemption will occur when all peoples are separated from ungodly ways and live in accord with the holy. Redemption is the transformation of the world, which now contains both the holy and the unholy, into a world where only holiness abounds. Redemption will be final when there are no more ungodly ways from which to be set apart.

Jewish faith entails faithfulness to God, by way of the Torah, in the context of Israel, for the redemption of humankind.

PART
THREE

The Antecedents of Faith

6

Wonder and Awe

The way to faith leads through acts of wonder and radical amazement.[1]
Awe precedes faith; it is at the root of faith. We must grow in awe in
order to reach faith. We must be guided by awe to be worthy of faith.[2]

The sublime mystery of existence is a source of religious faith insofar as it evokes acts and attitudes of wonder and awe, which are for Heschel antecedents of faith.

Just as the sublime and mystery are two aspects of one reality, wonder and awe are often two sides of one experience of reality. But no matter how closely related, wonder and awe are distinguishable. We will therefore examine the meaning of each in turn, focusing on their significance for the genesis of faith.

Wonder

"What seems to be natural is wondrous."[3] And wonder is the human response to the wondrous, which is another name for the sublime dimension of reality. As described in chapter 3, the sublime or the wondrous is, for Heschel, that aspect of nature which alludes to a transcendent meaning which may in turn be perceived as divine. Since the sublime suggests the divine, wonder nurtures faith, our response to the divine. Thus, says Heschel, "awareness of the divine begins with wonder."[4] It is for this reason that Heschel considers wonder an antecedent of faith.

To say that "awareness of the divine begins with wonder" is not the same as saying that wonder itself constitutes a response to the divine. Wonder is the response to the sublime dimension of reality that alludes to

153

the divine. Thus, the awareness of God begins in wonder only in the sense that it is rooted in wonder as the response to that which alludes to God. Heschel is quite clear on this point when he says: "The sense of wonder . . . does not give us a knowledge of God. It only leads to a plane where the question about God becomes an inescapable concern."[5]

THE WILL TO WONDER

While the sublime invites wonder, its presence does not guarantee the emergence of wonder. For wonder, like the faith it precedes, is both a gift and a response. When struck with wonder we realize that wonder is not our own achievement and we are grateful for the experience. Yet when devoid of wonder we know that we ourselves are somehow at fault and that we must strive for the experience of wonder. For even more universal than wonder is the imperative to wonder.[6] The experience of wonder is a gift we must seek through "deeds of wonder," through acts of love. "What we lack is not a will to believe but a will to wonder."[7] But if we do learn how to live in wonder perhaps we will then learn what it is like to live in faith.

It is wonder not only as *an experience* but also as *an attitude* that fosters religious faith. This attitude of wonder is developed and sustained through constant acts of wonder. There may be times when, unprepared, we are struck with wonder, yet it is up to us to keep the spirit of wonder alive. Like love, wonder is both an effortless happening and the result of constant effort. We fall in love and we create love. Love happens to us and we make love happen. So it is with wonder.

We may at times be overwhelmed with wonder, but "we must keep alive the sense of wonder through deeds of wonder."[8] The sublimity of nature and of our neighbor will be noticed when we treat all as precious and unique. Wonder will seize us when we take nothing and no one for granted, when the concern for nature and the concern of others becomes our own.

The will to wonder is opposed to the will to power, and deeds of wonder are opposed to deeds of exploitation. Thus, Heschel contrasts the way of wonder with the way of expediency: "Most of our attention is given to the expedient, to that which is conducive to our advantage and which would enable us to exploit the resources of our planet. . . . However, as we have seen, there is more than one aspect of nature that commands our attention. We go out to meet the world not only by way of expediency but also by way of wonder. In the first we accumulate information in order to dominate; in the second we deepen our appreciation in order to respond."[9] Heschel conveys this same idea when he contrasts the way of appreciation with the way of manipulation as two primary ways in which we relate ourselves to the world that surrounds us. In the first way we see in what surrounds us "things to be handled, forces to be managed, objects to be put to use." In the second way we see in what surrounds us "things to be acknowledged, understood, valued, or admired."[10]

Thus, the will to wonder is the endeavor to face reality with grateful appreciation. To live in a spirit of wonder is to live with an attitude of appreciation. The extreme importance that Heschel places upon a life of appreciation and wonder is evident when he says: "Mankind will not perish for want of information; but only for want of appreciation. The beginning of our happiness lies in the understanding that life without wonder is not worth living."[11]

The reason why Heschel decries life without wonder is because the opposite of wonder, which is manipulation or exploitation, causes alienation. Wonder, however, fosters harmony. When we live in a spirit of wonder, "we become alive to our living in the great fellowship of all beings, we cease to regard things as opportunities to exploit."[12] And if we are to meet the world in this spirit, it is especially the case when we meet other human beings. This is because, in Heschel words, "many things on earth are precious, some are holy, humanity is holy of holies."[13]

TWO ATTITUDES TOWARD REALITY: ACCEPTANCE AND WONDER

While the way of wonder is opposed to the way of expediency and exploitation, it is also in contrast to an attitude that merely accepts the givenness of reality. Fritz Rothschild points out the difference between these two attitudes toward reality: "Acceptance stops with whatever is perceived and sees no good reason for going beyond it. The object is admitted as a given (datum) and that is all there is to it. Wonder, on the other hand, is an attitude which, far from being set at ease by a fact, takes it as a stimulus which points beyond what is immediately given."[14]

According to Heschel, the intimation of the beyond is given with the same immediacy as the facts themselves. The intimation is not simply as much a fact as any other, "it is a fact within the facts."[15] But if our attitude is one that merely accepts the apparent, we will fail to discern the intimation of transcendent meaning. "Wonder alone is the compass that may direct us to the pole of meaning."[16] To sense the beyond in the evident, the transcendent meaning of natural objects, we must live in a spirit of wonder, in a state of mind that takes nothing for granted: "Spiritually we cannot live by merely reiterating borrowed or inherited knowledge. Inquire of your soul, what does it know, what does it take for granted. It will tell you only no-thing is taken for granted; each thing is a surprise, *being is unbelievable*. We are amazed at seeing anything at all; amazed not only at particular

values and things but *at the unexpectedness of being as such,* at the fact
there is being at all."[17] This sense of amazement or wonder at the
unexpectedness of being, and with it the sense for the world's transcendent
meaning, is vividly described by Heschel:

> To a mind unwarped by intellectual habit, unbiased by what it already
> knows; to unmitigated innate surprise, there are no axioms, no dogmas;
> there is only wonder, the realization that the world is too incredible, too
> meaningful for us. The existence of the world is the most unlikely, the most
> unbelievable fact. Even our ability for surprise is beyond expectation. In
> our unmitigated wonder, we are like spirits who have never been conscious
> of outside reality, and to whom the knowledge of the existence of the
> universe has been brought for the first time. Who could believe it? Who
> could conceive it? We must learn to overcome the sleek certainty and learn
> to understand that the existence of the universe is contrary to all reasonable
> expectations.[18]

When in fact we refuse to take the world for granted, to merely accept it as
given, and when, instead, we attempt to face the world as if "for the first
time," then we begin to understand what Heschel means when he says: "The
world is not just here. It shocks us into amazement."[19]

TWO KINDS OF WONDER: CURIOSITY AND RADICAL AMAZEMENT

It should be clear by now that the wonder of which Heschel speaks is
not the same as intellectual curiosity, which though a step beyond mere
acceptance of the given is not a matter of being stunned "at the
unexpectedness of being as such." Heschel's wonder is an *ultimate wonder*
which he calls *radical amazement,* as such distinct from *rational wonder*
which he identifies with *curiosity.*[20] Curiosity refers to segments of reality
and to their relations; radical amazement pertains to reality as such. So
while curiosity may give rise to science, radical amazement—which the
scientist may indeed experience—leads to a religious concern for the
ultimate source and meaning of life. For since "there is no answer in the
world to man's ultimate wonder at the world," we are driven to look beyond
the world for an answer to the world. "The world is a mystery, a question,
not an answer," and therefore "the most pressing problem is, what does it
stand for? What is its meaning?"[21]

When we live in a spirit of wonder we are overcome by the realization
that nature has not endowed itself with its own grandeur, nor have we
endowed the world with the meaning to which it alludes. In such a situation
we cannot circumvent the supreme question, "Who is the great author?
Why is there a world at all?"[22] In a spirit of wonder we come to realize that

the great miracle of life is something we witness and generate rather than something we ourselves create. It is this realization, provoked by wonder, that enables us to believe that the Living God to whom biblical religion bears witness is the great author of life, that it is this God who is the transcendent meaning of the world.

To realize that the world is a question, not an answer, is to realize that the world is not self-sufficient. The religious quest begins when, in radical wonder, we question the self-sufficiency of the world. Religious faith begins when we realize and appreciate the fact that the foundation of the world is not of this world, that the world's foundation is divine. Such a realization is at the core of the biblical doctrine of creation which is deeply rooted in the experience of wonder. The premise of this doctrine is the radical amazement "at the unexpectedness of being as such."[23]

The question about the creation of the world is "*a question of amazement,* not of curiosity." In fact, the question—as Isaiah put it, "Who created these?" (40:26)—is "an answer in disguise," it is "a question that contains the impossibility of giving a negative answer." From a biblical perspective, then, "there is a way of asking the great question which can only elicit an affirmative answer."[24] Heschel articulates the answer this way: "God called the world into being, and that call goes on. There is a present moment because God is present. Every instant is an act of creation."[25]

When contrasting curiosity and radical amazement as two kinds of wonder, Heschel implies that curiosity is the root of philosophy and science while radical amazement is the root of religion. Indeed, curiosity itself may give rise to speculative philosophy and science but this does not mean that radical amazement may not also be at the root of these disciplines. And Heschel is well aware of this, although he is not clear about it in his brief section entitled "Two Kinds of Wonder" in *God in Search of Man*.[26] Elsewhere, however, Heschel says that it is "on the level of wonder and radical amazement" that "the unique insights of art, religion and philosophy come into being" and that "under the running sea of our theories and scientific explanations lies the aboriginal abyss of radical amazement."[27] It seems, then, that the purpose of Heschel's contrast is not to deny that radical amazement is at the root of philosophy and science, but to point out that the curiosity that may give rise to these disciplines must be distinguished from the ultimate wonder which—although it too may be at the root of them—is more than a prelude to philosophical and scientific knowledge.[28]

WONDER AND KNOWLEDGE

While many people admit that wonder is a stimulant to thinking or a condition for knowledge, Heschel goes much further. For him, wonder is not only a prelude to knowledge, it is also a state of knowledge and an act that goes beyond knowledge, an act or attitude that does not cease with the acquisition of the knowledge sought.

WONDER AS THE ROOT OF KNOWLEDGE

Wonder is the root of knowledge because it is, as we have seen, the act of taking nothing for granted, not even our inherited knowledge. "Wonder is a state of mind in which we do not look at reality through the latticework of our memorized knowledge."[29] Heschel also says: "The greatest hindrance to knowledge is our adjustment to conventional notions, to mental clichés. Wonder or radical amazement, the state of maladjustment to words and notions is, therefore, a prerequisite for an authentic awareness of that which is."[30] Thus, to overcome the tendency of taking things for granted and thereby being enslaved to "conventional notions," we must learn to "unthink many thoughts and recall the innate sense of wonder, systematically extirpated by false wisdom."[31] This is the only way we are able to attain *real knowledge* rather than a merely *notional knowledge*. It is the only way we can enjoy *personal knowledge* rather than simply repeating *inherited knowledge*.

This is not to say, however, that inherited knowledge cannot become personal knowledge, but that if we are to truly understand an inherited insight which was itself born in wonder, we ourselves must live in a state of wonder; we must have personal insight into our "heritage of insight."[32] So wonder is the root of knowledge not only because it is the act of taking nothing for granted but, more positively, because it is an act in which insight is born, whether it be an *original insight* in the history of a tradition or, as is more usually the case, a *personal insight* into the knowledge which tradition has accumulated and bequeaths to those who seek it.

It must, of course, be understood that for Heschel the conventional wisdom to which wonder or radical amazement is a "state of maladjustment" is not the same as the traditional wisdom or "the heritage of insight." But it must also be understood that for Heschel just as it is wrong to be adjusted to conventional notions, it is likewise wrong merely to memorize and repeat genuine inherited wisdom. Conventional notions are thoughts which we must *unthink* in order to attain the insights of wonder. The heritage of insight contains those thoughts which we must *rethink* by living in a state of wonder. It was wonder that gave rise to our heritage of insight and it is only in wonder that this heritage shall endure.

Heschel's impatience with conventional notions, as well as his conviction that wonder is the seed of insight and, further, that this insight is the root of all knowledge, including rational philosophy, is perhaps most vividly expressed in the following excerpt:

It is impossible to be at ease and to repose on ideas which have turned into habits, on "canned" theories, in which our own or other people's insights are preserved. We can never leave behind our concern in the safe-deposit of opinions, nor delegate its force to others and so attain vicarious insights. We must keep our own amazement, our own eagerness alive. And if we ever fail in our quest for insight, it is not because it cannot be found, but because we do not know how to live, or how to beware of the mind's narcissistic tendency to fall in love with its own reflection, a tendency which cuts thought off its roots.

The tree of knowledge and the tree of life have their roots in the same soil. But, playing with winds and beams, the tree of knowledge often grows brilliant, sapless leaves instead of fruits. Let the leaves wither, but the sap should not dry up. What is subtle speculation worth without the pristine insight into the sacredness of life, an insight which we try to translate into philosophy's rational terms, into religion's ways of living, into art's forms and visions? To maintain the stir and flow of that insight in all thoughts, so that even in our doubts its sap should not cease to flush, means to draw from the soil of what is creative in civilization and religion, a soil which only artificial flowers can dispense with.

The sense of the ineffable does not hush the quest of thought, but, on the contrary, disturbs the placid and unseals our suppressed impressionability. The approach to the ineffable leads through the depth of knowledge rather than through ignorant animal gazing. . . . Souls that are focused and do not falter at first sight, falling back on words and ready-made notions with which the memory is replete, can behold the mountains as if they were gestures of exaltation. To them all sight is suddenness, and eyes which do not discern the flash in the darkness of a thing perceive but series of clichés.[33]

While Heschel is impatient with the reiteration of conventional notions, or even with the mere recollection of traditional wisdom, he by no means underestimates the importance of committing the insights of tradition to memory. Such remembrance is essential for the acquisition of knowledge. Heschel would simply object to a mere memorizing of these ideas. The insights and doctrines of tradition must be both remembered and rethought. Memory alone is not enough to keep a tradition alive, nor is it an adequate way for us to attain real understanding.

In Heschel's view, memory and personal insight must always be intertwined. If we were to rely on memory alone, our thinking would lack depth; our knowledge may be broad, but it would also be shallow. If we were to rely on personal insight alone, our thinking would lack perspective; it may be deep, but it would also be narrow. Personal insight stands in need of the critique of the tradition that is remembered. Memory stands in need of the experience of personal insight. This is so because we are neither strictly solitary nor strictly communal beings. Each person needs the tradition of the community and each community needs the insight of its members. This is particularly true with regard to religious faith, for the insight of faith is not simply a private matter. Each of us, to some degree or another, may share the faith-insight of the community to which we belong. Yet to share that faith-insight is to interiorize it, which involves more than just memorizing the language in which the insight is communicated. Each of us must perceive for ourselves the meaning of the faith-insight of the community, we must envision the vision that lies at the foundation of our community of faith. And since wonder is a source of insight, and because the memory of wondrous moments can evoke or rekindle wonder, then memory and wonder are intimately related. Their harmony is well expressed by Heschel in the following passage: "Reminders of what has been disclosed to us are hanging over our souls like stars, remote and of mind-surpassing grandeur. They shine through dark and dangerous ages, and their reflection can be seen in the lives of those who guard the path of conscience and memory in the wilderness of careless living. Since those perennial reminders have moved into our minds, wonder has never left us."[34]

In asserting the fact that wonder is the source of knowledge, Heschel opposes the claim that knowledge or philosophy begins with doubt, the principle of *dubito ut intelligam*. Wonder, or the insight of wonder, lies at the origin of thought. Doubt is a subsequent movement within the process of thinking. The insight of wonder is a primary or immediate awareness, an intuitive or perceptive understanding. Only after this insight has been conceptualized does doubt have a role to play within the process of thinking or in the acquisition and testing of knowledge. First comes the perception or insight of wonder; then comes the process of conceptualizing this insight; thereafter doubt may emerge, not about whether we really perceive but about whether what we perceive is a true reflection of what really exists, whether our wonder is a reliable source of knowledge and whether our concepts or theories are an adequate expression of wonder's insight. This process is clearly described by Heschel as follows: "Even before we conceptualize what we perceive, we are amazed beyond words, beyond doubts. We may doubt anything, except that we are struck with amazement."[35] Thus: "Wonder rather than doubt is the root of knowledge. Doubt comes in the wake of knowledge as a state of vacillation between two contrary or contradictory views; as a state in which a belief we had embraced begins to totter. It challenges the mind's accounts about reality and calls for an examination and verification of that which is deposited in the mind."[36]

Heschel's epistemology, in which wonder is accorded priority over doubt, is rooted in the biblical world view. As he himself explains: "There is no word in Biblical Hebrew for doubt; there are many expressions for wonder. Just as in dealing with judgments our starting point is doubt, wonder is the Biblical starting point in facing reality. The Biblical man's sense for the mind-surpassing grandeur of reality prevented the power of doubt from setting up its own independent dynasty. Doubt is an act in which the mind inspects its own ideas; wonder is an act in which the mind confronts the universe."[37] It is clear from the last few quotations that, although Heschel maintains that doubt has a subsequent rather than a primary function within the process of thinking, he does not underestimate the value of doubt in the quest for knowledge and truth. On the contrary, says he: "The mind in its honesty tolls its doubts" and, therefore, "the sense of wonder . . . must not stifle doubt where doubt is legitimate."[38]

Doubt has a vital role to play in the life of thought, according to Heschel, but it must never be considered a substitute for wonder. "He who is sluggish will berate doubt; he who is blind will berate wonder."[39] So it is not the value of doubt that Heschel questions but only its timing and the place it is accorded. There is indeed a time when doubt is out of place.

> At the moment in which a fire bursts forth, threatening to destroy one's home, a person does not pause to investigate whether the danger he faces is real or a figment of his imagination. Such a moment is not the time to inquire into the chemical principle of combustion, or into the question of who is to blame for the outbreak of fire. The ultimate question, when bursting forth in our souls, is too startling, too heavily laden with unutterable wonder to be an academic question, to be equally suspended between yes and no. Such a moment is not the time to throw doubts upon the reason for the rise of the question.[40]

If doubt is not the beginning of knowledge, and if it is out of place during moments of "unutterable wonder," then doubt must not be accorded the primary position in the philosophical task. The fact that doubt has a critical function in philosophical thought is not doubted; but that it can ever adequately replace wonder as the starting point of philosophy is flatly denied by Heschel.

Heschel's denial is important, I believe, for the following reasons: First, a philosophy that begins in wonder will be much more inclusive than a philosophy that begins in doubt. For instance, a philosophy that begins in wonder does not exclude doubt; but a philosophy that begins in doubt will find it difficult, if not impossible, to include wonder. This is because wonder or the insight of wonder spontaneously tends toward speculation which may include doubt, but speculation and doubt do not spontaneously tend toward wonder. Second, a philosophy that begins in wonder has a greater chance for reality-contact than a philosophy that commences in doubt. This is because wonder is a primary experience while speculation and doubt are secondary moments within experience and might even become substitutes for real experience. And if reality is known either in experience or not at all, then it is important for a philosophy to begin with experience and not with something that can only question experience and that might even become a substitute for experience. And if experience is the primary subject matter for philosophical reflection, then wonder, as a real experiential happening, is an appropriate starting point for philosophy. Finally, since philosophy, at least metaphysics, is concerned with the question of being, it is wise for a philosophy to begin with wonder, which is, as we have seen Heschel describe it, the act of being amazed "at the unexpectedness of being as such."

Heschel's claim that wonder is the root of knowledge also leads him to the assertion that wisdom is not simply the outcome of reasoning but that reason itself is founded upon the wisdom attained through the insights of wonder. While discursive thinking may enable us to grow in wisdom, it is not, according to Heschel, the primary source of wisdom. He states this conviction most clearly in the following excerpt:

> Much of the wisdom inherent in our consciousness is the root, rather than the fruit, of reason. There are more songs in our souls than the tongue is able to utter. When detached from its original insights, the discursive mind becomes a miser, and when we discover that concepts bring no relief to our outraged conscience and thirst for integrity, we turn to the origin of thought, to the endless shore that lies across the logical. Just as the mind is able to form conceptions supported by sense perception, it can derive insights from the dimension of the ineffable. Insights are the roots of art, philosophy and religion, and must be acknowledged as common and fundamental facts of mental life.[41]

WONDER AS A STATE OF KNOWLEDGE AND MORE

Wonder is not only the root of knowledge; it is also a state of knowledge because it is a cognitive act or insight and "a form of thinking" that sustains insight.[42] Moreover, wonder is "an act that goes beyond knowledge" because it is an attitude that "does not come to an end when knowledge is acquired."[43] In fact, according to Heschel, wonder or "radical amazement is enhanced rather than reduced by the advancement of knowledge," so that, "at whatever climax of thinking we may arrive, we face transcendent significance."[44] Thus, we can also say that wonder is an act that goes beyond knowledge because it is a state of mind in which we are aware of a meaning we cannot fully comprehend. "This, then, is an insight we gain in acts of wonder: not to measure meaning in terms of our own mind, but to sense a meaning infinitely greater than ourselves."[45] Now this statement is very important for understanding the relation between wonder and knowledge in Heschel's thought. It indicates that the two claims under present consideration—that wonder is a state of knowledge and an act that surpasses knowledge—cannot be separated, precisely because the insight attained in wonder is the knowledge that we are in contact with a meaning that exceeds our knowledge. In other words, wonder is a state of mind wherein we know that we are confronted with that which eludes our intellectual grasp, with a meaning that "we apprehend but cannot comprehend."[46] Heschel says: "We must apply all we know about what is given to man's higher incomprehension, to his naked wonder, and what the intuition of the ineffable conveys to our consciousness. Let us remember the fundamental fact of a universal non-discursive perception of the ineffable which is a sense of transcendent meaning, of an awareness that something is meant by the universe which surpasses our power of comprehension."[47] This "perception of the ineffable" or "sense of transcendent meaning" which is given in wonder is "a cognitive insight, since the awareness it evokes adds to our deeper understanding of the world."[48] As such, wonder is an act or state of real knowledge. What is of fundamental importance is the fact that what we cannot comprehend is nonetheless conveyed to our consciousness and that we are aware of transcendent meaning.

The reason why transcendent meaning cannot be comprehended yet can nonetheless be consciously experienced is explained by Heschel in the following way:

> It would be a contradiction in terms to assume that the attainment of transcendent meaning consists in comprehending a notion. Transcendence can never be an object of possession or of comprehension. Yet man can relate himself and be engaged to it. He must know how to court meaning in order to be engaged to it. Love of ultimate meaning is not self-centered but rather a concern to transcend the self. . . . Transcendent meaning must not be reduced to an object of acknowledgment, to saying 'yes' to an idea. The experience of meaning is an experience of vital involvement, not having an idea in mind but living within a spirit surpassing the mind; not an experience of a private reference of meaning, but sharing a dimension open to all human beings. We meet in a stillness of significance, disclosing a fellowship of being related to a concern for meaning. The longing for such experience is part of man's ultimate vocation. . . . The relationship of a human being to ultimate meaning can never be conceived as a possession. . . . Our words do not describe it, our tools do not wield it. But sometimes it seems as if our very being were its description, its secret tool.[49]

For Heschel, then, wonder is a state of knowledge in the sense that it is a cognitive experience, though not an act of comprehension. As such, it is a moment of apprehension, awareness, intuition, and understanding.

So when Heschel speaks of wonder being a form of knowledge, he is referring especially to preconceptual or trans-rational knowledge. Often he uses the term "understanding" rather than "knowledge" in this regard, since "knowledge" tends to imply discursive and notional thinking. Thus, he says:

> We know through induction or inference, we understand through intuition; we know a thing, we understand a personality; we know a fact, we understand a hint. Knowledge implies familiarity with, or even the mastery of something; understanding is an act of interpreting something which we only know by its expression and through inner agreement with it. There is no sympathetic knowledge but there is sympathetic understanding. Understanding, significantly, is a synonym for agreement. It is through agreement that we find a way of understanding.[50]

While in this text Heschel makes a clear distinction, and even a contrast, between knowledge and understanding, and while he often prefers to speak of understanding rather than of knowledge when he discusses the insight attained in wonder, sometimes he does use the word "knowledge" in a less restricted sense and thus, as we have seen, speaks of wonder as a state of knowledge.

When discussing the relation between wonder and knowledge, Heschel refers to wonder not only as a cognitive act or insight but also as a form of thinking. However, in the one instance where he does call wonder a form of thinking he does not offer an explanation of what he means. Nevertheless, the sentence that follows his assertion may be considered a good indication of what he means. That sentence reads as follows: "It [wonder] is not the beginning of knowledge but an act that goes beyond knowledge; it does not come to an end when knowledge is acquired; it is an attitude that never ceases."[51] Now since Heschel says that wonder is "an act that goes beyond knowledge," he seems to mean that wonder as a form of thinking is a way of being consciously aware of transcendent meaning. But if this is all he means, then wonder as a form of thinking is not different from wonder as a preconceptual (though cognitive) insight. Yet elsewhere Heschel speaks not only of preconceptual insight but also of preconceptual thinking. But even in these instances it is difficult to see any difference between the two. In his brief section entitled "Preconceptual Thinking" in *God in Search of Man*,[52] and indeed elsewhere throughout his writings, Heschel seems to use the terms "preconceptual insight" and "preconceptual thinking" synonymously. Yet these terms do possess slightly different connotations. The insights of wonder may come and go; yet wonder as a form of thinking "is an attitude that never ceases." Now whether or not wonder ever ceases, what is important is that wonder as a form of thinking is "an attitude." So we may distinguish between occasional acts of wonder and an enduring attitude of wonder. But why does Heschel call an attitude of wonder a form of thinking? I suggest that he does so precisely because such an attitude is a state of mind, a way of being consciously related to the world; and, furthermore, because thinking for Heschel is nearly co-extensive with living, so that our attitude can be said to be our form of thinking. Concerning the range of thinking, Heschel writes: "We think with all our faculties; our entire living is involved in our thinking. Thus our way of thinking is affected by our way of living, and contemplation is the distillation of one's entire existence. Thinking is a summing up of the truth of our own living."[53] Thus, if we live in a spirit of openness to reality, and with an attitude of concern and amazement, then it can be said that this spirit or attitude is a form of thinking that can be called wonder. And if from time to time in our attitude of wonder we attain flashes of insight, then we can also speak of the insights of wonder. Thus, the word "wonder" can be used to designate both a cognitive insight and a form of thinking.

That insight is something both fleeting and abiding is well stated by Heschel in the following sentence: "Creative insights grow a life-time to last a moment, and yet they last forever."[54] A moment of insight is an experience of wonder; the growth and abidance of insight is wonder as a form of thinking. Both as act and attitude, as a cognitive insight and a form of thinking, wonder is a state of knowledge as well as an experience that goes beyond knowledge.

WONDER AND FAITH

In light of the foregoing presentation and analysis, it is easy to see why Heschel considers wonder an antecedent of religious faith. For as we have seen, it is in wonder that we are amazed "at the unexpectedness of being as such" and thus begin to question the self-sufficiency of the world. When this happens we also begin to perceive the world as an allusion to transcendent meaning. And this awareness of transcendent meaning induces a yearning to transcend our own understanding. It is, therefore, a prerequisite of faith, for as Heschel says, "the soul's urge *to rise above its own wisdom* is the root of religious faith."[55] Wonder initiates such an urge, it is a prerequisite of faith because it is a way toward self-transcendence. And according to Heschel, "faith is an act of man who *transcending himself* responds to him who *transcends the world.*"[56]

In this sense, our concern for God and our understanding for the reality and meaning of God begin in wonder. As Heschel says, "only those who have experienced . . . the voicelessness of a soul struck by wonder are able to enter into the meaning of God, a meaning greater than the mind."[57] Thus, again, the awareness of God begins in wonder, not because wonder alone yields an understanding for the meaning of God but because wonder is a state of soul that nurtures such understanding. Faith, not wonder alone, is that which yields understanding of God. Wonder is a premise; faith, a climax.

Yet wonder not only precedes faith but is also a constitutive element of faith. For any experience that cultivates faith is also an aspect of the experience and life of faith. The experience of wonder is the soil in which faith is rooted, as well as the climate in which faith endures and grows. So while wonder alone does not constitute faith, it is nevertheless an essential feature of faith.

Thus we may conclude that it is in wonder that we see life as sublime and life's origin divine. It is in wonder that we ask, "What are the foundations of the world?" and, when we overcome "conventional notions" and are present to "that which is," it is again in wonder that we begin to sense indebtedness rather than ownership and we come to realize that "the earth is the Lord's" and we the Lord's loved ones. In wonder we hear God's call to cultivate the earth and care for one another. In wonder our response begins. Indeed, wonder is an antecedent of faith.

Awe

In moments of wonder, when we sense the sublime dimension of existence, it is upon mystery that we come and in reverence that we stand. Life's grandeur directs our attention to its mystery; our amazement turns to awe.

Although Heschel does not state it explicitly, there are two levels of awe discernable in his writings: awe as a *response to mystery* and awe as a *response to God*. Since God is a mystery, awe of God includes awe of mystery. But because the mystery is not God, it is possible to feel awe before the mystery of created reality without yet realizing awe of God. Nevertheless, since life's mystery evokes an attitude of awe in which the question of God is raised and is the setting in which the presence of God is disclosed, awe before mystery often gives way to awe of God.

FEAR AND AWE

The Hebrew word *yirah* has two meanings: fear and awe. Heschel makes a clear distinction between them:

> Fear is the anticipation and expectation of evil or pain, as contrasted with hope which is the anticipation of good. Awe, on the other hand, is the sense of wonder and humility inspired by the sublime or felt in the presence of mystery. . . . Awe, unlike fear, does not make us shrink from the awe-inspiring object, but, on the contrary, draws us near to it. This is why awe is compatible with both love and joy. In a sense, awe is the antithesis of fear. To feel "The Lord is my light and my salvation" is to feel "Whom shall I fear?" (Psalms 27:1).[58]

Heschel would agree with Rudolf Otto's celebrated depiction of the *mysterium* as at once *tremendum* and *fascinosum*.[59] Therefore, although Heschel says that awe is "in a sense" the antithesis of fear because it "draws us near to" the awe-inspiring object, he does not reduce awe to *fascination* alone. A feeling of what Otto calls *tremor* is for Heschel also an aspect of awe; not a tremor that "makes us shrink from" the awesome but which humbles us in its presence.[60] In awe we are drawn toward the mystery before which we are diffident and devout. Awe includes both attraction *and* veneration, rapture *and* reserve. It is a yearning love for the divine in whose presence we shudder with adoration. Awe may supersede fear, but it does not remove our blush in the presence of the holy. The type of fear which is the antithesis of awe is that which fills us with horror or despair. But if by "fear" is meant the state of being struck still by life's mystery, silenced by God's overwhelming presence, then in this sense fear is not the antithesis of awe but an aspect of it. Thus we distinguish between profane and reverential fear.

It is indeed important to realize that awe includes both fascination and tremor. Fascination without tremor would result in familiarity without esteem; tremor apart from fascination would be sheer dread. Religious awe in Heschel's sense is not dread, nor is it mere familiarity. Rather it is both captivation and respect, intimacy and acquiescence. This is why Heschel uses the word "reverence" as a synonym for "awe."

A CATEGORICAL IMPERATIVE

It is in the context of discussing awe as a response to mystery that Heschel calls awe "a *categorical imperative*."[61] It is not simply a significant experience, it is a universal requirement for being human. Reality, abounding in mystery, demands such a response. Just as wonder is the appropriate human response to what is wondrous, awe is the only fitting reply to what is awesome or mysterious.

As a categorical imperative, awe is evidence for the realness of the ineffable dimension of life and for its transcendent meaning: "The awareness of transcendent meaning comes with the sense of the ineffable. The *imperative of awe* is its certificate of evidence, a universal response which we experience *not* because we desire to, but because we are stunned and cannot brave the impact of the sublime."[62] By affirming that awe is an imperative of human existence, Heschel avoids the charge that he is inferring an ontological fact (ineffable, transcendent meaning) from a psychological state (awe). "More important than the feeling of awe is the validity and requiredness of awe which remains unchallenged by the mind of man."[63] In an effort to indicate the ontological reality of transcendent meaning, Heschel says: "The feeling of awe may often be the result of a misunderstanding of an ordinary fact; one may be overawed by an artificial spectacle or display of evil power. That objection is, of course, valid. Yet what we infer from is not the actual feeling of awe but the intellectual certainty that in the face of nature's grandeur and mystery we must respond with awe; what we infer from is not a psychological state but a fundamental norm of human consciousness, a *categorical imperative.*"[64]

This statement is important from the standpoint that it shows, in case we need to be reminded, that our experiences are not infallible; thus it awakens us to the fact that beliefs derived solely from experience are subject to error. Furthermore, it shows that despite our fallible experiences and interpretations, we can be assured that the ineffable is real because we know that awe is an imperative. Yet the knowledge that awe is imperative is, in the broad sense, an experience. Why is such experiential knowledge more reliable than the experience of awe itself? As our feelings can be misleading, so can our "intellectual certainty." Yet the fact that this intellectual certainty is shared by so many of the noblest minds in the world suggests the realness of the ineffable meaning before which human beings are certain they must stand in awe.

But Heschel usually suggests that it is apprehension of the divine, not the thought or the intellectual certainty of the divine, that leads us to an awareness of God's reality.[65] Do we have the reverse with regard to the ineffable? Perhaps such a reverse is suggested here, but some pages before the quotation under consideration, Heschel suggests that it is an experience that is the evidence of the reality of the ineffable.[66]

Recognizing this prompts another critical reflection. There is a sense in which, no matter how valuable the argument under consideration, it seems inconsistent with Heschel's basic approach. He says: "What we *infer* from is . . . the intellectual certainty . . . that we must respond with awe." Yet Heschel normally insists that we do not become aware of the ineffable—or certain of its realness—by way of inference but by way of immediate encounter and insight.[67] Of course he never says that insight is infallible. Nonetheless, it is not by way of inference that we become certain of the realness of the ineffable. Perhaps Heschel is using the method of inference here only because he is answering a possible objection. Thus, he invokes an apologetic that is accidental to his own experience and understanding, but which can serve to vindicate rationally his experiential certainty. In this case, he is not being inconsistent, but simply using a different method and terminology in his post-experiential dialogue with those who may raise objections. Even if this is the case, however, it seems that instead of saying that "what we infer from is not the actual feeling of awe but the intellectual certainty that . . . we must respond with awe," it would be more "Heschelian" for Heschel to say that "we do not infer from the actual feeling of awe but we have an understanding for the realness of the ineffable that is given with our knowing that we must respond with awe." It is important to realize that the understanding is "given with," not derived from, our knowing that we must respond with awe. For the ineffable itself must somehow be known if we are to know that, in response to the ineffable, awe is imperative. However, some of us may be more conscious of having to respond with awe than we are of the ineffable itself; that is, we may be conscious of the fact that we should be more aware of mystery, of transcendent meaning. "Many who cannot revere feel reverence for reverence,"[68] says Heschel. "What we feel primarily is our inability to feel adequately."[69] For this reason it is wise to point to the existential requirement of awe as an indication of the ontological fact of the ineffable. So the value of recognizing that awe is a categorical imperative lies mainly in the fact that regardless of how intense or imperfect our response to the ineffable is, we are nevertheless aware of an obligation to respond with awe and to thereby transcend ourselves. We thus attain assurance that the reality which obliges us is meaningful and real.

Another criticism may be advanced. In the quotation we have been considering, Heschel says that "the feeling of awe may often be the result of misunderstanding" and that "one may be overawed by an artificial spectacle or display of evil power." Yet in the light of the fact that Heschel elsewhere describes awe as more than a feeling, as an insight into transcendent meaning,[70] it seems that it would be more appropriate to say: "The feeling we *suppose* to be awe may often be the result of misunderstanding. . . ." Surely, the "awe" that one feels before "a display of evil power" is radically different than the awe one has in the presence of transcendent meaning. Heschel would, of course, agree. In fact, that is his point: there are authentic and inauthentic experiences. So the question is: How can we be certain of the genuineness of our awe? How can we be sure that what we regard as awe is of admirable quality? Heschel would probably reply with one of the answers he proposes for testing the veracity of religious insights: "Oneness is the norm, the standard and the goal. If in the afterglow of a religious insight we can see a way to gather up our scattered lives, to unite what lies in strife—we know it is a guidepost on His Way."[71] If our awe is genuine, if it promotes oneness within ourselves and between ourselves and others, then we can be confident that the mystery to which our awe is a reply is not only real but is replete with transcendent, life-giving meaning.

Thus far it has been shown that awe is a categorical imperative because reality, abounding in mystery, demands such a response. But there is another reason: awe before the mystery of being is imperative because its lack leads to the destruction of being. Without reverence for life, life will soon be no more. "Forfeit your sense of awe, let your conceit diminish your ability to revere, and the universe becomes a market place for you."[72]

Elsewhere, Heschel writes: "Horrified by the discovery of man's power to bring about the annihilation of organic life on this planet, we are today beginning to comprehend that the sense for the sacred is as vital to us as the light of the sun; that the enjoyment of beauty, possessions and safety in civilized society depends upon man's sense for the sacredness of life, upon his reverence for this spark of light in the darkness of selfishness; that once we permit this spark to be quenched, the darkness falls upon us like thunder."[73] Awe, then, or reverence, is a categorical imperative; it is a prerequisite of ethical living, which is, in turn, a prerequisite for the survival of humanity. Where reverence for life abounds, so do justice, peace, and harmony—the goals of ethics. Where reverence is wanting, violence, injustice, and war prevail.

Moreover, awe is a categorical imperative because it is an act or attitude by which we relate to God and is, as such, "the beginning of wisdom." It is primarily when discussing the awe of God that Heschel treats awe as a way to wisdom.[74]

THE WAY TO WISDOM

"*The beginning of awe is wonder, and the beginning of wisdom is* awe."[75] Whereas some people might tend to regard awe as an intellectual resignation, an end to wisdom, in the Bible awe is regarded as a way to wisdom, a way of understanding. "The awe of the Lord is the beginning of wisdom," exclaims the Psalmist (111:10). And in the Book of Job (28:28) we find a complete equation: "The awe of the Lord, that is wisdom." Therefore, awe is more than an emotional reaction to the unknown and the overwhelming. "Awe is a way of being in rapport with the mystery of all reality," says Heschel, and "is itself an act of insight into a meaning greater than ourselves."[76]

"The foundations of the world are not of this world."[77] Nor can a true understanding of this world be confined to this world. In order to understand the world we must seek an understanding of its foundation. God is the world's foundation, and its ultimate meaning as well. True wisdom, therefore, cannot be found apart from God. "Ultimate meaning and ultimate wisdom are not found within the world but in God, and the only way to wisdom is . . . through our relationship to God. That relationship is *awe*."[78] It would be neither uncommon nor startling to hear someone claim that "a person who wants to understand God must seek to understand the world" or that "someone who wishes to relate to God must relate to the world." After all, it is in and through creation that we meet the Creator. Heschel obviously agrees with such a view. Yet his claim is more radical: "He who wishes to understand the world must seek to understand

God."[79] True wisdom about the world is, then, a matter of having an understanding of the source and the goal of the world which is God. Relationship with God, then, is a prerequisite for a genuine relationship with God's creation.

While it is true that to understand God we must seek to understand the world, it would be wrong to conclude that we can somehow attain an understanding of the world but stop short of an understanding of God. But why is such a conclusion wrong? It seems, rather, to be a confession of humility, and it may be just that. Yet it is incorrect to assume that we can understand the world apart from somehow understanding its foundation, apart from an understanding of God. This is because "all reality is involved in the will and thought of God."[80] The objection might be that there are many intelligent atheists who know a great deal about the world. Why, then, find fault with the conclusion that an understanding of the world can be attained apart from an understanding of God?

Here we must call to mind a fundamental distinction between knowing about the world and having an understanding for the significance of the world. Knowing the function of things is not the same as understanding their meaning. This is not meant to suggest that atheists have no understanding for the significance of the world. But it seems that a monotheist has to maintain that where an atheist does have such understanding there is an "unknowing" understanding of God. Heschel maintains that "we often know Him unknowingly and fail to know Him when insisting upon knowing."[81] Thus, the point is not that monotheists understand the world while atheists do not. Rather, wherever there is an understanding for the significance of the world there is an understanding for God—whether belief in God is professed or not.

The meaning of things is often disclosed to those who study their function; but knowing the function does not quarantee an understanding of what the things stand for, just as knowing many facts about another person does not assure an understanding of that person. Yet someone who knows very little about the data of another person's life may understand that person very well. Thus, it is possible to be an expert concerning the mechanics of things without understanding the God for whom these things stand, to whom these things point. And it is also possible to have an understanding of God while having little knowledge of the mechanics of the things of God's creation. True wisdom concerning the world is a matter of understanding the transcendent reality to which the world points and for which it stands, and that is a matter of understanding the reality of God upon which the world is founded and in which it is sustained. From this point of view we can begin to see why Heschel maintains that an understanding of God is the condition for the possibility of an understanding of the world.

There is, of course, a presumptuous way of claiming an understanding of God, but there is also a way of humble testimony. It is presumptuous to think that we can conquer the secret of God; it is a confession of gratitude and faith to say that God has graced us with an appreciation of God's concern and challenge. The understanding of God that is born in awe is not a matter of grasping the essence of God. It is an understanding that comes in the wake of love: a sympathy for divine dreams, an appreciation of divine deeds. To be in awe of God is to see things from a divine perspective, to share in a wisdom greater than our own. In Heschel's words: "True wisdom is participation in the wisdom of God. Some people may regard as wisdom 'an uncommon degree of common sense.' To us, wisdom is the ability to look at things from the point of view of God, sympathy with the divine pathos, the identification of the will with the will of God."[82] If left to our own striving we would never find God. But our quest for God is met by God's search for us. Indeed, it is God who incites our quest, reveals the way, and fulfills our destiny.

AWE AND FAITH

In light of the foregoing exposition, it is no wonder that Heschel sees a close connection between awe and faith. In fact, by saying that awe *is* our relationship to God, Heschel comes close to equating awe with faith.[83] This, of course, only applies to awe of God, not to awe of mystery itself. It is obvious that awe before mystery is not in itself a matter of faith, but may be an antecedent of faith if it sparks the awareness of divine presence in mystery. Yet awe of God seems to be not an antecedent but an element of faith. The question that arises is whether when Heschel says "awe precedes faith" he means not only awe of mystery but also awe of God. If he means that the latter also precedes faith in what sense can this be understood?

Since Heschel also maintains that "praise precedes faith"[84] he probably does mean that awe of God somehow precedes faith in God. Rather than now offer an explanation of how this might be understood, in the next chapter I shall deal with the question of how praise is an antecedent of faith. And since praise of God includes awe of God, this question will, by implication, include the question of how awe of God precedes faith.

7

Indebtedness and Praise

Religion has been defined as a feeling of absolute dependence. We come closer to an understanding of religion by defining one of its roots as a sense of personal indebtedness.[1]
Praise precedes faith. First we sing, then we believe. The fundamental issue is not faith but sensitivity and praise, being ready for faith.[2]

Wonder and awe are not the summit of human experience. As grandeur and mystery bespeak divine glory, wonder and awe give rise to grateful worship. The glory that fills the world is a source of religious faith because it moves those who perceive it to indebtedness and praise.

Although praise is an expression of indebtedness, and indebtedness a part of praise, we may distinguish between them and explore the meaning of each in turn, examining why they are for Heschel antecedents of faith.

Indebtedness

Within our wonder and awe before the sublime mystery of existence, we begin to realize that both the world we behold and our very selves who are privileged to perceive and be a part of its miraculous unfolding are precious gifts for which we must be forever grateful. Moreover, within our wonder and awe we begin to perceive more than the sublime mystery of being. This is because the sublime mystery alludes to a divine glory that is experienced as a transcendent concern and challenge. In the presence of such glory, wonder and awe alone are insufficient. In responding to the divine concern and challenge, our wonder and awe become suffused with indebtedness. "Endless wonder unlocks an innate sense of indebtedness. . . . Within our awe we only know that all we own we owe."[3]

173

WHAT TO DO WITH WONDER AND AWE

Wonder and awe are antecedents of religious faith because, as we have seen, they are moments charged with transcendent meaning, moments in which we wrestle with life's ultimate question and in which a sense of indebtedness wells up within our souls. According to Heschel, then, religion or religious faith is the result of what we do with our ultimate wonder and our moments of awe.[4] That is to say, religion is an answer to the ultimate question which arises in wonder and awe.[5] And since the ultimate question is experienced, not as one which we ourselves raise on our own accord, but as a question addressed to us,[6] for this reason we realize our indebtedness, our obligation to respond. If the question was merely our own we would not be required to answer, and our response would not constitute religion. However, according to Heschel, "the more deeply we meditate, the more clearly we realize that the question we ask is a question we are being asked; that *man's question about God is God's question of man*."[7] Because it is God's question, the answer is not a philosophical conjecture but a religious response. "Religion, the end of isolation, begins with a consciousness that something is asked of us. It is in that tense, eternal asking in which the soul is caught and in which man's answer is elicited."[8]

> The soul is endowed with a sense of indebtedness, and wonder, awe and fear unlock that sense of indebtedness. Wonder is the state of our being asked.
>
> In spite of our pride, in spite of our acquisitiveness, we are driven by an awareness that something is asked of us; that we are asked to wonder, to revere, to think and to live in a way that is compatible with the grandeur and mystery of living.
>
> What gives birth to religion is not intellectual curiosity but the fact and experience of our being asked.
>
> All that is left to us is a choice—to answer or to refuse to answer. Yet the more deeply we listen, the more we become stripped of the arrogance and callousness which alone would enable us to refuse. We carry a load of marvel, wishing to exchange it for the simplicity of knowing what to live for, a load which we can never lay down nor continue to carry not knowing where.
>
> If awe is rare, if wonder is dead, and the sense of mystery defunct, then the problem what to do with awe, wonder and mystery does not exist, and one does not sense being asked. The awareness of being asked is easily repressed, for it is an echo of the intimation that is small and still. It will not, however, remain forever subdued. The day comes when the still small intimation becomes "like the wind and storm, fulfilling His word."[9]

Without wonder and awe we would never sense our being asked the ultimate question—"what to live for"?—and never would we realize our personal indebtedness. Yet while wonder and awe admit of varying degrees of intensity during our lives, the spirit of indebtedness can remain strong even when wonder and awe are less intense. What we do with wonder and awe is a matter of what we do to keep them aflame: "we are asked to wonder, to revere." It is also a matter of what we do with our lives even when wonder and awe burn low. The moments may be rare when we are wonderfully and awe-fully alive to the ultimate question, but the way of indebtedness aroused by wonder and awe should remain constant. What we do with our wonder and awe is a matter of what we do in wonder and awe—that is, how we respond to the question confronting us therein—and it is a matter of how we remain faithful to that response.

TO BE IS TO BE INDEBTED

When in the face of the grandeur and mystery of reality we are struck with wonder and awe, we begin to realize that "the foundations of the world are not of this world."[10] Coinciding with this realization is the awareness that the self is not its own, nor is any part or even the whole of the universe the ultimate source of the self.[11] And when we experience this world and ourselves as precious gifts, then we know that to be is to be indebted. Furthermore, it is not only the awareness of the world's transcendent origin that leads us to a spirit of indebtedness; it is even more so the awareness of a transcendent and gracious presence that makes us indebted for being alive. According to Heschel, "to sense that all existence is embraced by a spiritual presence" is to learn "that life is not a property of the self."[12] Moreover, the awareness of this transcendent, spiritual presence also involves the awareness of an existential challenge or demand: "The certainty of being exposed to a presence not of the world is a fact of human existence. But such certainty does not find its fulfillment in esthetic contemplation; it is astir with a demand to live in a way that is worthy of that presence."[13] Heschel's logic is clear: the fact that we are exposed to a gracious and challenging transcendent presence fills us with the realization that life is something for which we are indebted, and this realization carries with it the awareness of a requirement to live responsively and responsibly.

Countering the contemporary mood and what many may regard as natural or human instinct, Heschel asserts: "The world is such that in its face one senses owingness rather than ownership."[14] And what we owe is not only what we have but also what we are. Even what is most intimately ours is not ultimately ours: "I am endowed with a will, but the will is not mine; I am endowed with freedom but it is a freedom imposed on the will. Life is something that visits my body, a transcendent loan; I have neither initiated nor conceived its worth and meaning. The essence of what I am is not mine. *I am what is not mine.*"[15] This statement arises from a profound experience of moral and religious conscience. It is by no means a statement of determinism; it is a recognition of being created. Heschel affirms a life of freedom for which we are indebted, and he also recognizes it to be a life that demands responsibility. Being human is neither the result of chance nor of necessity; nor is it a combination of the two. Being is the result of creation, and creation is the expression of divine concern.[16] With this realization dawns the awareness of being indebted. Heschel's view is explained by way of a response to Martin Heidegger:

> Heidegger's rhetorical question, "Has the Dasein, as such, ever freely decided and will it ever be able to decide as to whether to come into existence or not?" has been answered long ago: "It is against your will that you are born, it is against your will that you live, and it is against your will that you are bound to give account. . . ." The transcendence of human being is disclosed here as life imposed upon, as imposition to give account, as imposition of freedom. The transcendence of being is commandment, being here and now is obedience.
>
> I have not brought my being into being. Nor was I thrown into being. My being is obeying the saying "Let there be!"
>
> Commandment and expectation lie dormant in the recesses of being and come to light in the consciousness of being human. What Adam hears first is a command.
>
> Against the conception of the world as something just here, the Bible insists that the world is creation. Over all being stand the words: Let there be! And there was, and there is. To be is to obey the commandment of creation. God's word is at stake in being. There is a cosmic piety in sheer being. What is endures as a response to a command.
>
> Philosophically the primacy of creation over being means that the "ought" precedes the "is." The order of things goes back to an "order" of God. . . .
>
> The loss of the sense of significant being is due to the loss of the commandment of being. Being is obedience, a response. "Thou art" precedes "I am." I am because I am called upon to be.[17]

The command "Let there be!" is not only a call into being; it is a call into "significant being," into meaning and value. "Being created implies being born in value, being endowed with meaning, receiving value."[18] Moreover, the command has not only to do with the origin of being and meaning. It is, rather, a continual call into significant being, into meaningful living. Indeed, it is this persistent command that awakens us to the fact that life is a gift from the very beginning. It is because we sense the fact that we are commanded on all levels of our existence that we realize even the origin of our existence is a result of a command.

> Of one thing . . . I am sure. There is a challenge that I can never evade, in moments of failure as in moments of achievement. Man is inescapably,

essentially challenged on all levels of his existence. It is in his being challenged that he discovers himself as a human being. Do I exist as a human being? My answer is: *I am commanded—therefore I am.* There is a built-in *sense of indebtedness in the consciousness of man,* an awareness of *owing grátitude,* of being *called upon* at certain moments to reciprocate, to answer, to live in a way which is compatible with the grandeur and mystery of living.[19]

Thus, for Heschel, the sense of indebtedness is more than a mere feeling; it is, rather, an essential component of being human. He explains this as follows:

Indebtedness is given with our being human because our being is not simply being, our being is being created. Being created means, as said above, that the "ought" precedes the "is."

Indebtedness is given with our very being. It is not derived from conceptions; it lives in us as an awareness before it is conceptualized or clarified in content. It means having a task, being called. It experiences living as receiving, not only as taking. Its content is gratitude for a gift received. It is more than a biological give-and-take relationship.

Indebtedness is the pathos of being human, selfawareness of the self as committed; it is given with the awareness of existence. Man cannot think of himself as human without being conscious of his indebtedness. Thus it is not a mere feeling, but rather a constitutive feature of being human. To eradicate it would be to destroy what is human in man.[20]

INDEBTEDNESS AND REQUIREDNESS

It is clear from the above that Heschel's sense of indebtedness includes or is accompanied by what he calls "the sense of requiredness."[21] The distinction between the two is not as clear-cut in Heschel's writings as may at first be assumed. True, indebtedness, the state of owing gratitude, may seem to pertain more to the realm of being, while requiredness pertains to the realm of doing; that is, we are indebted for being created, for receiving life as a gift, and we are consequently required to live in such a way that we recognize life as a gift, we are required to live responsively and responsibly. Yet in Heschel's view, as we have seen explained in response to Heidegger, we are also, in a sense, required to be; that is, we are commanded or called into being. On the other hand, we are indebted for being required, for being called upon, since it is in response to the transcendent requirement that we realize the transcendence of being human. While it may commonly be thought that we are indebted for having our needs satisfied, for being cared for, Heschel suggests that we are, or should be, primarily indebted for being needed, for being asked to care, for being called upon to serve the authentic needs of others and to assist God in the redemption of the world.[22] Thus does Heschel speak of "gratefulness . . . for the gift of our unearned right to serve, to adore, and to fulfill."[23]

Since the glory of God is revealed and experienced both as a divine concern and a divine challenge,[24] it is only appropriate that the response thereto be described in terms of a sense of indebtedness and requiredness. We are indebted for the divine concern and required to answer the divine challenge. And just as the divine concern is always accompanied by a challenge or just as the divine challenge is always a signal of concern, so is indebtedness always accompanied by requiredness which is in turn an indication of indebtedness.

Since the sense of requiredness is an essential feature of indebtedness— or intrinsically related to it—it is just as true to say of this sense of requiredness what has been said of the sense of indebtedness: it is more than a feeling; it is an essential component of being human. Heschel explains his view as follows:

> The sense of requiredness is as essential to being human as his capacity for reasoning. It is an error to equate the two as it is a distortion to derive the sense of requiredness from the capacity for reasoning.
>
> The sense of requiredness is not an afterthought; it is given with being human; not added to it but rooted in it.
>
> What is involved in authentic living is not only an intuition of meaning but a sensitivity to demand, not a purpose but an expectation. Sensitivity to demands is as inherent in being human as physiological functions are in human being.
>
> A person is he of whom demands can be made, who has the capacity to respond to what is required, not only to satisfy his needs and desires. Only a human being is said to be responsible. Responsibility is not something man imputes to himself; he is a self by virtue of his capacity for responsibility, and he would cease to be a self if he were to be deprived of responsibility.
>
> The qualities that constitute personhood, such as love, the passion for meaning, the capacity to praise, etc., can hardly be regarded as demands of reason, though reason must offer direction as to what is worthy of being loved or praised. Their justification is in their being required for being human.
>
> Here is the basic difference between the Greek and the biblical conception of man. To the Greek mind, man is above all a rational being; rationality makes him compatible with the cosmos. To the biblical mind, man is above all a commanded being, a being of whom demands may be made. The central problem is not: What is being? but rather: What is required of me?[25]

Being created means that we are required to live in a way that attests to the grace of life for which we are indebted. Being human, therefore, is impossible without a sense of indebtedness and requiredness.

The most important experience in the life of every person is, then, the discovery that something is asked of that person.[26] Some people encounter the question at every turn; it is as evident as the things through which it echoes: "There is a question that follows me wherever I turn. What is expected of me? What is demanded of me? What we encounter is not only flowers and stars, mountains and walls. Over and above all things is a sublime expectation, a waiting for. With every new child born a new expectation enters the world."[27]

But even those for whom the question is less obvious are somewhat aware of their being called upon. "Every human being has had a moment in which he sensed a mysterious waiting for him."[28] This is life's most important experience because "we cannot survive unless we know what is asked of us"[29] and because "meaning is found in understanding the demand and responding to it."[30] The essence of being human is not only in what we are but in what we are able to be.[31] As human beings we realize ourselves in transcending ourselves; we discover the meaning and dignity of being human by transcending our own interests, needs, and desires and by responding to the transcendent challenge with which we are faced. This transcendent challenge is, in Heschel's view, a divine challenge, which is perceived primarily in and through human situations. Throughout his writings Heschel stresses the fact that the divine challenge—the challenge to overcome inequity, injustice, suffering and oppression—is discerned primarily in the pleading of other human beings, in the anguished cry of the oppressed and the prophetic outcry made on their behalf. In responding to their appeal we are, knowingly or not, responding to God's command to "love thy neighbor as thyself." And in loving other persons we are, knowingly or not, also loving God. "True love of man," says Heschel, "is clandestine love of God."[32] Such love is not a mere feeling, it is a response to an objective requirement to be sensitive to other people's feelings, particularly to their suffering. It is, then, "the index of one's own humanity,"[33] a requirement for being human. Thus, "the reality of being human depends upon man's sense of indebtedness being a response to transcendent requiredness."[34]

Throughout Heschel's writings, and from what has been presented here, it is clear that to be indebted is, in his view, to be indebted to God; to be commanded is to be commanded by God. In experiencing life as a gift that comes with demands we experience the Giver of life who requires us to live in accord with the sublime mystery of life.

It is true, and Heschel recognizes this, that some of us may be aware of our indebtedness and requiredness without being consciously aware of the gracious and commanding God. Some of us may be grateful for life and have a real sense of moral responsibility without explicitly recognizing the living God from whom life with its demands proceeds. But then Heschel would ask, To *whom* are we indebted and by *whom* are we commanded? Since a gift implies a giver and a command implies someone who commands, Heschel's question obviously would not be, to *what* are we indebted and by *what* are we commanded? To be sure, giving and commanding imply a subject who is alive, personal, and concerned. And the subject of this concern is the living God. Thus, to sense our indebtedness and requiredness is to realize that we dwell not only in the realm of space and time but also in the sphere of God's concern and challenge. And this realization, more than anything else, is what characterizes authentic religious consciousness. Therefore, in an obvious reply to Friedrich Schleiermacher, Heschel maintains that rather than defining religion as "a feeling of absolute dependence" (though this is an aspect of it) "we come closer to an understanding of religion by defining one of its roots as a sense of personal indebtedness."[35] And since the sense of indebtedness includes or is accompanied by the sense of requiredness, it might also be said that religion has as one of its antecedents the sense of requiredness. Indeed, Heschel says as much when he claims that "religion begins with the certainty that something is asked of us, that there are ends which are in need of us,"[36] that "faith comes with the discovery of being needed, of having a vocation, of being commanded"[37] and that "faith is . . . the response to a challenge which no one can forever ignore."[38]

INDEBTEDNESS AND EMBARRASSMENT

The sense of indebtedness is accompanied not only by the sense of requiredness but also by what Heschel calls "the sense of embarrassment."[39] By this he is not referring to any ordinary bashfulness or timidity but to the humbling awareness of the disparity between the splendor of what is and the poverty of our appreciation thereof, or between the misery of what is and the grandeur of what ought to be.

> How embarrassing for man to be the greatest miracle on earth and not to understand it! How embarrassing for man to live in the shadow of greatness and to ignore it, to be a contemporary of God and not to sense it. . . .
> Embarrassment is the awareness of an incongruity of character and challenge, of perceptivity and reality, of knowledge and understanding, of mystery and comprehension. . . .
> Embarrassment is a response to the discovery that in living we either replenish or frustrate a wondrous expectation. It involves an awareness of the grandeur of existence that may be wasted, of a waiting ignored, of unique moments missed. It is a protection against the outburst of inner evils, against arrogance, *hybris,* self-deification. The end of embarrassment would be the end of humanity.[40]

Since Heschel believes that "the end of embarrassment would be the end of humanity," he obviously regards the sense of embarrassment, like that of indebtedness and requiredness, as an essential component of being human. It is the countercheck to our *"false sense of sovereignty* which fills the world with terror."[41] As such, "what the world needs is a sense of embarrassment."[42] Cause for embarrassment abounds: "A world full of grandeur has been converted into a carnival. There are slums, disease, and starvation all over the world, and we are building more luxurious hotels in Las Vegas. . . . Modern man has the power and the wealth to overcome poverty and disease, but he has no wisdom to overcome suspicion. We are guilty of misunderstanding the meaning of existence; we are guilty of distorting our goals and misrepresenting our souls."[43] Not only are we guilty, but "the guilt is endless," says Heschel, for "the world is drenched in blood."[44] Yet we need not despair, since "there is always a way that leads out of guilt: repentance or turning to God."[45]

Embarrassment is the beginning of repentance. "Sensitivity to God is given to a broken heart."[46] And since faith includes sensitivity to God, it may be said that "faith begins in embarrassment."[47]

INDEBTEDNESS, CONSCIENCE, AND GOD

The sense of indebtedness, accompanied as it is by the sense of requiredness and embarrassment, is another term for moral and religious conscience.[48] Louvain's Jan H. Walgrave has shown that "there is a philosophical tradition according to which conscience is a privileged locus of religious experience."[49] This tradition, claims Walgrave, includes the likes of Kant, Newman, Kierkegaard, Scheler, and Tolstoy. To this list may be added Heschel's name.

"In the wake of religious insight," says Heschel, "we retain an awareness that the transcendent God is *He to whom our conscience is open.*"[50] That is to say, "God is *He to whom we are accountable.*" Heschel vividly describes this experience of God through conscience in the following way:

> We are exposed to the challenge of a power that, not born of our will nor installed by it, robs us of independence by its judgment of the rectitude or depravity of our actions, by its gnawing at our heart when we offend against its injunctions. It is as if there were no privacy within ourselves, no possibility of either retreat or escape, no place in us in which to bury the remains of guilt-feelings. There is a voice that reaches everywhere, knowing no mercy, digging in the burial-places of charitable forgetfulness.[51]

But the question may be asked, How do we know that the "voice" which reaches our conscience is really the "voice" of God? Could it not simply be our own inner voice or the voice of society within us (the voice of internalized social demands)? To be sure, the *specific demands* of conscience may be either self-induced or stem from society, but this does not mean that we are accountable only to self or society. Heschel realizes that the origin of these specific demands is ambiguous; yet the fact that we and society as a whole are obliged to answer for our conduct is indubitably certain. We know for certain that we are called upon to protect and enhance human life, to embrace goodness and truth and to promote peace on earth. And we also know that if this is to be accomplished justice and love are required of us. Yet we are not always so sure of how justice and love are to be actualized in given situations: "Man's consciousness of requiredness is, of course, no proof that the particular forms in which he tries to attain his moral or religious ends are absolutely valid. However, the fact of such consciousness may serve as an index of his being committed to striving for valid ends. Man's conception of these ends is subject to change; his being committed endures forever."[52]

Some of the demands of our conscience may indeed be self-imposed. But the someone to whom we are ultimately accountable cannot be the self, for "the essential admission of the soul is that the self is not its final authority."[53] This, of course, is because the self is not self-sufficient; it is not its own source nor can it stand alone. Nor is society the final authority to whom we are accountable, because society likewise is not its own source of meaning and worth. "Human existence cannot derive its ultimate meaning from society, because society itself is in need of meaning."[54] While human beings are indeed accountable to each other, society—and the whole of humankind—is ultimately accountable to its transcendent source of meaning.

So the authority to whom we are ultimately accountable must transcend both self and society. And that authority cannot be simply an abstract law or an impersonal force. For, as already mentioned, the authority to whom we are accountable must be a personally concerned giver of life to whom we are indebted and by whom we are commanded.[55] Each of us, and the whole of society and humankind, must therefore be accountable to a living and personal Creator, to Someone who cares enough to grant us life and to challenge us to promote freely and responsibly the life with which we have been graced.

Heschel is emphatic about this: our conscience is not God.[56] God is beyond our conscience, yet our conscience may be open to God. Our conscience may be misguided (and misguiding), but it may also be a locus of experiencing God: "A force from beyond our conscience cries at man, reminding and admonishing that the wanton will fail in rebellion against the good. He who is willing to be an echo to that pleading voice opens his life to the comprehension of the unseen in the desert of indifference. It is God who sues for our devotion, constantly, persistently, who goes out to meet us as soon as we long to know Him."[57]

Our conscience is not God, but the goal of moral and religious living is to let God guide our conscience. Our task is to form our conscience according to God's design for humankind; not to project our own concerns onto God, but to make God's concern our own. This is why, for Heschel, Paul Tillich's definition of religion or faith as "a state of being ultimately concerned" must be corrected when it comes to prophetic religion. In an obvious, though unnoted response to Tillich, Heschel claims that "prophetic religion may be defined, not as what man does with his ultimate concern, but rather what man does with God's concern."[58] As Heschel points out, and Tillich himself realizes, human beings might unfortunately be concerned ultimately with what is not truly ultimate.[59] Prophetic religion, on the contrary, is a way of being ultimately concerned with God and radically committed to God's concern for justice, compassion, and love—a concern revealed through the prophets and to our conscience.

The experience of God through conscience—through a conscience formed by Torah and the prophets—not only enables us to correct our understanding of religious faith but also to understand more deeply the meaning of the God to whom our faith is a response. "Knowledge of God is knowledge of living with God,"[60] a knowledge born in a conscience open to God's presence and formed by God's Word. And the knowledge thus attained enables us to realize that God is not simply a notion arrived at through speculative thinking but an eternal challenge confronting us on all levels of our existence. In Heschel's own prophetic outcry: "The word God is an assault, a thunder in the soul, not a notion to play with."[61] Moreover, this God of conscience is not simply "being itself" or—to use Tillich's metaphorical expression for this same definition—"the ground of being." Rather, according to Heschel, God is "the transcendent care for being."[62] This "transcendent care" is what really matters to us: "The supreme issue is not the question whether in the infinite darkness there is a ground of being which is an object of man's ultimate concern, but whether the reality of God confronts us with a pathos—God's ultimate concern with good and evil; whether God is mysteriously present in the events of history; whether being is transcended by creation; whether creation is transcended by care; whether my life is dependent on God's care; whether in the course of my life I come upon a trace of His guidance."[63] Defined as "being itself" or as "the ground of being," God is all-inclusive, embracing both good and evil. Yet as "the transcendent care for being," God is the source of goodness, challenging us to share in the divine redemptive task of overcoming evil with good, falsehood with truth, hatred with love.

In his last book, appropriately entitled *A Passion for Truth,* Heschel compares the ground of being with the God of conscience:

Those who teach that God is the ground of being have been acclaimed. We need feel no discomfort when God is called the ground of being. But those who insist that He is above the ground of being, that He is the source of qualms, conscience, and compassion, find very few ears.

Truth is severe, harsh, demanding. We would rather hide our face in the sand than be confronted by it. "To live means to be indebted"—who wants to hear this? "I am commanded, therefore I am"—who knows how to cherish it?[64]

Heschel warns us that "an idea or a theory of God can easily become a substitute for God, impressive to the mind when God as a living reality is absent from the soul."[65] If we close our conscience to God's assault, then God will be absent from our soul—no matter what idea of God we may entertain. Heschel was anguished by the demise of conscience and the absence of God. His words continue to haunt us today: "The decay of conscience fills the air with a pungent smell. Good and evil, which were once as distinguishable as day and night, have become a blurred mist. But that mist is man-made. God is not silent. He has been silenced."[66]

INDEBTEDNESS AND FAITH

For some people, a conscious awareness of God's presence may be given with the sense of indebtedness, requiredness, and embarrassment. For others, the sense of indebtedness, requiredness, and embarrassment may lead to the awareness that it is to God that we are ultimately indebted, it is from God that the ultimate requirement proceeds, and it is before God that we cannot belie our ultimate embarrassment at the inadequacy of our gratitude, the infrequency of our responsiveness.

It is obvious that the sense of indebtedness in and of itself, without an explicit awareness that it is God to whom we are ultimately indebted, is not yet religious faith but may be an antecedent of faith insofar as it prepares us to seek the whence of our indebtedness. But what of conscious indebtedness to God, the explicit awareness that it is God to whom we are ultimately indebted? Is this but an antecedent of faith? Might this not be an aspect of faith? These are questions that Heschel himself does not raise. But we can imagine him answering them thus: Is faith in God not more than the sense of owing gratitude to God? Is it not more than the sense of having to respond to the challenge of God? Is faith not the active expression of gratitude, the actual acceptance of the divine challenge? As already stated, religion has as "one of its roots . . . a sense of personal indebtedness." But the sense of indebtedness is not yet religion. Even the sense of indebtedness to God precedes faith in God. Faith is the expression of indebtedness, not just the sense of it. And while faith is a response to a divine challenge, the awareness of that challenge, the sense of requiredness, is not yet faith. Even the realization that the challenge proceeds from God is not quite the same as faith in God. Faith is the response to the God from whom the challenge proceeds. And embarrassment before God? This is not faith, even though "faith begins in embarrassment." The sense of indebtedness, requiredness, and embarrassment—even as felt in relation to God—is not faith itself but is an antecedent of faith in God. But after faith emerges, the sense of indebtedness, requiredness, and embarrassment that sparked it continues to enlighten it. What was an antecedent of faith becomes, after the dawn of faith, one of its essential features. This is why, for example, Heschel is able to claim that "embarrassment not only precedes religious commitment; it is the touchstone of religious existence."[67] The sense of indebtedness, including or accompanied by the sense of requiredness and embarrassment, not only precedes religious faith but also nurtures it. The sense of indebtedness is, therefore, both an antecedent of faith and an ingredient in the life of faith.

"To the sense of indebtedness, the meaning of existence lies in reciprocity."[68] And since "faith is reciprocity,"[69] the meaning of existence lies in faith, in the attempt "to pay the existential debt."[70] As an act of reciprocating for the love of God disclosed in our existence, "Faith is," says Heschel, "a dynamic, personal act, flowing between the heart of man and the love of God."[71] As such, faith presupposes the sense of indebtedness to God. Indeed, it is this sense of indebtedness that fosters the genesis of faith.

Praise

"The whole earth is full of His glory" and "praise is our first response," says Heschel. "Aflame with the inability to say what His presence means, we can only sing, we can only utter words of adoration."[72] Being human involves the sense of indebtedness as well as the expression of it. Praise is indebtedness proclaimed; it is the response to the glory in relation to which we sense our ultimate indebtedness.

AN ACT OF ULTIMATE CONCERN

There are many things for which to be indebted, first of all for the very fact of being. But being would lack meaning—in fact it would not be—were it not for the glory in which it abides. "The glory is not an exception but an aura that lies about all being, a spiritual setting of reality."[73] As we have seen, the glory of which Heschel speaks is the presence of God. Moreover, the presence of God which fills the world and in which the world abides is, in effect, the reality of God's concern for the world. The word "glory" is synonym for divine concern. It is fitting, then, that the ultimate act of praise or worship, which is our "first response" to the glory, is described by Heschel as an act of "ultimate concern."[74]

Every human being is ultimately concerned with something or someone. "Such ultimate concern is an act of worship, an act of acknowledging in the most intense manner the supremacy of the issue."[75] Therefore, worship is "a fundamental fact of human existence."[76] Every human being must have an ultimate object of worship, though each is free to decide what or who that might be. "No one is without a sense of awe, a need to adore, an urge to worship," asserts Heschel. "The question only is what to adore, or more specifically, what object is worthy of our supreme worship."[77] Since we are ultimately indebted to God, God alone is worthy of our worship. We may be concerned with many things, with many people. In fact, being human involves a myriad of such concerns. But if we are monotheists, our ultimate concern is with God. Many things and many people may merit our praise. But God alone is worthy of our worship, our ultimate praise.

THE HARVEST OF LOVE

Human concern for God is the only appropriate response to God's concern for humanity. Praise, as an act of such concern, is the fitting human response to divine glory, the presence of God's concern. "Engagement to His concern comes about through attachment to the essentials of worship. Its meaning is disclosed in acts of worship."[78]

Since praise is an act of concern, and since love is another word for concern, Heschel is able to say that "praise is the harvest of love."[79] To be indebted for the glory that pervades and embays all being is to be indebted for the divine love with which existence is graced. And the only way "to pay the existential debt" for divine love is to love God in return. "He whose soul is charged with awareness of God earns his inner livelihood by a passionate desire to pour his life into the eternal wells of love."[80] Praise, as an act of love, is a privileged way of doing just this, of communing with divine love.

"We praise for the privilege of being."[81] Yet our hearts crave more than being. What we long for is the meaning of being, and this is "a quest for that which surpasses being, expressing insufficiency of sheer being."[82] We worship for the wonder of living. "Living is a situation, the content of which is much richer than the concept of being."[83] Nevertheless, "living is not enough by itself."[84] "Life would be preposterous if not for the love it confers."[85] The meaning of being and of living is found in love. So we praise and worship God not only for being alive but, even more, for receiving love and for the ability to give love. "Love is what brings the world forward," says Heschel.[86] "In loving we intone God's unfinished song."[87]

Since love is the meaning of life, and "praise is the harvest of love," it may be said of praise that "it is the quintessence of life."[88]

A KINSHIP OF PRAISE

As an act of love for God, praise is always a personal, and in some sense even a private, response to God. It is to be understood, in Heschel's words, "as an enterprise of the individual self, as a personal engagement, as an intimate, confidential act."[89]

But praise is never a merely solitary act. For instance, "a Jew never worships as an isolated individual but *as a part of the Community of Israel. Yet it is within the heart of every individual that prayer takes place.*"[90] And not only does a Jew—or anyone else—pray as an individual in the context of a particular community but also in league with all other human beings who do now or who ever have raised their hearts to God. "Every act of worship is an act of participating in an eternal service, in the service of all souls of all ages."[91]

Moreover, the "eternal service" of praise in which we partake extends beyond the realm of the human community. "We are not alone in our acts of praise. Wherever there is life, there is silent worship," declares Heschel.[92] "Our kinship with nature is a kinship of praise. All beings praise God. We live in a community of praise."[93]

It is our privilege and our vocation as human beings to articulate the "silent worship" of all things, to intone the score of eternal cosmic praise. "The cosmos is a congregation in need of a Cantor. . . . It is man who is the Cantor of the universe, and in whose life the secret of cosmic prayer is disclosed."[94] Heschel says: "When we sing, we sing for all things. Essentially music does not describe that which is, rather it tries to convey that which reality stands for. The universe is a score of eternal music, and we are the cry, we are the voice."[95]

INSIGHT AND PRAISE

"There is no knowledge without love, no truth without praise."[96] But where love is, there too is knowledge; and when love breaks into praise, there is an understanding of truth.

The knowledge born of love involves insight or sympathetic understanding. And since "praise is the harvest of love," it is also the fruit of love's insight. It is not just the feeling or emotion of love, but the understanding or wisdom of love, that moves the soul to praise. "This is decisive: worship comes out of insight."[97] Heschel explains:

> A certain understanding or awareness, a definite attitude of the mind is the condition *sine qua non* of all prayer. Prayer cannot live in a theological vacuum. *It comes out of insight.*
> Prayer must not be treated as if it were the result of an intellectual oversight, as if it thrived best in the climate of thoughtlessness. One needs understanding, wisdom of spirit to know what it means to worship God.[98]

And what is the insight of love out of which worship comes? Is it not precisely the realization that the meaning of existence is found in love; that we are indebted for existence graced with love and called upon to pour our lives "into the eternal wells of love"? This is the great insight that provokes our praise: "Beyond all mystery is the mercy of God. It is a love, a mercy that transcends the world, its value and merit. To live by such a love, to reflect it, however numbly, is the test of religious existence."[99] The love and mercy of God, the divine concern by which all things exist, this is the glory that fills the world. And the awareness of this glory is the supreme insight out of which flows praise.

What is more, praise in turn cultivates insight, enriches understanding. "The beginning of prayer is praise. The power of worship is song. First we sing, then we understand."[100] True, some understanding is at the root of praise. As we have seen, love's insight is the source of praise. But the insight of love will never flourish, indeed may even perish, if love does not blossom into praise. Praise is celebration, and as the celebration of love enhances love, the celebration of love's wisdom enriches that wisdom.

"Though not born of an urge to learn, [prayer] often endows us with insights not attainable by speculation. It is in prayer that we obtain the subsidy of God for the failing efforts of our wisdom."[101] One of the great insights of prayer, particularly of praise, that goes beyond what speculation can grasp is an insight already quoted: "We are not alone in our acts of praise. Wherever there is life there is silent worship." As Heschel points out: "What reason fails to conceive, our prayer makes clear to our souls. It is a higher truth, to be grasped by the spirit: *All thy works praise thee.*"[102] The spirit is more than reason, and its insight is greater than speculation. "The soul rarely knows how to raise its deeper secrets to discursive levels of the mind."[103] Prayer is an exercise of the spirit or soul that enables us to perceive what reflection might not attain. "The truth of holiness is not a truth of speculation—it is the truth of worship."[104]

"There are moments," says Heschel, "in which there is a lifting of the veil at the horizon of the known, opening a vision of what is eternal in time."[105] Those moments, that vision, obtain especially during worship. Yet acts of worship are not always, and might rarely be, imbued with such insight or vision. For religious insight does not occur without spiritual preparation, and worship is at times unprepared. "Unless living is a form of worship, our worship has no life."[106] Thus prayer must be well grounded: "Prayer is not a hothouse plant of temples, but a shoot that grows in the soil of life, springing from widespread roots hidden in all our needs and deeds. Vicious needs, wicked deeds, felt or committed today, are like rot cankering the roots of tomorrow's prayer."[107] Yet even if we do strive to make our living a form of worship, even if the roots of our prayer are in the fertile soil of authentic needs and gracious deeds, prayerful illumination may be rare and fleeting. In any case, we must *pray for the ability* to pray," for "it is the continuity of trying to pray, the unbroken loyalty to our duty to pray, that lends strength to our fragile worship."[108] And what lends strength to our fragile worship may illumine it with insight as well.

AN ONTOLOGICAL NECESSITY

But why do we have a "duty to pray"? For Heschel, it is because "all existence is coexistence with God"[109] and prayer is the act of acknowledging that coexistence. And since "the meaning of existence lies in reciprocity," prayer is *"an ontological necessity,* an act that constitutes the very essence of man."[110] Thus, human dignity consists not in the possession of knowledge, wealth, or skill but in the ability to worship God, in "being endowed with the gift of addressing God," says Heschel. "It is this gift which should be a part of the definition of man."[111] So prayer is not only our duty, it is our greatest privilege, it is the act by which we reflect the dignity with which we are endowed.

Lest religious believers be inclined to think that while they fulfill the ontological necessity of praying, unbelievers do not, it is well to recall that those who do not consciously address themselves to God may nevertheless praise God by their lives. Indeed there are people who do not believe in God, yet who in their search for truth and their deeds of love disclose and extol God's glory. "We often know Him unknowingly and fail to know Him when insisting upon knowing."[112]

PRAISE AND FAITH

Since "praise is our first response" to the presence of God and is an act that generates religious insight, Heschel maintains, as we have seen, "praise precedes faith." As such, "the premise of praise" is one of "the antecedents of faith."[113] Yet for Heschel praise is also "the quintessence of spiritual life, that is, the climax of aspirations."[114] Now the question that arises—a question that Heschel himself did not raise—is: How can praise be both an *antecedent* of faith *and* the *quintessence* or *climax* of religious life?

When Heschel calls praise an antecedent of faith does he perhaps mean that it is *logically*—not necessarily chronologically or psychologically— prior to faith? That it is a necessary condition of faith, an essential component of faith? In this case faith may be psychologically prior to worship but would not survive without it. While this may be a suitable explanation for the statement "praise precedes faith," it does not adequately explain Heschel's qualifying sentence—"*First* we sing, *then* we believe"— which implies that praise has more than logical priority. Indeed, while Heschel would agree that praise logically precedes faith, his writings repeatedly suggest that praise chronologically and psychologically precedes faith as well. [115]

Perhaps the answer to our question lies in the realization that a chronological and psychological antecedent of faith may also become a constitutive element of faith, even its supreme element. So while praise is faith's essential and climactic moment, it may also have been the act out of which faith emerged. In this view praise is the initial response to the glory of God while faith is faithfulness to that response. Thus, praise precedes and sustains faith; it is both an antecedent of faith and the essence or climax of faith.

Yet another question arises: Is not the initial act of praise also a moment of faith? Does not the term "faith" include both the *initial response* to God as well as the *faithfulness* to that response? If so, then praise as the initial response precedes only the latter aspect of faith but is identical with the former. In this case praise is an *experience of faith* that precedes the *life of faith.* But is this what Heschel means when he says "praise precedes faith"?

To be sure, while there is for Heschel one sense in which "*faith is faithfulness,* loyalty to an event, loyalty to our response,"[116] he does not reduce faith to faithfulness alone. The initial event or response is also for Heschel an act of faith: "Faith itself is *an event,* . . . a *moment* in which the soul of man communes with the glory of God."[117] So although Heschel does not state it explicitly, praise is an event or a moment of faith that precedes faith as faithfulness. To support this interpretation we need only to compare two of Heschel's apparently contradictory statements. On the one hand, Heschel says "faith is *sensitivity, understanding, engagement* and *attachment.*"[118] On the other hand he says "the fundamental issue is not faith but sensitivity and praise, being ready for faith."[119] Now in the first statement *sensitivity* is considered an aspect of faith, while in the second statement it is distinguished from faith and is conjoined with praise as a prerequisite of faith. It seems plausible to conclude that in the latter statement Heschel is using the term "faith" as *faithfulness* which grows out of sensitivity and praise, whereas in the former statement he is using the term "faith" in a broader sense to include sensitivity and—by association—praise. So where Heschel says "praise precedes faith" we can read him to mean that praise, like sensitivity to God, is an aspect of faith, an initial moment of faith, which precedes faithfulness, the life of faith. Perhaps it is in this sense that we are to understand another of Heschel's provocative insights: "The way *to* faith is the way *of* faith."[120] The way to a life of faith is by way of acts or moments of faith such as praise.

8

Remembrance and Mitsvah

Memory is a source of faith. To have faith is to remember.[1]
The gates of faith are not ajar, but the mitsvah is a key. By living as Jews
we may attain our faith as Jews. We do not have faith because of deeds;
we may attain faith through sacred deeds.[2]

"Faith is the achievement of ages"[3] and "unless we remember, . . . the holiness of ages will remain a secret of God."[4] The Jewish tradition conveys the faith and the holiness of Judaism that has been acquired throughout many ages. And this tradition, like others, is kept alive by remembrance. Since the Jewish tradition is a source of Jewish faith, the remembrance of that tradition is an antecedent of this faith.

But the Jewish tradition is meant not only to be remembered, just as the Jewish faith is meant not only to be repeated. "Authentic faith is more than the echo of a tradition. It is a creative situation, an event."[5] Such faith is meant not only to reflect the tradition but to enhance it, to "enrich the legacy of ages."[6] Concerning "the acquisition of faith," Heschel claims that "only he who is a pioneer is worthy of being an heir."[7] And how might a person become a pioneer en route to Jewish faith or a pioneer in the life of Jewish faith? According to Heschel, it is by way of the *mitsvah,* the good and holy deed.

The Jewish tradition is both remembered and enriched by way of the mitsvah. And Jewish faith is both acquired and nurtured by way of remembrance and mitsvah. The first part of this chapter examines the meaning of remembrance as a way to faith. While it deals with certain mitsvot that are vehicles of remembrance, it is the second part of the

192

chapter that explicitly examines the meaning of mitsvah and what Heschel means by claiming that a mitsvah is a way to faith, not only an expression of faith. Moreover, the second part also deals with mitsvah as a way toward redemption. Hence, the first part is entitled "Remembrance" and the second part "Mitsvah." But there is an overlapping of the two, since it is through certain mitsvot that the tradition is remembered and since it is remembrance that inspires the performance of mitsvot that enrich the tradition and advance the process of redemption.

Remembrance

Why and in what sense does Heschel regard remembrance as an antecedent of faith? And what are the primary vehicles of the remembrance that leads to faith? These are the questions dealt with in the first part of this chapter.

REMEMBRANCE AND FAITH

The Jewish faith draws on both the remembrance of historic events and the remembrance of personal experiences.

REMEMBRANCE OF HISTORIC EVENTS

"Judaism is *a religion of history,* a religion of time."[8] Events, not only doctrines and principles, are among its basic categories. The exodus from Egypt and the revelation of the Torah at Sinai, not only the idea of liberty and the principle of justice, are fundamental to its existence.[9] In fact, the act of liberating the oppressed is more significant than the art of entertaining the idea of liberation, and the acceptance of law is more important than theorizing about it. An idea of liberation and a theory of law are meaningful to the extent that they reflect or ignite concrete actions or historic events. The remembrance of temporal events is, therefore, as crucial to Judaism as is the affirmation of eternal truths: "We must remember that God is involved in our doings, that meaning is given not only in the timeless but primarily in the timely, in that task given here and now."[10]

The ideas and principles of Judaism are derived from sacred events, and the acceptance of these ideas and principles is nurtured by remembrance of those events. The Jewish understanding of God, for instance, is derived from the realm of events, not from abstract ideas. The realization that "God is in search of man" and that "He is a lover engaged to His people" comes about not by way of philosophical speculation but by way of discerning "instances of God's care in history": "The God of the philosopher is a concept derived from abstract ideas; the God of the prophets is derived from acts and events. The root of Jewish faith is, therefore, not a comprehension of abstract principles but an inner *attachment to sacred events;* to believe is to remember, not merely to accept the truth of a set of dogmas."[11]

While Jewish faith is cultivated by "attachment to sacred events," it is also nourished by acceptance of the truths conveyed in and by those events. Since "the moment of revelation must not be separated from the content or substance of revelation," Heschel insists that "loyalty to the norms and thoughts conveyed in the event is as essential as the reality of the event":[12] "Judaism demands the acceptance of some basic thoughts or norms as well as attachment to some decisive events. Its ideas and its events are inseparable from each other. The spirit manifests itself through God's presence in history, and the acts of manifestation are verified through basic thoughts or norms."[13]

Faith involves commitment and loyalty. And the faith of an enduring people involves "the memory of a commitment" made in former generations as well as "loyalty to a moment" of revelation to which such commitment was a response. "Revelation lasts a moment, acceptance continues," says Heschel. "We accept events that happened at moments gone by, as if those moments were still present, as if those events were happening now."[14] We also accept truths and commandments conveyed in and by sacred events; we accept doctrines and obligations pledged by our forebears as a result of these events. By such acceptance we enter into the covenant of Israel and thereby discover that "the meaning of Jewish history revolves around faithfulness of Israel to the covenant."[15] Jewish history does not endure unawares but as a conscious fidelity of the Jewish people to a covenant long since made at Sinai. "Had Israel been disloyal subsequent to Sinai, the great moment would have been deprived of all meaning."[16] And had Sinai lost its meaning, the great history of the Jewish people would have been deprived of meaning as well. "The reality of genuine history" is found in the "ongoing faithfulness to the Covenant of the past."[17]

Now a question that arises is this: "Does one generation have the right to commit all generations to a covenant?"[18] What God revealed at Sinai was not only for the generation of people there but for subsequent generations as well; it was a "word which He pledged for a thousand generations to come" (I Chronicles 16:15b). For this reason the people of Israel are asked to "remember His covenant for ever" (I Chronicles 16:15a). As a revelation meant for all generations, "Sinai is both an event that happened once and for all, and an event that happens all the time."[19] Accordingly, the people at Sinai responded not only for themselves but for subsequent generations for whom the revelation there was also meant. "The contemporaries of Moses succeeded in transcending the present and committed the subsequent generations to the word of God because of their ability to think of life in terms of time."[20]

Nevertheless, later generations have the freedom to renew or to deny the commitment made on their behalf. As noted in our chapter on tradition, faith is not automatically transmitted from person to person, nor from one generation to the next.[21] Each person and each generation is faced with the question of covenantal renewal, as were those whom Joshua the prophet, successor of Moses, addressed at the great assembly at Schechem: "If you be unwilling to serve the Lord, choose this day whom you will serve, whether the gods your fathers served in the region beyond the River, or the gods of the Amorites in whose land you dwell; but as for me and my house, we will serve the Lord" (Joshua 24:15). The problem the Israelites faced was the problem of faith: in what or in whom to place their faith. The choice was between the gods of their neighbors, the gods their ancestors worshiped before Abraham's conversion, and the God of their more recent ancestors, Abraham, Isaac, Jacob, Moses. Their problem was not unlike the problem every generation faces. Whom to serve? The idols of the time? The idols that some of their ancestors served? Or the living God whose redemptive revelation forged the Hebraic tradition by which their other ancestors lived? "To be a Jew is to renounce allegiance to false gods," says Heschel; "to be sensitive to God's infinite stake in every finite situation; to bear witness to His presence in the hours of His concealment."[22]

Each person and each generation is faced with the question of covenantal renewal because, although there is a heritage of faith, there is a sense in which faith cannot simply be inherited. Faith involves a personal decision, the ability and condition for which is inherited but not the act itself. Therefore, there is no such thing as merely "handing on the faith" from person to person or from one generation to the next. But faith can nonetheless be roused and cultivated by faithful persons or by generations of believers. A tradition cannot simply bequeath faith, but it can inspire the covenantal renewal of faith. But to do so, it must be kept alive. This means that the sacred events that have generated and sustained the tradition must be remembered. "Jewish faith is a recollection of that which happened to Israel in the past. . . . Much of what the Bible demands can be comprised in one word: *Remember*."[23]

REMEMBRANCE OF PERSONAL EXPERIENCES

While Jewish faith has its source in the wellspring of history, it is also "a fountain that rises with the influx of personal experience."[24] Just as events of history endure by way of remembrance, the personal experience that quickens faith "survives as a recollection of how we have once been blessed by the manifestation of divine presence in our life."[25] And just as Jewish faith is rooted in "the memory of a commitment" made in Israel's past and in "loyalty to a moment" of revelation from that past, so is it nurtured by the remembrance of our own past religious experience and by loyalty to the pledge given in the wake of that experience. Heschel explains it thus:

> In every man's life there are moments when there is a lifting of the veil at the horizon of the known, opening a sight of the eternal. Each of us has at least once in his life experienced the momentous reality of God. . . . But such experiences or inspirations are rare events. To some people they are like shooting stars, passing and unremembered. In others they kindle a light that is never quenched. The remembrance of that experience and the loyalty to the response of that moment are the forces that sustain our faith. In this sense, *faith is faithfulness,* loyalty to an event, loyalty to our response.[26]

There are times when we are aware of the "momentous reality of God" and other times when God seems terribly absent from our lives. It is so easy to forget the moments gone by when we were graced with the light of divine presence. "The spiritual memory of many people is empty," laments Heschel.[27] This is causing a "spiritual blackout" that "is increasing daily."[28] His remedy: "to preserve single moments of radiance and keep them alive in our lives."[29] These moments—and the faith prompted therein—are kept alive by remembrance. Faith arises and survives not only as a response to the light of God's presence but also in the remembrance of that light and as faithfulness to God in the midst of spiritual darkness.

AN ANTECEDENT OF FAITH

The fact that Heschel says "to have faith is to remember" might suggest that, for him, remembrance is more an aspect of faith than an antecedent thereof. But Heschel also says "memory is a source of faith," that it is "a stream . . . from which souls must constantly drink *before* entering the realm of faith."[30] Moreover, although Heschel says "to have faith is to remember," he never says "to remember is to have faith." Remembrance is a prerequisite of faith, an act without which faith would never arise. But remembrance in and of itself—even the remembrance of God's presence in history or in our lives—is not faith. After faith arises, remembrance, which was one of faith's antecedents, becomes one of its constitutive features. Remembrance precedes faith and fosters its growth. It brings it to be and sustains it. Perhaps more than anything else, remembrance accounts for the genesis of faith.

VEHICLES OF REMEMBRANCE

Since remembrance is a prerequisite of faith, and since our concern is to understand how faith emerges, we must also inquire as to how remembrance is fostered. For history to be kept alive it must be remembered. But how is remembrance itself kept alive? The Jewish answer is simple: ritual and study. These are vehicles of remembrance, hence pathways to faith.

Although there is a sense in which religious study is a ritual in Judaism,[31] a mitsvah observed dutifully, regularly, and devoutly by pious Jews, we shall here make a distinction between ritual and study and discuss each in turn.

RITUAL

While there are many different kinds of ritual in Judaism that spark the remembrance that nurtures faith, we shall concentrate on ritual worship or prayer, for this type of ritual is most explicitly a vehicle of remembrance.

As we have seen, "Judaism is a religion of history." And, according to Heschel, "genuine history is enshrined in our rituals."[32]

> Once a light had been kindled in the temple of our history, it was never extinguished. We are the keepers of ancient events. The immortal past of our people has survived with sustaining vitality in our thoughts, in our hearts, in our ritual.[33]
>
> Reminders of what has been disclosed to us are hanging over our souls like stars, remote and of mind-surpassing grandeur. Heedfully we stare through the telescope of ancient rites lest we lose the perpetual brightness beckoning to our souls.[34]

Many rites or rituals in Judaism are ways recalling and celebrating significant historic events, such as the exodus from Egypt and the revelation at Sinai. It is important to stress the fact that Jewish rites *celebrate* these events, not simply commemorate them. For to celebrate them is, in a sense, to make them present, to feel their eternal relevance. Heschel claims that "there are events which never become past,"[35] that "days of spirit never pass away."[36] Yet in order for such events and days to be kept alive they must be remembered. And ritual is one of the principal ways to remember and thus keep alive the past. "Jewish liturgy in text and song is a spiritual summary of our history," says Heschel.[37] Partaking in liturgy is thus a primary way of remembering Jewish history. It is, thus, a way of growing toward or in Jewish faith which is rooted in history.

Just as we cannot live without a future, we also cannot live significantly without a past.[38] The true meaning of the present moment cannot be found if divorced from the past moments that led to its occurrence. We must recall the meaning of moments gone by in order to appreciate the full significance of the present moment. Just as in the course of an individual's life there are certain moments, certain events, that give meaning and direction to the whole of that person's life, so in the course of history there are certain moments or events that give meaning and direction to the whole of history. Religious ritual is an important way of recalling and celebrating such moments and events.

What gives significance to the whole of history surely gives significance to our lives, for we are immersed in history. We are not simply now-creatures but historical beings—beings with a past, a present, and a future. "The authentic individual is neither an end nor a beginning but a link between ages, both memory and expectation."[39] Religious ritual is a vital way of expressing our memory of events that give meaning to the whole of history and thereby authenticate our lives. Moreover, it is a way of expressing our expectation and hope that history will lead to a fulfillment of the meaning proleptically realized in those great events. Indeed, it is because of the memory that we are able to have the expectation or hope. Heschel explains: "As parts of Israel we are endowed with a very rare, a very precious consciousness, the consciousness that we do not live in a void. We never suffer from harrowing anxiety and fear of roaming about in the emptiness of time. We own the past and are, hence, not afraid of what is to be. . . . We remember the beginning and believe in an end. We live between two historic poles: Sinai and the Kingdom of God."[40]

It is primarily in the rites of worship that Jews explicitly "remember the beginning and believe in an end." Jewish ritual fosters the remembrance of Sinai and the anticipation of God's Kingdom. As such, Jewish ritual is always concerned with the realm of time. "Judaism is a *religion of time* aiming at *the sanctification of time.*"[41] Jewish ritual provides a means of sanctifying time, as Heschel explains: "Jewish ritual may be characterized as the art of significant forms in time, as *architecture of time.* Most of its observances—the Sabbath, the New Moon, the festivals, the Sabbatical and the Jubilee year—depend on a certain hour of the day or season of the year. It is, for example, the evening, morning, or afternoon that brings with it the call to prayer. The main themes of faith lie in the realm of time."[42]

The realm of time with which Jewish ritual is concerned is not only the historic time of the Jewish people but also the lifetime of the individual Jew. Jewish rites not only celebrate the events of the people's historic past and anticipate the coming of God's kingdom in this world; they also remember and anticipate the experiences of an individual's personal past and future. Moreover, the personal past and future of an individual Jew is, through ritual, illumined in the light of Jewish history.

Perhaps not all prayer is a matter of ritual, but Jewish ritual is primarily a matter of prayer. And since Jewish ritual is largely an act of remembrance, the prayers that constitute Jewish ritual are comprised of "words sanctified by ages of worship."[43]

"Words of prayer are repositories of the spirit."[44] And to understand the spirit of Judaism, "we must learn to face the grandeur of words"[45] found in

Jewish prayers: "In Judaism study is a form of worship, but it may also be said that worship is in a sense a form of study; it includes meditation. It is not enough to rely on one's voice. It takes a constant effort to find a way to the grandeur of the words in the Prayer Book."[46] Studying the words of the Jewish Prayer Book, reciting them, chanting them, remembering what they represent, a person may be transported to the threshold of faith. "He who knows how to carry a word in all its splendor is carried away by the word."[47]

> We do not realize how much we acquire by dwelling upon the treasures of the liturgy until we learn how to commune with the spirit of Israel's prophets and saints. It is more inspiring to let the heart echo the music of the ages than to play upon the broken flutes of our own hearts. . . . On the other hand, one may ask: Why should we follow the order of the liturgy? Should we not say, one ought to pray when he is ready to pray? The time to pray is all the time. There is always an opportunity to disclose the holy, but when we fail to seize it, there are definite moments in the liturgical order of the day, there are words in the liturgical order of our speech to remind us. These words are like mountain peaks pointing to the unfathomable. Ascending their trails we arrive at prayer.[48]

Implicit in this last excerpt is a distinction between two types of prayer which Heschel elsewhere makes explicit: "prayer as *an act of expression* and prayer as *an act of empathy*."[49] The first type is spontaneous prayer, unbosoming oneself to God in one's own words, or in sighs beyond words. The second type is prescribed prayer, ritual praying, empathizing with "words sanctified by ages of worship." Heschel realizes that "prayer is an outburst of the heart, an act of spontaneity and self-expression."[50] He even claims that "spontaneity is the goal"[51] of prayer. But he also realizes that prayer may "begin by turning to the words of the liturgy"[52] and that "continuity is the way"[53] unto the goal of prayer. "It is the continuity of trying to pray, the unbroken loyalty of our duty to pray, that lends strength to our fragile worship."[54] What better way to try to pray than to attempt to empathize with prayerful words?

Prayer of expression comes about when we feel the urge to pray. But we might not feel such an urge as often as it would be good for us to pray. Prayer of empathy needs no such urge to commence, just the realization that we have a "duty to pray," or just the suspicion that through prayer we may find something of life's purpose.

> There need be no prayerful mood in us when we begin to pray. It is through our reading and feeling the words of the prayers, through the imaginative projection of our consciousness into the meaning of the words, and through empathy for the ideas with which the words are pregnant, that this type of prayer comes to pass. Here the word comes, the feeling follows. . . . We

must, therefore, remember that the experience of prayer does not come all at once. It grows in the face of the word that comes ever more to light in its richness, buoyancy, and mystery. Gradually, going out to meet its meaning, we rise to the greatness of prayer. On the way to the word, on its slopes and ridges, prayer matures—we purify ourselves into beings who pray.[55]

While Heschel makes a distinction between prayer as an act of expression and prayer as an act of empathy, he also realizes that there is no absolute contrast between the two: "In human experience they are intimately intertwined; the one cannot happen without the other. An act of empathy is involved in genuine expression, and profound empathy generates expression."[56] Ritual prayer, comprised of words that evoke the remembrance of God's great acts in history, is also for the purpose of evoking our heartfelt expression of gratitude to God, our praise of God, and our longing for God. "Praying [by means of empathy] means to take hold of a word, the end, so to speak, of a line that leads to God."[57] As such, "prayer is a way to faith."[58]

In the previous chapter we concluded that when Heschel says "praise precedes faith" it should be taken to mean that praise, as an initial moment or experience of faith, precedes faithfulness or the life of faith.[59] But now it seems that what is being suggested is that faithfulness—"continuity in trying to pray" or the constant effort to empathize with established words of prayer—precedes the spontaneous expression of prayer which may be called a moment or an experience of faith. We may indeed reaffirm the conclusion reached in chapter 7, because to give heartfelt praise to God— which is more than reciting the words of ritual prayer, more even than trying to empathize with them—is nothing if not an expression of faith in God, an expression which in turn fosters faithfulness to God. But there is also a faithfulness in attempting to pray, a faithful effort at empathy, that precedes and provokes the heartfelt praise of God. Heschel suggests as much when he says that "there is a way that leads from piety to faith."[60]

To really praise God is an act of faith in God that nurtures faithfulness to God. But there is a form of praying that precedes such praise. The prayer of empathy, the attempt to feel the meaning of ritual words, may be a prayer for the ability to praise, a prayer for the birth of faith. "The words are often givers, and we the recipients. They inspire our mind and awaken our hearts."[61] With what do they inspire our minds? To what do they awaken our hearts? "These words are like mountain peaks pointing to the unfathomable. Ascending their trails we arrive at prayer."[62] After empathizing with the words—which is a form of prayer—we arrive at the kind of prayer that is a form of faith. "A prayer for truth may evoke the dawn of God."[63] Prayer as an act of empathy involves the remembrance of Godly events that may in turn evoke the dawn of faith in God. Remembrance is a prerequisite of faith, and prayer—ritual prayer—is a vehicle of remembrance. Ritual prayer is, therefore, an antecedent of faith.

And what was an antecedent of faith may become an element of faith. We may ride the tide of ritual prayer with the hope of arriving at the shore of faith. And once upon the shore we may continue to plunge into ritual prayer in order to purify our faith. Even after the flowering of faith we might not always feel the urge to express our faith. Ritual prayer is an obligation to recall the source of faith, to cultivate the soil of faith. Ritual prayer—as an act of remembrance—thus accounts for the genesis and growth of Jewish faith.

STUDY

The Jewish tradition is enshrined not only in Jewish rituals but also in countless texts, foremost among them being the Bible and the rabbinic midrashim. It is also incarnated in the lives of those who live by the Torah contained in and interpreted by those texts. The remembrance of Jewish history, a remembrance that fosters faith, is therefore quickened and sustained not only by way of ritual participation but also by way of religious study, primarily the study of biblical and rabbinic literature and the study of living based thereon. Hence is sacred study, like sacred liturgy, an antecedent of Jewish faith.

"Judaism is a confrontation with the Bible."[64] But it is also more than that, for "Judaism is not only a Biblical religion," insists Heschel.[65] "The concern for God continued throughout the ages, and in order to understand Judaism we must inquire about the way and the spirit of that concern in post-Biblical Jewish history as well."[66] Confrontation with the Bible and inquiry into post-biblical Judaism are prerequisites not only of Jewish understanding but also of the faith that arises in the wake of such understanding. As a means by which the confrontation and inquiry are carried out, study is, to repeat, an antecedent of Jewish faith.

Revelation, the Bible, and rabbinic commentary are, as pointed out in chapter 5 of this book, wellsprings of the Jewish tradition.[67] The remembrance of that tradition must first and foremost be nurtured by drinking from these holy springs. We remember revelation because it was recorded and interpreted in the Bible which in turn has been interpreted throughout the ages by Jewish sages. The remembrance of revelation, and the understanding thereof and the faith therein, are therefore facilitated by studying the Bible and the subsequent midrashim—as well as by studying the lives of the sages themselves.

To recall the wellsprings of the Jewish tradition is to concentrate on the principal foci of that tradition: God, Torah, and Israel.[68] Such concentration, by way of study, may well evoke Jewish faith which is, after all, faith in God, by way of Torah, in the context of Israel.

The sacred study that precedes and nurtures faith is not detached from the ritual prayer that leads to faith, though it may be distinct from it. To function as an antecedent of faith, sacred study must be either rooted in or suffused with wonder, awe, and prayer. Says Heschel: "Authentic theology is . . . scholarly, disciplined thinking grafted upon prayer."[69] He even goes so far as to say that "study is *a form of worship.*"[70] Religious study that is simply a matter of curiosity or performed simply for the acquisition of knowledge will not lead to faith. "Study, learning must coincide with striving for intimate attachment to the Lord. It must be raised to the level of prayer, become a kind of praying, not merely understanding."[71] If this is the spirit in which study is carried out, how can it but bring on the dawn of faith?

Although study without prayer will not lead to faith, students need not wait until they have the urge to pray before engaging in study. In fact, study may be a pathway to prayer or, in Heschel's words, it may be "a gate whereby one enters . . . the life of piety and awe."[72] In turn, piety, awe, and prayer may provoke more fruitful study. When study precedes prayer it may function much like prayer of empathy which precedes heartfelt prayer of expression. And genuine heartfelt prayer may be an impetus to engage not only in ritual but also in further study. In either case, study may be considered an antecedent of faith. Study that precedes awe and prayer is a remote antecedent of faith; study that is the harvest of prayer is a proximate antecedent of faith.

Religious study is genuine if it is a search for "the truth of religion" and an attempt to understand "man's capacity to sense the truth of religion."[73] "The inquiry must proceed both by delving into the consciousness of man and by delving into the teachings and attitudes of the religious tradition."[74] This is a twofold inquiry rather than two disparate projects, as was pointed out in chapter 2 of this work. "Delving into the consciousness of man" involves a study of the traditions people have consciously assumed. "Delving into the teachings and attitudes of the religious tradition" requires a penetration of the human consciousness in which those teachings and attitudes were formed.

Religious study is for the sake of remembering, of bringing to mind, the religious tradition as well as for the sake of personal insight into the meaning and truth of religious existence. Since remembrance and insight—the insight born in the wake of wonder, awe, and praise—are, as we have seen, antecedents of faith, it follows that study which fosters remembrance and insight may be called an antecedent of faith.

Since study is so important to Jewish faith, so too is teaching, for genuine study is inspired by authentic teaching. Such teaching must first and foremost convey a deep appreciation for study: "Genuine reverence for the sanctity of study is bound to invoke in the pupils the awareness that study is not an ordeal but an act of edification; that the school is *a sanctuary*, not a factory."[75] According to Heschel, "learning is holy, an indispensable form of purification as well as ennoblement."[76] And by learning he does not mean knowledge or erudition but "the very act of studying, of being involved in wisdom."[77] Thus, says he, "the unique attitude of the Jew is not the love of knowledge but the love of studying."[78] The teacher's vocation is to inspire the love of studying and to thereby implant the seed of faith that grows in the soil of sacred study.

Himself one of Judaism's foremost teachers, Heschel valued the teaching profession with utmost esteem: "The teacher is . . . the representative as well as the interpreter of mankind's most sacred possessions."[79] When speaking of Judaism in particular, he says of the teacher: "He is the intermediary between the past and the present. . . . Yet he is also the creator of the future of our people. He must teach the pupils to evaluate the past in order to clarify their future."[80] He elaborates the teacher's task as follows:

> The task of the teacher is to be a midwife to the student and midwife to our tradition. At the hands of a clumsy practitioner, ideas will be stillborn. . . . At the hands of a master, a new life will be born.
> The secret of effective teaching lies in making a pupil a contemporary of the living moment of teaching. . . . It is not enough for the pupil to appropriate the subject matter; the pupil and the teacher must go through significant moments, sharing insight and appreciation.[81]

To be all that Heschel says the teacher of Judaism is meant to be, the teacher must not only possess knowledge but also strive for wisdom. And this wisdom must be conveyed not only in words but also in living: "It is the duty of every teacher to teach and to live the claim that every man is capable of genuine love and compassion, of discipline and universality of judgment, of moral and spiritual exaltation."[82] In short, says Heschel, "what we need more than anything else is not *textbooks* but *textpeople*. It is the personality of the teacher which is the text that the pupils read; the text that they will never forget."[83]

For all of the esteem in which Heschel holds the teaching profession, he nonetheless claims that "education is a matter which rests primarily with the parent."[84] He is as earnest as ever, and perhaps most self-revealing, when speaking about the "supreme educational duty" of the parent:

> The mainspring of tenderness and compassion lies in reverence. It is our supreme educational duty to enable the child to revere. The heart of the Ten Commandments is to be found in the words: *Revere thy father and thy mother.* Without profound reverence for father and mother, our ability to

observe the other commandments is dangerously impaired. The problem we face, the problem I as a father face, is why my child should revere me. Unless my child will sense in my personal existence acts and attitudes that evoke reverence—the ability to delay satisfactions, to overcome prejudices, to sense the holy, to strive for the noble—why would she revere me? . . . Only a person who lives in a way which is compatible with the mystery of human existence is capable of evoking reverence in the child.[85]

From the above it is clear that, for Heschel, education is meant first and foremost to be an "education for reverence."[86] And since "reverence precedes faith" and "is at the root of faith,"[87] Heschel's educational program is, ultimately, aimed at the cultivation of faith.

"The Hebrew term for education means not only to train but also to dedicate, to consecrate. And to consecrate the child must be our goal."[88] To consecrate the Jewish child is to enable that child "to participate in and share the spiritual experience of Jewish living."[89] Since Jewish living is rooted in and sustained by Jewish faith, to consecrate the Jewish child is to educate that child in the life of Jewish faith.

It follows from what we have seen that, for Heschel, "a goal of Jewish education [is] that every Jew become a representative of the Jewish spirit."[90] Yet this goal must be sought while at the same time cultivating the individual uniqueness of every Jew. "To educate means to meet the inner needs, to respond to the inner goals of the child. We dare not commit human sacrifice by immolating the individual child upon the altar of the group."[91] For Heschel, the realization of personal uniqueness is an essential component of being human, and Judaism is committed to fostering such a realization. "No two human beings are alike. . . . Every human being has something to say, to think, or to do which is unprecedented."[92] Jewish education must communicate the spiritual substance of Judaism in such a way as to inspire unprecedented individual contributions that will enrich the Jewish community. The following statement of Heschel's sheds light on the connection between being a representative of Jewish spirit and being a unique Jew: "Identification with what is undying in Israel, the appreciation of what was supremely significant throughout the ages, the endeavor to integrate the abiding teachings and aspirations of the past into our own thinking will enable us to be creative, to expand, not to imitate or to repeat."[93]

As a covenantal religion, Judaism is the antithesis of individualism. Yet "it would be suicidal to reduce Judaism to communalism, collectivism, or nationalism."[94] Judaism is both the faith of a people and "the religion of the individual."[95] Therefore, "religious education must . . . pay attention to both the individual and the people."[96] It must help the individual to become a representative of the people and teach the people to accept and promote the uniqueness of each individual. Jewish education must teach the individual what it means to be an heir to the Jewish tradition while at the same time it must help that person to become a pioneer within that tradition.[97] Genuine study, true learning, stimulates "ingenuity and independence of mind."[98] Thus does it promote individuality. At the same time it "counteracts *tribalism* and *self-centeredness*" and "is a way of relating oneself to something which is both *eternal* and *universal.*"[99]

Because Judaism is a religion of the individual as well as of the people, and, more fundamentally, because individuality and community are essential characteristics of the human condition, Jewish education must foster solitude and solidarity, both of which are essential modes of being human.[100] There is no sense of individual identity, no sense of human dignity, without a sense of solitariness, without "the capacity to stand apart, to differ, to resist, and to defy."[101] And there is no sense of communal identity without actual solidarity. "We must all live in two spheres—in society and in privacy. To survive in society we must thrive in privacy."[102] Therefore, Heschel is committed to the belief that education must reach the inner life of individual students and help them "know what to do in privacy," not only "know how to act in public."[103]

"Judaism is a way of action, but it is also a way of inner living," says Heschel.[104] "Hence it is the inner life that is a problem for us, Jewish educators, and particularly the inner life of the child."[105] The inner life is enriched by cultivating the antecedents of faith, the experiences and attitudes that have been discussed throughout this book: wonder, awe, indebtedness, praise and remembrance. Yet since Judaism is also a way of action, mitsvah must also be fostered. But not mitsvah as pure external deed. "External performance is important, but it must be accompanied by the soul. The mind, the heart are not exempted from being engaged in the service of God."[106] Even an education for public life, for public actions, demands an education of the inner life. Ultimately, Jewish education, with all the rigorous study it requires, is "character education" which is described by Heschel "as *cultivation of total sensitivity.*"[107] In short, says Heschel, "to educate means to cultivate the soul, not only the mind."[108]

Although we have noted Heschel's insistence on the importance for Jewish educators "to respond to the inner goals of the child," and "to consecrate the child"; although we have cited his view on the educational duty of the parent toward the child, we must acknowledge the fact that, for Heschel, education is "a life-long process rather than a passing state" and that, therefore, he stresses the dire need for "adult education" and even "education for retirement."[109] Adult education is a necessity because "the attainment of wisdom is the work of a life time."[110] Another of the essential features of being human, according to Heschel, is "nonfinality," about which he writes: "The being of a person is never completed, final. The status of a person is a *status nascendi*. The choice is made moment by moment.

There is no standing still."[111] Consequently, education must never be completed, never final. In Heschel's words: "It is wrong to define education as *preparation* for life. Learning *is* life, a supreme experience of living, a climax of existence. . . . The meaning of existence is found in the experience of education. Termination of education is the beginning of despair. Every person bears a responsibility for the legacy of the past as well as the burden of the future."[112] Concerning the need of an education for retirement, Heschel is as insightful as ever, and his practical suggestions could, if heeded, revolutionize life for senior citizens and consequently for the whole of society:

> May I suggest that man's potential for change and growth is much greater than we are willing to admit and that old age be regarded not as the age of stagnation but as *the* age of *opportunities for inner growth?* . . . The years of old age may enable us to attain the high values we failed to sense, the insights we have missed, the wisdom we ignored. They are formative years, rich in possibilities to unlearn the follies of a lifetime, to see through inbred self-deceptions, to deepen understanding and compassion, to widen the horizon of honesty, to refine the sense of fairness. . . .
>
> At every home for the aged there is a director of recreation in charge of physical activities; there ought to be also a director of learning in charge of intellectual activities. We insist upon minimum standards for physical well-being, what about minimum standards for intellectual well-being?
>
> What the nation needs is senior universities, universities for the advanced in years where wise men should teach the potentially wise, where the purpose of learning is learning itself.[113]

Just as all of Heschel's insights, original as they may be, are rooted in the Jewish tradition, so it is with his view of education, particularly of how this should be an ongoing adventure of the spirit for all members of society. Reminiscing about the style of Jewish life in Eastern Europe before the Holocaust, Heschel writes:

> In almost every Jewish home in Eastern Europe, even in the humblest and the poorest, stood a bookcase full of volumes, proud and stately folio tomes together with shy, small-sized books. Books were neither an asylum for the frustrated nor a means for occasional edification. They were furnaces of living strength, timeproof receptacles for the eternally valid coins of spirit. Almost every Jew gave his time to learning, either in private study or by joining one of the societies established for the purpose of studying the Talmud or some other branch of rabbinic literature. . . . Poor Jews, whose children knew only the taste of "potatoes on Sunday, potatoes on Monday, potatoes on Tuesday," sat there like intellectual magnates. They possessed whole treasures of thought, a wealth of information, of ideas and sayings of many ages. . . . The stomachs were empty, the homes barren, but the minds were crammed with the riches of Torah.[114]

"The riches of Torah" are known to those who study it with care. And the treasures of a tradition based on Torah are remembered to a great extent by devoted study. The supreme importance that Heschel ascribes to sacred study must not be underestimated. While he realizes, with the Baal Shem, that "a man could devote himself to Torah yet remain distant from God," he also recalls another of the Baal Shem's teachings: "Torah study is a way of coming upon the presence of God."[115] The outcome depends on the motive for and the approach to study. If study is pursued for the sake of self-aggrandizement, the student of Torah might "remain distant from God." If pursued for the sake of discovering truth and living by it, the student may begin to sense the presence of God. Since "the way that always leads to God is Truth,"[116] the search for truth is, knowingly or not, a search for God. The search for truth prepares us to perceive the revelation of truth. And since, "Truth is always with God,"[117] the revelation of truth is a revelation from God. Faith is a response to the truth recognized as divine. Genuine study, as a quest for truth, may prepare the way for such a response and thereby foster faith in God.

Mitsvah

Ritual and study, like all mitsvot, are meant not only to remember the tradition but to enhance it, not only to convey an ancient faith but to cultivate a pioneering faith. And, more than that, these mitsvot are meant not only to celebrate redemptive events from the past but to advance the drama of redemption in the present and the future. In the remainder of this chapter we consider first the relationship between mitsvah and faith and then the relationship between mitsvah and redemption, the goal of faith.

MITSVAH AND FAITH

Throughout his writing Heschel suggests that mitsvot are expressions of faith. Yet he also claims that they may be pathways to faith and, therefore, calls upon his readers to take "a leap of action" in order to reach the threshold of faith. We shall consider the relationship between mitsvah and faith from both of these angles and then discuss Heschel's "ladder of observance" of halachic mitsvot proposed as a "pedagogy of return" to the Jewish faith.

AN EXPRESSION OF FAITH

Standing in wonder and awe before the sublime mystery of being; sensing our indebtedness for being and for the divine concern invested in being;

praising God for life and grace; remembering the revelation of God and the tradition that flows therefrom, we are moved to act in accord with God. A mitsvah is such an act.[118] "A mitsvah is an act which God and man have in common."[119]

Acting in accord with God may be a deliberate response to the revelation of God's concern and challenge and thus be an expression of faith. Sensing the concern and challenge is only the beginning, a prerequisite of faith. Faith is responsiveness to what is sensed. Since praise is an act of responding to God, it is not only an antecedent of faith but an expression of it.[120] But faith also expresses itself in deeds other than praise, in mitsvot that are "carried out as variations on the theme of prayer."[121] Says Heschel: "God asks for the heart, and we must spell our answer in terms of deeds. . . . God asks for the heart, but the heart is oppressed with uncertainty in its own twilight. God asks for faith, and the heart is not sure of its own faith. It is good that there is a dawn of decision for the night of the heart; deeds to objectify faith, definite forms to verify belief."[122] As much as faith is an act of the heart it must be more than that as well. Jewish faith is "*an answer* to Him who is asking us to live in a certain way" and "deeds are the language of living."[123] To be sure, we each have an "inner living" and we "perform" internal deeds, acts of the mind, heart, and soul. And faith is to a great extent comprised of such internal acts. Yet faith is also a symphony of internal and external deeds, of bodily acts done with spirit. "Faith is not a silent treasure to be kept in the seclusion of the soul, but a mint in which to strike the coin of common deeds."[124] Moreover, Jewish faith is not just a matter of single deeds performed here and there, now and then, but of a pattern of deeds that constitutes an order of living, the goal of which is "a life compatible with the presence of God."[125]

Since Heschel says that "piety is a life compatible with God's presence,"[126] and since Jewish faith is meant to be such a life, we might expect Heschel to equate piety with faith. But in one instance he says: "Piety is usually preceded by faith, and it is then faith's achievement."[127] But if there is no faith apart from deeds—whether purely internal or inspirited bodily deeds—and if deeds of faith are acts of piety, then what can Heschel mean by suggesting that faith may precede piety? Does he perhaps mean that there may be acts of faith—pious acts—that nonetheless precede the *life* of piety, acts that precede "a *life* compatible with God's presence"? If so, this would seem to be an important reminder to those who have attained some degree of faith, who perform occasional deeds of faith, that a life of piety, an integrated life of faith, is still a task and yet a goal.

But it seems that when Heschel says "piety is usually preceded by faith" he is in this instance referring to faith as belief, for he adds that piety is "an effort to put faith's ideas into effect, to follow its suggestions."[128] Now the ideas of faith are beliefs, but faith itself is more than belief; it is personal consent to the reality believed.[129] Jewish faith, therefore, is not just the belief that God exists, it is the personal consent to God's Word and ways. Such consent, it would seem, is nothing if not responsiveness. Yet, in the context wherein Heschel suggests that faith precedes piety, he also suggests that piety is the response to God made in the wake of faith. So what is faith? Is it simply belief or, as Heschel also suggests here, "to meet God"? If this is what Heschel means in this instance, then it is not faith as he usually describes it. By faith Heschel usually means the responsiveness to God, not just the belief in God's existence or the encounter with God's presence. And responsiveness to God is normally what he means by piety. So it is not as if piety is a response added to faith—as Heschel implies in the instance under consideration—but a response in faith or a way of faithfully responding to God.

At any rate, faith or piety is the result of having discerned the concern and challenge of God. Mitsvot are acts of faith and piety made in response to God's acts of concern and challenge.

A LEAP OF ACTION

While mitsvot are commonly viewed as expressions of faith, as our author himself views them, Heschel contends that they are also pathways to faith. In his words: "By living as Jews we may attain our faith as Jews. We do not have faith because of deeds; we may attain faith through sacred deeds."[130]

Some of Heschel's critics are perplexed by the fact that he, who so often stresses the importance of *kavanah* (inner devotion) in the performance of sacred acts, calls upon Jews to take "*a leap of action*"[131] and perform mitsvot as a way of attaining faith in God.[132] "Is it conceivable," asks Harold Kasimow, "that Heschel, the man of agada, is asking us to take a 'leap of action' before we attain inner devotion?"[133] He then quotes Maurice Friedman who asks: "But if we who are not observant Jews do not *now* feel ourselves commanded by God to perform the law, how shall we perform it with integrity even on the strength of Heschel's assurance that we *shall* know this to be God's will for us through our observance?"[134]

Kasimow responds correctly to his own question by contending that Heschel "tells us to perform the mitsvot even if we do not feel the intention,"[135] that is, the proper sense of devotion. But Kasimow is wrong to suggest with Friedman that deed before devotion implies action without integrity. Heschel calls for a leap of action, realizing that only those who suspect that the action may be valuable or who seek to attain faith through action will take the leap. The fact that, in Heschel's words, "one must continue to observe the law even when one is not ready to fulfill it 'for the sake of God'"[136] does not mean that one does so without any integrity but that one may even see value in keeping the law—and thus act with integrity—prior to the belief that the law is of God. Moreover, the fact that, in the context of speaking of attaining faith through deeds, Heschel defines faith as "vision, sensitivity and attachment to God" and claims—reversing what we saw in the previous section—that "piety [doing mitsvot] is an attempt to attain such sensitivity and attachment"[137] shows that his call for a leap of action is addressed primarily to those who are already striving for faith. He is calling upon those who long for faith to do things faithful in order to give faith a chance to flower. Performing mitsvot in the hope of attaining faith is like studying the Bible in the hope of finding God. Neither need lack integrity. In fact both are mitsvot, acts of piety in search of faith.

Also, the fact that in other contexts Heschel implies that yearning for faith is itself a matter of faith[138] suggests that when Heschel speaks of taking a leap of action to attain faith he perhaps means that the leap itself is the beginning of faith which may lead to a life of faith. Thus can we understand Heschel's statement, not quoted by Kasimow, that "the way *to* faith is the way *of* faith."[139]

A mitsvah may function as an antecedent of faith in two senses. 1) It may be an act of faith that precedes loyalty to the pledge made by that act or to the God to whom the pledge was made. As such a mitsvah may be the beginning of faith that leads to a life of faith. 2) But a mitsvah may precede even an initial expression of faith. It may be enacted not as a sign of faith in God but simply because it is perceived as a good deed or as something that may lead to faith discerned as a value.

Even though pious Jews believe that mitsvot are commanded by God, others may see value in doing mitsvot prior to the belief that God commands them. A mitsvah is an antecedent of the act of faith inasmuch as its performance may lead to the discovery of God. As an initial conscious response to God, a mitsvah is an aspect of faith that is an antecedent of faithfulness.

A LADDER OF OBSERVANCE

In our study of the meaning of Torah in chapter 5 we saw that Heschel rejected the notion that all halachic laws are of equal importance.[140] Going hand in hand with that notion is "the assumption that either you observe all or nothing."[141] In analyzing Heschel's rejection of the former notion we recalled his claim that "there were ages in Jewish history when some aspects of Jewish ritual observance were not adhered to by people who had otherwise lived according to the law."[142] We also examined one reason why this was the case: not all halachic laws are of perennial significance or equal merit.[143] Now, to explain Heschel's rejection of the "all or nothing" approach to halacha, we must mention another reason why some halachic mitsvot have not been adhered to by otherwise faithful Jews: that "the power to observe depends on the situation."[144] Heschel explains:

> The industrial civilization has profoundly affected the condition of man, and vast numbers of Jews loyal to Jewish law feel that many of the rabbinic restrictions tend to impede rather than to inspire greater joy and love of God.
>
> In their zeal to carry out the ancient injunction, "make a hedge about the Torah," many Rabbis failed to heed the warning, "Do not consider the hedge more important than the vineyard." Excessive regard for the hedge may spell ruin for the vineyard. The vineyard is being trodden down. It is all but laid waste. Is this the time to insist upon the sanctity of the hedges?[145]

Heschel is critical of the intransigent attitude with regard to halacha not only because it is neither historically nor theologically justified but also because it lacks sensitivity and understanding for the majority of contemporary Jews who have abandoned "Torah as *a total way of living.*"[146] Heschel's impatience with the intransigent and his concern for Jews who have forsaken the traditional way is evident in a statement he made to the Jerusalem Ideological Conference in 1957:

> The intransigent refuse to surrender a single iota, yet are ready to surrender the multitudes of Israel. Is it the way of Torah to say to the majority of our people: "Put the idea out of your minds that you have a share in the God of Israel"? Let us not trample on the heads of the people. We must not write off those who have left, those who are sunk in ignorance. Saving a soul sets aside the Sabbath, and the word "soul" has a double meaning. Let us bring in the estranged. Even those who have only a minimum of attachment have a capacity for greatness.[147]

Heschel goes on to suggest that Jewish leaders "must evolve *a pedagogy of return*" and "must devise *a ladder of observance.*"[148] He then offers the following advice: "Extremism, maximalism is not the way. Elasticity, flexibility is the way."[149] Concerning those who are able to return to the life of Torah, Heschel says: "To each individual our advice should be: 'Observe as much as you are able to, and a little more than you are able to. And this is essential: *A little more than you are able to.*'"[150] In a letter to David Ben-Gurion, then Prime Minister of Israel, Heschel reiterated his position as well as his concern for those who find halachic life too burdensome:

> You are of the opinion that in the State of Israel "there is no danger of Jews assimilating among non-Jews." I think that the danger of spiritual assimilation lurks everywhere; even the holiness of rebuilding the land of Israel will not afford protection. I am well aware of the difficulties involved,

and can feel the anguish of those who find the world of Halakah too narrow for them. The trouble is that some see all of Judaism in its law; in their concern for the letter of the law they give up the Jewish spark. They make the fence more important than the tradition it is meant to protect. Such extremism and severity do us great harm; even the Creator of the world, finding that a world could not exist by justice alone, combined the quality of justice with the quality of mercy. Flexibility, not fanaticism, is needed.

We cannot force people to believe. Faith brought about by coercion is worse than heresy. But we can plant respect in the hearts of our generation. Like the wicks of the candle, many wait to hear the tidings that the spirit of God is hovering on the face of the deep, and to enjoy the light of that spirit. The trouble is that they do not know the light that is in Judaism. Many of us who recoil from the shadows have never in their lives seen the lights.

Some of the public heretics are secret believers, but we have not yet found a way to express ourselves to them who despise faith learned by rote. Struck by confusion they stray in worlds not ours.[151]

Yet Heschel knows that his advice, lenient as it is compared to the intransigent approach, will go unheeded unless there is a reawakening of religious sensitivity. "A pedagogy of return" and "a ladder of observance" ultimately rests upon a revival of reverence: "Without a return to reverence, without a revival of the sensitivity of faith, the call to discipline will sound hollow. . . . We must learn how to initiate Jewish acts by kindling a light in the home and a light in the soul, by evoking an insight into the great love story between God and the Community of Israel."[152] The reverence and the insight of which Heschel speaks may be kindled by agada, which relates the love story between God and Israel. The return to halacha is sparked by agada, not by halacha itself.[153]

In rejecting the "all or nothing" approach to the observance of Jewish mitsvot, in calling for "a pedagogy of return" which would involve "a ladder of observance," and in stressing the primary importance of a revival of insight and reverence to spark the enactment of the mitsvot, Heschel is clearly favoring a qualitative rather than a quantitative approach to halacha. "The problem is not *how much* but *how to* observe."[154] Such an approach is the practical result of the belief that, as noted in chapter 5, "halacha is ultimately dependent upon agada."[155] In and of itself, halacha is concerned with "how *much* we must perform in order to fulfill our duty"; agada, on the other hand, tells us "*how* rather than *how much* we must do to fulfill our duty."[156] Heschel's wager is that by kindling an appreciation of agada, the observance of halacha will follow. He believes that by sparking a revival of insight and reverence, those estranged from Judaism will be inspired to perform the mitsvot that lead to and express the Jewish faith.

MITSVAH, FAITH, AND JOY

Although the observance of halacha, the enactment of mitsvot, takes discipline and at times even involves sacrifice, it may also be a source of joy. In fact, since meaning may be found in fulfilling the mitsvot, the discipline and the sacrifice entailed may become suffused with joy. Those responsible for evolving a "pedagogy of return" to the life of Torah should be aware of the fact that "one of the goals of Jewish education" is "to learn how to sense the ineffable delight of good deeds."[157] Though it be "a scandal to dullards," let it be known to those searching for life's meaning that "joy lies at the very heart of worship," that it is "the very heart of religious living, the essence of faith."[158]

Because the demands of the Torah are meant to help human beings live in accord with God, and since "all joy comes from God,"[159] the fulfillment of those demands renders joy, as obligatory and at times as difficult as those demands might be. Thus it is important to foster joy in doing mitsvot.

It has been said that the joy with which a deed is done is more precious than the deed itself. The good without the joy is a good half done; and the love and delight with which we do the good and the holy are the test of our spirit. "Thy Torah is my delight. . . . Oh, how I love Thy Torah" (Psalms 119: 77, 79).

"Morality inevitably involves pain. There can be no bliss in the good— there can only be bliss beyond good and evil." In contrast, Jewish experience is a testimony to *simhah shel mitsvah,* to "the joy in doing a mitsvah." Everyone knows that out of suffering goes a way that leads to Him. Judaism is a reminder that joy is a way to God. The mitsvah and the holy spirit are incompatible with grief or despair.

The experience of bliss in doing the good is the greatest moment that mortals know. The discipline, sacrifice, self-denial, or even suffering which are often involved in doing the good do not vitiate the joy; they are its ingredients.

Daily we pray: "Happy are we! How good is our destiny, how pleasant our lot, how beautiful our heritage." There is joy in being a Jew, in belonging to Israel, to God, in being able to taste heaven in a sacred deed. There is joy in being a link to eternity, in being able to do His will.[160]

Although elsewhere Heschel speaks of "the pleasure of good deeds,"[161] in the context from which the above excerpt is taken he makes a distinction between joy and pleasure. He quotes W. R. Boyce Gibson on the subject:

I am pleased with an object when it gratifies some interest of mind or some instinctive impulse. It gives me pleasure if it fulfills my need. . . . But joy is not self-centered like pleasure. No doubt there is pleasure in it, for all our emotions are toned by pleasure or pain, but such pleasure is but the pleasure of the joy. There is also a self-enlargement in joy, but this is not of its essence. The joy itself attaches not to the subject but to the object, and to have joy in an object is to value it for its own sake. Joy is thus an active disinterestedness, and its instinctive impulse is not only to maintain its object, but to surrender itself to it and rest freely in it as in something of intrinsic value and promise.[162]

In the light of this, it might be thought that when Heschel speaks of "the pleasure of good deeds" he is using the word "pleasure" as a synonym for "joy". But that need not be the case since, according to him, Judaism "rejects the idea that the good should be done in self-detachment, that the satisfaction felt in doing the good would taint the purity of the act."[163] Throughout his writings Heschel is insistent about the fact that we should act not only, nor primarily, to satisfy ourselves, our own needs, but to serve worthy ends that are in need of us.[164] But he also thinks that we need feel no qualms if we derive satisfaction from serving these ends. In fact, says he, "Jewish religious education consists in converting ends into personal needs rather than in converting needs into ends."[165] Thus, he adds, "Divine ends ought to become human needs."[166] If those ends are not assimilated as needs but remain mere duties, uncongenial to the heart, incumbent but not enjoyed, then there is a state of tension between the self and the task."[167] And, according to Heschel, "the right relationship of the self to the good [the task] is not that of tension but that of inner agreement and accord."[168] The development of personal integrity requires the reconciliation of ends and needs. When this happens, both joy and pleasure may be felt in the fulfillment of duties, in serving ends that go beyond the self. Mitsvot are ways of fulfilling duties, of serving noble ends, while experiencing pleasurable joy.

Since "joy is a way to God," and since there is "joy in dong a mitsvah," then surely a mitsvah done on the "ladder of observance" may be a step toward the life of faith. And if Jewish faith is nurtured thus, it will then be a life of joy: "Jewish faith," says Heschel, "is an attitude, the joy of living a life in which God has a stake, or being involved with God."[169]

MITSVAH, FAITH, AND REDEMPTION

Ultimately, what is the purpose of doing mitsvot? What is the goal of faith? Is it joy? Perhaps, if by this answer is meant the granting of joy, bringing joy to God and to others. But the purpose of doing mitsvot and the goal of living in faith is not, primarily, to attain personal joy, cherished as this should be. To claim that personal joy is the goal is the same as claiming personal salvation as the goal. But this is not a Jewish claim. "The ultimate concern of the Jew is not personal salvation but universal redemption."[170] And every person has a part to play in this great drama. "Every person participates at all times in the act of either destroying or redeeming the world."[171] How is this so? "By whatever we do, by every act we carry out, we either advance or obstruct the drama of redemption."[172] What kinds of acts advance the drama of redemption? The Jewish answer; Heschel's answer: mitsvot, good and holy deeds. "The Hebraic tradition insists upon the *mitsvah* as the instrument in dealing with evil. At the end of days, evil will be conquered by the One; in historic times evils must be conquered one by one. . . . Redemption is not an event that will take place all at once at 'the end of days' but a process that goes on all the time. Man's good deeds are single acts in the long drama of redemption, and every deed counts."[173] Thus, "By each sacred deed we commit, by each word we hallow, by each thought we chant, we render our modest part in reducing distress and advancing redemption."[174] But is not God supposed to be the Redeemer? And is not God going to send the Messiah to carry out the mission of redemption? Yes, God is the Redeemer, the source of all redemption. But "man holds the keys that can unlock the chains fettering the Redeemer."[175] Perhaps God will even raise up an individual messiah to usher in the messianic age of universal peace. This has been the hope of pious Jews throughout the ages. But Heschel reminds us of this: "Redemption, scholars insisted, was not to be conceived of solely as an act that will come about all at once and without preparation."[176] We must prepare for the coming of the Messiah. Better still, we must prepare the world for the coming of the Messiah, prepare it so that the Messiah will come. And this we can do, for "the Messiah is in us."[177]

This being so, "God is waiting for us to redeem the world."[178] "Every man is called upon to be a redeemer, and redemption takes place every moment, every day."[179] If we succeed, however humbly, in advancing redemption, it will be "by the grace of God."[180] But just as we need God's grace to redeem the world, so God needs us, our responsiveness, if that grace is to abound.

"The world is unredeemed and deficient, and God is in need of man to be a partner in completing, in aiding, in redeeming."[181] Since God needs human beings so, Heschel can claim that "to exist as a human is to assist the divine."[182] Heschel even goes so far as to say, "I would define man as a divine need."[183] The meaning of human existence is to satisfy a divine need. Since that need is the redemption of the world, to help satisfy it is to realize the greatest of human goals. "The meaning of man's life lies in his perfecting the universe."[184] To satisfy the divine need is to achieve the human end. The divine need is a human interest. "The pagan gods had selfish needs, while the God of Israel is only in need of man's integrity. The need of Moloch was the death of man, the need of the Lord is the life of man."[185]

Why does God need us to carry out the divine dream of a world redeemed? Is God not all powerful? This is Heschel's answer: "His need is a self-imposed concern. God is now in need of man, because He freely made him a partner in His enterprise."[186] Moreover, "the idea of Divine omnipotence, meaning, holding God responsible for everything, expecting him to do the impossible, to defy human freedom, is a non-Jewish idea."[187] What makes God divine is not infinite control, almighty power, but infinite mercy, unending love.

"God's mercy is too great to permit the innocent to suffer. But there are forces that interfere with God's mercy, with God's power. This is a dreadful mystery as well as a challenge: God is held in captivity."[188] This is the supreme responsibility of being human: to release God from captivity. This is our only task: to let the divine mercy flow through our lives to heal the innocent who suffer.

There are those who do not believe in God because the innocent suffer. Why not have so much faith in God as to free God to redeem the innocent from their suffering? Faith is not only the acceptance of God's grace and compassion. "Faith is the beginning of compassion, of compassion for God."[189]

Yet "God needs not only sympathy and comfort but partners, silent warriors."[190] God needs not only those who rely on God, but also those on whom God may rely for help.

> God does not need those who praise Him when in a state of euphoria. He needs those who are in love with Him when in distress, both He and ourselves. This is the task: in the darkest night to be certain of the dawn, certain of the power to turn a curse into a blessing, agony into a song. To know the monster's rage and, in spite of it, proclaim to its face (even a monster will be transfigured into an angel); to go through Hell and to continue to trust in the goodness of God—this is the challenge and the way.[191]

Mitsvot, sacred deeds of justice, mercy, and love, these are the weapons of war against the evil that ousts God from this world. They are the instruments by which "to turn a curse into a blessing, agony into a song." Mitsvot are the vehicles of redemption and the true signs of faith in the God who needs our help in redeeming the world.

If the divine is absent from our world, if our lives are dreadfully unredeemed, we must not blame God. God creates a world sublime, but we fail to appreciate it; a world full of mystery that we mistake for absurdity. The glory of God fills the earth, but we do our best to conceal it; God's will has been revealed to the prophets, interpreted by the sages, conveyed by the tradition, but we fail to remember it. God assaults our conscience with the demand for justice and love, and we ignore the outcry. Accusing God for being absent, as if we have been present; blaming God for the ills that plague us, as if we have been laboring to redeem the world, is not the way. "In a world where God is denied, where His will is defied, Truth flouted, compassion sloughed, violence applauded; in a world where God is left without allies—is it meaningful to court-martial Him?"[192] No, what is meaningful is to put an end to evil, to welcome God back into our lives, into our deeds. "The will of God is to be here, manifest and near. . . . God did not depart of His own volition; He was expelled. *God is in exile.*"[193]

To do a mitsvah is to bring God back from exile, for "the mitsvah is a way of God, a way where the self-evidence of the Holy is disclosed."[194] And by bringing God back into our deeds, into our lives, we advance the work of redemption. This, in the end, is the goal of faith: to make our lives and our world more compatible with the glory of God.

Appropriate to the conclusion of this last chapter are the last words of an address by Heschel, given not many years before he died:

> This is an age of spiritual blackout, a blackout of God. We have entered not only the dark night of the soul, but also the dark night of society. We must seek out ways of preserving the strong and deep truth of a living God theology in the midst of the blackout.
>
> For the darkness is neither final nor complete. Our power is first in waiting for the end of darkness, for the defeat of evil; and our power is also in coming upon single sparks and occasional rays, upon moments full of God's grace and radiance.
>
> We are called to bring together the sparks to preserve single moments of radiance and keep them alive in our lives, to defy absurdity and despair, and to wait for God to say again: Let there be light.
>
> And there will be light.[195]

Conclusion

The purpose of Abraham Heschel's depth theology is to study the act of faith and its antecedents, to explore the experiences, insights, emotions, attitudes, and acts out of which faith arises. These antecedents of faith are subjective responses to objective sources of faith. In this book I have systematized and analyzed Heschel's insights concerning faith's sources and antecedents.

Rather than foisting an alien system upon Heschel's mosaic of insights, I have attempted to explicate the inner coherence and consistency as well as the dynamic movement of his thought on the genesis of faith. Along the way, I have offered explanations of why Heschel regards certain realities as sources of faith and why he regards certain experiences and acts as antecedents of faith. I have raised questions that Heschel himself did not raise and have offered answers that are implied in his writings or, where no such implications can be found, are either in the spirit of his thinking or, at least, in the spirit of his search for truth. Although this book may, in large part, appear to be a disciple's systematization and interpretation of his master's message, there are instances where I have expressed disagreement with Heschel and have even been audacious enough to suggest how he might have expressed himself in more "Heschelian" ways on certain matters. In doing so, I have followed the advice he gave to another of his critics: "If you want to make a contribution you must be independent. . . . You have a right to disagree with me even when you interpret my thoughts."[1] I take this to mean that the critic has a right to disagree with Heschel on *how* to interpret his insights or on the ramifications of those insights. Although Heschel saw more deeply than I into the meaning of life and faith, perhaps I have seen some of the ramifications of his thought that he himself did not see. Among other things, this book has dealt with those ramifications.

One of the main questions raised in this book is that of the difference between antecedents of faith and aspects of faith. Heschel uses the phrase "antecedents of faith" both for those experiences and acts that obviously are not in themselves aspects of faith and for those that at first sight are aspects of faith. Even an experience or act that Heschel speaks of in one context as the quintessence or climax of religious existence is referred to by him in another context as an antecedent of faith. How can an experience or act that is a constitutive element of faith, even a quintessential aspect of faith, be an antecedent of faith? This study has offered an answer to that question, explaining why certain experiences and acts that are commonly viewed as aspects of faith are also considered antecedents of faith by Heschel. It also has shown why other experiences and acts that are not in themselves aspects of faith do function, in Heschel's view, as antecedents of faith.

Wonder and awe before the sublime mystery of nature and remembrance of the Jewish tradition are not in themselves aspects of Jewish faith, since this faith is a response to God, not to nature and tradition. Such wonder, awe, and remembrance may occur prior to the emergence of faith. These may also ignite the flame of faith, for while faith is a response to God, it is not God alone that gives rise to faith. Realities through which God is revealed, like nature and tradition, may be considered sources of faith—even if God is the primary source. And responses to these realities, even prior to the perception of God's revelation in them, may be considered antecedents of faith insofar as they occasion and quicken the perception of and response to God. Wonder and awe before the sublime mystery of nature and remembrance of the Jewish tradition—even when God is not yet perceived in them—are therefore experiences or acts that may be considered antecedents of Jewish faith. When faith in God emerges, then what were antecedents of the act of faith become aspects of the life of faith. Wonder, awe, and remembrance facilitate the flourishing of faith and they also express the fruitfulness of faith.[2]

Indebtedness, praise, and mitsvah, the other experiences or acts which Heschel claims give rise to faith, might at first be considered aspects of faith rather than antecedents of faith. It is clear that wonder and awe before nature and that remembrance of a religious tradition may precede any explicit response in faith to God. But the indebtedness of which Heschel speaks is a response to God, not to nature or tradition. So how can it be said to precede faith? Is not such indebtedness an aspect of faith rather than an antecedent of faith? Heschel can speak of indebtedness as an antecedent of faith because, whereas for some people a conscious awareness of God's presence is given with the sense of indebtedness, he suggests that for others there is a sense of indebtedness that is felt even prior to the explicit recognition of God as the reality to whom we are ultimately indebted. This sense of indebtedness is an antecedent of faith insofar as it prepares us to seek the whence of our indebtedness and leads to a conscious indebtedness to God.

But what of conscious indebtedness to God, the explicit awareness that it is God to whom we are ultimately indebted? Is this but an antecedent of faith? Might this not be an aspect of faith? These are questions that Heschel himself does not raise. But as suggested in chapter 7, we can imagine him answering them thus: Is faith in God not more than the sense of owing gratitude to God? Is it not more than the sense of having to respond to the challenge of God? Is faith not the active expression of gratitude, the actual acceptance of the divine challenge? The sense of indebtedness is one of the roots of faith, but it is not in itself a matter of faith. Even the sense of indebtedness to God precedes faith in God. Faith is the expression of indebtedness, not just the sense of it. The sense of indebtedness—even as felt in relation to God—is not faith itself but is an antecedent of faith in God. But after faith emerges, the sense of indebtedness that sparked it continues to enlighten it. What was an antecedent of faith becomes, after the dawn of faith, one of its essential features. The sense of indebtedness not only precedes religious faith but also nurtures it. Therefore, it is both an antecedent of faith and an ingredient in the life of faith.[3]

But what of praise and mitsvah? The praise which Heschel says precedes faith is an explicit praise of God. Is not such praise an aspect of faith? In what sense can it be an antecedent of faith? Does Heschel simply mean that praise logically precedes faith? It has been shown at the end of chapter 7 that when Heschel speaks of praise as an antecedent of faith he means that it is not only logically but chronologically and psychologically prior to faith. But it has also been shown, by means of an exegesis of Heschel's use of the word "faith," that the faith that praise precedes is faith as faithfulness and that the act of praise is a moment of faith that precedes such faithfulness. The meaning of the word "faith" is rich and varied, and in Heschel's writings it is not limited to one definition. It is neither just an experience, a moment of responding to God, nor simply a matter of faithfulness in the wake of a religious experience; it is both. So where Heschel says "praise precedes faith," we can interpret him to mean that praise, as a moment of responding to God, is an aspect of faith that precedes the loyalty of faith. Wonder, awe, remembrance, and indebtedness may precede even the initial act of faith; praise is an act of faith that precedes the life of faith.[4]

But this is not to say that there is no form of prayer that might precede the initial act of faith. To really praise God is an act of faith in God—an act that nurtures faithfulness to God. But there is a form of praying that precedes such praise. What Heschel calls the prayer of empathy, which is the attempt to feel the meaning of ritual words, may be a prayer for the ability to praise and believe in God. After empathizing with the words we may arrive at the kind of prayer that is a form of faith. This is because prayer as an act of empathy with sacred words involves the remembrance of sacred events that may inspire faith. Then, after faith is born, the ritual prayer of empathy continues to nourish its life. Ritual prayer thus functions as both an antecedent of faith and an aspect of faith.[5]

In this respect, ritual prayer functions like many other mitsvot. A mitsvah may be the beginning of faith that leads to a life of faith. It may be an act of faith that precedes fidelity to the pledge made by that act. But a mitsvah may precede even an initial act of faith in God. It may be enacted simply because it is perceived as a good deed. Even though pious Jews believe that mitsvot are commanded by God, others may see value in doing these deeds prior to the belief that God commands them. A mitsvah is an antecedent of the act of faith inasmuch as its performance may lead to the discovery of God. As an initial conscious response to God, a mitsvah is an aspect of faith that is an antecedent of faithfulness.[6]

There are various acts and experiences that serve as pathways to faith, and this book has examined what are, for Heschel, the principal ones. But no matter what sparks the genesis and growth of faith, it is clear that Heschel believes that, in order to attain faith and to grow in faith, we can not simply wait passively for such experiences; we must actively foster the antecedents of faith. This raises the question of whether faith is something with which we are favored or whether it is the result of our own decided efforts in its favor, whether faith is a gift or whether it is earned.

"Faith is the fruit of hard, constant care and vigilance," insists Heschel.[7] "Faith cannot come of itself; one must work at it."[8] "There is no faith without strenuous effort, effort in thought and deed."[9] These statements suggest that Heschel does not regard faith as a gift but as something earned. To the point, says he: "Faith is neither a gift we receive undeservedly nor a treasure to be found inadvertently."[10]

Yet, on the other hand, Heschel maintains that "faith is not the product of our will."[11] Likewise, he claims: "You do not attain faith by your own effort alone. Faith is a gift of God."[12] Is Heschel simply contradicting himself? How can he have it both ways?

The answer lies in this assertion: "Faith is only given to him who lives with all his mind and all his soul. . . . Faith is found in solicitude for faith."[13]

The fact that faith is not a gift "we receive undeservedly" does not mean that it is not a gift at all. Faith is a gift we must seek, a gift we must struggle to receive and retain. The reason Heschel sees faith as a gift is because even though we have to search for faith, when we find it we realize it is not simply the result of our search. Yet the fact remains that without searching for it, without soliciting it, we would fail to discover the gift. "Faith comes about in a collision of an unending passion for Truth and the failure to attain it by one's own means."[14] We do not acquire faith simply by means of our own search for Truth, but without seeking Truth, without searching for God, we would not find God approaching us. Faith is the fruit of God's approach to us and our longing for God. The quest for God does not guarantee the emergence of faith, but it prepares in us the disposition that makes faith possible. By actively cultivating the antecedents of faith we prepare ourselves for the genesis of faith which, ultimately, is caused by the grace of God.

And what, after all, does it mean to have faith in God? In a word, faith is enacted sympathy for the pathos of God; it means joining God's struggle against evil and falsehood, laboring in the divine cause of redemption. Faith is responding in love to the love of God.

The last word belongs to the rebbe himself, Abraham Joshua Heschel, whose very name has become a reminder of God and a summons to faith in God: "Faith is the beginning of compassion, of compassion for God. It is when bursting with God's sighs that we are touched by the awareness that *beyond all absurdity* there is meaning, Truth, and love."[15]

Abbreviations

The following are the abbreviations for Heschel's books used in the notes after the first reference to each in which bibliographical data is conveyed. Other books by Heschel are cited by full title even after the first reference to them, as are his articles unless a shortened form of their title is given in the first citation. Books and articles by authors other than Heschel are, after the first reference to each, cited by means of the author's name and the title only.

Earth	*The Earth Is the Lord's*
Freedom	*The Insecurity of Freedom*
Israel	*Israel: An Echo of Eternity*
Not Alone	*Man Is Not Alone*
Prophets	*The Prophets*
Quest	*Man's Quest for God*
Saadia	*The Quest for Certainty in Saadia's Philosophy*
Sabbath	*The Sabbath*
Search	*God in Search of Man*
Truth	*A Passion for Truth*

Notes

Introduction (pp. xvi–xix)

1. Abraham Joshua Heschel, *Man Is Not Alone: A Philosophy of Religion* (New York: Farrar, Straus, and Young, 1951), pp. 230–231; hereafter cited as *Not Alone.*
2. Reinhold Neibuhr, quoted by Byron Sherwin, "Abraham Joshua Heschel," *The Torch,* Spring 1969, 7.
3. Reuven Kimelman, "Abraham Joshua Heschel (1907–1972)," *Response,* 16 (Winter 1972–1973), 21.
4. Abraham Joshua Heschel, "Faith," part 2, *The Reconstructionist,* 10 (November 17, 1944), 12.
5. Abraham Joshua Heschel, "The Jewish Notion of God and Christian Renewal," in *Theology of Renewal,* vol. 1, *Renewal of Religious Thought,* ed. by L. K. Shook, C.S.B. (New York: Herder & Herder, 1968), pp. 115–116.
6. Abraham Joshua Heschel, *The Insecurity of Freedom: Essays on Human Existence* (New York: Schocken Books, 1966), p. 68; hereafter cited as *Freedom.*
7. Abraham Joshua Heschel, *God in Search of Man: A Philosophy of Judaism* (New York: Farrar, Straus, and Cudahy, 1955), p. 6; hereafter cited as *Search.*
8. Fritz A. Rothschild, "Abraham Joshua Heschel (1907–1972): Theologian and Scholar," in *American Jewish Yearbook,* 74, ed. by Morris Fine and Milton Himmelfarb (Philadelphia: Jewish Publication Society of America, 1973), p. 533.
9. Jacob Neusner, "The Tasks of Theology in Judaism: A Humanistic Program," *The Journal of Religion,* 59 (January 1979), 78.

Chapter 1 (pp. 3–26)

1. Abraham Joshua Heschel, *The Prophets* (New York: Harper and Row, 1962), p. 22; hereafter cited as *Prophets.*
2. Robert McAfee Brown, "Abraham Heschel: A Passion for Sincerity," *Christianity and Crisis,* December 10, 1973, 257–258.
3. Byron Sherwin, "Abraham Joshua Heschel, Master," *Sh'ma: A Journal of Jewish Responsibility,* 3 (January 19, 1973), 44. The *Shekinah* is the presence of God to the world.
4. Balfour Brickner, "Abraham Joshua Heschel, Chasid," *Sh'ma: A Journal of Jewish Responsibility,* 3 (January 19, 1973), 47.
5. Jacob Y. Teshima, "My Memory of Professor Abraham Joshua Heschel," *Conservative Judaism,* 28 (Fall 1973), 80. *Zaddik:* righteous person; in Hasidism: a master (*rebbe*) of a Hasidic community. (While *rebbe* is Yiddish for rabbi and thus literally means master or teacher, in Hasidism it is synonymous with *zaddik.*)

6. Jacob Neusner, "Faith in the Crucible of the Mind," *America,* March 10, 1973, 209.

7. Ibid.

8. Heschel reveals these facts in an interview published in Patrick Granfield's *Theologians at Work* (New York: Macmillan, 1967), p. 77. Hasidism is a Jewish communal mystical movement, forged in Eastern Europe during the eighteenth century, that emphasizes the immanence of God and joy as a way to God. It cultivates ecstatic devotion to God. Although Hasidism recognizes that study is a Jewish way to God and although many scholars have come from its ranks, Hasidism teaches that awe of God is more important than Torah study and that the simplest believer may be as close to God as the greatest scholar of Torah. While not dispensing with *halacha* (Jewish law), Hasidism tends to emphasize *agada* (Jewish lore) as of equal importance. It also has institutionalized the role of the *zaddik* or *rebbe,* ascribing to him an authority quite distinct from that of the rabbi. The rabbi is ordained by a talmudic scholar or in a rabbinic seminary and is authorized to decide on questions of Jewish law. The *rebbe* may also be ordained as a rabbi, but his authority comes not from ordination but from his special relationship to God, his profound piety and insight, or his *yiḥus* or lineage. The *rebbe* functions as a spiritual master and intermediary between God and his hasidim. Heschel's male ancestors were not only rabbis but also *rebbes,* several of whom are considered among the most eminent in the history of Hasidism.

9. Cf. Martin Buber, *Tales of the Hasidim: Later Masters* (New York: Schocken Books, 1948), p. 15. *Rav:* master, teacher, head of the law court; *Maggid:* preacher.

10. Elie Wiesel, *Souls on Fire: Portraits and Legends of Hasidic Masters* (New York: Vintage Books, 1973), p. 143.

11. Martin Buber, *Tales of the Hasidim: Early Masters* (New York: Schocken Books, 1947), p. 19.

12. Elie Wiesel, *Souls on Fire,* p. 90.

13. Louis Finkelstein, "Three Meetings with Abraham Heschel," *America,* March 10, 1973, 203.

14. Abraham Joshua Heschel, *A Passion for Truth* (New York: Farrar, Straus, and Giroux, 1973), p. xiv; hereafter cited as *Truth.*

15. Ibid.

16. Ibid.

17. Abraham Joshua Heschel, *Kotzk: In gerangl far emesdikeit (Kotzk: The Struggle for Integrity),* Yiddish, 2 vols. (Tel-Aviv: Hamenora Publishing House, 1973), p. 10. This quotation was translated and cited by Harold Kasimow, *The Divine-Human Encounter: A Study of Abraham Joshua Heschel* (Washington D.C.: University Press of America, 1979), p. 3; hereafter cited as *Divine-Human Encounter.*

18. Abraham J. Heschel, quoted from an interview with Jack D. Spiro held in October 1971, in Jack D. Spiro's "Rabbi Abraham Joshua Heschel: An Appreciation," *Religious Education,* 68 (March–April 1973), 220.

19. Cf. Fritz A. Rothschild, Introduction, *Between God and Man: An Interpretation of Judaism from the Writings of Abraham J. Heschel,* ed. by Fritz A. Rothschild (New York: The Free Press, 1959), p. 7; hereafter cited as *Between God and Man.* On the *Kabbalah,* see Abraham J. Heschel, "The Mystical Element in Judaism," in *The Jews: Their History, Culture, and Religion,* ed. by Louis Finkelstein (New York: Harper and Brothers, 1949), pp. 620–623.

20. Fritz A. Rothschild, *Between God and Man,* pp. 7–8. Rothschild's statement includes a quotation from Heschel's *The Earth Is the Lord's: The Inner World*

of the Jew in East Europe (New York: Henry Schuman, 1950), p. 56; hereafter cited as *Earth.*

21. Franklin Sherman, *The Promise of Heschel,* The Promise of Theology Series, ed. by Martin E. Marty (Philadelphia and New York: J. B. Lippincott Co., 1970), p. 15.

22. Abraham Joshua Heschel, *Man's Quest for God: Studies in Prayer and Symbolism* (New York: Charles Scribner's Sons, 1954), pp. 94–95; hereafter cited as *Quest.*

23. Fritz A. Rothschild, "Abraham Joshua Heschel (1907–1972): Theologian and Scholar," p. 537

24. *Prophets,* pp. xiv–xv.

25. Abraham J. Heschel, "Teaching Jewish Theology in the Solomon Schecter Day School," *The Synagogue School,* 28 (Fall 1969), 7; hereafter cited as "Teaching Jewish Theology." The article is followed by a discussion, pp. 18–33.

26. Cf. Ibid., p. 10.

27. Fritz A. Rothschild, "Architect and Herald of a New Theology," *America,* March 10, 1973, 211.

28. For an English translation of seven of these poems see Zalman M. Schachter, "Abraham Joshua Heschel, Poet," *Sh'ma: A Journal of Jewish Responsibility,* 3 (January 19, 1973), 45–47. About the entire corpus of Heschel's Yiddish poems, Schachter writes: "To anyone acquainted with the other writings of Heschel, his use of metaphor, the evocation of images, the way in which the world's problems always place him in the situational mode of thought, his deep wish to relate, to repair, to soothe and heal, to bring light to a suffering world are all presaged in these poems" (p. 45). An English version of the entire book, entitled *Man-God's Ineffable Name,* translated by Zalman M. Schachter (Winnipeg, 1971) has been privately circulated by the translator in a mimeographed edition.

29. In "Abraham Joshua Heschel (1907–1972): Theologian and Scholar," p. 534, Fritz A. Rothschild claims that "the Hochschule appointed him a lecturer after his ordination in 1934." Although Heschel went through an official ordination with his class at the Hochschule, he had already been recognized as a rabbi in his youth in Warsaw. In a meeting with members of the Faculty of Theology of the Katholieke Universiteit te Leuven (Catholic University of Louvain) held in Louvain's Theology Library in February 1976, Heschel's daughter, Susannah, claimed that "his ordination came when he was very young, from Hasidic rabbis." Byron Sherwin in his book *Abraham Joshua Heschel,* Makers of Contemporary Theology Series (Atlanta: John Knox Press, 1979), p. 1, confirms Ms. Heschel's claim: "In his late teens, already ordained a rabbi, the precocious prodigy left the confines of Warsaw to study philosophy at the University of Berlin."

30. Fritz A. Rothschild, *Between God and Man,* p. 8.

31. Abraham J. Heschel, "No Religion Is an Island," *Union Seminary Quarterly Review,* 21 (January 1966), 117.

32. Edward K. Kaplan, "The Spiritual Radicalism of Abraham Joshua Heschel," *Conservative Judaism,* 28 (Fall 1973), 42.

33. Abraham Joshua Heschel, *The Quest for Certainty in Saadia's Philosophy* (New York: Philip Feldheim, 1944), p. 2; hereafter cited as *Saadia.*

34. Susannah Heschel made this claim about her father's observance of Jewish law during the meeting at Louvain mentioned above, note 29. Concerning Heschel's resignation from Hebrew Union College, cf. Alfred Gottschalk, "Abraham Joshua Heschel: A Man of Dialogues," *Conservative Judaism,* 28

(Fall 1973), 24–25. Heschel's letter of resignation is reprinted on these latter pages.

35. Reuven Kimelman, a former student of Heschel, told me this at a visit we had in Louvain during the World Conference on Religion and Peace in September 1974.

36. Sylvia Heschel told me this when I visited with her at her home in New York in November 1976.

37. Cf. chapter 8, note 154.

38. Robert McAfee Brown, "Abraham Heschel: A Passion for Sincerity," p. 258.

39. *Freedom*, p. 246.

40. J. A. Sanders, "An Apostle to the Gentiles," *Conservative Judaism*, 28 (Fall 1973), 62.

41. Cf. Franklin Sherman, *The Promise of Heschel*, p. 18.

42. Moshe Starkman, "Abraham Joshua Heschel: The Jewish Writer and Thinker," *Conservative Judaism*, 28 (Fall 1973), 75.

43. J. A. Sanders, "An Apostle to the Gentiles," p. 61. Sanders makes another statement that would be interesting to investigate. Concerning Heschel's impact, he writes: "In fact, my own private thesis is that Karl Barth's most penetrating single essay, *The Humanity of God*, which appeared in 1956, was influenced by Heschel's *God in Search of Man*, which appeared the year before" (Ibid.).

44. W. D. Davies, "Conscience, Scholar, Witness," *America*, March 10, 1973, 215.

45. Cf. Seymour Siegel, "Divine Pathos, Prophetic Sympathy," *America*, March 10, 1973, 216; Siegel says of Heschel: "He immensely enriched the scholarly understanding of the history of religious thought—especially Jewish religious thought." Cf. also Siegel's "Abraham Joshua Heschel's Contributions to Jewish Scholarship," *Proceedings of the Rabbinical Assembly*, 32 (1968), 72–85, where the author discusses several areas in which Heschel has "enriched the storehouse of Jewish learning in our generation with works of originality and comprehensiveness" (p. 72).

46. Jacob Neusner, "Faith in the Crucible of the Mind," p. 208.

47. Reuven Kimelman, "Abraham Joshua Heschel (1907–1972)," p. 19.

48. Franklin Sherman, *The Promise of Heschel*, p. 18.

49. *Earth*, pp. 9–10.

50. Jacob Neusner, *The Way of Torah: An Introduction to Judaism*, The Religious Life of Man Series, ed. by Frederick J. Streng (Belmont, California: Dickenson Publishing Company, Inc., 1970), p. 105.

51. Will Herberg, review of *God in Search of Man: A Philosophy of Judaism*, *America*, April 14, 1956, 68.

52. Franklin Sherman, *The Promise of Heschel*, p. 19.

53. Reinhold Niebuhr, "Masterly Analysis of Faith," *New York Herald Tribune Book Review*, April 1, 1951, 12.

54. Fritz A. Rothschild, "Abraham Joshua Heschel (1907–1972): Theologian and Scholar," p. 533.

55. Reinhold Niebuhr, "Masterly Analysis of Faith," p. 12.

56. Reinhold Niebuhr, "The Mysteries of Faith," *Saturday Review*, April 21, 1956, 18.

57. Jacob Neusner, *The Way of Torah*, p. 104. Cf. also Neusner's *American Judaism: Adventure in Modernity* (Englewood Cliffs, N. J.: Prentice-Hall, Inc., 1972), p. 156, where the author hails *God in Search of Man* as "the single, most sophisticated, profound, and comprehensive statement within modern Judaic theology."

58. A third volume may yet be published posthumously. The English title of these

volumes is not a translation of the Hebrew but is *Theology of Ancient Judaism.*

59. Seymour Siegel, "Abraham Joshua Heschel's Contributions to Jewish Scholarship," pp. 80–81.

60. Jacob Neusner, review of *Torah min ha-shamayim,* vol. 2, *Conservative Judaism,* 20 (Spring 1966), 71.

61. Bernhard W. Anderson, "Confrontation with the Bible," *Theology Today,* 30 (October 1973), 270.

62. Maurice Friedman, "Abraham Heschel Among Contemporary Philosophers: From Divine Pathos to Prophetic Action," *Philosophy Today,* 18 (Winter 1974), 299.

63. Will Herberg, review of *Man's Quest for God, Theology Today,* 12 (January 1956), 404.

64. Charles F. Whiston, review of *Man's Quest for God, Religious Education,* 61 (July–August 1966), 316.

65. Abraham J. Heschel, "The Moral Outrage of Vietnam," in *Vietnam: Crisis of Conscience,* by Robert McAfee Brown, Abraham J. Heschel, and Michael Novak (New York: Herder and Herder, 1967), p. 49; hereafter cited as *Vietnam.*

66. Robert McAfee Brown, "Abraham Heschel: A Passion for Sincerity," p. 257.

67. Judith Herschlag Muffs, "A Reminiscence of Abraham Joshua Heschel," *Conservative Judaism,* 28 (Fall 1973), 53.

68. Leon Stitskin, review of *A Passion for Truth, Library Journal,* August 1973, 2314. About this book, Jacob Neusner writes: "His last book, and in many ways his most sophisticated, brought together the Kotzker and Kierkegaard, a tour de force not likely to have its parallel in our day." Jacob Neusner, "The Tasks of Theology in Judaism: A Humanistic Program," p. 77, note. 6.

69. Jack Riemer, review of *A Passion for Truth, Commonweal,* January 11, 1974, pp. 372, 373.

70. Ibid., p. 372.

71. Eugene Borowitz, review of *A Passion for Truth, New York Times Book Review,* January 13, 1974, 22.

72. Reuven Kimelman, "Abraham Joshua Heschel (1907–1972)," pp. 20–21.

73. *Truth,* p. 323.

74. Byron L. Sherwin, *Abraham Joshua Heschel,* p. 8.

75. *Freedom,* p. 248.

76. Fritz A. Rothschild, "Architect and Herald of a New Theology," p. 211.

77. Edward K. Kaplan, "Form and Content in Abraham J. Heschel's Poetic Style," *Central Conference of American Rabbis Journal,* 18 (April 1971), 29.

78. Sylvia Heschel told me this when I visited with her at her home in New York in November 1976.

79. Balfour Brickner, "Abraham Joshua Heschel, Chasid," p. 47.

80. Judith Herschlag Muffs, "A Reminiscence of Abraham Joshua Heschel," pp. 53–54.

81. *Quest,* p. 27.

82. Kenneth L. Woodward, "A Foretaste of Eternity," *Newsweek,* January 8, 1973, 50.

83. Reinhold Niebuhr, as quoted in my introduction, p. xvii.

84. *Prophets,* p. xiii.

85. "A Conversation with Doctor Abraham Joshua Heschel," transcript of "The Eternal Light" program, presented by the National Broadcasting Company, February 4, 1973, p. 6; hereafter cited as "Conversation with Heschel." Heschel

was interviewed by Carl Stern, NBC News United States Supreme Court Correspondent.

86. Ibid.
87. Bernhard W. Anderson, "Confrontation with the Bible," p. 271.
88. W. D. Davies, "Conscience, Scholar, Witness," p. 213.
89. *Freedom*, p. 92.
90. Byron L. Sherwin, *Abraham Joshua Heschel*, p. 47.
91. An expanded version of this address was published in a 1943 issue of the *Hebrew Union College Bulletin;* a final version is in *Quest*, pp. 147–151.
92. Cf. Byron L. Sherwin, *Abraham Joshua Heschel*, p. 5.
93. This address was delivered on the opening day of the Conference on January 14, 1963, in Chicago. It is published in *Freedom*, pp. 85–100.
94. *Freedom*, p. 86.
95. Robert McAfee Brown, "Abraham Heschel: A Passion for Sincerity," p. 256.
96. *Vietnam*, p. 49.
97. John C. Bennett, "Agent of God's Compassion," *America*, March 10, 1973, 206.
98. In connection with the war in Vietnam, Heschel was also deeply concerned about the fate of American draft resisters. In 1967 he pledged to risk fine or imprisonment to aid those who resisted the military draft on the basis of conscience. Moreover, he strongly pleaded for amnesty. At the inter-religious Conference on Amnesty in Washington, D.C., March 26–27, 1972, he delivered a talk entitled "On the Theological, Biblical and Ethical Considerations of Amnesty" (unpublished).
99. Reuven Kimelman, "Abraham Joshua Heschel (1907–1972)," p. 18.
100. Maurice Friedman, "Abraham Heschel Among Contemporary Philosophers," p. 302.
101. *Freedom*, pp. 272–273.
102. Fritz A. Rothschild, "Abraham Joshua Heschel (1907–1972): Theologian and Scholar," p. 535.
103. W. D. Davies, "Conscience, Scholar, Witness," p. 213.
104. Fritz A. Rothschild, "Abraham Joshua Heschel (1907–1972): Theologian and Scholar," pp. 535–536.
105. Ibid., p. 536. Concerning the details of Heschel's involvement at Vatican II, cf. Marc H. Tanenbaum, "Heschel and Vatican II: Jewish–Christian Relations," an unpublished paper delivered at the Jewish Theological Seminary, February 21, 1983. Cf. also Eva Fleischner, "Heschel's Significance for Jewish–Christian Reconciliation," in *Abraham Joshua Heschel: Exploring His Life and Thought,* ed. by John C. Merkle, to be published by Macmillan.
106. Jacob Neusner, "The Tasks of Theology in Judaism: A Humanistic Program," p. 76.
107. Robert McAfee Brown, "Abraham Heschel: A Passion for Sincerity," p. 257.
108. W. D. Davies, "Conscience, Scholar, Witness," p. 214.
109. John C. Bennett, "Agent of God's Compassion," p. 205.
110. Ibid.
111. Harold Kasimow, *Divine–Human Encounter*, p. 75.
112. Ibid.
113. Ibid., p. 90.
114. "No Religion Is an Island," p. 126.
115. Ibid., p. 127.
116. Ibid., pp. 119, 125–126.
117. W. D. Davies, "Conscience, Scholar, Witness," p. 215.

118. "No Religion Is an Island," p. 129.
119. *Not Alone*, p. 92; *Quest*, p. xiii; *Search*, p. 153.

Chapter 2 (pp. 27–52)

1. *Freedom*, p. 124.
2. *Search*, p. 7; *Freedom*, pp. 117–118, 116.
3. *Truth*, p. 159.
4. *Search*, p. 11.
5. Cf. *Freedom*, pp. 116–117, where Heschel recognizes the importance of deeds (ritual or otherwise), teachings (through myth, scripture, and creed), and institutions in religious existence while at the same time he claims that "the innerness of religion" ("faith, inwardness, the direction of one's heart") is "the vital ingredient" of religious life. The exploration of this "dimension of privacy" is indispensable in the search for the meaning and truth of religion.
6. *Search*, p. 10.
7. Ibid., p. 3. Cf. *Freedom*, p. 3, where Heschel states: "The trouble is that religion has become 'religion'—institution, dogma, ritual. It is no longer an event."
8. *Search*, p. 3.
9. *Freedom*, pp. 115–116.
10. Cf. *Search*, pp. 25–27.
11. Ibid., pp. 140–141.
12. Ibid., p. 26.
13. *Freedom*, pp. 118–119.
14. *Search*, p. 31.
15. Ibid., p. 275.
16. *Not Alone*, p. 164.
17. Jacob Neusner, "Faith in the Crucible of the Mind," p. 208.
18. *Not Alone*, p. 229.
19. Ibid., p. 230.
20. Ibid., pp. 230–231.
21. *Search*, p. 8.
22. Ibid.
23. *Prophets*, p. xi.
24. *Search*, p. 251.
25. *Prophets*, p. xii.
26. Ibid., pp. xii–xiii.
27. In a statement quoted below, p. 33, Heschel acknowledges the fact that the method of study he employed "in important aspects reflects the method of phenomenology." Although he makes no reference in his writings to the influence of Husserl himself, in an interview with Robert Earl Clark, Los Angeles, California, August 1962, Heschel did acknowledge Husserl's influence on his own methodology. (Cf. Robert Earl Clarke, "The Biblical Philosophy of Abraham Joshua Heschel," dissertation presented to the Faculty of the School of Theology, Southwestern Baptist Theological Seminary, Fort Worth, Texas, July 1965, p. 20, note 4.) Fritz A. Rothschild, who both as a student and a colleague knew Heschel well, also claims that Husserl's writings "were of decisive influence on Heschel in his student days in Berlin." Rothschild adds the following observation: "I think that some of the most solid and enduring achievements of Heschel's work, which have become classics of their kind, are

the results of his phenomenological research: his phenomenology of prophetic
consciousness which earned him his doctorate, the phenomenological descriptions of man's threefold approach to the awareness of God, . . . his phenomenological understanding of the Sabbath experience as sanctification of
time, and his typology of prayer." (Fritz A. Rothschild, "The Religious
Thought of Abraham Joshua Heschel," *Conservative Judaism*, 23 (Fall 1968),
22.) For an introduction to Husserl and the phenomenological movement, see
Herbert Spiegelberg, *The Phenomenological Movement: A Historical Introduction*, second ed., 2 vols. (The Hague: Martinus Nijhoff, 1965).

28. *Prophets*, p. xii.
29. Ibid.
30. *Not Alone*, p. 20.
31. Ibid., p. 71.
32. *Prophets*, p. xiii.
33. *Search*, p. 5.
34. Abraham J. Heschel, *Who Is Man?* (Stanford, Calif.: Stanford University
Press, 1965), p. 1. Hereafter cited as *Who Is Man?*
35. Ibid., p. 2.
36. Ibid., pp. 14, 94.
37. *Search*, pp. 7, 130.
38. Ibid., p. 7; cf. *Not Alone*, p. 55.
39. *Prophets*, p. xiii. Cf. *Search*, p. 251: "It is not enough to think *about* the
prophets; we must think through the prophets. It is not enough to read the
Bible for its wisdom; we must *pray the Bible* to comprehend its claim."
40. *Search*, p. 252. Cf. Ibid., p. 131: "Acts of love are only meaningful to a person
who is in love, and not to him whose heart and mind are sour. The same
applies to the categories of religion." How true is this statement of Heschel's?
Are acts of love only meaningful to a person who is in love? What of a person
who, though not in love, longs to be in love, whose heart and mind are not sour
but searching? Are not acts of love meaningful to someone longing to be in
love? Similarly, are categories of religion only meaningful to a religious
person? What of a person who, though not so very pious, longs to be pious? Is
not religion meaningful to someone who feels its absence? True, "to
understand love it is not enough to read tales about it." The understanding of
love presupposes a feeling for love. "Unless we are in love, or remember vividly
what happened to us when we were in love, we are ignorant of love" (*Search*, p.
5). But cannot the love of which one is experientially ignorant still be
meaningful to one who feels its want? Likewise, cannot religion be meaningful
to one who feels its lack? Heschel himself has claimed: "What we feel primarily
is our inability to feel adequately" (*Search*, p. 316), and: "Many who cannot
revere feel reverence for reverence" (*Freedom*, p. 215). Yes, we may feel for
love by feeling how inadequate our love is, and thus is love meaningful to us.
Many who are not religious feel respect for religion, and to that extent religion
and its categories are meaningful to such people. Perhaps Heschel would say
that if one longs for love or for religion, then, to that extent, one already loves
or is religious. While this may be true, is seems that love may be meaningful to
a person who has craved it more than known it; religion may be meaningful to
a person who has sought it more than practiced it. But even if love or religion
may be meaningful to one who knows neither except in longing, still if one is
truly to understand either, then one must begin living with love or piety. And
this, I trust, is Heschel's point.
41. *Not Alone*, p. 180; *Search*, p. 111. The relationship of thought to concern is of

great importance in Heschel's philosophy: "Thought is born out of concern and should remain linked to it; when the umbilical cord between them is cut, thought forfeits authenticity" (*Truth,* p. 315).

42. *Freedom,* p. 116. Cf. *Search,* p. 111: "Thinking is not an isolated phenomenon: it affects all of one's life and is in turn affected by all one knows, feels, values, utters, and does. The act of thinking about God is affected by one's awe and arrogance, humility and egotism, sensitivity and callousness."

43. *Search,* pp. 130–131.

44. Cf. *Theologians at Work* (wherein Heschel is interviewed by Patrick Granfield), p. 79.

45. *Search,* pp. 8, 10, 18.

46. Ibid., p. 8.

47. Ibid.

48. Ibid., pp. 8–9.

49. Ibid., p. 9.

50. *Not Alone,* p. 160.

51. Cf. *Truth,* pp. 93–96.

52. *Search,* p. 9.

53. Cf. Ibid., pp. 10–11.

54. Ibid., p. 10.

55. Ibid., p. 20.

56. Ibid., p. 19.

57. *Not Alone,* pp. 172–173; cf. *Saadia,* p. 53.

58. *Not Alone,* p. 171.

59. Ibid., pp. 172, 173.

60. *Search,* p. 10.

61. Ibid., p. 12.

62. Ibid.

63. Ibid., p. 17.

64. Ibid., p. 18.

65. *Not Alone,* p. 170.

66. *Truth,* p. 196.

67. *Search,* p. 18.

68. Ibid.

69. Cf. ibid., pp. 13–14.

70. Cf. ibid., pp. 11–12.

71. Since philosophy is not a genuine substitute for religion, reason, while having a role to play in the realm of religion, cannot perform the task of religion. Cf. *Search,* p. 354: "Reason in the realm of religion is like a whetstone that makes iron sharp, as the saying goes, though unable itself to cut."

72. Ibid., pp. 11–12.

73. Ibid., p. 18. Cf. ibid., p. 272: "The ultimate task of philosophy of religion is to lead us to a higher plane of knowledge and experience, to attachment through understanding."

74. Cf. *Theologians at Work,* p. 79, where Heschel explicitly cites the first two of these functions of philosophy of Judaism (though modifying the second description): "The task of philosophy of Judaism is twofold: radical self-understanding in terms of its own spirit as well as critical reassessment of Judaism from the point of view of both our total knowledge and our immediate situation." Cf. *Quest,* p. 95, where Heschel makes a statement that indicates his agreement with the third function of philosophy of Judaism: "There is much that philosophy could learn from Jewish life." Cf. *Search,* p. 17: "There is much that philosophy could learn from the Bible."

75. Cf. *Search*, p. 22: "Our method in this book is primarily, though not exclusively, that of self-understanding, and the term Judaism in the subtitle of the book is used primarily as a subject."
76. Abraham J. Heschel, "The Biblical View of Reality," in *Contemporary Problems in Religion*, ed. by Harold A. Basilius (Detroit: Wayne University Press, 1956), pp. 57–76.
77. *Search*, p. 23, note 8.
78. Bernhard W. Anderson, "Confrontation with the Bible," p. 268.
79. Jacob Neusner, "The Tasks of Theology in Judaism: A Humanistic Program," p. 76.
80. Fritz A. Rothschild, "Abraham Joshua Heschel (1907–1972): Theologian and Scholar," p. 538.
81. *Search*, pp. 25–26.
82. Ibid., p. 6.
83. Fritz A. Rothschild, "The Religious Thought of Abraham Heschel," p. 23.
84. Edward K. Kaplan, "Form and Content in Abraham J. Heschel's Poetic Style," *Central Conference of American Rabbis Journal*, 18 (April 1971), 30, 33, 33, 38–39. Kaplan is the foremost interpreter of Heschel's use of language, particularly his poetic style. For a more extensive study of the subject see: Edward K. Kaplan, "Language and Reality in Abraham J. Heschel's Philosophy of Religion," *Journal of the American Academy of Religion*, 41 (March 1973), 94–113, and "Heschel's Poetics of Religious Thinking," in *Abraham Joshua Heschel: Exploring His Life and Thought*, ed. by John C. Merkle, to be published by Macmillan. In another article, "Toward a Poetics of Faith," *Response*, 10 (Spring 1971), 44–46, which deals not only with Heschel, Kaplan makes a most significant remark about Heschel (pp. 45–46):

> The writings of Abraham Joshua Heschel probably best exemplify the poetic approach to religious tradition available in our time. This great religious philosopher and poet writes with an intelligence sustained by loving piety, and his often incandescent poetry conveys to sensitive readers the passion of his experience of Judaism. The most mystical and morally committed of modern Jewish documents, Heschel's books seem rather unappreciated by most rabbis. . . . Our relationship to Heschel's writings may be said to reflect the quality of our inner participation in a Jewish experience of religion. For the pious reader privileged with traditional faith, Heschel represents an example of the wisdom of accepted observance, for the believer is blessed with a preestablished power of empathy with the sacred content of religious writings. But even the reader deprived of solid faith may still find in Heschel a spiritual ideal to be pursued. Both require an understanding of poetic language: the former, to project his intimate emotions into traditional behavior so often desiccated and rendered unconscious by habit; the latter, to enable him to experience empathically and imaginatively the emotions of faith contained in written prayers. The harmony of religious language and spiritual experience is attained when both such individuals can meet in a tacit awareness of how God might function in their lives.

Other insightful articles by Kaplan on Heschel are: "The Spiritual Radicalism of Abraham Joshua Heschel," *Conservative Judaism*, 28 (Fall 1973), 40–49, which treats briefly of Heschel's poetic style (pp. 43–45), and "Mysticism and Despair in Abraham J. Heschel's Religious Thought," *The Journal of Religion*, 57 (January 1977), 33–47, which deals primarily with Heschel's apologetics vis-à-vis nonbelievers.

It is significant that Kaplan, unlike some of Heschel's critics who recognize the poetic grandeur of his writings, does not view Heschel simply as a religious poet but as a "great religious philosopher and poet." Moreover, Kaplan shows how Heschel uses poetry in the service of his philosophical *apologia*. Some of Heschel's critics fail to appreciate the nature and the achievement of his apologetics. While Kaplan demonstrates how "Heschel's apologetics embraces the realistic anguish of despair or disbelief and leads us to the frontier of mystical faith" ("Mysticism and Despair," p. 38), Emil Fackenheim, in his review of *Man Is Not Alone, Judaism,* 1 (January 1952), 86, claims that Heschel "lacks understanding for the tragedy of unbelief," a view shared by Arthur Cohen, *The Natural and the Supernatural Jew* (New York: Pantheon Books, 1962), p. 252, and William Kaufman, *Contemporary Jewish Philosophers* (New York: Reconstructionist Press, 1976), p. 161. These latter critics therefore believe that Heschel's writings serve only to enhance the faith of believers but fail to communicate with non-believers. Another reason that each of these critics cites for Heschel's failure to reach non-believers is his lack of rational argumentation. Fackenheim, in a review of *God In Search of Man, Conservative Judaism,* 15 (Fall 1960), 53, claims that Heschel's work is "religious thinking, and nothing else," suggesting that Heschel does not even attempt to persuade his readers philosophically but simply celebrates his own religious convictions. Cohen (op. cit., p. 259) suggests that Heschel's "rhetoric" is "a substitute for theology" or philosophical argumentation. Kaufman (op. cit., p. 160) claims that Heschel fails to supply his readers "with a coherent and systematic explication of his *conception* of the universe and of God." Kaplan and Rothschild obviously differ, as do a number of other interpreters of Heschel's thought, including myself, who recognize his rational and coherent world view (even if it is not presented in a rigidly systematic way) and his attempt to persuade others of its validity. This book is an endeavor to present systematically Heschel's coherent world view and the cogency of his apologetics.

A statement of Kaufman's demands a response. He says (op. cit., p. 161): "It is because of his lack of conceptual clarity that Heschel's availability to the atheist and the agnostic is doubtful." In the first place, Kaufman never establishes any "lack of conceptual clarity" on Heschel's part. Moreover, even if Heschel could improve upon his conceptual clarity it would not, of itself, make Heschel's philosophy more available to the atheist and the agnostic. Religious concepts make sense only in the context of religious situations that give rise to the concepts. Thus, Heschel attempts to evoke religious situations for those who disbelieve or who suspend belief in God. Kaufman himself acknowledges that "the aim of Heschel's work is precisely to evoke in man an awareness of the religious situation" (op. cit., p. 147). It is the evocation of such awareness, accompanied by what Kaplan calls Heschel's "clear intellectual position" ("Form and Content," p. 33), that does make Heschel's message available to the atheist and the agnostic.

85. *Search,* p. 7; *Freedom,* p. 118.
86. Cf. *Search,* p. 7; *Freedom,* pp. 117–118.
87. *Search,* p. 116.
88. Ibid., p. 117.
89. *Not Alone.* p. 59.
90. *Search,* pp. 34, 58; cf. ibid., p. 160.
91. Ibid., p. 116.
92. Ibid., p. 131.

93. *Quest*, p. 41.
94. *Search*, p. 116.
95. *Not Alone*, p. 60; cf. *Search*, p. 8.
96. Heschel's recognition of the polarity and disparity between insight (or experience) and expression has been misinterpreted by S. Daniel Breslauer in "Theology and Depth-Theology: A Heschel Distinction," *Central Conference of American Rabbis Journal*, 21 (Summer 1974), 81–86. According to Breslauer, "Heschel's dichotomy between religious experience and its expression implies that the psychological data and the sociological data are in some way independent of each other" (p. 83), that they are separated in "a radical way" (p. 84). However, from the evidence presented in this section, as in the section on "Faith and Creed" below, it is clear that while Heschel does recognize the disparity between experience and expression, he does not present them in terms of radical duality. On the contrary, genuine religious language must be born in and remain linked to religious experience, according to Heschel.
97. *Not Alone*, p. 60.
98. Ibid., p. 98.
99. Ibid., p. 99.
100. *Search*, p. 154.
101. Ibid.
102. *Not Alone*, p. 166.
103. Heschel sometimes uses the terms "belief" and "faith" interchangeably, but when he does, "belief" always carries the connotations ascribed to "faith" (trust, fidelity, etc.); it always is meant to express the idea of believing in a reality, not simply believing that it exists or that a proposition is true.
104. *Not Alone*, p. 166.
105. *Search*, pp. 34, 58; cf. ibid., p. 160. In his discussion of the distinction between faith and belief, Heschel asserts: "Unlike belief (which is the accompaniment of knowledge or apprehension, the assent given to what we know), faith surges beyond knowledge and apprehension; if refers not to the knowable but to that which transcends knowledge" (*Not Alone*, p. 166). Here he is probably using "knowledge" as a synonym for "comprehension" while using "apprehension" to mean "the assent given to what we know" or comprehend. So when he says "faith surges beyond knowledge and apprehension" he means that the object of faith is not comprehensible. Usually, however, Heschel speaks of our being able to apprehend God, meaning that we can spiritually perceive the presence of God. And sometimes he speaks of our being able to attain knowledge of God, meaning that we can have an existential understanding for the reality of God. Thus, Heschel's statement that "faith surges beyond knowledge and apprehension" is an example of linguistic inconsistency, probably not conceptual inconsistency. As far as I can tell, Heschel consistently maintains that we can apprehend and know God in the sense that we can spiritually sense and existentially understand God, however inadequately. But sometimes, as in the text here cited, he suggests that God is beyond our knowledge because he is thinking of knowledge in terms of comprehension. And in this one instance, Heschel suggests that we do not apprehend God, the object of our faith, because he has given a different meaning to the term "apprehension."
106. *Not Alone*, p. 166.
107. Unfortunately, when contrasting faith and belief in this context (*Not Alone*, p. 166) Heschel says "belief is *personal* conviction," implying that faith is not a

personal act. But as I have explained, an act that transcends the awareness of the self is no less personal than an act accompanied by self-awareness. From the thrust of Heschel's writings, there is no reason to believe that Heschel would object to my explanation.

108. *Search,* pp. 330, 331.
109. *Not Alone,* p. 87; *Search,* p. 138.
110. *Not Alone,* p. 167.
111. Ibid., p. 169; *Freedom,* p. 121.
112. *Not Alone,* p. 168.
113. *Search,* p. 103.
114. *Freedom,* pp. 176–177; cf. ibid., pp. 120–121; cf. *Not Alone,* pp. 168–169.
115. *Search,* p. 331.
116. Cf. *Not Alone,* p. 169; *Freedom,* p. 121.
117. Cf. "No Religion Is an Island," pp. 121–122.
118. Cf. *Freedom,* pp. 121, 123.
119. *Not Alone,* p. 170.
120. A careful reading of Heschel's discussion of the matter reveals that the distinction between depth theology and theology is *based on* the distinctions we have just examined rather than synonymous with those distinctions. Yet Heschel leaves himself open to misinterpretation by making some statements that suggest the equation of the distinction between depth theology and theology with the prior distinctions I have cited. For example: "Theology is in the books; depth theology is in the hearts. The former is doctrine, the latter an event" (*Freedom,* p. 119). It is perhaps a statement like this that led S. Daniel Breslauer (in the article cited above, note 96) to misinterpret Heschel by dissolving the distinction between depth theology and theology into the distinction between experience and expression, faith and creed. Breslauer claims that for Heschel "'theology' was the content of religion, . . . while 'depth-theology' represented spontaneity, the creative moment of religiousness." Now while Heschel may have sometimes implied this, he more consistently showed that theology is not so much the content of religion as it is the study of that content (creed is the content of religion; theology also becomes the content inasmuch as it is a sound elaboration of the dogmas of creed); and it is not depth theology that is the spontaneous and creative moment of religiousness, but rather it is wonder, awe, insight, faith. Depth theology is not a primordial religious experience; rather it deals with such experience. Theology is not primary religious language, but the systematic explication of such language. Depth theology and theology are inquiries into the acts and the content of religion (cf., e.g., *Search,* p. 7, where Heschel calls depth theology a "method," and *Freedom,* p. 117, where he calls it an "inquiry"; in both of these places Heschel speaks of the content of believing as "the theme" of theology and the act of believing as "the theme" of depth theology). The distinctions between experience and expression, between faith and creed, between "the creative moment of religiousness" and "the content of religion" precede the distinction between depth theology and theology.
121. *Freedom,* p. 121.
122. Ibid., pp. 116, 176, 181.
123. Ibid., p. 118.
124. Ibid., p. 177.
125. "The Jewish Notion of God and Christian Renewal," pp. 115–116.
126. *Freedom,* p. 68.
127. Cf. *Who Is Man?* p. 118; *Quest,* p. 78.
128. Cf. *Quest,* p. 94.

Chapter 3 (pp. 55–77)

1. *Not Alone,* p. 89.
2. *Search,* p. 117.
3. Ibid., p. 33.
4. Ibid. Cf. ibid., p. 397: "The essence of man, his uniqueness, is in his power to surpass the self." The grand premise of religion, therefore, has to do with the essence of being human and, as we shall see, human beings are, for Heschel, essentially religious beings.
5. Religion is here said to begin with the sense of the sublime not because the sublime is the same as the divine reality to which religion is a response, nor because it is a characteristic of the divine, but because, as we shall see, the sublime aspect of nature alludes to the divine. Thus, the sense of the sublime may, but does not necessarily, give way to an awareness of the divine, to a sense of God's glory. I stress this point particularly because Alfred McBride, in *Heschel: Religious Educator* (Denville, N. J.: Dimension Books, 1973), while offering the only detailed treatment of Heschel's idea of the sublime prior to this book, misinterprets Heschel by identifying the sublime with the divine or with a characteristic of the divine. McBride calls the sublime, mystery, and glory "divine approaches" and says that, according to Heschel, "God seeks him out, disclosing himself to man in terms of the sublime, the mysterious, the glory" and that "the sublime characterizes God's otherness" (p. 31). McBride gives no reference to support this interpretation and I maintain that none could be given to support it. According to Heschel's technical meaning and general usage of the term "the sublime" as a synonym for the "allusiveness" of nature, it is not God who is revealed as sublime, it is God's creation that is sublime. Thus, "the sublime" is not the term by which Heschel "characterizes God's otherness." "Transcendence" or "mystery" are Heschel's synonyms of God's "otherness" (though these terms are also used by Heschel in connection with created realities). In short, the sublime is that which, according to Heschel, alludes to the divine; it is not the otherness of the divine.
6. *Not Alone,* p. 3; cf. *Search,* pp. 33–34, and *Freedom,* p. 40, where Heschel uses the word "beauty" in place of "loveliness" in a paraphrase of the above quotation. Note also that throughout his writings Heschel uses "grandeur" and "the sublime" synonymously. But the synonymity is not always clear. The fact that in the above quotation Heschel says "grandeur fills him with awe" seems to imply that grandeur is more synonymous with mystery than with the sublime, since throughout his writings he cites wonder as the response to the sublime and awe as the response to mystery. However, since Heschel considers wonder as the beginning of awe (cf. *Search,* p. 74) the above statement could be taken to indicate that grandeur, rather than being synonymous with mystery, is a broader term encompassing the categories of both sublimity and mystery. Thus, the statement "grandeur fills him with awe" would be an inclusive way of saying that grandeur fills man with wonder and awe, since wonder gives way to awe. (Dr. Rothschild, in his introduction to *Between God and Man,* says that the sublime, mystery, and glory are, for Heschel, "terms that describe grandeur" [p. 12]. But, as we shall see, for Heschel, the glory is more than grandeur. And, in my judgment, Heschel does not even use "grandeur" as a term encompassing the sublime and mystery, nor as a term synonymous with mystery, though, as mentioned, both of these interpretations could seem plausible.) However, Heschel's general usage, I maintain, manifests the synonymity of grandeur and the sublime (e.g.: "The theme of Biblical poetry is not the charm or beauty of nature; it is the grandeur, it is the *sublime* aspect of

nature. . . ."*Search,* p. 37). On the other hand, Heschel generally makes a distinction between grandeur and mystery (e.g.: "Who will tell us how to live in a way that is compatible with the grandeur, the mystery, and the glory?" Ibid., p. 163; here the three terms are clearly not used in apposition because glory is always distinct from grandeur and mystery in Heschel's writings). Why, then, does Heschel say that "grandeur fills him with awe" instead of saying "grandeur fills him with wonder"? It simply might be that it makes for a more poetic sentence, and that Heschel was not conscious at the time of the distinctions under discussion. It might also be because wonder and awe are not separate experiences but aspects of one experience (as the sublime and mystery are dimensions of one reality) that Heschel can speak of grandeur (sublimity) evoking awe. It is important to realize that while Heschel uses different categories (power, beauty, sublimity, mystery) with regard to nature he does not compartmentalize them. These different categories refer to elements of one reality (as, for example, enjoyment, wonder, and awe refer to aspects of one experience of that reality), and it is only through a process of mental abstraction that we can separate them. Thus, while this book treats Heschel's transcendental categories separately, in reality they cannot be separated.

Since, according to Heschel, nature is mysterious as well as sublime, and since he makes a distinction between sublimity and mystery, he could have said that there are four aspects of nature that command human attention: power, beauty, the sublime (grandeur), and mystery. Or since, for Heschel, both sublimity and mystery are categories of the ineffable, and since they are so closely related, he could have cited ineffability as the third aspect of nature, which upon analysis is found to have the distinct characteristics of sublimity and mystery.

7. Despite the great difference between their accounts of beauty and sublimity, both Edmund Burke, in *A Philosophical Inquiry into the Origin of Our Ideas of the Sublime and the Beautiful* (1756), and Immanuel Kant, in *Kritik der Urteilskraft* (1790), identified the sublime with the vast and powerful and opposed it as such to the beautiful considered as that which has the qualities of delicacy, form, and color. For Heschel's critique of their descriptions see *Search,* pp. 38–41. I might add that Burke and Kant were quite traditional in their identifying the sublime with the grand and that they were also not unique in contrasting the sublime with the beautiful. Therefore, Heschel's critique of Burke and Kant represents, in effect, a critique of the whole tradition which equates the sublime with the grand and opposes it to the beautiful. Likewise, Heschel's interpretation of the sublime is a critique of those who reduce the sublime to an aesthetic category. Thus, in maintaining that not only the grand is sublime, but that all things are, and that, as we will see, it is the allusiveness of things to transcendent meaning that constitutes their sublimity, Heschel advances an original interpretation of the sublime, though one that he acknowledges to be based on the biblical view of reality.

8. While Heschel's chapter entitled "The Sublime" in *God in Search of Man* centers on the sublimity of nature (undoubtedly because this is the focus of the classical discussions of the sublime to which Heschel responds), all of his works attest even more to the sublimity of human life (which, of course, can to an extent be understood as part of nature) and to human creativity (for example, in language, music, and noble deeds), as well as to the sublimity of time and historic events. To mention but a few examples: *Who Is Man?* is an eloquent testimony to the grandeur of being human, as is "Sacred Image of Man" in *The Insecurity of Freedom,* pp. 150–167. *The Earth Is the Lord's,* which depicts the spirituality of Eastern European Jews before the Holocaust, is a moving portrayal of human living that was indeed sublime. "The Vocation of the

Cantor," also in *Freedom,* is a reflection on "sublime words" (p. 248) and on music as "the only language that seems compatible with the wonder and mystery of being" (p. 245). Part 2 of *Man Is Not Alone,* entitled "The Problem of Living," and part 3 of *God in Search of Man,* entitled "Response," are studies of the sublime dignity of human deeds. *The Prophets* recalls the grandeur of historic events and *The Sabbath* is concerned with the sublimity of time.

9. *Search,* p. 39. Elsewhere Heschel employs a synonymous poetic image by saying that things stand out like "silent witnesses." He explains this image by saying: "All things carry a surplus of meaning over being—they mean more than what they are in themselves. Even finite facts stand for infinite meaning" (*Not Alone,* pp. 40–41). Cf. also *Who is Man?* chapter 4, pp. 50–80, which is concerned with questions of being and meaning; most pertinent are the sections entitled "Being and Meaning" (pp. 67–68) and "Transcendent Meaning" (pp. 77–80).

10. *Not Alone,* p. 22.

11. Ibid., p. 4; *Search,* p. 39.

12. *Freedom,* pp. 41–42; cf. *Not Alone,* p. 285, and *Who Is Man?* p. 88.

13. *Who Is Man?* p. 86.

14. *Freedom,* p. 47.

15. *Who Is Man?* p. 86. Cf. *Not Alone,* p. 36: "Power is the language of expediency."

16. *Freedom,* p. 47.

17. Cf. *Not Alone,* pp. 36–37, on "the way of expediency" and "the way of wonder" as two ways by which "we go out to meet the world"; cf. also *Who Is Man?* pp. 81–83, on "manipulation and appreciation" as the "two primary ways in which man relates himself to the world."

18. Abraham Joshua Heschel, "What We Might Do Together," *Religious Education,* 62 (March–April 1967), 136.

19. *Not Alone,* p. 281.

20. Although a careful reading of Heschel gives rise to the interpretation of the sublime as a nonphysical aspect of nature, there are statements of his which taken on their own could suggest that, for him, the sublime was a physical category. For instance, in *Search,* p. 83, he says: "The glory is neither an esthetic nor a physical category. It is sensed in grandeur, but it is more than grandeur." This seems to imply that grandeur is either an aesthetic category, which in his chapter on the sublime he rejects (cf. note 7 above), or a physical category, which if it is a "spiritual suggestiveness" or a "spiritual radiance" cannot be the case. (It could be, however, that Heschel is not here using "grandeur" in apposition to "esthetic" or "physical" but simply as a third term which, like these, falls short of what is meant by "glory.") This apparent inconsistency demonstrates the need to read Heschel very carefully in order to know when a particular passage of his does not truly represent his overall perspective, which is broader and more penetrating than that of his critics, but which may not always be as clearly presented. The fact that Heschel's writings are so poetic and replete with polarized images and concepts may account for the fact that the terms he uses are subject to a change of meaning in different contexts.

21. Alfred North Whitehead, *Science and the Modern World* (New York: Macmillan, 1926), p. 286.

22. William Wordsworth, "Ode: Intimations of Immortality from Early Childhood" (first published, 1807), in *The Poetical Works of Wordsworth,* ed. by T. Hutchinson, revised ed. (London, 1936), p. 460.

23. *Not Alone,* p. 5.

24. Ibid., p. 22; *Search*, p. 106.
25. *Not Alone*, pp. 40, 44.
26. John Baillie, from whom I have borrowed the phrase "nonsensuous perception," also stresses the fact that our awareness of spiritual reality is a perception in the sense that it enables us "to perceive something not otherwise perceptible; to *perceive* it, I say, and not merely to conceive it as a concept to which we are led by argument." John Baillie, *The Sense of the Presence of God* (New York: Charles Scribner's Sons, 1962), p. 53.
27. *Not alone*, p. 35.
28. Ibid., p. 63.
29. Ibid.
30. Ibid., p. 20.
31. Ibid., p. 32.
32. Ibid., p. 33.
33. Ibid., p. 58.
34. Ibid., p. 39.
35. Ibid., p. 33.
36. *Search*, p. 36.
37. Ibid.
38. "The Jewish Notion of God and Christian Renewal," p. 116.
39. *Not Alone*, p. 21.
40. Ibid., p. 39.
41. *Who Is Man?* p. 46.
42. The oldest treatise on the subject, entitled *On the Sublime*, has long been attributed to Cassius Longinus, a third-century Greek philosopher, but is now generally believed by scholars to be by an unknown writer of the first century C.E. who is often designated as Pseudo-Longinus. Although this treatise primarily treats the sublime as a quality of literary style, Heschel notes that Longinus refers also to the sublimity in nature and that he sees the inward greatness of the human soul in terms of the ability to respond to it (cf. *Search*, pp. 37–38).
43. *Freedom*, p. 47 (emphasis mine).
44. *Who Is Man?* p. 3. While all of Heschel's works seem to be born out of anguish—as well as exaltation—he explicitly says that pain and anguish were the condition for his writing *Who Is Man?*; cf. "Conversation with Heschel," p. 18, where Heschel also says: "Now what I tried to do in this book is to counter, to fight the ongoing dehumanization of man, which I see in every step, everywhere."
45. *Who Is Man?* p. 22. Heschel does not deny the fact that there is a certain animality about human being. Nevertheless, he claims: "In asking the question about man our problem is not the undeniable fact of his animality but the enigma of what he does, because and in spite of, with and apart from his animality" (ibid., p. 21).
46. Ibid., p. 29. Cf. ibid., p. 23:

> Is it not possible that, in following the example of Aristotle and contemplating man in terms of the animal species, we have been looking at man from the wrong perspective? The sense in which the term "animal" is used in defining the whole man is far from being clear and exact. Do we really know the inner life of the animals? Is it possible for us to sense pure animality, unmixed with humanity? Is the animality of a human being the same as the animality of the animal? . . . The zoomorphic conception of man enables us to assign his place in the physical universe, yet it fails to account for the infinite dissimilarity between man and the highest animal

below him. . . . In addition to its descriptive inadequacy, the suggestive and evocative meaning of the word "animal" in the term "thinking animal" distorts as much as it clarifies.

47. Ibid., p. 25. Cf. ibid., p. 27, where Heschel claims there is a "creeping self-disparagement" in the contemporary literature about humanity and adds: "Moral defamation of man may spell the doom of all of us. Moral annihilation leads to physical extermination. If man is contemptible, why be upset about the extinction of the human species?"
48. Ibid., p. 29.
49. Ibid., p. 66. Cf. Abraham Heschel, "Choose Life!" *Jubilee*, 13 (January 1966), 37: "What makes a man human is his openness to transcendence, which lifts him to a level higher than himself."
50. *Search*, p. 105.
51. *Not Alone*, p. 67.
52. Ibid., p. 70.
53. *Who Is Man?* p. 73.
54. Ibid.
55. Ibid., p. 72.
56. *Freedom*, p. 163. Cf. *Who Is Man?* p. 73: "Man is in need of meaning, but if ultimate meaning is not in need of man, and he cannot relate himself to it, then ultimate meaning is meaningless to him. As a one-sided relationship, as a reaching-out or searching for, the meeting of man and meaning would remain a goal beyond man's reach."
57. *Who Is Man?* p. 64.
58. Ibid., p. 74.
59. Ibid., p. 69.
60. *Not Alone*, p. 71.
61. "Choose Life!" p. 37.
62. *Search*, p. 158.
63. *Freedom*, pp. 49, 125.
64. *Who Is Man?* p. 77.
65. *Freedom*, p. 259.
66. *Search*, p. 182.
67. *Quest*, p. 39.
68. *Freedom*, p. 248.
69. Ibid., p. 246.
70. *Quest*, p. 105; *Search*, p. 351.
71. *Search*, p. 356.
72. "No Religion Is an Island," p. 121. The holiness or sanctity of human life, the affinity of the divine and the human, and the disclosure of the divine in the human, are the most consistently emphasized themes in and throughout Heschel's writings.
73. *Freedom*, p. 97.
74. *Quest*, pp. 124–125.
75. *Freedom*, p. 44.
76. *Search*, p. 37.
77. Ibid., pp. 95, 97.
78. Ibid., p. 89.
79. Ibid., pp. 90–91. On the "desanctification of nature," cf. Heschel's *The Sabbath: Its Meaning for Modern Man* (New York: Farrar, Straus, and Young, 1951), p. 79; hereafter cited as *Sabbath*.
80. *Search*, p. 181.
81. Ibid., p. 40. The idea that "what seems to be natural is wondrous" is a recurrent

theme in Heschel's writings. Cf., e.g., ibid., p. 51, where Heschel cites the following quotation from Nahmanides: "All things and all events in the life of the individual as well as in the life of society are miracles. There is no such thing as a natural course of events." And in ibid., p. 45, Heschel says that it is alien to the religious spirit to regard events as a natural course of things. On p. 63 of the same book he says: "For this is the essence of faith: even what appears to us as a natural necessity is an act of God" (citing Rabbi Isaac Meir Alter of Ger). The same theme is echoed in Heschel's *Israel: An Echo of Eternity* (New York: Farrar, Straus, and Giroux, 1968), p. 51; hereafter cited as *Israel:* "Things look natural and conceal what is a radical surprise." This does not mean, however, that the religious person is unaware of the laws that regulate the course of natural processes. In *Search,* p. 45, Heschel says: "He is aware of the regularity and pattern of things. However, such knowledge fails to mitigate his sense of perpetual surprise at the fact that there are facts at all. Looking at the world he would say, 'This is the Lord's doing, it is marvelous in our eyes' (Psalms 118:23)."

82. Cf. *Who Is Man?* pp. 90–92.
83. *Not Alone,* p. 267.
84. *Quest,* p. 121. It may appear that Heschel contradicts this above-stated position when, in *Not Alone,* p. 144, he says: "Creation in the language of the Bible is an act of expression." But from the context it is clear that he means not that created reality is God's self-expression (the view that he opposes in the quotation from *Quest,* p. 121) but that by the act of creation God expresses concern for the created reality.
85. *Sabbath,* p. 101.
86. Cf. *Quest,* p. 118: "A *real symbol* is a visible object that represents something invisible. . . . A real symbol represents, e.g., the Divine because it is assumed that the Divine resides in it or that the symbol partakes to some degree of the reality of the Divine." Since the world is not of God's essence, "it would be alien to the spirit of the Bible to assert that the world is a symbol of God" (ibid., p. 120).
87. *Search,* p. 97.
88. *Quest,* p. 124; cf. *Freedom,* p. 124.
89. *Freedom,* p. 151.
90. *Quest,* p. 126.
91. To say that it is in and through our contact with the sublime that we begin to perceive the divine is not to suggest that the reality of the divine is immediately known as such. Explicit awareness of the divine may be the result of reflective wonder and understanding. Yet this does not mean that the reality of God is conceived rather than perceived. It simply means that it may take some time to become explicitly aware of the reality that is perceived.
92. *Search,* p. 250.
93. *Not Alone,* p. 206.
94. *Search,* p. 95.
95. Quoted by Heschel, ibid., p. 41.
96. *Not Alone,* p. 44.
97. Ibid., p. 68.
98. *Search,* p. 41 (includes Psalms 66:3).
99. Ibid.
100. *Not Alone,* p. 22; *Search,* p. 106.
101. *Search,* p. 41 (includes Psalms 23:4).
102. *Not Alone,* pp. 4–5.
103. *Search,* p. 58; cf. Ibid., pp. 34, 160.

104. *Who Is Man?* p. 77.
105. Ibid., p. 78.
106. *Search,* p. 110.
107. *Ibid.,* p. 118.
108. *Who Is Man?* p. 31.
109. *Search,* p. 54. Cf. ibid., p. 57: "In using the term mystery we do not mean any particular esoteric quality that may be revealed to the initiated, but the essential mystery of being as being." Cf. *Not Alone,* pp. 57–58, and *Who Is Man?* pp. 87–88.
110. *Search,* p. 161.
111. *Not Alone,* pp. 30–31.
112. *Search,* p. 57.
113. Ibid., p. 59. By saying "The world is both . . . a matter of fact and a mystery" and, therefore, "we know and we do not know," Heschel perhaps leaves himself open to the misinterpretation that he means there are both nonmysterious facts that we know and mysterious facts that we do not know. But, as we have seen, Heschel sees the mystery everywhere. For him, all being is mysterious. Yet the same being, and each being encountered in the realm of being, though an unknown mystery, is also somehow a known reality.
114. Ibid., p. 114.
115. *Not Alone,* p. 61.
116. *Search,* pp. 114–115.
117. Ibid., p. 56.
118. Ibid., p. 57.
119. Ibid., p. 107.
120. Ibid., p. 105. Cf. *Not Alone,* pp. 22–23: "While the ineffable is a term of negation indicating a limitation of expression, its content is intensely affirmative, denoting an *allusiveness* to something meaningful, for which we possess no means of expression."
121. *Not Alone,* p. 22; *Search,* p. 106.
122. *Not Alone,* pp. 94–95.
123. Cf. above, p. 62.
124. *Who Is Man?* p. 71.
125. *Search,* pp. 57–58.
126. *Not Alone,* p. 46.
127. Ibid., p. 44.
128. Ibid., p. 16.
129. Ibid., pp. 48, 47, 48.
130. Ibid., pp. 202–203.
131. *Who Is Man?* p. 60.
132. Ibid., p. 111.
133. Ibid., p. 83.
134. *Search,* p. 89; cf. *Not Alone,* p. 106.
135. *Search,* p. 110.
136. *Who Is Man?* p. 76.
137. Ibid.
138. Abraham Joshua Heschel, "Faith," part 1, *The Reconstructionist,* 10 (November 3, 1944), 12.
139. *Not Alone,* pp. 226–227.
140. Cf. *Search,* pp. 67–68.
141. Ibid., p. 67. For example, Heschel mentions the Maat of the Egyptians, Pta and Ash among the Indians and Persians, and the Moira among the Greeks. Cf. *Prophets,* pp. 238–241, where Heschel contrasts the biblical doctrine of

divine pathos with the Greek doctrine of moira and distinguishes between pathos and power.
142. *Who Is Man?* pp. 76–77.
143. *Search,* p. 66.
144. Ibid., p. 74.
145. Ibid.
146. "The Jewish Notion of God and Christian Renewal," p. 108.
147. *Search,* p. 26. The question of the realness of God and the human ability to believe in and have an understanding of God is raised throughout *Search;* cf., e.g., pp. 101, 114, 117, 120–122, 131, 159.
148. Ibid., p. 114.
149. "What We Might Do Together," p. 137.

Chapter 4 (pp. 78–103)

1. *Search,* p. 82.
2. *Freedom,* p. 60.
3. *Search,* p. 83.
4. Ibid., p. 90.
5. Ibid., p. 97.
6. Ibid., p. 66.
7. Cf. chapter 3, p. 58, where it is argued that the sense of the sublime is a nonsensuous perception.
8. *Search,* p. 130 (emphasis mine).
9. *Prophets,* pp. 265–266. Without mentioning his name, Heschel is obviously replying to William James who, in *The Varieties of Religious Experience* (New York: Longmans, 1902), p. 58, says: "It is as if there were in the human consciousness a *sense of reality, a feeling of objective presence, a perception of* what we may call 'something there.' . . ." In all fairness to James it should be pointed out that his intention in this statement is not to suggest that God is an impersonal reality but that God *is a reality,* not a subjective projection of the human mind (or at least that it seems as if God is a reality). Heschel's concern is not to suggest that James's God is impersonal, but to point out that religious experience, at least in the biblical tradition, is not properly depicted as "a perception of . . . 'something there'." Yet even if James's God is a personal agent, this God, as "something there," is not perceived to transcend the universe but is a "cosmic power" within it, as we shall see in the next note.
10. Notice that for James, God, as an "objective presence," as "something there," is *"a MORE of the same quality,"* the "higher part" of ourselves, *"which is operative in the universe"* or, in other words, is the "higher part of the universe" (*The Varieties of Religious Experience,* pp. 508 and 516). As such, God is indeed a spiritual reality but does not transcend the spiritual dimension of the universe. Thus, God is not experienced *in contrast to* nature but as the spiritual power inherent within nature. For James, then, this finite God is not distinguishable from the transcendent dimension of nature. But, for Heschel, God, as the "subjective presence," as the Transcendent Subject, is beyond the transcendent dimension of the world, since such a dimension, spiritual as it may be, is not a personal reality, not a Transcendent Person. The transcendent dimension is "something more" than the material constitution of the world, but it is not a Transcendent Subject. Unlike James, Heschel, conscious as he is of a Transcendent Subject, is aware of what von Hügel calls "the Contrasting

Other," contrasting because this Other, God, is not only apprehended "in, and with, and on occasion of" our apprehending other realities, but "also in contrast to" those other realities. These are oft-repeated assertions of von Hügel; cf., e.g., Friedrich von Hügel, *Essays and Addresses on the Philosophy of Religion,* first series (London, 1921, 1963), p. 188; *Essays and Addresses on the Philosophy of Religion* second series (London, 1926, 1963), p. 143; *Letters from Baron Friedrich von Hügel to a Niece,* ed. by Gwendolen Plunket Greene (London, 1928, 1965), p. 13.

11. *Prophets,* p. 487.
12. *Not Alone,* p. 113.
13. Cf. ibid., where Heschel says:

> Xenophanes, looking at the universe, said: "All is one." Parmenides, in taking the one seriously, was bound to deny the reality of everything else. Moses, however, did not say: "All is one," but: "God is One." Within the world there is the stubborn fact of plurality, divergence and conflict. . . . The vision of the One, upon which we stake our effort and our ultimate hope, is not to be found in contemplations about nature or history. It is a vision of Him who transcends the scenes of both, subdued yet present everywhere, giving us the power to aid in bringing about ultimate unification.

14. Ibid., p. 114 (emphasis mine).
15. Ibid., p. 68.
16. Maurice Friedman, "Divine Need and Human Wonder: The Philosophy of Abraham J. Heschel," *Judaism,* 25 (Winter 1976), 76.
17. *Search,* p. 26.
18. Ibid., pp. 174–175.
19. *Between God and Man,* p. 16.
20. *Search,* p. 162.
21. Ibid., p. 66.
22. *Not Alone,* pp. 71–72.
23. "Choose Life!" p. 37.
24. *Search,* p. 158.
25. Ibid., p. 162.
26. Abraham J. Heschel, "On Prayer," *Conservative Judaism,* 25 (Fall 1970), 5.
27. *Search,* p. 160.
28. "Choose Life!" p. 37.
29. *Not Alone,* p. 138. Cf. *Prophets,* p. 486: "To be a person is to have concern for the nonself."
30. *Who Is Man?* p. 74 (emphasis mine).
31. *Prophets,* p. 440 (emphasis mine).
32. *Not Alone,* p. 259.
33. Ibid., p. 139.
34. Ibid., p. 142.
35. Ibid.
36. *Search,* p. 138.
37. Ibid., p. 131.
38. Cf. chapter 1, p. 3.
39. *Not Alone,* p. 282.
40. *Search,* p. 132. Cf. *Not Alone,* p. 76: "Philosophy begins with man's question; *religion begins with God's question and man's answer.*"
41. *Prophets,* p. 266. This is an obvious, though unnoted, reply to Paul Tillich, *Systematic Theology,* vol. 1 (Chicago: Chicago University Press, 1951), p. 166.

42. *Not Alone*, p. 20.
43. Ibid., p. 78.
44. Ibid., p. 73.
45. Ibid., p. 61.
46. Ibid., pp. 64, 65.
47. Cf. *Search*, p. 231, where Heschel says: "To assume that prophetic revelation was the expression of an urge, hidden in the heart of the prophet, of which he not only was unaware but which he resisted, would presuppose the action of a spiritual power so wise and so holy, that there would be no other name for it but God."
48. *Prophets*, p. 266. Cf. *Search*, p. 120: "God cannot be sensed as a second thought, as an explanation of the origin of the universe. He is either the first and the last, or just another concept."
49. *Search*, p. 137.
50. *Not Alone*, p. 72.
51. Ibid., p. 70.
52. *Prophets*, p. 484.
53. *Search*, p. 412.
54. *Not Alone*, p. 226.
55. Ibid., p. 112.
56. Ibid., p. 109.
57. *Search*, p. 161; cf. *Not Alone*, p. 109.
58. *Freedom*, p. 95.
59. *Who Is Man?* p. 70.
60. *Not Alone*, p. 12.
61. *Who Is Man?* p. 71; cf. *Prophets*, pp. 263–264.
62. *Who Is Man?*, p. 91.
63. Cf. *Search*, p. 413: "The divine concern is not a theological afterthought but a fundamental category of ontology."
64. *Who Is Man?* pp. 91–92.
65. That Heschel admits a rational distinction between the existence and the essence of God is clear, for example, in *Truth*, p. 292, where he says: "The belief in God does not come through anthropocentric speculation, but in overwhelming moments of the awareness of His existence. These lead to an understanding of His essence."
66. *Search*, p. 81.
67. *Sabbath*, p. 100.
68. *Search*, pp. 81, 85.
69. *Israel*, p. 10.
70. *Not Alone*, p. 84. It seems to me that Heschel could have challenged the particular Kantian doctrine in question in its application to the question of God's existence, precisely because the term "existence" is used in qualitatively different senses when applied to God and when applied to other beings: when applied to God, existence is conceived as necessary; when applied to other beings, existence is conceived as contingent. While I find the Kantian doctrine that existence cannot be deduced from thought to be acceptable with regard to finite or contingent beings, I find it questionable when applied to God's existence. In other words, while I agree that it is not valid to deduce the existence of a contingent object from the idea of it, I do consider it valid to infer the existence of a necessary reality from the idea of such a reality. Thus do I accept Anselm's "ontological argument" for God's existence and agree with David Tracy who, in *Blessed Rage for Order: The New Pluralism in Theology* (New York: Seabury Press, 1975), p. 185, writes: "If one can coherently

conceive the concept 'necessary existent,' he must, short of self-contradiction, affirm its reality." And again, p. 186: "In this single instance, the instance of coherently conceiving the necessary reality of God, meaning [the idea] and truth [the reality] are logically identical." Tracy is here explaining the position advanced by Charles Hartshorne in various writings, especially in *Anselm's Discovery* (LaSalle, Ill.: Open Court, 1965). Compare John E. Smith, who, in *Experience and God* (New York and London: Oxford University Press, 1968), p. 128, maintains that the principal objection against the ontological argument "is not conclusive because of the dual sense of existence involved."

The ontological argument is particularly valid, I believe, when used in conjunction with the cosmological approach, for the idea of a necessary existent is given with the realization that for contingent beings to exist there must be a necessary reality upon which they depend for their existence. But while the ontological argument is logically cogent, I also admit that it is an insufficient ground upon which to build religious faith (and this seems to be Heschel's reason for not following it). I therefore agree with Smith that the classical objection to the ontological argument does carry a certain force. The reason why it is not a sufficient foundation for religious faith (or for genuine religious understanding) is, as Smith also points out, that while it provides us with a *"rational encounter,"* it *"does not provide us with the actual encounter* in experience" (op. cit., p. 128). So while I disagree with Heschel when he suggests that it is not valid to deduce the existence of God from the idea of God, I do nevertheless agree with him that genuine knowledge of God in the biblical sense—i.e., the sense required as a foundation for faith—is the result of the experience of God's presence, not the result of the speculative approach.

I may also point out that the very fact that Heschel speaks of "an idea which we may find ourselves *obliged to think*" indicates, contrary to what he suggests, that the idea does "hold true of a reality that lies beyond the reach of the mind." For we are not *obliged* to have an idea of a finite object that we have not encountered. But it does seem to me that we are obliged to have an idea of a necessary existent if we are aware of existence at all. And if such an idea is one that we are obliged to think, then it seems to me valid to deduce from this idea "a reality that lies beyond the reach of the mind."

71. *Search*, p. 121. This is a slight revision of what Heschel already wrote in *Not Alone*, p. 84.
72. *Not Alone*, pp. 84–85; *Search*, p. 121.
73. *Truth*, p. 292 (emphasis mine).
74. Cf. *Search*, p. 121, where Heschel says that "our belief in His reality . . . *is an ontological presupposition*"; and compare two pages later where he says, "We said that God is an ontological presupposition." As I interpret it, both God *and* our belief in God's reality are ontological presuppositions because: 1) The reality of God is the ontological presupposition of our experience of God; and 2) our belief in God, which arises in such experience, is the ontological presupposition of our ideas and statements about God. The experience of God, and in some sense even the belief in God (if in this case "belief" can be used as a synonym for "faith" or "trust"), may be preconceptual or prereflective. This prereflective experience or tacit belief is the presupposition of our reflective idea of God and our explicit affirmation of divine reality. But in any case, the ontological presupposition about which Heschel speaks is not, as Maurice Friedman claims in "Divine Need and Human Wonder," p. 77, "only another name for the awareness of the ineffable itself." It is *God* or our experiential *belief in God* that is the ontological presupposition of our affirmation of God's existence. Nor is Heschel's ontological presupposition "the defeat of reason,"

as Arthur Cohen claims in *The Natural and Supernatural Jew*, p. 247. Heschel's point is precisely that *it is reasonable* to assume that our awareness of the empowering and confronting presence which we call the presence of God presupposes the reality of that for which there is no other name but God. So too is it reasonable to assume that our explicit affirmation of God presupposes our belief in God's reality, so that "our thought is but an after-belief." For those who have had the experiences that Heschel describes, it is reasonable to assume that God and our experiential belief in God's reality precede and provoke our reasoning about God and our explicit affirmation of God's existence.

75. *Not Alone*, p. 91.
76. *Search*, pp. 121–122.
77. Ibid., p. 82.
78. *Not Alone*, p. 145.
79. Ibid., pp. 143–144.
80. Ibid., pp. 67–68. Cf. *Truth*, p. 292, where Heschel says that "the awareness of His existence" leads "to an *understanding of His essence*" (emphasis mine).
81. *Not Alone*, p. 135.
82. Ibid., p. 136.
83. Cf. ibid., pp. 142–143.
84. *Search*, pp. 181–182.
85. *Prophets*, p. 277. Cf. ibid., p. 273: "Impropriety is the mark of all expression that presumes to convey what is meant by the divine. Fortunately, creative thinking is not always hurt by the awareness of impropriety, nor does it dread the frown of the critic. In trying to set things right, we must not forget the anguish of sensing things altogether." Cf. also *Quest*, p. 41: "The sense for the power of words and the sense for the impotence of human expression are equally characteristic of the religious consciousness."
86. Cf. *Prophets*, p. 270.
87. Ibid., p. 271.
88. Ibid., p. 276.
89. Ibid., pp. 271–272.
90. Ibid., p. 229.
91. Cf. *Search*, p. 125: "What is the minimum of meaning that the word God holds for us? It is first the idea of *ultimacy*."
92. "Choose Life!" p. 37.
93. *Who Is Man?* p. 69. Transcendence as such is not God, but God is "a living transcendence." If the transcendence we encounter were not alive, it would not be called God, for "we cannot in religious thinking say God and deny at the same time that He is alive" (*Search*, p. 127). This is because "the living soul is not concerned with a dead cause but with a living God" (ibid., p. 125). "This, then, is the minimum of meaning which the word God holds for us: God is alive" (ibid, p. 126).
94. *Prophets*, pp. 218, 225.
95. *Not Alone*, p. 244.
96. *Prophets*, p. 277.
97. Ibid., pp. 297, 220.
98. Ibid., p. 225.
99. *Not Alone*, p. 78.
100. The first two quotations in this sentence are from *Who Is Man?* p. 91. In *Not Alone*, pp. 237–238, Heschel seems to be using the terms "God" and "the holy dimension" synonymously. In a separate essay I have argued that, while

Heschel is inconsistent in his use of the term "the holy dimension" (sometimes using it as a synonym for God, sometimes as a term for the sacred aspect of all being), he does not intend to suggest that God, as the holy dimension, is an aspect of the universe, but that the presence of God is the ultimate sphere in which the universe abides.

101. *Prophets,* p. 486.
102. The first two quotations in this sentence are from ibid., p. 486. Heschel often refers to God as the Supreme Being; cf., e.g., *Not Alone,* pp. 132 and 143.
103. *Prophets,* p. 364; pp. 222, 237, 366.
104. Franklin Sherman, *The Promise of Heschel,* p. 29.
105. Ibid., p. 37.
106. Edmond La B. Cherbonnier, "Heschel's Time-Bomb," *Conservative Judaism,* 28 (Fall 1973), 17. Cherbonnier makes no reference to Sherman. His point is to defend Heschel's biblical understanding of God as a personal agent against those who claim that, although God may include the personal, God is not a person. Cherbonnier does not mention Paul Tillich, but it seems that he has him in mind when he says: "Should the student of the Bible have any misgivings about the claim that the personal God of the Bible is really only a symbol for being-itself, the symbolist patiently explains that there is nothing to worry about, since, to use the currently fashionable jargon, 'the personal element is not left out, but is included in being-itself.'" Cf. Paul Tillich, *Systematic Theology,* vol. 1 (Chicago: Chicago University Press, 1951), p. 245 (p. 271 in British edition): "'Personal God' does not mean that God is *a* person, but he is not less than personal. . . . 'Personal God' is a confusing symbol." In other words, as one of Tillich's interpreters puts it: God "is 'the Personal-Itself.' . . . Man, of necessity, must communicate with God by using personal language, only because man knows no other more profound instrument of communication. But this communication does not proceed from one individual person center (man) to another (God)" (L. Gordon Tait, *The Promise of Tillich* [Philadelphia: J. B. Lippincott Co., 1971], pp. 54–55). That this is in line with Tillich's own position is clear in that Tillich himself says (in *Systematic Theology,* vol. 1, pp. 244–245): "God cannot be called a self, because the concept 'self' implies separation from and contrast to everything which is not self. . . . The divine life participates in every life as its ground and aim. God participates in everything that is. . . . Certainly such statements are highly symbolic. They can have the unfortunate logical implication that there is something alongside God in which he participates from the outside." In other words, for Tillich, God, as being-itself, is "the power of being in which everything participates" or "the power inherent in everything" (ibid., pp. 230 and 236). According to Cherbonnier, the view that the personal element is included in that which is not a person "conceals fuzzy thinking"—for the reason he expresses in the above quotation. Moreover, Cherbonnier rejects the view that the personal God of the Bible is merely a symbol (and a "confusing" one at that) for being-itself; in other words, he rejects the view that God is not a self: "If the conception of God as Someone is taken figuratively, the whole Bible becomes unintelligible. . . . To love, to create, to judge, to choose—these are all verbs, with God as subject. Subtract the Subject and they become meaningless" (op. cit., pp. 17–18). That Tillich does indeed "subtract the subject" is clear when, in *The Courage to Be* (New Haven: Yale University Press, 1952), p. 187, he says: "God is neither object nor subject and is therefore above the scheme into which theism has forced him." Heschel would never say that God is not a subject; on the contrary, he maintains that God is "all-

subject" (*Prophets,* pp. 218, 486). For Heschel, God is "the supreme Subject" (ibid., p. 485). In my judgment, then, Cherbonnier's argument is thoroughly Heschelian.

107. *The Promise of Heschel,* p. 37. While this misrepresents Heschel's view, it is in accord with Tillich's. Cf., e.g., *The Courage to Be,* p. 187.
108. *Freedom,* p. 151.
109. *Prophets,* p. 273.
110. Ibid., p. 486.
111. Ibid., p. 277.
112. Ibid., p. 263; *Who Is Man?* p. 71.
113. *Prophets,* p. 366.

Chapter 5 (pp. 104–149)

1. *Not Alone,* p. 161.
2. Cf. *Search,* p. 16.
3. *Freedom,* p. 119.
4. *Search,* p. 43.
5. *Not Alone,* p. 160.
6. Quoted in Jacob Neusner, *History and Torah: Essays on Jewish Learning* (New York: Schocken Books, 1965), p. 29.
7. *Search,* p. 423.
8. Ibid., p. 298.
9. Michael Polanyi, *The Tacit Dimension* (New York: Doubleday and Co., 1966), p. 67.
10. *Search,* p. 141.
11. Michael Polanyi, *Personal Knowledge: Towards a Post-Critical Philosophy* (London: Routledge and Kegan Paul, 1962), p. 53.
12. *Quest,* p. 112.
13. Michael Polanyi, *Personal Knowledge,* p. 53.
14. *Who Is Man?* p. 99.
15. *Israel,* p. 128.
16. *Not Alone,* p. 161; cf. *Freedom,* p. 203.
17. Cf. *Earth,* pp. 8–9, and *Freedom,* p. 72.
18. *Israel,* p. 137.
19. *Not Alone,* p. 165; *Freedom,* p. 198.
20. *Search,* p. 152.
21. *Who Is Man?* p. 99.
22. *Not Alone,* p. 164. Cf. *Truth,* p. 188, where, concerning "the acquisition of faith," Heschel writes: "Only he who is a pioneer is worthy of being an heir."
23. *Search,* p. 424.
24. *Not Alone,* pp. 164–165; cf. *Freedom,* p. 198.
25. *Truth,* p. 192.
26. Cf., e.g., *Search,* p. 321, and *Truth,* p. 311.
27. *Search,* p. 199.
28. *Prophets,* p. 438.
29. Ibid., p. 202.
30. Cf. chapter 4, p. 98.
31. *Search,* p. 198.
32. *Prophets,* p. 438; cf. *Search,* p. 136.
33. *Prophets,* p. 436.

34. *Search,* p. 209; *Prophets,* p. 431; *Who Is Man?* p. 42.
35. *Prophets,* p. 431.
36. Ibid., p. 436.
37. Despite the fact that Heschel empathically denies that there is a continuous revelation, he does, in one instance, speak of there being "one revelation" of which there are various "installments" (*Prophets,* p. 366). But Heschel does not mean to suggest that this one revelation is continuous, only that there is "a continuity, an all-embracing meaning" that welds the various revelatory events into one. Cf. ibid., pp. 389, 472.
38. *Not Alone,* p. 153.
39. Cf. *Search,* p. 207: In the happenings of history "we hear the voice as well as the silence of God."
40. Ibid., p. 155.
41. *Not Alone,* p. 151.
42. *Israel,* p. 135.
43. "On Prayer," p. 11.
44. *Search,* p. 85.
45. Ibid., p. 81.
46. Ibid., p. 255.
47. Ibid.
48. Ibid., p. 188; cf. ibid., pp. 201–202, 221.
49. Ibid., p. 174.
50. Cf. ibid., pp. 169–174.
51. Cf. ibid., pp. 169–170.
52. Cf. ibid., p. 171; cf. *Freedom,* p. 162; *Who Is Man?* p. 66.
53. *Search,* pp. 172–173.
54. Ibid., pp. 126, 173.
55. *Prophets,* p. 227.
56. *Not Alone,* p. 133; *Search,* p. 164.
57. *Who Is Man?* p. 77.
58. Cf. *Prophets,* pp. 227–228, where Heschel claims that God is not "The Wholly Other," a being "shrouded in unfathomable darkness," but "The Holy One" whose will may be known.
59. *Search,* p. 173.
60. Ibid., p. 250.
61. Ibid., p. 189.
62. Ibid., p. 184.
63. Ibid., p. 189.
64. Ibid., pp. 185–186.
65. Ibid., pp. 178–179.
66. *Not Alone,* p. 168; *Freedom,* p. 177.
67. *Search,* p. 187.
68. Ibid., p. 180.
69. Ibid., pp. 182–183.
70. Cf. chapter 4, p. 99.
71. Cf. *Search,* p. 185.
72. Cf. ibid.
73. Cf. ibid., p. 249.
74. Cf. ibid., p. 247.
75. Cf. ibid., pp. 233–234.
76. Cf. ibid., p. 247. Cf. Michael Polayni, *Meaning* (Chicago and London: Chicago University Press, 1975), p. 180: "What genuinely . . . opens doors to greater meaning is what we can only verbally refuse to believe."

77. *Theologians at Work*, p. 77.
78. *Search*, p. 252; cf. *Freedom*, p. 172.
79. *Search*, p. 243.
80. Ibid., pp. 241–242.
81. Ibid., p. 252.
82. Ibid.
83. Cf. *Prophets*, pp. 206, 214–215.
84. *Search*, p. 232.
85. Ibid., p. 250.
86. Ibid., p. 181.
87. *Not Alone*, p. 129.
88. *Search*, p. 265.
89. *Israel*, p. 58.
90. *Search*, p. 261.
91. Ibid., p. 264.
92. Cf. ibid., pp. 26 and 260.
93. Ibid., p. 260; cf. *Earth*, p. 98.
94. *Search*, p. 260.
95. *Israel*, p. 45.
96. Cf. below, pp. 144–146.
97. *Israel*, p. 47.
98. *Search*, pp. 252, 238.
99. *Israel*, p. 47; cf. *Freedom*, p. 172.
100. "The Jewish Notion of God and Christian Renewal," p. 111.
101. "No Religion Is an Island," p. 118.
102. "The Jewish Notion of God and Christian Renewal," p. 113.
103. Ibid., pp. 113–114.
104. *Who Is Man?* p. 119.
105. *Freedom*, p. 172.
106. *Search*, p. 274.
107. Ibid., p. 27.
108. Ibid., p. 185.
109. Ibid., p. 273.
110. Ibid., p. 274.
111. Ibid., p. 239; *Israel*, p. 46.
112. *Search*, p. 274.
113. Ibid.
114. Ibid., pp. 272–273.
115. Abraham J. Heschel, "God, Torah, and Israel," in *Theology and Church in Times of Change: Essays in Honor of John Coleman Bennett* (Philadelphia: Westminster Press, 1970), p. 71.
116. "Teaching Jewish Theology," p. 12.
117. Cf. chapter 4, p. 98, where transitive concern is cited as an essential attribute of God, and cf. *Prophets*, pp. 223–224, where Heschel speaks of divine pathos as God's being "moved and affected by what happens in the world," even "intimately affected."
118. *Prophets*, p. 226.
119. Ibid., p. 224.
120. Ibid., p. 259.
121. Cf. *Not Alone*, pp. 136–139.
122. Cf. *Ibid.*, p. 245, and *Prophets*, pp. 225–226.
123. *Prophets*, p. 224.
124. Ibid., p. 256.

125. Ibid., p. 225.
126. Ibid., p. 237.
127. Ibid., p. 260.
128. Ibid., p. 247.
129. Ibid., pp. 262, 264. Here we may note a parallel between Heschel's thought and that of Alfred North Whitehead, the patriarch of modern process philosophy. Although Heschel never addresses the question of an affinity between process philosophy and his own biblical philosophy, it seems clear from the above that, whatever differences there may be between the two, Heschel would be able to concur with one of Whitehead's central tenets: "God is not to be treated as an exception to all metaphysical principles, invoked to save their collapse. He is their chief exemplification." Cf. Whitehead's *Process and Reality: An Essay in Cosmology* (Cambridge University Press, 1929), p. 521.
130. *Not Alone*, p. 245.
131. Fritz A. Rothschild, *Between God and Man*, p. 25. Several authors have used this designation for God as if it were either Heschel's or their own phrase, failing to credit Rothschild with coining this phrase to interpret Heschel's understanding of God.
132. *Prophets*, p. 277.
133. Ibid., p. 231.
134. Ibid., p. 485.
135. *Not Alone*, p. 244.
136. *Prophets*, p. 248.
137. Ibid., p. 250.
138. Ibid.
139. Ibid., p. 316.
140. Ibid., p. 258.
141. Ibid., p. 238.
142. Ibid., pp. 258–259.
143. Ibid., pp. 308, 313, 314.
144. *Search*, p. 249.
145. For further elaboration of Heschel's doctrine of divine pathos, including a defense of it against its principal critic, Eliezer Berkovits ("Dr. A. J. Heschel's Theology of Pathos," *Tradition: A Journal of Orthodox Thought*, 6 [Spring–Summer 1964], 67–104), cf. John C. Merkle, "Heschel's Theology of Divine Pathos," in *Abraham Joshua Heschel: Exploring His Life and Thought*, ed. by John C. Merkle, to be published by Macmillan.
146. *Search*, p. 288.
147. Ibid.
148. Ibid.
149. Cf. ibid., pp. 289–290, and *Freedom*, pp. 160–161.
150. *Search*, p. 290.
151. Ibid.
152. Recall that Jacob Neusner's introduction to Judaism is entitled *The Way of Torah*. That Heschel would agree with this definition of Judaism is clear from *Search*, p. 167: "Judaism may be described as a relation between *man with Torah* and *God*."
153. *Freedom*, p. 198; cf. *Search*, pp. 328 and 338.
154. *Search*, p. 307.
155. Ibid., p. 306.
156. *Freedom*, pp. 219–220.
157. *Search*, p. 338.
158. Ibid., p. 308; cf. ibid., pp. 296, 321.

159. Ibid., p. 315; cf. ibid., p. 338.
160. Ibid., p. 344.
161. Ibid., p. 299.
162. Ibid., p. 298. Cf. ibid., p. 197: "At Sinai we have learned that spiritual values are not only aspirations in us but a response to a transcendent appeal addressed to us."
163. *Quest*, p. 101; *Search*, p. 302.
164. *Search*, pp. 274–275.
165. Ibid., p. 303.
166. Ibid., p. 302.
167. *Quest*, p. 102.
168. Ibid., pp. 100–101; cf. *Freedom*, p. 205.
169. *Quest*, p. 101; *Freedom*, p. 205.
170. *Search*, pp. 272, 270.
171. Ibid., p. 269; in ibid., pp. 269–270, Heschel cites two classical examples of such challenges.
172. "God, Torah, and Israel," p. 78; cf. *Truth*, pp. 59–60.
173. *Search*, p. 268.
174. *Quest*, p. 94; cf. *Not Alone*, p. 270.
175. *Quest*, p. 93.
176. Ibid., p. 102.
177. Ibid., p. 103.
178. *Earth*, p. 63.
179. *Not Alone*, pp. 266–267.
180. *Search*, p. 307.
181. Ibid., p. 356.
182. "God, Torah, and Israel," pp. 75, 78, 81.
183. Ibid., p. 74.
184. Ibid., pp. 76, 82.
185. Ibid., p. 79; cf. *Truth*, p. 59.
186. *Freedom*, p. 212.
187. Ibid., p. 202.
188. *Search*, pp. 422, 425.
189. Ibid., p. 424.
190. *Freedom*, p. 202.
191. *Search*, p. 424.
192. Ibid., p. 167.
193. Ibid.; *Freedom*, p. 201.
194. *Freedom*, p. 233.
195. *Search*, p. 422.
196. This letter has been reprinted in *Jewish Identity*, ed. by Sidney B. Hoenig (New York, 1965), pp. 229–231. The quotation cited occurs on p. 231.
197. *Israel*, p. 45; cf. *Not Alone*, pp. 243–244; *Freedom*, p. 202; "God, Torah, and Israel," p. 86; "Teaching Jewish Theology," p. 17.
198. *Freedom*, p. 202; "No Religion Is an Island," p. 117. It is clear that by "the fate of God" Heschel does not mean the future of God's existence but the future of God's impact on the world.
199. *Earth*, p. 98.
200. *Theologians at Work*, pp. 77, 78.
201. Ibid., p. 78; cf. "God, Torah, and Israel," p. 84; "No Religion Is an Island," p. 125.
202. "No Religion Is an Island," p. 118.

203. "Conversation with Heschel," p. 13.
204. Cf. *Freedom*, pp. 169–171; "No Religion Is an Island," p. 124.
205. "The Jewish Notion of God and Christian Renewal," p. 111.
206. Ibid., p. 113; *Theologians at Work*, pp. 77, 78.
207. Cf. "The Jewish Notion of God and Christian Renewal," p. 114.
208. "No Religion Is an Island," p. 129; cf. *Search*, p. 246.
209. *Search*, pp. 425–426.
210. "The Jewish Notion of God and Christian Renewal," p. 110.
211. "No Religion Is an Island," p. 121.
212. *Freedom*, p. 164.
213. "Conversation with Heschel," p. 4.
214. "No Religion Is an Island," p. 127.
215. Ibid., p. 126; cf. "Conversation with Heschel," p. 13.
216. "No Religion Is an Island," p. 126. Concerning Heschel's acceptance of the validity of other religions, one critic, Harold Kasimow, in *Divine-Human Encounter*, claims that "Heschel's view comes into *direct conflict* with classical sources of Judaism" (p. 83). Kasimow bases his claim on the belief that Heschel grants validity "to all the world religions" (p. 79) and regards other faiths as "equally true." After quoting Immanuel Jakobivits, "the recognition of other faiths as 'equally true' is branded an apostasy in Jewish law" (p. 84), Kasimow says: "Given this evidence, we must therefore conclude that Heschel's attitude toward other religions is in conflict with the position of classical Judaism" (p. 85). Yet nowhere does Heschel suggest that *all* religions are valid or that other faiths are equally true. All Heschel claims is that "in this aeon diversity of religions is the will of God" and that, interpreting Malachi 1:11, "it seems that the prophet proclaims that all men all over the world, though they confess different conceptions of God, are really worshipping One God, the Father of all men, though they may not be aware of it" ("No Religion Is an Island," p. 127; quoted by Kasimow, pp. 79–80). Heschel sees value in a number of religions, as do Maimonides and other sages in Israel's history. He therefore considers the diversity of religions a sign of God's will. This does not mean that Heschel regards *all* religions as valid or thinks other faiths reflect truth to the degree of Judaism. Kasimow also suggests that Heschel's position on other religions seems inconsistent, though really paradoxical, within his own theological structure because Heschel "would like to see all the world open its heart and mind to the words of the prophets" (p. 86). But desiring this is not the same as wanting the world to convert to Judaism. Heschel may desire that the words of the prophets be heeded while at the same time be open to the fact that people may heed these words in the context of their own traditions. Kasimow suggests another reason for Heschel's apparent inconsistency is the fact that "for Heschel, 'the renewal of man' can occur if only man would come to grips with the biblical view of the world" (p. 86). But coming to grips with the biblical view is not the same as becoming a Jew. Moreover, Heschel does not suggest that "the renewal of man" can occur "only if" human beings come to grips with the biblical view but "if only" they would. Therefore, Heschel's view need not be considered inconsistent or paradoxical. Rather, it is one of commitment to Judaism while being open to the validity within other religions.
217. *Search*, pp. 289–290.
218. Cf. John L. McKenzie, S.J., S.V. "Holy," *Dictionary of the Bible* (Milwaukee: Bruce Publishing Company, 1965), p. 365.
219. Cf. *Freedom*, p. 226.
220. "No Religion Is an Island," p. 130.

221. *Quest*, p. 124.
222. "On Prayer," p. 8.
223. "No Religion Is an Island," p. 130.

Chapter 6 (pp. 153–172)

1. *Search*, p. 47.
2. Ibid., p. 77; cf. ibid., p. 153, and *Who Is Man?* p. 89.
3. *Search*, p. 40.
4. Ibid., p. 46.
5. Ibid., pp. 118–119. Cf. *Not Alone*, p. 68: "The sense of the ineffable does not give us an awareness of God. It only leads to a plane, where no one can remain both callous and calm, unstunned and unabashed." Recall that it was in this sense that religion was said to begin with the sense of the sublime, not because the sublime is divine but because it alludes to the divine (cf. above, chapter 3, note 5).
6. Cf. *Not Alone*, pp. 3–4: "Perhaps more significant than the fact of our awareness of the cosmic is our consciousness of *having to* be aware of it, as if it were an *imperative*, a compulsion to pay attention to that which lies beyond our grasp." Here Heschel is using "the cosmic" as synonymous with "grandeur" or "the sublime." Note that Heschel also speaks of awe as being imperative; cf. ibid., pp. 27 and 63; *Search*, p. 106; *Who Is Man?* p. 77; cf. also my analysis of this below, pp. 167–170.
7. *Not Alone*, p. 37; *Search*, p. 46.
8. *Search*, p. 349.
9. *Not Alone*, p. 36.
10. *Who Is Man?* p. 82.
11. *Not Alone*, p. 37.
12. Ibid., p. 39.
13. "No Religion Is an Island," p. 121.
14. Fritz A. Rothschild, *Between God and Man*, pp. 11–12.
15. *Not Alone*, p. 63.
16. Ibid., p. 16.
17. Ibid., p. 12.
18. Ibid., p. 58.
19. *Who Is Man?* p. 87.
20. For Heschel's contrast between curiosity and radical amazement, cf. *Not Alone*, p. 73, and *Search*, pp. 45–46, 99.
21. *Search*, p. 110.
22. *Not Alone*, p. 44.
23. Cf. Chapter 4, p. 92.
24. *Search*, p. 99.
25. *Sabbath*, p. 100.
26. *Search*, pp. 45–46.
27. Ibid., p. 117; *Not Alone*, p. 13.
28. I wish to emphasize the fact that Heschel does not deny that radical amazement is the root of philosophical and scientific thought because this is the erroneous interpretation advanced by Arthur Cohen in *The Natural and Supernatural Jew*, pp. 239–240. In order to support his claim that Heschel discards "the forms of traditional philosophic cognition . . . in favor of their Biblical antecedents,"

Cohen says: "Heschel, to be sure, is well aware that Plato believed that 'philosophy begins in wonder.' He is at pains nevertheless to demonstrate that the 'wonder' of Plato, to judge by the subsequent history of philosophy, results in a species of doubt which inhibits man's fresh encounter with the world, and issues finally in that 'radical despair' which is the predicament of modern man. Presumably philosophy is a dead end" (pp. 239–240). In a footnote, Cohen adds: "Heschel quotes Plato's affirmation ['Philosophy begins in wonder'] in the *Theatetus,* 155D, but it is very unclear in the gloss that follows his quotation whether he really believes Plato's 'wonder' is so different from his own, or whether he in fact means what he says when he contends that Plato's wonder is a species of doubt which 'ends in radical despair'" (ibid).

In response to Cohen, I should like to point out that while he is right about the fact that there is a gloss or mistaken translation which follows Heschel's quotation of Plato's statement, it is merely that—a mistaken translation—and not a misunderstanding on Heschel's part. Although Heschel translates *thaumazein* as "to doubt" whereas it should be translated as "to wonder," it is obvious from the context that this is merely a slip on Heschel's part (or on his editor's) and that he in fact means to translate *thaumazein* as "to wonder." In order to prove my point I quote the paragraph in which the gloss appears: "A philosophy that begins with radical doubt ends in radical despair. It was the principle of *dubito ut intelligam* that prepared the soil for modern gospels of despair. 'Philosophy begins in wonder' (Plato, *Theatetus* 155D), in a state of mind which we should like to call thaumatism (from *thaumazein*—to doubt) as distinguished from skepticism" (*Not Alone,* p. 13). Now *"dubito ut intelligam"* is Cartesian, not Platonic; and Heschel is contrasting this philosophic starting-point with Plato's "thaumatic" point of departure. As he clearly points out in the last sentence, thaumatism must be distinguished from skepticism. Skepticism is the result of *"dubito ut intelligam";* thaumatism is the result of *admiror ut intelligam.* So from the context in which the gloss appears, as well as from statements which Heschel has made elsewhere (some of which I have quoted), it is clear that Heschel is not contending (as Cohen says) "that Plato's wonder is a species of doubt which 'ends in radical despair.'"

For Heschel, philosophy in its richest sense is the result of ultimate wonder, not only the outcome of curiosity. In the paragraph that follows his quotation of Plato, Heschel maintains that radical amazement underlies "our theories and scientific explanations." Elsewhere he claims that such wonder "was the wellspring of Kant's basic insights" and that it is "the spring of all creative thinking" (*Search,* p. 51). Heschel does not discard philosophic cognition; he only criticizes philosophies that either begin in doubt or deal only with concepts rather than dealing with experiences and situations. So Cohen is wrong when he says that for Heschel "presumably philosophy is a dead end." Only those philosophies which begin in doubt or are merely concerned with concepts are dead ends. Philosophy that begins in wonder is openended. In fact, Heschel himself says: "Philosophy is, in a sense, a kind of thinking that has a beginning but no end. . . . Its answers are questions in disguise; every new answer giving rise to new questions" (ibid., p. 4). Cohen has obviously made too much out of a slip of pen, has overlooked the context in which that slip took place, and has ignored those of Heschel's statements that clearly suggest an affinity between radical amazement and philosophy. I repeat, then, that Heschel's radical wonder is related to philosophical and scientific knowledge.

29. *Not Alone,* p. 12.
30. Ibid., p. 11, and *Search,* p. 46; cf. *Who Is Man?* pp. 115–116.
31. *Search,* p. 251.

32. Cf. chapter 5, p. 105.
33. *Not Alone,* pp. 14–15.
34. *Search,* pp. 140–141.
35. *Not Alone,* p. 13.
36. Ibid., p. 11. Cf. ibid., p. 12:

> Doubt, then, is an interdepartmental activity of the mind. First we see, next
> we judge and form an opinion and thereafter we doubt. In other words, to
> doubt is to question that which we have accepted as possibly true a moment
> ago. Doubt is an act of appeal, a proceeding by which a logical judgment is
> brought from the memory to the critical faculty of the mind for re-
> examination. Accordingly, we must first judge and cling to a belief in our
> judgment before we are able to doubt. But if we must know in order to
> question, if we must entertain a belief in order to cast doubt upon it, then
> doubt cannot be the beginning of knowledge.

37. *Search,* p. 98.
38. *Not Alone,* p. 81; *Search,* p. 51.
39. *Not Alone,* p. 12.
40. Ibid., p. 69.
41. Ibid., pp. 16–17; cf. *Search,* p. 115.
42. Cf. *Who Is Man?* p. 78, where Heschel calls wonder and awe "cognitive acts."
    On the same page, as well as in *Not Alone,* p. 19, Heschel calls the sense of the
    ineffable a "cognitive insight." Since wonder is a way of sensing the ineffable,
    Heschel is in effect saying that wonder is a cognitive insight. Cf. ibid., p. 20,
    where he speaks of "the awareness of radical amazement." Cf. also *Search,* p.
    46, where Heschel calls wonder "a form of thinking."
43. *Search,* p. 46.
44. Ibid., pp. 30, 31.
45. Ibid., p. 107.
46. Ibid., pp. 34, 58; cf. ibid., p. 160. Cf. also *Not Alone,* p. 20, where Heschel says
    that man "is endowed with the ability to know that there is more than what he
    knows."
47. *Not Alone,* p. 62.
48. *Who Is Man?* p. 78.
49. Ibid., pp. 79–80. Cf. *Truth,* p. 294: "The opposite of absurdity is not always
    intelligible. . . . Our goal is not to come upon ultimate solutions to all problems
    but to find ourselves as part of a context or meaning."
50. *Not Alone,* p. 133. Cf. *Prophets,* pp. 221–223, where Heschel maintains that it is
    more suitable to speak of an understanding of God rather than of a knowledge
    of God. Yet Heschel himself does often use the term "knowledge of God." When
    he does so, however, he is using the term in a broader sense than a merely
    speculative or discursive knowledge. For instance, in ibid., p. 223, he says: "To
    the prophet, knowledge of God was fellowship with Him, not attained by
    syllogism, analysis or induction but by living together." And in *Search,* p. 281,
    he says: "Knowledge of God is knowledge of living with God." Note also that at
    times Heschel even uses the word "understanding" not as "a synonym for
    agreement" (as in the quotation above) but as a synonym for "comprehension"
    and thus as an even narrower term than "knowledge." Hence, in *Freedom,* p. 61,
    he says: "Man knows more than he understands." In this case to know is to
    apprehend, to intuit; knowledge is not reduced to discursive and conceptual
    knowledge; but to understand seems to mean to know conceptually. Indeed,
    Heschel's use of words is not always consistent. But his intention or meaning is
    consistent. The consistent meaning which he conveys when speaking of the

insight attained in wonder is that we are conscious of more than we can comprehend, aware of more than we can grasp.

51. *Search*, p. 46.
52. Cf. ibid., pp. 115–116.
53. *Who Is Man?* p. 81; cf. *Not Alone*, p. 180, and *Search*, p. 111.
54. *Not Alone*, p. 206.
55. *Search*, p. 117.
56. Ibid.
57. Ibid., p. 140.
58. Ibid., p. 77. Cf. ibid., p. 78 (n. 6): "In regard to God, *yirah* is used in the Bible primarily in the sense of awe." Yet "in some places, *yirah* does indeed mean dread of God's punishment." While most English translations of the Bible use the expression "fear of God," the attitude to which this expression refers is qualitatively different from ordinary fear. Thus Heschel's translation "awe of God" is less apt to distort the meaning that the Biblical authors wished to convey: humble reverence before God.
59. Although Heschel does not refer to Rudolf Otto's *The Idea of the Holy* (London, 1923) in his discussion of awe, his writings show that he, like Otto, views mystery as both overwhelming and fascinating.
60. Tremor and fascination are the two aspects that form the dual character of numinous consciousness analyzed by Otto in *The Idea of the Holy*. Note, however, that while for Heschel tremor and fascination are aspects of awe, Otto uses "tremor" and "awe" synonymously (cf. pp. 13–14) in contrast to "fascination" and "wonder" (cf. p. 41). Though Heschel does not systematically explicate the relationship between fascination and tremor, his discussion of awe shows that he views both as aspects of awe (cf., e.g., *Search*, pp. 106–107, where he explicitly conjoins them as aspects of awe). Note also that Otto, like Heschel, uses the term "tremor" analogically to refer to an experience that is "wholly distinct from that of being afraid" (p. 13) and that there are various gradations of tremor according to the different stages of religious development. Heschel's treatment of awe concerns the highest stage that Otto discusses.
61. Cf. *Not Alone*, p. 27.
62. *Who Is Man?* p. 77.
63. *Search*, p. 106.
64. *Not Alone*, p. 27.
65. Cf., e.g., *Search*, p. 160.
66. Cf. *Not Alone*, p. 20.
67. Cf., e.g., ibid., p. 19, and *Who Is Man?* p. 77.
68. *Freedom*, p. 225.
69. *Search*, p. 316.
70. Cf., e.g., ibid., pp. 74 and 106, and *Who Is Man?* pp. 78 and 88.
71. *Search*, p. 161; cf. *Not Alone*, p. 109.
72. *Search*, p. 78.
73. *Not Alone*, p. 146.
74. Cf. *Search*, pp. 73–74. It is clear from the above discussion, however, that Heschel also considers awe of mystery a beginning of wisdom inasmuch as he regards it as an entrance into the realm of meaning.
75. Ibid., p. 74.
76. Ibid.; cf. ibid., p. 106, and *Who Is Man?* pp. 78, 88.
77. *Search*, p. 92.
78. Ibid., p. 74.
79. Ibid., p. 73.
80. Ibid.

81. *Not Alone,* p. 130.
82. *Search,* p. 75.
83. Cf. ibid., p. 74.
84. *Who Is Man?* p. 116.

Chapter 7 (pp. 173–191)

1. *Who Is Man?* p. 109.
2. Ibid., p. 116.
3. *Not Alone,* p. 69.
4. Cf. ibid., pp. 57–58, 68–69; *Search,* pp. 111–113, 162; *Who Is Man?* p. 110.
5. Cf. *Search,* p. 3, where Heschel advances one of his several complementary definitions of religion: "Religion is an answer to man's ultimate questions." And throughout his writings it is clear that, for Heschel, ultimate questions (or what he often refers to in the singular as "the ultimate question") arise especially in moments of wonder and awe.
6. Cf. chapter 4, pp. 88–90, for an explanation of why the ultimate question is experienced as a question addressed to us rather than as one that we raise on our own accord.
7. *Search,* p. 132; cf. ibid., p. 137: "Religion consists of God's question and man's answer. . . . Unless God asks the question, all our inquiries are in vain." Cf. also *Not Alone,* p. 76: "Philosophy begins with man's question; *religion begins with God's question and man's answer.*" Thus, to say that religion is an answer to the ultimate question which arises in wonder and awe is to say that God's presence and challenge are discerned especially in those moments of wonder and awe before the grandeur and mystery of reality. Therefore, in *Quest,* p. xiv, Heschel also defines religion as "what man does with the presence of God"—an obvious, though unnoted, reply to Whitehead's definition of religion as "what man does with his own solitariness" (Alfred North Whitehead, *Religion in the Making* [New York: The Macmillan Co., 1926], p. 16). Still other complementary definitions or descriptions of religion will be quoted elsewhere in this chapter.
8. *Not Alone,* pp. 68–69.
9. *Search,* pp. 112–113; *Who Is Man?* pp. 110–111.
10. *Search,* p. 92.
11. Cf. chapter 3, pp. 74–76.
12. *Not Alone,* p. 64.
13. *Search,* p. 162.
14. *Who Is Man?* p. 108; *Truth,* p. 259.
15. *Not Alone,* pp. 47–48.
16. Cf. chapter 4, pp. 92–93.
17. *Who Is Man?* pp. 97–98.
18. Ibid., p. 98.
19. Ibid., p. 111; cf. *Search,* p. 112.
20. *Who Is Man?* p. 108; cf. *Truth,* p. 259, and *Freedom,* p. 44.
21. Heschel uses this phrase frequently throughout his writings but gives particular attention to it in *Who Is Man?* pp. 106–107.
22. Cf. especially *Not Alone,* pp. 193–195, and *Who Is Man?* pp. 57–61 and 103–112.
23. *Quest,* p. 5.

24. Cf. chapter 4, pp. 84–92.
25. *Who Is Man?* pp. 106–107.
26. Cf. ibid., p. 108, and *Truth*, p. 259.
27. *Who Is Man?* p. 108; cf. *Truth*, p. 259.
28. *Who Is Man?* p. 108. Cf. *Not Alone*, p. 245: "An air of expectancy hovers over life. Something is asked of man, of all men."
29. *Search*, p. 113, and *Who Is Man?* p. 111.
30. *Truth*, p. 259; cf. *Who Is Man?* p. 108.
31. Cf. *Not Alone*, p. 209.
32. Ibid., p. 139.
33. *Who Is Man?* p. 46; cf. *Freedom*, p. 272.
34. *Who Is Man?* p. 112.
35. Ibid., p. 109. Cf. ibid., p. 75:

> Ever since Schleiermacher it has been customary in considering the nature of religion to start with the human self and to characterize religion as a feeling of dependence, reverence, etc. What is overlooked is the unique aspect of religious consciousness of being a recipient, of being exposed, overwhelmed by a presence which surpasses our ability to feel. What characterizes the religious man is faith in God's transitive concern for humanity, faith in God's commitment to man, in terms of which he seeks to shape his life and attempts to find sense in history.

> Cf. also *Prophets*, p. 440: "The unique quality of the awareness that characterizes biblical religion goes beyond what Schleiermacher called 'absolute dependence.' It is rather an awareness of a God who helps, demands, and calls upon man." For Schleiermacher's description of the feeling of absolute dependency, which he says is "the same thing" as "to be conscious of being in relation with God," cf. his study entitled *The Christian Faith*, English trans. of the second German ed. (1830), ed. by H.R. Mackintosh and J.S. Steward (Edinburgh: T. & T. Clark, 1928), pp. 12–18.

36. *Not Alone*, p. 215; *Who Is Man?* p. 109; *Freedom*, p. 63.
37. *Freedom*, p. 66.
38. *Search*, p. 117.
39. This is another phrase that Heschel employs frequently throughout his writings; his most sustained treatment of it occurs in *Who Is Man?* pp. 112–114. Heschel at times speaks of "a *sense of ultimate embarrassment*" (ibid., p. 112) or "our ultimate embarrassment" (*Freedom*, pp. 124–125).
40. *Who Is Man?* pp. 112–113.
41. *Freedom*, p. 164.
42. *Who Is Man?* p. 114.
43. Ibid.
44. *Freedom*, p. 165.
45. Ibid.
46. *Search*, p. 159.
47. *Freedom*, p. 67. Cf. ibid., p. 201: "The sense of wonder, amazement, and embarrassment precedes faith."
48. Cf. *Who Is Man?* pp. 108–109, where Heschel claims that the sense of indebtedness may be translated as conscience.
49. J. H. Walgrave, O.P., "Religious Experience Through Conscience," *Louvain Studies*, 4 (Fall 1972), 114.
50. *Search*, p. 158.
51. Ibid.
52. *Not Alone*, p. 223. Heschel would agree with Walgrave's description of

conscience as "an heterogeneous complex" or "a complex alloy"; as an "objective rule" into which "alien elements are grafted." Furthermore, he would endorse Walgrave's argument that, while admitting the travesties of conscience, "it would be wrong to reduce conscience to its travesties or to ignore the vein of gold in the dubious alloy" (Walgrave, "Religious Experience Through Conscience," p. 101).

53. *Search*, p. 159. Cf. Walgrave, "Religious Experience Through Conscience," p. 95: "To say that something is right because I will it, whatever it may be, is to proclaim the absoluteness or divine character of the self. We cannot but say that it is a kind of demonic pride. But in trying to sustain such a claim we soon begin to feel somewhat unreal and not a little mad."

54. *Not Alone*, p. 197, and *Who Is Man?* p. 59.

55. Heschel also claims that the someone to whom we are accountable "cannot be an abstract law or blind force" because in violating such a law "we never feel any guilt" (*Search*, p. 159). This argument, however, is not so cogent considering the fact that there are experiences of both religious guilt (sin) and non-religious guilt. I would agree with Heschel that in violating such an impersonal law we could never feel any religious guilt, i.e., we could have no sense of sin—and this is probably what Heschel means. Yet other forms of guilt may indeed be experienced, no matter what kind of law we feel ourselves violating.

56. Cf. *Freedom*, p. 3, where Heschel says: "Confusion is not a rare disease. We are guilty of committing the fallacy of misplacement. We define self-reliance and call it faith, . . . conscience and call it God."

57. *Not Alone*, p. 76.

58. *Prophets*, p. 484.

59. Cf. *Search*, pp. 127–128. Cf. Paul Tillich, *Systematic Theology* vol. 1, p. 211.

60. *Search*, p. 281.

61. "What We Might Do Together," p. 137.

62. *Who Is Man?* p. 91.

63. "The Jewish Notion of God and Christian Renewal," pp. 107–108.

64. *Truth*, p. 159.

65. *Prophets*, p. 221.

66. *Not Alone*, p. 152.

67. *Who Is Man?* p. 113.

68. Ibid., p. 118.

69. *Not Alone*, p. 174.

70. *Who Is Man?* p. 118.

71. "Faith," part 1, p. 13.

72. *Quest*, p. 63.

73. *Search*, p. 85.

74. Ibid., pp. 118–119.

75. Ibid., p. 119.

76. Ibid.

77. Ibid., p. 88.

78. Ibid., p. 281. Cf. *Quest*, p. 18: "What is the meaning of praise if not to make His concern our own? Worship is an act of inner agreement with God. . . . To praise is to feel God's concern."

79. *Who Is Man?* p. 116.

80. "Faith," part 1, p. 13.

81. "On Prayer," p. 8.

82. *Who Is Man?* p. 67.

83. Ibid., p. 68.

84. "On Prayer", p. 8.
85. "Faith," part 1, p. 13.
86. *Search,* p. 329.
87. Ibid., p. 290.
88. "On Prayer," p. 8. Cf. *Quest,* pp. 12, 93–94, and *Freedom,* p. 254.
89. "On Prayer," p. 1.
90. *Quest,* p. 55. Cf. ibid, p. 46, where Heschel claims that "prayer is primarily an event in the individual souls" and yet "we never pray as individuals, set apart from the rest of the world."
91. Ibid., p. 46.
92. Ibid., p. 82; *Freedom,* p. 245.
93. *Search,* p. 95.
94. *Quest,* p. 82; *Freedom,* p. 245.
95. *Not Alone,* p. 41.
96. "On Prayer," p. 8.
97. *Quest,* p. 60.
98. Ibid., p. 59.
99. *Search,* p. 162.
100. "On Prayer," p. 7.
101. *Quest,* p. 13.
102. Ibid., p. 82 (includes Psalms 145:10); cf. *Freedom,* p. 125.
103. *Search,* p. 138.
104. *Quest,* p. 60.
105. *Search,* p. 138; cf. *Not Alone,* p. 165.
106. *Search,* p. 384. Cf. *Freedom,* p. 255: "For prayer to live in man, man has to live in prayer" and "We pray the way we live." Cf. also "On Prayer," p. 5: "Prayer must not be dissonant with the rest of living. The mercifulness, gentleness, which pervades us in moments of prayer is but a ruse or a bluff, if it is inconsistent with the way we live at other moments. The divorce of liturgy and living, of prayer and practice, is more than a scandal; it is a disaster."
107. *Quest,* p. 12.
108. *Search,* pp. 407–408. Cf. *Quest,* p. 40: "God hears not only prayer but also the desire to pray." Cf. also "On Prayer," pp. 4 and 3 respectively, where Heschel says: *"I pray because I am unable to pray"* and "Though I do not know how to pray, I can still say: Redeem me from the agony of not knowing what to strive for, from the agony of not knowing how my inner life is falling apart."
109. *Not Alone,* p. 240.
110. *Quest,* p. 78.
111. Ibid. Cf. Ibid., p. 18: "The privilege of praying is man's greatest distinction."
112. *Not Alone,* p. 130.
113. Ibid., p. 74; *Search,* p. 120. Cf. *Quest,* p. 72, where Heschel claims "prayer is a way to faith."
114. *Quest,* p. 94.
115. For example, in *Not Alone,* p. 74, Heschel says: "When mind and soul agree, belief is born. But first our hearts must know the shudder of adoration." And in *Freedom,* p. 198, he claims that "from yearning and song, the faith in God bursts forth."
116. *Not Alone,* p. 165; *Freedom,* p. 198; cf. *Search,* p. 155.
117. *Search,* p. 138.
118. Ibid., p. 154; *Freedom,* p. 198. Cf. *Search,* p. 282: "Faith is vision, sensitivity, attachment to God."
119. *Who Is Man?* p. 116.
120. *Search,* p. 137; *Freedom,* p. 199.

Chapter 8 (pp. 192–217)

1. *Not Alone,* p. 162.
2. *Search,* p. 282; cf. *Quest,* p. 106.
3. *Not Alone,* p. 161.
4. *Earth,* p. 107.
5. *Not Alone,* p. 165, and *Freedom,* p. 198.
6. *Earth,* p. 107.
7. *Truth,* p. 188.
8. *Search,* p. 200. Although here placed in apposition, the words "time" and "history" are not synonymous for Heschel. Cf., e.g., *Search,* p. 423, where he says: "The meaning of history is to be a sanctuary in time." History is what we do with God's time. We must revere time but not history, since history is often the abuse of time. Time is God's gift, and must be revered as such. History is our response to that gift; it is what we do with that gift and is not always to be revered.
9. Cf. ibid., p. 201.
10. Ibid., p. 206.
11. Ibid., p. 213.
12. Ibid., p. 217.
13. Ibid., p. 201.
14. Ibid., pp. 213, 214.
15. Ibid., p. 216.
16. Ibid., p. 217.
17. *Israel,* p. 129.
18. *Search,* p. 215.
19. Ibid.
20. Ibid., p. 216.
21. Cf. chapter 5, pp. 108–109.
22. *Search,* p. 416.
23. *Not Alone,* p. 162. Cf. *Israel,* p. 200: "The commandment of faith in the Torah is *Remember.*"
24. "Faith," part 2, p. 12.
25. Ibid.
26. *Not Alone,* p. 165.
27. "On Prayer," p. 11.
28. Ibid., p. 12.
29. Ibid.
30. *Not Alone,* p. 163; *Israel,* p. 60 (emphasis mine).
31. Cf. Jacob Neusner, *The Way of Torah,* p. 37, where Neusner claims that study is "the central *ritual* of the Judaic tradition."
32. *Israel,* p. 223.
33. "Faith," part 2, p. 12; cf. *Not Alone,* pp. 162–163.
34. *Search,* pp. 140–141.
35. Ibid., p. 211. Cf. *Israel,* p. 128: "Certain moments in history never vanish."
36. *Sabbath,* p. 98; *Search,* p. 215.
37. *Freedom,* p. 251.
38. Cf. *Israel,* p. 128, and chapter 5, p. 107.
39. *Who Is Man?* p. 99.
40. *Search,* p. 426; cf. *Earth,* p. 108.
41. *Sabbath,* p. 8. Cf. *Freedom,* p. 20: "Judaism claims that the way to nobility of the soul is the art of sanctifying time."
42. *Sabbath,* p. 8. On this same page, Heschel writes: "Judaism teaches us to be

attached to *holiness in time,* to be attached to sacred events, to learn how to consecrate sanctuaries that emerge from the magnificent stream of a year. The Sabbaths are our great cathedrals; and our Holy of Holies is a shrine that neither the Romans nor the Germans were able to burn; a shrine that even apostasy cannot easily obliterate: The Day of Atonement."

43. *Quest,* p. 33.
44. Ibid., p. 25.
45. *Freedom,* p. 260.
46. Ibid., p. 249.
47. Ibid., p. 251.
48. *Quest,* p. 33.
49. Ibid., p. 28.
50. Ibid., p. 30.
51. Ibid., p. 47. This is the title of chapter 3 of this book on prayer. Although Heschel says that "spontaneity is the goal" of prayer, and even though he says, as we have seen, that "prayer is . . . an act of spontaneity and self-expression," he does not mean to imply that self-expression is the goal of prayer. Cf. ibid., p. 31: "The self gains when absorbed in the contemplation of the non-self, in the contemplation of God, for example. Our supreme goal is *self-attachment* to what is greater than the self rather than *self-expression.*"
52. Ibid., p. 28.
53. Ibid., p. 91. This is the title of chapter 4 of *Quest.*
54. *Search,* p. 408.
55. *Quest,* p. 28.
56. Ibid., p. 31.
57. Ibid., p. 30.
58. Ibid., p. 72.
59. Cf. chapter 7, pp. 190–191.
60. *Search,* p. 282.
61. *Quest,* p. 32.
62. Ibid., p. 33.
63. "On Prayer," p. 2.
64. *Search,* p. 25.
65. Ibid., p. 274.
66. Ibid., p. 27.
67. Cf. chapter 5, pp. 112–129.
68. Cf. chapter 5, pp. 129–149.
69. "On Prayer," p. 2.
70. *Freedom,* pp. 42 and 57; cf. ibid., p. 237.
71. *Truth,* p. 56.
72. Ibid., p. 55. Cf. "God, Torah, and Israel," p. 82: "Again and again we are taught that the Torah is not an end in itself. It is the gate through which one enters the court in which one finds awe of heaven."
73. *Freedom,* p. 116.
74. Ibid.
75. Ibid., p. 42.
76. Ibid.
77. Ibid.
78. Ibid., p. 237.
79. Ibid., p. 42.
80. Ibid., p. 237.
81. Ibid., p. 55.
82. Ibid., p. 50.

83. Ibid., p. 237.
84. Ibid., p. 54.
85. Ibid., pp. 39–40.
86. Ibid., pp. 21, 215.
87. Ibid., p. 20.
88. Ibid., p. 236.
89. Ibid.
90. Ibid.
91. Ibid., p. 226.
92. *Who Is Man?* p. 37.
93. *Quest,* p. 112.
94. *Freedom,* p. 192.
95. Ibid., p. 226.
96. Ibid., p. 65.
97. Cf. chapter 5, pp. 109–112.
98. *Earth,* p. 54.
99. *Freedom,* p. 42.
100. Cf. *Who Is Man?* pp. 44–45.
101. Ibid., p. 44.
102. *Freedom,* p. 60.
103. Ibid., p. 73.
104. Ibid., p. 235.
105. Ibid., p. 232.
106. Ibid., p. 231.
107. Ibid., p. 59. On "character education," cf. *Who Is Man?* p. 99.
108. *Freedom,* p. 59.
109. Ibid., pp. 50, 43, 79.
110. Ibid., p. 84.
111. *Who Is Man?* p. 41.
112. *Freedom,* pp. 42–43.
113. Ibid., pp. 78–79.
114. *Earth,* pp. 42–44.
115. *Truth,* pp. 58, 63.
116. Ibid., p. 164.
117. Ibid.
118. Praising God and the remembrance of revelation and tradition are also mitsvot, acts in accord with God. But these acts move us to other acts, to acts of mercy and justice, for example.
119. *Search,* p. 287. Cf. ibid., pp. 289–290, and *Freedom,* pp. 160–161, where Heschel speaks of the Bible suggesting not only an analogy of being, but also an analogy of doing between the divine and the human; cf. chapter 5, p. 136.
120. Cf. chapter 7, pp. 190–191.
121. "On Prayer," p. 2.
122. *Search,* p. 297.
123. Ibid., p. 293; *Who Is Man?* p. 95.
124. *Search,* p. 295.
125. *Not Alone,* p. 283. On Judaism as an order of living, cf. ibid., p. 270, *Quest,* p. 100, and *Search,* pp. 301–302.
126. *Not Alone,* p. 284.
127. Ibid., p. 281.
128. Ibid.
129. On Heschel's distinction between belief and faith, cf., e.g., *Not Alone,* pp. 165–167, and chapter 2, pp. 47–48.

130. *Search,* p. 282; cf. *Quest,* p. 106.
131. *Quest,* p. 106; *Search,* p. 283.
132. Cf., e.g., Marvin Fox, "Heschel, Intuition and the Halakah," *Tradition,* 3 (Fall 1960), 5–15, especially pp. 9–11; Maurice Friedman, "Liberal Judaism and Contemporary Jewish Thought," *Midstream* (Autumn 1959), 24; Harold Kasimow, *Divine-Human Encounter,* pp. 53–60. Since I shall deal with Friedman and Kasimow in the text, I will respond to Fox in this note.

After pointing out that Heschel calls upon Jews to take "a leap of action" in order to find their way to faith, Fox claims that faith must precede the performance of mitsvot: "Without the commitment of faith a man is most unlikely to undertake the performance of 'sacred deeds,' and if he should they will be mere posturings without any spiritual effect" (op. cit., p. 9). He also asks: "If a man performs deeds without any sense of their spiritual significance whatsoever how can they be effective in leading him to God?" (ibid.), as if Heschel's call for action regardless of faith implies that the deeds would then be done without any sense of spiritual significance. Heschel never suggests this at all, as I shall presently point out in the text. Fox says that "Professor Heschel's position would be far sounder if he consistently put the main emphasis on the initial act of faith" rather than on action and the intuition that comes thereby as a way to faith. But even if Heschel did put the emphasis on the initial act of faith rather than on the pathway to faith, he still would be concerned to show the grounds for that faith. And, according to him, actions, whereby we realize that *"the wonder of doing* is no less amazing than the marvel of being," (*Search,* p. 285) may prompt us to discover *"the divinity of deeds"* (ibid., p. 288). In other words, in doing sacred deeds we may begin to realize that there is more in our doing than ourselves, that in our doing there is something—nay, someone—divine. And this realization may provoke the dawn of faith.

After dismissing Heschel's approach, Fox proceeds to say: "By way of halacha, Judaism grasped in a clear and communicable form the profoundest religious insights. . . . Jewish tradition has always taught that halacha is the only reliable way of finding God in life" (op. cit., p. 12). Now although Heschel would not say that halacha is the *only* reliable way of finding God, his point precisely is that it is a most reliable way of finding God, that it is a vehicle of "the profoundest religious insights," to use Fox's words. Heschel himself says that "through the ecstasy of deeds"—halachic deeds—we learn "to be certain of the hereness of God" (*Search,* p. 283) and that, speaking personally, "the foremost sources of my own religious insight lie in reverence for halacha" (*Freedom,* p. 219). That Fox could claim that "Dr. Heschel fails to see this" (op. cit., p. 12), fails to see that halacha is a source of profound religious insights and is a way of finding God, indicates his misreading of Heschel. The extent of his misunderstanding of Heschel is revealed further when, as if offering an alternative to Heschel's approach, he says: "Instead of being asked to look for evidences of God in nature or in the Bible, he [a human being] must be confronted with the greatest of all challenges—the challenge to find meaning in his own life. He must be forced to see that without God and his Torah men are reduced to being animals and automata" (op. cit., p. 10). As is clear from this entire book, this is precisely Heschel's reason for attempting to help people see "evidences of God" in nature, in the Bible, and in mitsvot: that they may discover meaning in life and realize that God is the source of all meaning.

133. Harold Kasimow, *Divine-Human Encounter,* p. 56.
134. Maurice Friedman, "Liberal Judaism and Contemporary Jewish Thought," p. 24; quoted by Harold Kasimow, op. cit., p. 56.

135. Kasimow, op. cit., p. 56.
136. *Search*, pp. 403–404 and *Freedom*, p. 140; quoted by Kasimow, op. cit., p. 57.
137. *Search*, p. 282.
138. Cf., e.g., *Freedom*, p. 66: "Even he who merely strives for faith in the living God is on the threshold of faith" and "Faith implies striving for faith." Cf. ibid., p. 199: "Faith is not a system but an ongoing striving for faith."
139. *Search*, p. 137; *Freedom*, p. 199.
140. Cf. chapter 5, pp. 140–141.
141. *Quest*, p. 100; cf. *Freedom*, p. 205.
142. *Quest*, p. 101; *Freedom*, p. 205.
143. Cf. chapter 5, p. 140.
144. *Search*, p. 303. Heschel attributes this statement to Rabbi Moshe Cordovero, "a great Jewish authority" of the nineteenth century.
145. Ibid., pp. 302–303.
146. *Freedom*, p. 206.
147. Ibid., pp. 205–206.
148. Ibid., p. 206.
149. Ibid.
150. Ibid., p. 207.
151. Letter dated December 18, 1958, reprinted in *Jewish Identity*, ed. by Sidney B. Hoenig (New York, 1965), p. 230.
152. *Freedom*, p. 209.
153. On the Torah as comprised of both agada and halacha, cf. chapter 5, p. 136, on the polarity of the two, cf. pp. 137–138.
154. *Quest*, p. 101. The fact that Heschel favors a qualitative rather than a quantitative approach to halacha prompts the question as to which branch of Judaism he was most closely aligned. Once when asked what type of Jew he was, Orthodox, Conservative, or Reform, Heschel replied that he "was not a noun in search of an adjective" (cf. chapter 1, note 37). Yet we may still muse about the branch of Judaism with which Heschel's life-style and views were most compatible. Heschel himself was punctilious in his observance of halacha, which would place him among the Orthodox. His view that the interpretations of the sages are as important as the inspirations of the prophets and that "we approach the laws of the Bible through the interpretation and the wisdom of the Rabbis" (*Search*, p. 274) is a perspective compatible with Orthodoxy. Yet the fact that Heschel does not accept the view that all of the Torah was revealed to Moses (cf. chapter 5, pp. 139–140) and, moreover, the fact that he accepts the relativity of certain halachic laws (cf. chapter 5, pp. 140–141) and de-emphasizes the quantitative approach to observance, places him to the left of the modern Orthodox movement, i.e. within the fold of Conservative Judaism. (Certainly he is not as far left as the Reform movement.) Indeed, Heschel himself identified with the Conservative movement by teaching for the last 27 years of his life at the Jewish Theological Seminary of America, the world center of Conservative Judaism. According to his widow, Sylvia Heschel, "He supported the Conservative movement; he thought it necessary for Judaism" (cf. chapter 1, p. 12). Perhaps he viewed the Orthodox position as being to the right of the tradition itself. According to Herbert Parzen, Heschel concurred with the view that Conservative Judaism "is the only modern interpretation that has retained respect and reverence for the authority of the Halacha, the Law, and is concerned to recover its dynamism for Jewish life" (Herbert Parzen, "Abraham Joshua Heschel: A New Teacher and Personality in the Conservative Movement," in *Roads to Jewish Survival*, ed. by Milton Berger, Joel Geffen, and M. David Hoffman

[New York: Bloch Publishing Co., 1967], p. 81). But surely Orthodox Judaism has respect and reverence for halacha. If what Parzen says is true, Heschel must have felt that the most genuine expression of respect for the authority of the Torah requires a greater appreciation of its dynamism. This is precisely the Conservative approach as stated by one of its spokespersons: "Indeed, it is our view that there is no better way to preserve the integrity and the authority of the law than by revising it when it needs revision" (Seymour Siegel, "Ethics and the Halacha," in *Conservative Judaism and Jewish Law*, ed. by Seymour Siegel [New York: The Rabbinical Assembly, 1977], p. 127).

155. *Search*, p. 338.
156. Ibid.,, p. 337.
157. Ibid., p. 385.
158. *Truth*, p. 52.
159. *Search*, p. 384.
160. Ibid., p. 385. The quotation at the beginning of the second paragraph of this excerpt is from Nicolas Berdyaev, *The Destiny of Man* (London: Geoffrey Bles, 1935), p. 30.
161. *Not Alone*, p. 250.
162. W. R. Boyce Gibson, *Encyclopaedia of Religion and Ethics*, vol. 8, p. 152a; quoted in *Search*, pp. 385–386.
163. *Not Alone*, p. 250.
164. Cf., e.g., ibid., p. 215; *Search*, p. 297; *Who Is Man?* p. 110; *Freedom*, p. 63.
165. *Not Alone*, p. 249; cf. *Search*, pp. 397–398; *Freedom*, pp. 8, 63.
166. *Not Alone*, p. 250.
167. Ibid., p. 249.
168. *Search*, p. 400.
169. *Freedom*, p. 66.
170. Ibid., p. 146, and *Israel*, p. 160. Cf. "The Jewish Notion of God and Christian Renewal," p. 119: "What is urgent for the Jew is not the acceptance of salvation but the preparing of redemption, the preparing *for* redemption. . . . The urgent issue is not personal salvation but the prevention of mankind's surrender to the demonic."
171. *Freedom*, pp. 237–238.
172. *Who Is Man?* p. 119. Cf. *Search*, p. 357: "Every deed is either a clash or an aid in the effort of redemption."
173. *Freedom*, pp. 145–146; cf. *Israel*, p. 160.
174. *Truth*, p. 299.
175. *Earth*, p. 72; cf. *Israel*, p. 159.
176. *Israel*, p. 158.
177. *Freedom*, p. 238.
178. *Quest*, p. 151.
179. *Search*, p. 313.
180. *Quest*, p. 151.
181. "The Jewish Notion of God and Christian Renewal," p. 119. The theme of "God's need for man" is prevalent throughout Heschel's writings. Cf., e.g., *Not Alone*, pp. 215, 241–248; *Who Is Man?* pp. 73–75; *Freedom*, pp. 8, 67, 97; *Truth*, p. 301. When Heschel speaks of God's being in need of human beings, he does not mean to imply that God's existence is dependent upon human beings but that God's redemptive activity requires human cooperation. God is ontologically self-sufficient but not soteriologically self-sufficient. And the only sense in which God is ontologically self-sufficient is that the divine being is neither derived from (created by) nor dependent on (sustained by) any other being. God is not ontologically self-sufficient in the Aristotelian sense that the

divine being is "resting purely within itself," unmoved by the plight of creatures and hence apathetic. On the contrary, God wills not to be alone and is intimately affected by the doings and sufferings of creatures. Cf. chapter 5, pp. 130–135, on the pathos of God.
182. *Freedom*, p. 49.
183. "Conversation with Heschel," p. 4.
184. *Earth*, p. 72.
185. *Not Alone*, p. 245.
186. Ibid., p. 243.
187. "Teaching Jewish Theology," p. 13.
188. "On Prayer," p. 4.
189. *Truth*, p. 301.
190. Ibid., p. 300.
191. Ibid., p. 301.
192. Ibid., p. 298.
193. *Not Alone*, p. 153.
194. *Search*, p. 312.
195. "On Prayer," p. 12. This article which we have cited so often was first delivered as an address to the United States Liturgical Conference in Milwaukee, Wisconsin, on August 28, 1969.

Conclusion

1. Quoted by Jack D. Spiro, "Rabbi Abraham Joshua Heschel: An Appreciation," p. 222.
2. Cf. chapter 6, pp. 165–166, and 172; chapter 8, p. 196.
3. Cf. chapter 7, pp. 184–185.
4. Cf. chapter 7, pp. 189–191.
5. Cf. chapter 8, pp. 200–201.
6. Cf. chapter 8, pp. 207–210.
7. *Not alone*, p. 88.
8. *Truth*, p. 56.
9. *Freedom*, p. 201; cf. *Truth*, p. 188.
10. *Not Alone*, p. 88; cf. *Search*, pp. 152–153.
11. *Not Alone*, p. 73.
12. *Truth*, p. 191.
13. *Not Alone*, p. 89.
14. *Truth*, p. 302.
15. Ibid., p. 301.

Bibliography

Books by Abraham Joshua Heschel (Complete)

The following is a complete list of the original editions of Heschel's books arranged chronologically. For a complete list of each edition of each book, as well as translations and anthologies through 1975, see Fritz A. Rothschild's bibliography of Heschel's books in *Between God and Man: An Interpretation of Judaism from the Writings of Abraham J. Heschel*, ed. by Rothschild (New York: The Free Press; London: Collier Macmillan Publishers, 1975; revised ed.), pp. 275–277. Concerning editions beyond 1975, Farrar, Straus, and Giroux is republishing nearly all of Heschel's English works.

Der Shem Hameforash: Mentsh (Yiddish). Warsaw: Farlag Indsl, 1933.
Maimonides: Eine Biographie (German). Berlin: Erich Reiss Verlag, 1935. English edition: *Maimonides: A Biography*. Trans. by Joachim Neugroschel. New York: Farrar, Straus, and Giroux, 1982.
Die Prophetie (German). Cracow: The Polish Academy of Sciences (Memoires de la Commission Orientaliste No. 22), 1936.
Don Jizchak Abravanel (German). Berlin: Erich Reiss Verlag, 1937.
The Quest for Certainty in Saadia's Philosophy. New York: Philip Feldheim, 1944.
The Earth Is the Lord's: The Inner Life of the Jew in East Europe. New York: Henry Schuman, 1950.
Man Is Not Alone: A Philosophy of Religion. New York: Farrar, Straus, and Young, 1951.
The Sabbath: Its Meaning for Modern Man. New York: Farrar, Straus, and Young, 1951.
Man's Quest for God: Studies in Prayer and Symbolism. New York: Charles Scribner's Sons, 1954.
God in Search of Man: A Philosophy of Judaism. New York: Farrar, Straus, and Cudahy, 1955.
Torah min ha-šhamayim be-ispaḳlaryah šhel ha-dorot (Hebrew). English title: *Theology of Ancient Judaism*. London and New York: Soncino Press, 1962 (vol. 1) and 1965 (vol. 2).
The Prophets. New York: Harper and Row, 1962.
Who Is Man? Stanford, California: Stanford University Press, 1965.
The Insecurity of Freedom: Essays on Human Existence. New York: Schocken Books, 1966.
Israel: An Echo of Eternity. New York: Farrar, Straus, and Giroux, 1968.
Kotzk: In gerangle far emesdikeit (Yiddish). 2 vols. Tel Aviv: Hamenora Publishing House, 1973.
A Passion for Truth. New York: Farrar, Straus, and Giroux, 1973.

Articles by Heschel (Selected)

The following is a selection of articles and essays by Heschel, arranged chronologically, which have not been republished in or excerpted from his books (though something of the items cited here may have found their way into or be drawn from his books). For an almost complete list of Heschel's articles through 1975, see Rothschild's bibliography in *Between God and Man*, pp. 278–291.

"Faith," part 1. *The Reconstructionist*, 10 (November 3, 1944), 10–14; "Faith," part 2. *The Reconstructionist*, 10 (November 17, 1944), 12–16.
"The Mystical Element in Judaism." In *The Jews: Their History, Culture, and Religion*, ed. by Louis Finkelstein, pp. 602–623. New York: Harper and Brothers, 1949.
"Toward an Understanding of Halacha." *Yearbook, the Central Conference of American Rabbis*, 62 (1953), 386–409.
"A Preface to the Understanding of Revelation." In *Essays Presented to Leo Baeck on the Occasion of His Eightieth Birthday*, pp. 28–35. London: East and West Library, 1954.
"The Biblical View of Reality." In *Contemporary Problems in Religion*, ed. by Harold A. Basilius, pp. 57–76. Detroit: Wayne University Press, 1956.
"Sacred Images of Man." *Religious Education*, 54 (March–April, 1958), 97–102.
"The Concept of Man in Jewish Thought." In *The Concept of Man*, ed. by S. Radhakrishnan and P. T. Raju, pp. 108–157. London: Allen and Unwin, 1960.
"The Meaning of the Spirit." *Claremont Dialogue*, 1 (Spring 1964), 16–35.
"The Moral Dilemma of the Space Age." *Space: Its Impact on Man and Society*, ed. by Lillian Levy, pp. 176–179. New York: W. W. Norton & Co., 1965.
"Choose Life!" *Jubilee*, January 1966, 37–39.
"No Religion Is an Island." *Union Seminary Quarterly Review*, 21 (January 1966), 117–134.
"The Moral Outrage of Vietnam." In *Vietnam: Crisis of Conscience*, by Robert McAfee Brown, Abraham J. Heschel, and Michael Novak, pp. 48–61. New York: Herder and Herder, 1967.
"What We Might do Together." *Religious Education*, 62 (March–April 1967), 133–140.
"From Mission to Dialogue?" *Conservative Judaism*, 21 (Spring 1967), 1–11.
"The Jewish Notion of God and Christian Renewal." In *Renewal of Religious Thought*, pp. 105–129. Vol. 1 of *Theology of Renewal*, ed. by L. K. Shook. New York: Herder and Herder, 1968.
"Teaching Jewish Theology in the Solomon Schecter Day School." *The Synagogue School*, 28 (Fall 1969), 4–18.
"On Prayer." *Conservative Judaism*, 25 (Fall 1970), 3–12.
"God, Torah, and Israel." In *Theology and Church in Times of Change: Essays in Honor of John Coleman Bennett*, pp. 71–90. Philadelphia: Westminster Press, 1970.
"Reflections on Death." *Conservative Judaism*, 28 (Fall 1973), 3–9.

Interviews With Heschel (Selected)

Finn, James. "Abraham Joshua Heschel." In *Protest: Pacifism and Politics, Some Passionate Views on War and Non-Violence*, pp. 154–162. New York: Random House, 1967.

Granfield, Patrick. "Abraham J. Heschel." In *Theologians at Work,* pp. 69–85. New York: Macmillan, 1967.

Stern, Carl. "A Conversation with Dr. Abraham Joshua Heschel," transcript of "The Eternal Light" program, presented by the National Broadcasting Company, February 4, 1973, under the auspices of the Jewish Theological Seminary of America.

Books About Heschel (Complete)

The following is a complete list of books dealing entirely with Heschel.

Babolin, Albino. *Abraham Joshua Heschel: Filosofo della Religione.* Perugia: Editrice Benucci, 1978.

Kasimow, Harold. *Divine-Human Encounter: A Study of Abraham Joshua Heschel.* Washington, D.C.: University Press of America, 1979.

McBride, Alfred. *Heschel: Religious Educator.* Denville, New Jersey: Dimension Books, 1973.

Merkle, John C., Editor. *Abraham Joshua Heschel: Exploring His Life and Thought,* to be published by Macmillan.

Sherman, Franklin. *The Promise of Heschel.* The Promise of Theology Series, ed. by Martin E. Marty. Philadelphia and New York: J. B. Lippincott Company, 1970.

Sherwin, Byron L. *Abraham Joshua Heschel.* Makers of Contemporary Theology Series. Atlanta: John Knox Press, 1979.

Articles on Heschel (Selected)

The following is a selected list of articles on Heschel, most of which have been cited in this book. For a more complete list, see Rothschild's bibliography in *Between God and Man,* though several of the items below are not found therein.

Anderson, Bernhard W. "Confrontation with the Bible." *Theology Today,* 30 (October 1973), 267–271.

Barnard, David. "Abraham Heschel's Attitude Toward Religion and Psychology." *The Journal of Religion,* 63 (Winter 1983), 26–43.

Bennett, John C. "Agent of God's Compassion." *America,* March 10, 1973, 205–206.

Berkovits, Eliezer. "Dr. A. J. Heschel's Theology of Pathos." *Tradition: A Journal of Orthodox Thought,* 6 (Spring–Summer 1964), 67–104.

Borowitz, Eugene. "Abraham Joshua Heschel and Joseph Baer Soloveitchik: The New Orthodoxy." In *A New Jewish Theology in the Making,* pp. 147–173. Philadelphia: Westminster Press, 1968.

———— "Abraham Joshua Heschel, Model." *Sh'ma: A Journal of Jewish Responsibility,* 3 (January 19, 1973), 41–42.

Breslauer, S. Daniel. "Abraham Joshua Heschel's 'Biblical Man' in Contextual Perspective." *Judaism,* 25 (Summer 1976), 341–344.

———— "Theology and Depth-Theology: A Heschel Distinction." *Central Conference of American Rabbis Journal,* 21 (Summer 1974), 81–86.

Brickner, Balfour. "Abraham Joshua Heschel, Chasid." *Sh'ma: A Journal of Jewish Responsibility*, 3 (January 19, 1973), 47.

Bridges, Hal. "Three Varieties of Mysticism." In *American Mysticism: From William James to Zen*, pp. 51–72. New York: Harper and Row, 1970.

Brown, Raymond E. "A Heritage from Israel." *American*, March 10, 1973, 221.

Brown, Robert McAfee. "Abraham Heschel: A Passion for Sincerity." *Christianity and Crisis*, December 10, 1973, 256–259.

Cherbonnier, Edmond La B. "A. J. Heschel and the Philosophy of the Bible." *Commentary*, 27 (January 1959), 23–29.

—— "Heschel as a Religious Thinker." *Conservative Judaism*, 23 (Fall 1968), 25–39.

—— "Heschel's Time-Bomb." *Conservative Judaism*, 28 (Fall 1974), 10–18.

Cohen, Arthur. "The Rhetoric of Faith: Abraham Joshua Heschel." In *The Natural and Supernatural Jew: An Historical and Theological Introduction*, pp. 234–259. New York: Pantheon Books, 1962.

Davies, W. D. "Conscience, Scholar, Witness." *America*, March 10, 1973, 213–215.

Dresner, Samuel H. "The Contribution of Abraham Joshua Heschel." *Judaism*, 32 (Winter 1983), 57–69.

Fierman, Morton C. "The Educational Philosophy of Abraham J. Heschel." *Religious Education*, 64 (July–August 1969), 272–279.

Finkelstein, Louis. "Three Meetings with Abraham Heschel." *America*, March 10, 1973, 203–204.

Friedman, Maurice. "Abraham Heschel Among Contemporary Philosophers: From Divine Pathos to Prophetic Action." *Philosophy Today*, 18 (Winter 1973), 293–305.

—— "Abraham Joshua Heschel: Toward a Philosophy of Judaism." *Conservative Judaism*, 10 (Winter 1956), 1–10.

—— "Divine Need and Human Wonder: The Philosophy of Abraham J. Heschel." *Judaism*, 25 (Winter 1976), 65–78.

Fox, Marvin. "Heschel, Intuition, and the Halakhah." *Tradition*, 3 (Fall 1960), 5–15.

Goldman, Norman S. "The Metapsychology of Abraham Joshua Heschel." *Journal of Religion and Health*, 14 (April 1975), 106–112.

Gottschalk, Alfred. "Abraham Joshua Heschel: A Man of Dialogues." *Conservative Judaism*, 28 (Fall 1973), 23–26.

Graeber, Bruce S. "Heschel and the Philosophy of Time." *Conservative Judaism*, 33 (Spring 1980), 44–56.

Haughey, John C. "Jewish Prayer: A Share in Holiness." *America*, March 10, 1973, 219–220.

Holtz, Abraham. "Religion and the Arts in the Theology of Abraham Joshua Heschel." Trans. from Hebrew by Harlan J. Wechsler. *Conservative Judaism*, 28 (Fall 1973), 27–39.

Kaplan, Edward K. "Form and Content in Abraham J. Heschel's Poetic Style." *Central Conference of American Rabbis Journal*, 18 (April 1971), 28–39.

—— "Contemplative Inwardness and Prophetic Action." In *Thomas Merton: Pilgrim in Process*, ed. by Donald Grayston and Michael W. Higgins, pp. 85–97. Toronto: Griffin House, 1983; Heschel–Merton Correspondence, pp. 98–105.

—— "Language and Reality in Abraham J. Heschel's Philosophy." *American Academy of Religion*, 41 (March 1973), 94–113.

—— "Mysticism and Despair in Abraham J. Heschel's Religious Thought." *The Journal of Religion*, 57 (January 1977), 33–47.

—— "The Spiritual Radicalism of Abraham Joshua Heschel." *Conservative Judaism*, 28 (Fall 1973), 40–49.

Kasimow, Harold. "Abraham Joshua Heschel and Interreligious Dialogue." *Journal of Ecumenical Studies*, 18 (Summer 1981), 423–434.

Katz, Steven T. "Abraham Joshua Heschel." In *Jewish Philosophers*, pp. 207–215. New York: Bloch Publishing Co., 1975.

——"Abraham Joshua Heschel and Hasidism." *Journal of Jewish Studies*, 31 (Spring 1980), 82–104.

Kaufman, William. "Abraham Joshua Heschel: The Meaning Beyond Mystery." In *Contemporary Jewish Philosophers*, pp. 142–174. New York: Reconstructionist Press, 1976.

Kimelman, Reuven. "Abraham Joshua Heschel (1907–1972)." *Response*, 16 (Winter 1972–1973), 15–22.

Lamm, Norman. "Abraham Joshua Heschel, Teacher." *Sh'ma: A Journal of Jewish Responsibility*, 3 (January 19, 1973), 42–43.

Lookstein, Joseph H. "The Neo-Hasidism of Abraham J. Heschel." *Judaism*, 5 (Summer 1956), 54–59.

Merkle, John C. "Abraham Joshua Heschel (1907–1972)." *Louvain Studies*, 6 (Spring 1976), 54–59.

—— "The Meaning and Status of Torah in the Theology of Abraham Joshua Heschel. *Religious Studies Bulletin*, 4 (January 1984), 9–18.

—— "Religious Experience Through Conscience in the Religious Philosophy of Abraham Joshua Heschel." *Louvain Studies*, 6 (Fall 1977), 354–365.

—— "The Sublime, the Human, and the Divine in the Depth-Theology of Abraham Joshua Heschel." *The Journal of Religion*, 58 (October 1978), 365–379.

—— "Tradition, Faith and Identity in Abraham Joshua Heschel's Religious Philosophy." *Conservative Judaism*, 36 (Winter 1982–1983), 13–25.

—— "Worship, Insight and Faith in the Theology of Abraham Joshua Heschel." *Worship*, 49 (December 1975), 583–596.

Morgan, John. "From Human Being to Being Human." The Creative Dialectic in Rabbi Heschel's Thought." *American Benedictine Review*, 28 (December 1977), 413–430.

Muffs, Judith Herschlag. "A Reminiscence of Abraham Joshua Heschel." *Conservative Judaism*, 28 (Fall 1973), 53–54.

Neusner, Jacob. "Faith in the Crucible of the Mind." *America*, March 10, 1973, 207–209.

Parzen, Herbert. "Abraham Joshua Heschel: A New Teacher and Personality in the Conservative Movement." In *Roads to Jewish Survival*, ed. by Milton Berger, Joel Geffen, and M. David Hoffman, pp. 79–84. New York: Bloch Publishing Company, 1967.

Petuchowski, Jakob J. "Faith as the Leap of Action: The Theology of Abraham Joshua Heschel." *Commentary*, 25 (May 1958), 390–397.

Rotenstreich, Nathan. "On Prophetic Consciousness." *The Journal of Religion*, 54 (July 1974), 185–198.

Rothschild, Fritz A. "Abraham Joshua Heschel (1907–1972): Theologian and Scholar." In *American Jewish Yearbook*, ed. by Morris Fine and Milton Himmelfarb, pp. 533–544. New York: Jewish Publication Society of America, 1973.

—— "Abraham Joshua Heschel." In *Modern Theologians: Christians and Jews*, ed. by Thomas E. Bird, pp. 169–182. Indiana: University of Notre Dame Press, 1967.

—— "Architect and Herald of a New Theology." *America*, March 10, 1973, 210–212.

——Introduction. *Between God and Man: An Interpretation of Judaism from the Writings of Abraham J. Heschel*, pp. 7–32. New York: The Free Press, 1959.

—— "God and Modern Man: The Approach of Abraham J. Heschel." *Judaism*, 8 (Spring 1959), 112–120.

—— "The Religious Thought of Abraham Heschel." *Conservative Judaism*, 23 (Fall 1968), 12–24.

Sanders, J. A. "An Apostle to the Gentiles." *Conservative Judaism*, 28 (Fall 1973), 61–63.

Schachter, Zalman M. "Abraham Joshua Heschel, Poet." *Sh'ma: A Journal of Jewish Responsibility,* 3 (January 19, 1973), 45–47.
——— "Two Facets of Judaism." *Tradition,* 3 (Spring 1961), 191–202.
Schneider, Herbert W. "On Reading Heschel's *God In Search of Man:* A Review Article." *Review of Religion,* 21 (November 1956), 31–38.
Schulweis, Harold M. "Charles Hartshorne and the Defenders of Heschel." *Judaism,* 24 (Winter 1975), 58–62.
Sherman, Franklin. "Abraham Joshua Heschel: Spokesman for Jewish Faith." *Lutheran World,* 110 (October 1963), 400–408.
Sherwin, Byron. "Abraham Joshua Heschel, Master." *Sh'ma: A Journal of Jewish Responsibility,* 3 (January 19, 1973), 43–45.
——— "Abraham Joshua Heschel." *The Torch,* Spring 1969, 5–8.
——— "Journey of a Soul: Abraham Joshua Heschel's Quest for Self-Understanding." *Religion in Life* (Fall 1976), 270–277.
Siegel, Seymour. "Abraham Joshua Heschel's Contributions to Jewish Scholarship." *Proceedings of the Rabbinical Assembly,* 32 (1968), 72–85.
——— "Contemporary Jewish Theology: Four Major Voices." *Church and State,* 13 (Spring 1971), 257–270.
——— "Divine Pathos, Prophetic Sympathy." *America,* March 10, 1973, 216–218.
Silberman, Lou H. "The Philosophy of Abraham Heschel." *Jewish Heritage,* 2 (Spring 1959), 23–26, 54.
Spiro, Jack D. "Rabbi Abraham Joshua Heschel: An Appreciation." *Religious Education,* 68 (March–April 1973), 218–225.
Starkman, Moshe. "Abraham Joshua Heschel: The Jewish Writer and Thinker." *Conservative Judaism,* 28 (Fall 1973), 75–77.
Synan, Edward A. "Abraham Heschel and Prayer." In *The Bridge: A Yearbook of Judaeo-Christian Studies,* ed. by John M. Oesterreicher, pp. 256–265. New York: Pantheon Books, 1955.
Tanenzapf, Sol. "Abraham Heschel and His Critics." *Judaism,* 23 (Summer 1974), 276–286.
Teshima, Jacob Y. "My Memory of Professor Abraham Joshua Heschel." *Conservative Judaism,* 28 (Fall 1973), 78–80.
Thomas, George F. "Philosophy and Theology." *Theology Today,* 30 (October 1973), 272–277.
Weborg, John. "Abraham Joshua Heschel: A Study in Anthropodicy." *Anglican Theological Review,* 61 (October 1979), 483–497.
Woodward, Kenneth L. "A Foretaste of Eternity." *Newsweek,* January 8, 1973, 50.

Reviews of Heschel's Books (Selected)

Listed below are only those reviews of Heschel's books that are cited in this book.

Borowitz, Eugene. Review of *A Passion for Truth. New York Times Book Review,* January 13, 1974, 22.
Fackenheim, Emil. Review of *God in Search of Man. Conservative Judaism,* 15 (Fall 1960), 50–53.
——— Review of *Man Is Not Alone. Judaism,* 1 (January 1952), 86.
Herberg, Will. Review of *God in Search of Man. America,* April 14, 1956, 68.
——— Review of *Man's Quest for God. Theology Today,* 12 (January 1956), 404–406.

Neusner, Jacob. Review of *Torah min ha-shamayim,* vol. 2. *Conservative Judaism,* 20 (Spring 1966), 66–73.

Neibuhr, Reinhold. "Masterly Analysis of Faith." Review of *Man Is Not Alone. New York Herald Tribune Book Review,* April 1, 1951, 12.

—— "The Mysteries of Faith." Review of *God in Search of Man. Saturday Review,* April 21, 1956, 18.

Reimer, Jack. Review of *A Passion for Truth. Commonweal,* January 11, 1974, 372–373.

Stitskin, Leon. Review of *A Passion for Truth. Library Journal,* August 1973, 2314.

Whiston, Charles F. Review of *Man's Quest for God. Religious Education,* 61 (July–August 1966), 316.

Other Books

The following are books other than those by or about Heschel which are cited in this book.

Baillie, John. *The Sense of the Presence of God.* New York: Charles Scribner's Sons, 1962.

Buber, Martin. *Tales of the Hasidism: Early Masters.* New York: Schocken Books, 1947.

—— *Tales of the Hasidism: Later Masters.* New York: Schocken Books, 1948.

Burke, Edmund. *A Philosophical Inquiry into the Origin of Our Ideas of the Sublime and the Beautiful.* London, 1756, 1958.

Greene, Gwendolen Plunket. *Letters from Baron Friedrich von Hügel to a Niece.* London, 1928, 1965.

Hartshorne, Charles. *Anselm's Discovery.* LaSalle, Ill.: Open Court, 1965.

Hügel, Friedrich von. *Essays and Addresses on the Philosophy of Religion.* First series. London, 1921, 1963.

—— *Essays and Addresses on the Philosophy of Religion.* Second series. London, 1926, 1963.

James, William. *The Varieties of Religious Experience.* New York: Longmans, 1902.

Kant, Immanuel. *Critique of Aesthetic Judgement.* Trans. by J. C. Meredith. Oxford, 1911.

Neusner, Jacob. *American Judaism: Adventure in Modernity.* Englewood Cliffs, N. J.: Prentice-Hall, 1972.

—— *History and Torah: Essays on Jewish Learning.* New York: Schocken Books, 1966.

—— *The Way of Torah: An Introduction to Judaism.* The Religious Life of Man Series, ed. by Frederick J. Streng. Belmont, California: Dickenson Publishing Company, 1970.

Otto, Rudolf. *The Idea of the Holy.* London, 1923. New York: Oxford University Press, second ed. 1950.

Polanyi, Michael. *Meaning.* Chicago and London: Chicago University Press, 1975.

—— *Personal Knowledge: Towards a Post-Critical Philosophy.* London: Routledge and Kegan Paul, 1962.

—— *The Tacit Dimension.* New York: Doubleday and Co., 1966.

Schleiermacher, Frederich. *The Christian Faith.* English trans. of the second German ed. (1830), ed. by H. R. Mackintosh and J. S. Steward. Edinburgh: T. & T. Clark, 1928.

Smith, John E. *Experience and God.* New York and London: Oxford University Press, 1968.
Spiegelberg, Herbert. *The Phenomenological Movement: A Historical Introduction.* 2 vols. Second ed. The Hague: Martinus Nijhoff, 1965.
Tait, Gordon L. *The Promise of Tillich.* Philadelphia: J. B. Lippincott Company, 1971.
Tillich, Paul. *The Courage To Be.* New Haven: Yale University Press, 1952.
—— *Systematic Theology.* Vol. 1. Chicago: University of Chicago Press, 1951.
Tracy, David. *Blessed Rage for Order: The New Pluralism in Theology.* New York: The Seabury Press, 1975.
Whitehead, Alfred North. *Process and Reality: An Essay in Cosmology.* Cambridge University Press, 1929.
—— *Religion in the Making.* New York: The Macmillan Co., 1926.
—— *Science and the Modern World.* New York: The Macmillan Co., 1926.
Wiesel, Elie. *Souls on Fire: Portraits and Legends of Hasidic Masters.* New York: Vintage, 1973.

Other Articles

The following are articles other than those by or devoted primarily to Heschel which are cited in this book.

Friedman, Maurice. "Liberal Judaism and Contemporary Jewish Thought." *Midstream,* 4 (Autumn 1959), 16–28.
Kaplan, Edward K. "Toward a Poetics of Faith." *Response,* 10 (Spring 1971), 44–46.
McKenzie, John L. S.V. "Holy." *Dictionary of the Bible.* Milwaukee: Bruce Publishing Company, 1965, 365–367.
Neusner, Jacob. "The Tasks of Theology in Judaism: A Humanistic Program." *The Journal of Religion,* 59 (January 1979), 71–86.
Siegel, Seymour. "Ethics and the Halacha." In *Conservative Judaism and Jewish Law,* ed. by Seymour Siegel, pp. 124–132. New York: The Rabbinical Assembly, 1977.
Walgrave, J. H. "Religious Experience Through Conscience." *Louvain Studies,* 4 (Fall 1972), 91–114.

Index

Index